Foreign Relations of the PRC

Foreign Relations of the PRC

The Legacies and Constraints of China's International Politics since 1949

Robert G. Sutter

ROWMAN & LITTLEFIELD PUBLISHERS, INC.
Lanham • Boulder • New York • Toronto • Plymouth, UK

Published by Rowman & Littlefield Publishers, Inc.
A wholly owned subsidiary of The Rowman & Littlefield Publishing Group, Inc.
4501 Forbes Boulevard, Suite 200, Lanham, Maryland 20706
www.rowman.com

10 Thornbury Road, Plymouth PL6 7PP, United Kingdom

British Library Cataloguing in Publication Information Available

Library of Congress Cataloging-in-Publication Data

Sutter, Robert G.
Foreign relations of the PRC : the legacies and constraints of China's international politics since 1949 / Robert G. Sutter.
pages cm
Includes bibliographical references and index.
ISBN 978-1-4422-2015-7 (cloth : alk. paper) — ISBN 978-1-4422-2016-4 (pbk. : alk. paper) — ISBN 978-1-4422-2017-1 (electronic)
1. China—Foreign relations—1949- 2. World politics—1945–1989. 3. World politics—1989- I. Title.
DS777.8.S879 2013
327.51—dc23
2013005103

∞™ The paper used in this publication meets the minimum requirements of American National Standard for Information Sciences Permanence of Paper for Printed Library Materials, ANSI/NISO Z39.48-1992.

Printed in the United States of America

Contents

Abbreviations

ABM	antiballistic missile
ACFTA	ASEAN-China Free Trade Agreement
ADB	Asian Development Bank
APEC	Asian-Pacific Economic Cooperation
ARATS	Association for Relations across the Taiwan Strait
ARF	ASEAN Regional Forum
ASEAN	Association of Southeast Asian Nations
BRICS	Brazil, Russia, India, China, South Africa group
C4ISR	command, control, communications, computers, intelligence, and strategic reconnaissance
CACF	China-Africa Cooperation Forum
CBMs	confidence-building measures
CCP	Chinese Communist Party
DPP	Democratic Progressive Party
EAS	East Asian Summit
ECFA	Economic Cooperation Framework Agreement
EU	European Union
FDI	foreign direct investment
FRELIMO	Liberation Front for Mozambique

FTA	free trade agreement
G-7	Group of Seven
G-20	Group of Twenty
GDP	gross domestic product
GSP	Generalized System of Preferences
IMF	International Monetary Fund
INF	intermediate nuclear forces
IPR	intellectual property rights
KMT	Kuomintang
LDP	Liberal Democratic Party
LOAC	line of actual control
MFN	most-favored-nation status
MOFA	Ministry of Foreign Affairs
MOFTEC	Ministry of Foreign Trade and Economic Cooperation
MTCR	Missile Technology Control Regime
NMD	national missile defense
NPC	National People's Congress
NSC	new security concept
NTR	normal trade relations
OAS	Organization of American States
OECD	Organization for Economic Cooperation and Development
PA	Palestinian Authority
PKI	Indonesian Communist Party
PKO	peacekeeping operations
PLA	People's Liberation Army
PLO	Palestine Liberation Organization
PNTR	permanent normal trade relations
PRC	People's Republic of China
RMA	revolution in military affairs

ROC	Republic of China
ROK	Republic of Korea
SCO	Shanghai Cooperation Organization
SEF	Taiwan's Straits Exchange Foundation
SETC	State Economic and Trade Commission
SOE	state-owned enterprise
SPC	State Planning Commission
SEZ	special economic zone
TMD	theater missile defense
TRA	Taiwan Relations Act
UNDP	United Nations Development Program
UNITA	National Union for the Total Independence of Angola
UNSC	United Nations Security Council
WHA	World Health Assembly
WMD	weapons of mass destruction
WTO	World Trade Organization

Chapter One

Assessing China's Role in World Affairs

China's ascendance as a world power represents the most important change in the still developing international dynamics of the twenty-first century. A wide range of expert commentaries and assessments judges that China in recent decades has established a clear strategy of developing wealth and power in world affairs. They see expanding Chinese economic, military, and political influence that entails a change in leadership in the Asia-Pacific region and a power shift in world affairs. The United States and its partners among developed countries are viewed in decline as China rises, and thus their choices are depicted in sometimes stark terms. They are advised by some to appease and accommodate China, and by others to resist.

This study joins some other specialists and commentators in judging that the above assessments of China's rise and its consequences are premature and probably mistaken. The following chapters focus first on a chronological examination of the actual impact, legacies, and constraints of the foreign relations of the People's Republic of China (PRC); later chapters assess Chinese relations with specific countries and regions for the same purpose. Overall, the review provides two main reasons for the conclusion that China's rise has not and probably will not result in the regional and international power shift that some predict.

The first reason has to do with conflicts evident in China's purported strategy for acquiring leadership in Asian and world affairs. The Chinese Communist Party and state apparatus has long fostered an image of China following correct principles in accord with international conditions that in-

sure a consistently effective foreign strategy. The Chinese effort has reinforced the assessments of foreign specialists that China in recent decades has
been pursuing a coherent strategy to develop wealth and power within the
evolving international system that many believe foreshadows Chinese international primacy and leadership as the influence of developed countries declines.

Yet the record of China's actual behavior in world affairs shown in this
volume demonstrates repeated changes, shifts in emphasis, and adjustments
that belie a coherent foreign strategy. Mao Zedong (d. 1976) shifted China
between violent revolutionary behavior and more pragmatic accommodation
to the existing world order. Deng Xiaoping (d. 1997) curbed revolutionary
excesses but shifted China's foreign approach repeatedly; he notably sought
advantage in alternative overtures to the United States and the Soviet Union.
Both leaders left a legacy among concerned countries, especially around
China's periphery, that China was an unpredictable actor, prone to changes in
course and periodic violence. Later Chinese leaders tried to focus on domestic economic development and on sustaining a peaceful international environment conducive to such nation building. Nevertheless, time and again,
they have shifted toward assertive, coercive, disruptive, and sometimes violent behavior, especially in the pursuit of disputed Chinese sovereignty
claims and security interests around China's periphery.

This book argues that the repeated shifts and hard-to-predict instances of
assertiveness, intimidation, and violence have seriously encumbered China's
rising influence in regional and world affairs. They have put China's neighbors and other concerned powers, including the United States, on guard; and
they have reinforced the tendencies of these powers to develop contingency
plans to deal with possible Chinese pressure and dominance in the years
ahead. Those plans pose a strong impediment to Chinese leadership in areas
around China's periphery, the part of the world that remains by far China's
top concern in international affairs.

The second reason for this study's judgment that China's rise remains
encumbered centers on the book's examination in some detail of the extent of
the actual influence China exerts among the countries along its rim and with
other large powers involved in those countries, notably the United States.
The study shows that the People's Republic of China has always exerted its
greatest influence in nearby Asia, and that this area has always received the
lion's share of Chinese foreign policy attention. The region is essential to
China's national security; it contains the disputed sovereignty issues that

remain of top importance to the Chinese leaders as well as to the strongly patriotic Chinese popular and elite opinion. Nearby Asia is more important than any other world area to China's economic development; it determines the peaceful international environment seen by post-Mao Chinese leaders as essential in China's pursuit of economic development, the primary source of legitimacy for continued Communist Party rule in China.

The examination of China's actual influence in nearby Asia shows widespread shortcomings, especially in relations along China's eastern and southern frontiers, despite impressive recent advances in Chinese economic, diplomatic, and military engagement with the region. These shortcomings often are rooted in the legacies of past violence and unpredicted shifts toward neighboring countries, which support wariness as these states respond to China's rise in the current period. Episodes in 2005, 2010, and 2012 of unexpected Chinese assertiveness, coercion, and violence toward Japan, along with similar behavior in recent years toward Southeast Asian states, South Korea, India, and the United States over disputed territorial claims and other issues underline regional concerns and strengthen contingency planning and preparations to deal with possible increased pressure and coercion from China as it gains in wealth and power.

The study finds that the Chinese party-state apparatus, fostering a positive image of Chinese foreign relations with the countries of nearby Asia, strongly influences thinking among the Chinese people that is far from reality, making it very difficult for China to acknowledge the grievances and concerns of neighbors with past and recent Chinese assertiveness and coercion. The party-fostered worldview also is accompanied by a strong nationalistic resentment against the exploitation of Chinese weaknesses by foreign powers in the nineteenth and much of the twentieth centuries. This victim mentality is accompanied by other patterns of behavior, explained below, that prompt China to overreact to foreign actions in many areas of nearby Asia. Such overreaction in turn reinforces the concern and contingency planning of neighbors and the United States that limit China's actual influence in the region.

Regarding China's positive international contributions, the record shows continued preoccupation among Chinese leaders with ongoing and serious domestic problems and priorities that reinforce their unwillingness to undertake risks, costs, or commitments supporting regional or broader "common goods." The narrow China-centered mind-set that has characterized PRC foreign relations is seen in the ubiquitous "win-win" principle guiding Chinese foreign deal making in the post–Cold War period. At bottom, China is reluctant to undertake obligations that it wouldn't ordinarily do unless there is a clear "win" for a narrowly defined win-set of Chinese interests. In nearby Asia, China's actual contributions to regional common interests appear small and reflective of a "cheap rider" that exploits the prevailing international order supported by others. They pale in comparison with the massive costs and great risks undertaken by the United States, which remains a security and economic partner of choice for the majority of governments in the region.

Against this background, the inventory of China's relationships with countries of nearby Asia provided in chapter 8 shows that even though China is advancing in power and influence, it has a long way to go to reach a point where it can seriously challenge U.S. leadership in the Asia-Pacific area. Chapter 9 shows advances in Chinese interests in other world areas, with the major caveat that the range of Chinese interests in these areas is much narrower and the interests themselves much less important to Chinese decision makers. In these areas, China is focused heavily on commercial concerns that mesh fairly well with the leaders and business elites in these countries. Chapter 10 concludes with a comparison of Chinese strengths and limitations with U.S. strengths and limitations to argue that there is far to go for a tipping point and power shift in China's favor in the all-important Asia-Pacific region. And without China's assurance of its interests in nearby Asia, it is judged that China will be in no position to challenge the United States or undertake leadership in other world areas of less importance to the PRC.

SOURCES OF POWER AND INFLUENCE

The manifestations of China's growing impact and salience in world affairs start with the remarkable growth of the Chinese economy, which is strongly integrated with international economic developments. Since the beginning of economic reforms following the death of Mao Zedong in 1976, China has been the world's fastest-growing major economy. From 1979 to 2011, the average annual growth rate of China's gross domestic product (GDP) was about 10 percent. By 2010, China became the world's second-largest economy, after the United States. It was the world's largest exporter and second-largest trader. In 2011, it became the largest manufacturer, surpassing the United States. China has become the second-largest destination of foreign investment, the largest holder of foreign exchange reserves, and the largest creditor nation. Per capita income surpassed $5,000 in nominal terms and was much higher using measurements of international financial institutions. [1]

Looking to the future, some Chinese government officials and specialists warned of significant Chinese economic weaknesses involving the inefficient practices of state-owned enterprises (SOEs) and the state banking system, resource and energy scarcities, massive environmental problems, and China's strong dependence on the health of the global trading economy that entered a series of crises in 2008. [2] On the whole, however, a broad range of expert opinion in China and abroad project continued growth. Several predictions say that China is on track to surpass the United States, the world's largest economy, within a decade. [3]

In foreign affairs, the growing importance of the Chinese economy is manifested most notably by the growth in economic interchange between China and foreign countries throughout the world. Most important in this regard is the growth of trade and foreign investment in China. Chinese investment abroad also is growing rapidly from a low base. Notable increases in Chinese commercial and concessional financing have assisted developing countries in Africa and Asia in particular.

The major share of Chinese trade and investment involves neighboring Asian countries, the European Union, and the United States. However, the demand for resources to support China's economic growth has deepened and broadened Chinese economic interchange with developing countries. Chinese purchases of raw materials and sales of manufactured goods in these markets have grown very rapidly. China in recent years became the most important trading partner for Africa, Brazil, and many developing countries in Asia. [4] Chinese financing, economic assistance, and construction have transformed the way many developing countries export commodities abroad, with a focus on the China market. Such Chinese-fostered development in these developing economies often overshadows the support offered by developed countries and the international financial institutions they support.

Against this background, a number of foreign specialists and commentators in recent years have portrayed China as a clear leader in international economic affairs, surpassing Japan, India, and the European powers, as it closes the gap with the United States. Thus, they commonly assert the following key judgments:

- China already is an economic superpower.

- It is likely to continue rapid growth and gather greater economic and geopolitical strength.
- China's growth is the main engine changing the post–Cold War Asian and international order, where the United States was dominant, into a more multipolar order where U.S. dominance is diminished by China's rising stature and importance.
- China's emergence is unique among major powers in that China has risen by being widely open to economic interaction with the rest of the world, building international dependence on China's economy.
- The speed, scope, and scale of China's economic expansion on the global stage create very strong adjustment pressures on the United States, other developed countries, and many developing nations as well.[5]

Chinese economic growth has supported concurrent advances in Chinese military power. Chinese military modernization programs have been under way for thirty years. They involve usually double-digit increases in annual defense budgets that pay for marked improvements in China's ability to project military power in nearby regions of Asia by modern air, naval, and missile forces. They also involve new capabilities to counter adversaries in space and cyber warfare. The modernization efforts have reached the point where they strongly suggest that the objective of the Chinese leadership is to build Asia's most powerful defense force. Overall, Chinese defense acquisition and advancement show broad ambitions for Chinese military power. While they appeared focused recently on dealing with U.S. forces in the event of a Taiwan contingency, these forces can be used by Chinese leaders as deemed appropriate in a variety of circumstances. The Chinese advances mean that no single Asian power can match China's military power on continental Asia. With the possible exception of Japan, no Asian country will be capable of challenging China's naval power and airpower in maritime eastern Asia. Should Beijing choose to deploy naval and air forces to patrol the sea-lanes in the Indian Ocean, only India conceivably would be capable of countering China's power.[6]

The sinews of economic and military power underline China's greater prominence in international governance and leadership. China's growing involvement with and dependence on the world economy heads the list of reasons explaining China's ever-broadening and deepening involvement with foreign governments and various multilateral organizations. There have been remarkable changes and increased Chinese activism in Asian regional multilateral organizations, with China in recent years taking a leading role in creating such structures as the ASEAN–China Free Trade Agreement and a regional security body that includes Russia and four central Asian states known as the Shanghai Cooperation Organization (SCO). The Chinese approach in these endeavors strives to meet the interests of the other participants while ensuring that Chinese interests of security, development, and stability are well served. China also has participated actively in recent years in loosely structured global groups, notably the G-20, involving the world's twenty leading powers, and the BRICS, involving Brazil, Russia, India, China, and South Africa.[7]

China's approach to multilateralism and broader foreign relations has changed markedly since China became a participant in such endeavors on entry into the United Nations in 1971. There has been a trend since then toward closer Chinese government cooperation with the United Nations and an ever-widening range of multilateral organizations and the international norms supported by the UN. The record of Chinese adherence to multilateral guidelines and norms remains somewhat mixed, however.

Chinese engagement with international economic organizations has been the most active and positive. The reasons seem obvious: these organizations provide numerous material benefits for China's development, and China's active participation ensures that China will play an important role in decisions affecting the world economy on which Chinese development depends. There are some limits on Chinese cooperation with international economic institutions. For example, China does not cooperate closely with international organizations that seek to regulate scarcities in the global oil market.

China's recently more active and positive approach in Asian regional economic, security, and political organizations seems to reflect the strong recent priority of the Chinese government to ensure that China's rising power and influence not be seen as a danger by China's neighbors and the region's leading outside power, the United States. Chinese leaders see the recent period as a "strategic opportunity" to advance China's modernization; they do not want to prompt these states, out of concern that China's rise could hurt their interests, to obstruct or complicate China's development. China's attentive diplomacy and periodic deference to the interests of its neighbors have helped to reassure most of them about Chinese intentions, giving rise to significant improvement in Chinese relations throughout its periphery. On the other hand, as noted above, many regional governments remain on guard. For example, they have judged that the recent rise of Chinese military power, along with China's economic power and positive multilateral diplomacy, is inconsistent with China's avowed peaceful intentions toward its neighbors and poses a serious threat to their security and regional stability.[8]

In the case of international regulation of environmental practices, China is reluctant to commit to international norms if they infringe on Chinese efforts to expand economic growth. The Chinese government's approach to international human rights regimes has long focused on engaging in protracted dialogues and cooperating where possible or needed in order to avoid international sanction. China nonetheless consistently avoids significant commitments that would impede its ability to coerce those in China who are seen as challenging the Communist administration. China's cooperation with international arms control measures has grown steadily in the past two decades, although the Chinese government continues to avoid commitments that would impede Chinese independence in certain areas important to Chinese interests.[9]

The impressive and continuing advance of Chinese economic, military, and political power and influence contrasts with prevailing and widely publicized difficulties facing developed nations, notably Japan, the European Union, and the United States. As noted at the start of this chapter, a range of specialists and forecasters aver that a power shift is under way in world affairs. They believe that the prevailing order in the Asian-Pacific region, the most economically important world region in the twenty-first century, is witnessing a decline in the power and influence of the United States, as well as Japan, while China has emerged on a steady course as the region's new dominant power. Many experts judge that the power shift will soon involve other areas of the world as well. China's massive size, rapid economic growth, strengthening military power, and growing political influence will increasingly determine world affairs as the United States and other developed nations deal with protracted problems.[10]

International relations scholars are well aware that power shifts are dangerous phenomena in world affairs; they often are accompanied by military conflict and major wars that determine leadership in the emerging new order. These and other concerns have prompted closer examination of forecasts of China's rise to Asian and world leadership. Some specialists, including this writer, find the forecasts lacking in several respects. In particular, they do a poor job of accurately assessing various Chinese domestic limitations with important foreign policy implications involving leadership legitimacy, corruption, widening income gaps, widespread social turmoil, highly resource-intensive economic development, environmental damage, and slowing reform of an economic model seen as unsustainable. In addition, they have a hard time showing how China actually exerts influence in world affairs, notably by getting other countries to do things they wouldn't ordinarily do.[11]

Because of pervasive secrecy surrounding Chinese leadership decision making and the absence of accurate data on salient domestic developments in China, there is wide-ranging debate about how the various domestic limitations noted in the previous paragraph actually influence Chinese foreign behavior. On one side are those who see these difficulties as severe and bringing China to the brink of protracted decline or even collapse. On the other side are those who see them as comparatively small given the success of China's modernization and international prominence.[12]

The impact of these domestic determinants in contemporary Chinese foreign relations can be assessed indirectly through careful study of actual Chinese behavior in international affairs. The latter approach also has the added benefit of providing more clear and concrete evidence regarding what Chinese representatives in fact are doing in various international arenas and how successful their efforts have been in meeting Chinese goals. Once such an assessment has been made, it can provide a comparatively sound basis for discerning how influential China is in contemporary world affairs and the prospects for a power shift in China's direction.

This book endeavors to provide such an assessment. It pays close attention to the context of contemporary Chinese foreign relations. To do otherwise would ignore legacies and patterns of past behavior that influence Chinese contemporary behavior in ways that enhance or detract from Chinese pursuit of international influence and particular foreign policy goals. And assessing in some detail contemporary Chinese foreign relations in light of the recent past provides good indications as to how much progress China actually is making in pursuit of its objectives and in regard to regional and global leadership.

After this first chapter, which introduces the purpose and scope and provides key findings of the book, chapters 2, 3, and 4 review the remarkable course of the foreign relations of the People's Republic of China (PRC) during its more than six decades of international involvement. While Chinese leaders have tended to emphasize the consistency of China's approach in foreign affairs, the record of change seems overwhelming.

Chapters 5 and 6 address, respectively, patterns of decision making of the Chinese elite and their world outlook along with that of broader Chinese constituencies, and China's changing importance in world affairs since the founding of the PRC in 1949. There follow three chapters dealing with international relationships considered in order of importance for China: the United States (chapter 7); countries located around China's rim (chapter 8); and other developing and developed countries (chapter 9). The conclusion in chapter 10 draws implications from the findings of the book and on that basis offers forecasts for China's growing role in Asian and world affairs and for a possible power shift in China's direction.

CHINA'S IMAGE IN FOREIGN AFFAIRS

The record of Chinese foreign relations since 1949 shows gaps between the image of China in foreign affairs fostered by the Chinese government and the actual practice seen in the events of Chinese foreign relations. One of the first issues a student or other observer encounters in dealing with Chinese foreign relations involves how much weight to give to China's image building in foreign affairs and what are its actual implications for Chinese foreign behavior.

Examining the record of Chinese foreign behavior shows long-standing efforts by Chinese officials to support the positive in China's pursuit of its objectives abroad. In recent years, China's salience as an international economic, military, and political power has been reinforced by attentive efforts by the Chinese Foreign Ministry; various other government, party, and military organizations that deal with foreign affairs; various ostensibly nongovernment organizations with close ties to the Chinese government; party and military offices; and the massive publicity/propaganda apparatus of the Chinese government. The opinions of these officials, nongovernment representatives, and media accounts provide sources used by international journalists, scholars, and officials in assessing Chinese foreign relations. On the whole, they boost China's international stature while they condition people in China to think positively about Chinese foreign relations. Such efforts have been common in past periods of Chinese foreign relations. Points of emphasis in these efforts include the following:

- China's foreign policy is consistent.
- It follows principles in dealing with foreign issues, which assures a moral position in Chinese foreign relations.

- The Chinese government deals effectively with international events and adopts policies and takes actions in accord with Chinese principles and moral leadership.
- Abiding by principles and seeking moral positions provide the basis for effective Chinese strategies in world affairs.
- Such strategies insure that China does not make mistakes in foreign affairs, an exceptional position reinforced by the fact that the People's Republic of China is seen to have avoided publicly acknowledging foreign policy mistakes or apologizing for its actions in world affairs.[13]

Many in China and some foreign observers base their analyses of Chinese foreign relations on the information provided by the above-noted Chinese outlets. Their analyses show how China's image-building efforts, which enjoy support from the Chinese people and various constituencies in China, support a leading role for China in Asian and world affairs. They conclude optimistically that China will follow a contemporary policy emphasizing recent themes stressed by the Chinese government. The themes include promoting peace and development abroad, eschewing dominance or hegemonic policies in dealing with issues with neighbors or others even as China's power grows, and following the purported record of historical Chinese dynasties in not seeking expansionism as China's power increases.[14]

Some specialists in China and many others abroad, including this writer, duly consider Chinese-provided information but also examine closely the actual behavior of China in dealing with foreign affairs, behavior that can be measured both from the perspective of China as well as the perspective of foreign governments and others concerned. This book also joins other assessments that show that Chinese image building may help China's pursuit of goals in foreign affairs in some ways, but it also represents a serious liability in China's pursuit of effective policies, especially toward its Asian neighbors and the United States.

Principles versus Interest-Based Foreign Policy

While China's foreign policy actions are usually said to be based on adherence to righteous and moral principles, there are notable weaknesses in China's long-avowed adherence to such morally correct principles. Chinese foreign policy expert Samuel Kim twenty years ago labeled China's "peculiar" operational code of conduct "firmness in principle and flexibility in application." The result for Kim and other foreign observers is a gap between principle and practice, with China repeatedly attempting to show through often convoluted discussion of a sometimes dizzying array of various and often newly created sets of principles governing Chinese foreign relations that China is an exception to the interest-based policies and practices of great powers. Chinese discourse does not address the net effect of all the different sets of Chinese principles, which, as seen by Kim and others, allows China to be all things to all nations on all salient international issues, and thereby provides little in the way of concrete guidance on how and why China behaves in a particular set of circumstances. [15]

The course of Chinese foreign relations is littered with examples where principles were reinterpreted or put aside in favor of other sets of principles as Chinese interests in a foreign relationship changed. Jawaharlal Nehru seemed truly surprised when his efforts to nurture a cooperative relationship with Zhou Enlai under the rubric of the Five Principles of Peaceful Coexistence seemed to count for little as China pursued border interests at odds with India's interests. Noncommunist Southeast Asian leaders could be forgiven for skepticism as they observed China's flawed observance of its principle of noninterference in another state's internal affairs at various times in their checkered relationships with China. For example, Deng Xiaoping reached out to improve relations with noncommunist Southeast Asian neighbors in the mid-1970s as China was constructing a broad front of nations to oppose Soviet-backed Vietnam's pending attack against the Chinese-backed Khmer Rouge government in Cambodia. Deng did so on the understanding that these governments would accept reconciliation with China while Beijing at the same time continued support for the tens of thousands of insurgents China had trained, supplied, and supported in their armed struggles against the very Southeast Asian leaders with whom Deng was seeking to improve relations. [16]

Albania's Enver Hoxa was more vocal than other more important Communist leaders in Hanoi and Pyongyang as well as less prominent Communist leaders aligned with Beijing whose interests were adversely impacted by China's surprising opening to the United States in the early 1970s despite long-standing Chinese commitments to them in the struggle against American imperialism. Meanwhile, Pakistan, the only country with which China has been able to sustain a close relationship since the early 1960s, has seen China's commitment to an "all-weather" relationship diminish as China in the post–Cold War period has backed away from previous support for

Pakistan's position in the Kashmir dispute in order to open the way for improved Chinese relations with India.[17]

China's Exceptional Exceptionalism

It is common for states to redefine their foreign policies as their interests change in light of changing circumstances at home or abroad. And when states follow those changed interests and shift stated policies and commitments deemed principled and moral in new directions to the detriment of others, they rarely apologize; they tend to only grudgingly acknowledge negative consequences and mistakes.

Leaders of my own country, the United States, are widely seen as prone to an arrogant sort of exceptionalism in foreign affairs. They are loath to apologize for policy changes or international actions that sometimes grossly hurt others or are at odds with American principles. Nonetheless, the American political process, open media, active interest groups, and regularly scheduled elections allow for recognition of foreign policy failings and proposed remedies. In contrast, Chinese exceptionalism in foreign affairs is much more exceptional than that of the United States. One reason is the continuing need for the Chinese Communist Party–led system to sustain its legitimacy partly through an image of correct behavior in foreign affairs consistent with Chinese supported principles. Another reason is that while there have been some recent debates on foreign policy issues in Chinese media, they fail to deal well with many Chinese legacies of egregious malfeasance in the past. And no corrective is provided by elections or a legitimate political opposition.

The unwillingness and seeming inability of the Chinese administration to address forthrightly some of the major negative features of the PRC history is well represented. Samuel Kim acknowledged that Chinese Communist leaders have addressed and corrected some of their large domestic policy failures, while sustaining an image of correctness in foreign affairs.[18] Reflecting a tendency to avoid attention to the negatives of the PRC's record, the Great Leap Forward and the Cultural Revolution merit only tiny displays in the otherwise detailed recounting of the history of the modern Chinese revolution in the large National Museum in Beijing.

This writer's frequent lectures to university audiences and otherwise well-informed citizen groups in China show very weak understanding of such sensitive issues as Chinese support for the Khmer Rouge as well as other Communist insurgencies in Southeast Asia during the latter years of Mao Zedong's leadership (1949–1976) and most of the period of Deng Xiaoping's leadership (1977–1997). Many Chinese elites and broad popular opinion truly believe that the People's Republic of China has always followed moral- ly correct foreign policies based on principles in support of progressive world forces. Against this background, it was not surprising that a senior Chinese foreign policy researcher associated with the Chinese Foreign Min- istry presented a written keynote address to a trilateral international meeting of Vietnamese, Chinese, and American specialists in 2011 that was attended by the author and emphasized that "the People's Republic of China has always been a stabilizing force in Asia." The speaker seemed oblivious to the reaction of the Vietnamese delegates as they squirmed in their seats. He showed little awareness that the Vietnamese are among China's neighbors with the strongest reasons to disagree.

EXPLAINING CHINA'S INTEREST-BASED BEHAVIOR IN FOREIGN AFFAIRS—CHANGE AND UNCERTAINTY

Whatever importance one gives to the wide array of principles and moral norms that are said by the Chinese government to govern Chinese foreign relations, the fact is that the private calculus of Chinese leaders in making key foreign and domestic policy decisions remains shrouded in secrecy. It is a crime subject to serious punishment to disclose such matters. Thus, the explanation of Chinese foreign policy decisions provided in this volume joins other studies in basing analysis mainly on patterns of Chinese behavior that can be observed and supported by evidence from Chinese and international sources.[19]

A defining feature of the foreign policy behavior of the People's Republic of China is change. As noted above, it seems impossible to explain these changes realistically on the basis of the muddled array of principles used in Chinese foreign relations over the past sixty years. The discussion in this book finds greater accuracy in explaining Chinese decisions as heavily inter- est based. As seen from the list below and as explained in later chapters, the Chinese foreign policies changed markedly and frequently, apparently driven by changing calculations of Chinese interests that were in turn driven by changing circumstances at home or abroad. Perceiving the reasons for the changes in the course of Chinese policy is easier in retrospect. At the time, the changes often came as a surprise, adding to China's reputation as a power prone to unpredictable change, often leading to coercion and violence.

Because of the secrecy that has continued to surround Chinese leaders' decision making, it is hard to know with precision why Chinese leaders shifted course in foreign policy at different times over the years. During Mao's rule (1949–1976), the interests seen driving Chinese foreign policy were often perceived as focused on fostering and promoting domestic and international revolution; though Mao also valued domestic development and made several policy initiatives, including the opening to the United States in the late 1960s, in pragmatic moves to buy time and gain leverage in order to protect China's national security. Deng Xiaoping's leadership (1977–1997) and following leaders had a clearer focus on the top priorities of sustaining Communist Party rule through effective economic development. Foreign policy was to serve these primary goals.

Nevertheless, the leaders wrestled periodically with conflicts in interests. Thus, for example, questions over how far to go in accommodating the United States in the interests of fostering a strong united front against Soviet expansion were superseded after the Cold War and collapse of the USSR (1991) with questions about how to balance Chinese goals to lead the international struggle against U.S. superpower "hegemonism" and seek a multipolar world order versus a more pragmatic pursuit of peace and development beneficial to China and others it interacted with. As the issue of Taiwan independence rose to prominence with Taiwan's president's visit to the United States in 1995, Chinese leaders struggled to balance imperatives to protect China's claim to Taiwan and prevent Taiwan independence with the need to sustain and deepen their advantageous economic and other ties with Taiwan's main protector, the United States. Most recently, since 2009, advocates of a more assertive Chinese posture on sensitive territorial and other issues involving the United States and many of China's neighbors have seriously complicated China's ongoing effort to reassure those and other concerned governments that China's rise would be peaceful and not adverse to their interests.

Key periods with intervening changes in Chinese foreign relations can be broken down as follows:

1949–1953—Amid domestic consolidation, China showed strong support for revolution at home and abroad in opposition to the United States. Against this background, miscalculations resulted in war with the United States in Korea.

1954–1957—Chinese-backed Viet Minh forces defeated French forces in Indochina. China echoed Soviet-backed peaceful coexistence and improved relations with India and other neighbors.

1958–1965—Mass domestic mobilization in the ultimately disastrous Great Leap Forward was accompanied by Chinese artillery attacks on islands held by Chiang Kai-shek forces in the Taiwan Strait. The United States reacted with threats of nuclear war and the Soviet Union chafed over China's provocative international behavior and irrational economic policies involving large amounts of Soviet assistance. Moscow ended aid in 1960 and Sino-Soviet polemics spread from the international communist movement to competition among newly independent developing countries and insurgents resisting colonial rule. Radical Chinese policies in support of various foreign groups and nations generally failed to make many lasting gains; growing Chinese influence in Indonesia collapsed with a bloody purge of Communists and pogroms against ethnic Chinese, killing half a million.

1966–1968—Excesses during a violent radical phase of "Red Guard diplomacy" in the early years of the Cultural Revolution saw the collapse of the senior levels of the foreign ministry. China's relations with all but a handful of states suffered serious setbacks. Chinese mobs assaulted Soviet diplomats and set fire to the British mission with foreign officers forced to flee the flames into the mob.

1969–1978—Soviet military pressure and the threat of nuclear attack forced China's opening to other states helpful in China's search for security. The United States for its own reasons was seeking reconciliation. Cooperation against Moscow would bind the United States and China together amid an intense leadership struggle in China that did not subside until the death of Mao and arrest of the Gang of Four in 1976 and the ascendance of Deng Xiaoping to leading power in 1978.

1979–1989—China repeatedly maneuvered for advantage between the United States and the Soviet Union. Most of the time, it found improvements with the Soviet Union less beneficial than the advantages of cooperative relations with the United States.

1989–2001—China used generally pragmatic means to climb back to international importance following the imposition of Western isolation of China after the Tiananmen crackdown in 1989, the decline of China's strategic importance to the West as a result of the end of the Cold War, and Taiwan's international prominence as a new democracy. In the mid-1990s, China's strong actions in defense of claims to Taiwan and territories in the South China Sea alarmed and alienated many neighbors. It then adopted a new set of principles in a "new security concept" (NSC) that recalled the Five Principles of Peaceful Coexistence in pledging a policy of reassurance to China's neighbors. Nevertheless, China's moderation was not directed to the United States. China persisted with steady attacks against perceived U.S. hegemonism and took careful aim against U.S. alliances in the Asia-Pacific.

2002–2012—Faced with an initially tough American stance against China under the George W. Bush administration, China broadened its reassurance efforts to now include the United States. Its objections to U.S. alliances subsided; China did not want to be seen pressing Asian neighbors to have to make a choice they didn't want to make between aligning with the United States and aligning with China. U.S.-China relations remained smooth until the first year of the Obama administration. During 2009–2011, there was an upsurge of Chinese opposition to U.S. security and other policies in the Asia-Pacific, more assertive Chinese positions and commentary directed at China's neighbors, and stepped-up Chinese support for North Korea during a period of leadership succession that also featured egregious North Korean attacks on South Korea. The Chinese behavior and assertiveness undermined China's influence throughout its eastern and southern flanks. The behavior was moderated in favor of a revival of reassurance directed at the United States and China's neighbors, but tensions continued to flare periodically, especially over disputed territories in the East China Sea and South China Sea.

FEATURES OF CHINA'S CHANGING FOREIGN POLICY PRIORITIES AND BEHAVIOR

In addition to recurring change and related uncertainty over the course of Chinese foreign relations during the sixty-year rule of the People's Republic of China, other aspects of Chinese foreign relations need to be considered when assessing the impact and effectiveness of China's varied approaches to the world.

Chinese-Centered Calculus

A common feature in the changing Chinese priorities and behavior in foreign affairs is that the changes seem to be China-centered—grounded in a fairly clear and narrow set of Chinese interests. Mao Zedong talked often about world revolution, but he generally focused on China-centered interests. For example, available scholarship shows how Mao was prepared to confront the American military–backed containment system designed to halt China's advance in Asia in the 1950s, in part in order to better mobilize support for domestic change and revolution in China.[20] Domestic Chinese interests also were involved in governing Chinese foreign policy at the end of the Maoist period. Recent disclosures show how Mao insured that considerations of Chinese domestic politics were reflected in defining the principles used by Deng Xiaoping in his inaugural speech at the United Nations in 1974 setting forth China's renowned "Three Worlds" theory in foreign affairs.[21]

Deng Xiaoping's first decade as China's most important leader beginning in 1978 focused foreign policy on protecting China in the face of Soviet pressure and coercion. Against this background, Deng turned out to be as supportive of the reviled Khmer Rouge as were Mao and the revolutionary leaders in China during the previous decade known as the Gang of Four. Deng's interest in backing this unsavory and radical Cambodian group seemed carefully calculated to support China's security interests, as the Khmer Rouge fielded the best fighting force available to counter Soviet-backed Vietnam's expansion along China's southeastern flank.[22]

Post-Deng leaders have created a new principle, the "win-win principle," which underlines their China-centered concerns. The formula is useful for reassuring neighboring countries and other nations China interacts with that China is interested in their development and concerns along with China's interest in its own development and concerns. China's partners like the approach as it generally does not require them to do anything they wouldn't ordinarily do. For its part, China also does not do anything it wouldn't ordinarily do, thereby avoiding initiatives that don't have a payoff for a narrowly defined Chinese win-set.[23]

Concern with the United States and Nearby Asia-Pacific Countries

The long record of the policy and behavior of the People's Republic of China in the Asia-Pacific region shows repeated maneuvering to keep China's periphery as free as possible from hostile or potentially hostile great-power pressure. Asia, especially the countries around China's periphery, has been the main arena of Chinese foreign relations. At bottom, this area has contained sovereignty issues and security issues that have been at the very top of the list of Chinese foreign policy priorities in most years. They involve such sovereignty issues as China's long-standing goal of reunifying Taiwan and the Chinese mainland, and such security issues as opposition to U.S. containment in the 1950s and 1960, followed by opposition to perceived Soviet use of military force and alignments with Vietnam, India, and others to "encircle" and constrain China during the 1970s and 1980s, followed in turn by renewed public opposition to U.S. alliances and military deployments in the 1990s and into the early twenty-first century.

Chinese efforts to keep this periphery free of potentially hostile great-power presence and pressure have represented a long-lasting trend that shows persistent wariness and sometimes overt hostility toward such large outside powers, notably the United States. China has used sometimes offensive and sometimes defensive measures to thwart the perceived great-power ambitions in the region, which is seen as central to Chinese security. This trend has continued, along with growing Chinese economic integration, increasing political and security cooperation, and active engagement with various multilateral organizations in the region, since the 1990s. Thus, as Chinese officials in recent years declare greater confidence and China rises in influence in Asia, they work assiduously in trying to ensure that the United States and its allies and associates do not establish influence along China's periphery that is adverse to Chinese interests. [24]

Victim Mentality

China's enduring concern with the United States (or in the past, the Soviet Union) working with countries near China to establish a strong presence around China's periphery has been reinforced by a strong sense among Chinese elites and public opinion that China has been the victim of foreign imperialism and dominance for much of the past two centuries and should work assiduously to prevent such dominance in the future. Chinese and foreign specialists acknowledge that citizens and leaders of the People's Republic of China have long been conditioned through the education system, government-sponsored media coverage, and various other means to think of China as having been victimized by international powers beginning in the early nineteenth century. Emphasis on this historical conditioning was strengthened after the Chinese Communist Party (CCP) crisis at the time of the Tiananmen demonstrations and bloody crackdown in 1989 and continues up to the present. Sensing that communism no longer provided adequate ideological support for continued CCP rule, the authorities instituted a patriotic education campaign and other measures that encouraged regime-supporting patriotism in China by recalling the more than one hundred years of foreign affronts to Chinese national dignity. On one hand, the victim mentality has been created and used by the Chinese authorities to foster unity and support for the regime in the face of foreign challenges. On the other hand, it has become so widespread and deeply rooted in Chinese elite and public opinion that it requires Chinese officials to deal with the United States and other powers, notably Japan, with an often prickly sense of nationalism that impedes collaboration, even in some areas of mutual interest. [25]

United Front Tactics, Seeking Leverage against the "Main Enemy"

In its maneuvers against the United States and the Soviet Union focused on the Asia-Pacific region, China resorted repeatedly to tactics used during the wars against Japan (1937–1945) and Chiang Kai-shek's Nationalist government (1945–1949). Mao Zedong and post-Mao leaders focused on the main enemy and sought leverage and influence against it through mobilization of support within China and cooperation with other states or international forces. Sometimes the search for support brought China into close contact with international radicals, like the Khmer Rouge, or abusive authoritarians including Zaire's Sese Mobutu, Chile's Augusto Pinochet, the Shah of Iran, and Serbia's Slobodan Milošević. China's depiction of its adversary as a threat often was exaggerated, presumably in order to foster greater domestic Chinese vigilance and international resolve. Thus, even though the end of the Cold War saw the People's Republic of China for the first time face no imminent threat of superpower military attack, the Chinese debate following the U.S. bombing of the Chinese embassy in Belgrade during the U.S.-led air war against the regime of Slobodan Milošević in 1999 featured authoritative Chinese media arguing for a strong international united front against President Bill Clinton whose actions in the war were equated with the atrocities and expansionist threat of Adolf Hitler. [26] Meanwhile, China on its part repeatedly employed building leverage and using united front tactics against lesser powers—notably Taiwan and Japan, but also including Vietnam, Burma, Thailand, and others—that were important targets for Chinese use of sometimes attractive and sometimes coercive levers of influence to bend these countries more to China's will.

The United States at the Center of Chinese Foreign Calculations

The subsequent chapters show that the United States was often the "main enemy" in Chinese foreign policy calculations. Even when China shifted focus to the Soviet Union as the main enemy as the United States seemed to be in significant decline beginning in the late 1960s, Chinese leaders remained focused on relations with the United States as the chief bulwark against feared Soviet expansion. Although foreign and Chinese specialists advise in the post–Cold War period that China is increasingly less focused on the United States, as American primacy is seen to be in decline and for other reasons, available evidence shows strong Chinese awareness of China's increasing dependence on international commons and key world regions controlled or heavily influenced by America, notably many of the oil-producing countries of the Persian Gulf. Meanwhile, the Obama administration's reengagement efforts around China's rim in the Asia-Pacific became notable in 2011 and are viewed with carefully measured Chinese concern as they impact areas of direct salience to Chinese security and sovereignty.[27]

China Often Reactive, Not in Control of Developments

In contrast with the image fostered by Chinese officials that Chinese foreign policy has been effective and moral under the guidance of far-seeing officials, more often than not the twists and turns in Chinese foreign policies and practices listed above resulted from unforeseen developments that required Chinese policy makers to make adjustments and shift course. China obviously was surprised by the U.S. reaction to China-supported North Korea's attack on South Korea in 1950, and it may not have anticipated Soviet threats to invade China and destroy its nuclear facilities following a series of border clashes on the Sino-Soviet border in 1969. Also, internal Chinese turbulence or other developments sometimes have spilled over into foreign affairs, causing Chinese policy officials to respond. Examples include reactions to the excesses of so-called Red Guard diplomacy at the start of the Cultural Revolution and on-again off-again efforts in the past two years to curb the assertiveness of a range of Chinese foreign policy actors whose commentaries and initiatives compromised Chinese efforts to reassure its neighbors and improve Chinese influence in the nearby Asia-Pacific region.

Competing Goals = Muddled Strategy

As explained earlier in this chapter, the zigzag pattern of adjustments and major changes in Chinese foreign relations suggests that China has had a hard time coming up with a coherent foreign policy strategy. A closer look at developments in the following chapters underlines this finding. Even with the more consistent policy priorities of Deng Xiaoping and later leaders, Chinese decision makers repeatedly wrestle with competing priorities that remain hard to reconcile in a national strategy worthy of the name.

LEGACIES AND VOLATILITY ADD TO COMPLICATIONS IN THE ASIA-PACIFIC

To repeat a key finding of the assessment of Chinese foreign relations in this book noted earlier, the Asia-Pacific region and its main outside power, the United States, represent the focus of Chinese foreign policy efforts. Unfortunately for contemporary Chinese influence in the region, the zigzag pattern of often intense and violent Chinese behavior toward the United States and neighboring Asia has not been forgotten. Available scholarship and other evidence have reinforced the findings of this writer's interviews with 210 officials in ten Asia-Pacific countries since 2004 to underscore the importance of this powerful and largely negative Chinese legacy to China's neighbors. The United States, meanwhile, has a very large intelligence and security apparatus as well as a variety of scholars and specialists who delve into the past as well as the future in discerning dangers to American interests. All Asia-Pacific governments were relieved and pleased as China after the Cold War embarked with some twists and turns on an approach emphasizing reassurance of its neighbors. There is no interest among regional officials in digging up major negative episodes from the past. Nevertheless, the past is not forgotten, and China has an awful lot to live down given the record of its changing and often violent behavior.[28]

For example, the People's Republic of China arguably was the most disruptive element in the Asia-Pacific for forty of its sixty years. Most bordering countries have experienced intrusion or invasion by PRC security forces. They and others somewhat further away have experienced armed insurgencies for decades whose strength depended on training, financial support, and arms from China.

The twists and turns of changing Chinese foreign policies in the region have baffled senior foreign leaders. Nehru was surprised and shamed by the Chinese border incursions and later armed attack on India. Nikita Khrushchev led the Soviet Union from 1954 to 1964. In 1958, he was appalled by Mao's reckless behavior confronting the United States in the Taiwan Strait crisis that year and by what the Soviet leader called Mao's "harebrained schemes" involving misuse and waste of Soviet aid during the disastrous Great Leap Forward. Ho Chi Minh in the 1960s sought a united Sino-Soviet front in his war against America, which China rebuffed. His successor, Le Duan, in the 1970s may not have expected China to invade Vietnam and create a Vietnamese government in exile in reaction to the Vietnamese war against the provocative Khmer Rouge regime in Cambodia. Chinese willingness to follow up well into the 1980s with years of periodic massive artillery attacks into Vietnamese border regions and other aggression underlined Chinese resolve to pursue its interests with determined use of military force and coercion.[29]

The United States was surprised with the Chinese-backed invasion by North Korea of South Korea in June 1950 and the subsequent massive Chinese intervention into the Korean conflict with the United States at the end of that year. After that negative experience, Americans tended to be careful to avoid direct war with China in following years, but they were surprised again with China's militant reaction to the Taiwan president's visit to the United States in 1995. They worried about further abrupt Chinese behavior and violence directed at the United States after the U.S. bombing of China's embassy in Belgrade in 1999, and after the crash between a Chinese fighter jet and an American surveillance plane in 2001. The harassment of a U.S. surveillance ship by several Chinese government vessels in 2009 and Chinese public warnings against any further deployments of U.S. aircraft carriers into the Yellow Sea in 2010 served as public warnings that China could react to perceived affronts from the United States or its allies and associates in disruptive and perhaps violent ways.[30]

Japan has reason to be very perplexed with China's changing priorities. China's pragmatic turn to Japan in the 1960s for economic support after the Chinese break with the Soviet Union and disastrous collapse of the Great Leap Forward was broadly welcomed in Japan, which maneuvered for exceptions regarding the U.S.-led economic embargo of China. Japan was surprised by the U.S.-China announcement in 1971 of Nixon's visit in 1972. The Japanese government changed leaders and quickly established diplomatic relations with China. China's strident opposition to Soviet expansion muted past worries about Japanese militarism, and Deng Xiaoping and his colleagues in the 1970s encouraged Japan to more strongly adhere to a Chinese-supported international front against the USSR. Japan was not seeking confrontation with Moscow and reluctantly signed a peace treaty with China in 1978 that contained a clause seen targeting Moscow. The strong Ronald Reagan-Yasuhiro Nakasone relationship fended off Soviet expansion in Asia in the 1980s to China's general satisfaction.

Disputes with Japan over history books and past Japanese atrocities in China during the first half of the twentieth century were put aside as China welcomed Japan's efforts in 1990–1991 to renew normal economic relations, including substantial foreign assistance, with China after the Tiananmen crackdown and subsequent allied isolation of China. The Japanese emperor—the living symbol of imperial Japan—was warmly welcomed by a grateful China in 1992. But relations soon declined as Chinese leaders reflected the stronger Chinese emphasis during the 1990s on patriotism and resolve to avoid any repetition of foreign, especially Japanese, infringement on China. Historical issues as well as territorial disputes and competition for Asian and international leadership saw relations decline; and they further deteriorated with Japanese prime minister Junichiro Koizumi (2001–2006) and his repeated visits to a controversial Japanese war memorial. How sour the overall relation had become was seen in mass and sometimes violent demonstrations in some Chinese cities that broke out without Chinese government support in 2005, resulting in extensive property damage. Japan was a major target of the Chinese assertiveness over territorial and related issues in 2009–2011, and Chinese government–backed mass demonstrations, considerable property damage, and Chinese threats against Japan marked the dispute over Japanese policy toward the disputed Diaoyu/Senkaku Islands in 2012.[31]

For their part, the South Koreans had worked hard in the post–Cold War period to win Chinese favor regarding issues on the Korean peninsula while building ever-closer economic relations. Relations were very close and growing in 2004, a time of major decline in South Korea's relations with the United States. Persisting differences over some historical issues and divergence over how to deal with North Korea checked further forward movement in China-South Korean relations, but the South Korean leadership and public were not prepared for China's strong support for North Korea during 2010, despite two North Korean military attacks on South Korea resulting in dozens of military personnel killed and some civilian casualties.

India too found that agreements during seemingly warm meetings with Chinese leaders in the past decade did not translate into significant progress on pending issues. The border dispute flared repeatedly with officials on both sides making strong accusations and military forces preparing for action.

Other countries moving from close convergence to wariness in dealing with China during the past decade include Australia and New Zealand. Vietnam, the Philippines, and others in the Association of Southeast Asian Nations (ASEAN) became deeply concerned with China's perceived assertiveness in recent years in the South China Sea and how that blocked their ambitions to use the sea's resources.

As will be discussed in chapters 7 and 8, the legacies of negative behavior and volatile change add to the many differences between China and its neighbors and the United States over issues fundamentally important to China's security, stability, development, and national ambition. China's exceptionalism and image building make dealing with these issues realistically and effectively very difficult. The result is prevailing suspicion and wariness in the United States and among China's neighbors as they deal with China's increasing power.

As explained in chapter 8, China's relations with central Asia are notably smoother than elsewhere around China's periphery.

PROGRESS IN AREAS FARTHER FROM CHINA

The discussion in chapter 9 will show various and sometimes serious complications and obstacles to expanding Chinese influence among countries beyond China's periphery. However, in these countries, legacies and volatility count for less, as China is often seen as a newcomer, without the negative historical baggage of other outside powers that have been interacting with them for many decades. Also, Chinese objectives in these areas appear more limited than Chinese objectives around China's rim. Security and sovereignty are not directly involved. China's main objectives focus on advantageous economic interchange; this focus appears broadly in line with the indigenous countries' interests in promoting mutual development.

CONCLUDING JUDGMENT

Chapter 10 endeavors to answer the question on whether or not a power shift is under way in Asia by explaining that China remains seriously constrained where it matters most to China—in the Asia-Pacific region. Chinese behavior and interactions with the states of this region and with the United States in the region do not show the confidence that one would assume would accompany a power shift in China's favor. China's unwillingness to move beyond the restricted win-sets of the prevalent win-win formula governing Chinese foreign relations means that it remains unwilling to undertake significant risks or costs for the sake of regional or broader common goods. Part of the reason for this continued reluctance to lead in substantive as opposed to rhetorical ways appears related to the various internal problems noted earlier requiring that resources be used at home, not abroad. Meanwhile, the conclusion demonstrates that the expanded footprint in regions further from China remains narrowly based and under the win/win rubric does not show much influence toward actually getting countries to do what they wouldn't ordinarily do.

NOTES

1. Wayne Morrison, *China's Economic Conditions*, Report RL 33534 (Washington, DC: Library of Congress, Congressional Research Service, June 26, 2012), pp. 2–10. Cui Liru, "A Multipolar World in the Globalization Era," *Contemporary International Relations* (Beijing) 20, Special Issue (September 2010): pp. 1–11.

2. Yu Yongding, "A Different Road Forward," *China Daily*, December 23, 2010, p. 9; "China's Reforms: The Second Long March," *Economist*, December 11, 2008, www.economist.com.

3. Arvind Subramanian, "The Inevitable Superpower: Why China's Rise Is a Sure Thing," *Foreign Affairs* 90, no. 5 (September/October 2011): pp. 66–78.

4. Trade figures used in this section are from the UN COMTRADE database at comtrade.un.org/db.

5. Carl Dahlman, *The World Under Pressure: How China and India Are influencing the Global Economy and Environment* (Stanford, CA: Stanford University Press, 2011).

6. U.S. Department of Defense, *Annual Report to Congress: Military and Security Developments Involving the People's Republic of China 2012* (Washington, DC: U.S. Department of Defense, May 2012).

7. Jing-Dong Yuan, "China's Role in Establishing and Building the Shanghai Cooperation Organization (SCO)," *Journal of Contemporary China* 19, no. 67 (November 2010): pp. 855–70; Wu Xinbo, "Chinese Perspectives on Building an East Asian Community in the Twenty-First Century," in *Asia's New Multilateralism*, ed. Michael Green and Bates Gill (New York: Columbia University Press, 2009), pp. 55–77.

8. Michael Yahuda, *The International Politics of the Asia-Pacific* (London: Routledge, 2011), pp. 195–202; Linda Jacobson, "Australia-China Ties: In Search of Political Trust," *Policy Brief*, Lowy Institute, June 2012.

9. Evan Medeiros, *Reluctant Restraint: The Evolution of China's Nonproliferation Policies and Practices, 1980–2004* (Stanford, CA: Stanford University Press, 2007); U.S. Department of State, *2011 Country Reports on Human Rights Practices*, May 24, 2012, www.state.gov.

10. Gideon Rachman, "American Decline: This Time It's for Real," *Foreign Policy* 184 (January/February 2011): pp. 59–65; Wu Xinbo, "Understanding the Geopolitical Implications of the Global Financial Crisis," *Washington Quarterly* 33, no. 4 (October 2010): pp. 155–63.

11. Michael Beckley, "China's Century? Why America's Edge Will Endure," *International Security* 36, no. 3 (Winter 2011/2012): pp. 41–78.

12. Minxin Pei, *China's Trapped Transition* (Cambridge, MA: Harvard University Press, 2007); David Michael Lampton, *The Three Faces of Chinese Power* (Berkeley, CA: University of California Press, 2008); Bruce Dickson, "Updating the China Model," *Washington Quarterly* 34, no. 4 (Fall 2011): pp. 39–58.

13. Denny Roy, *China's Foreign Relations* (Lanham, MD: Rowman & Littlefield, 1998), pp. 36–39; Samuel Kim, "China's International Organizational Behaviour," in *Chinese Foreign Policy: Theory and Practice*, ed. Thomas Robinson and David Shambaugh (New York: Oxford University Press, 1994), pp. 401–5; Harry Harding, "China's Changing Role in the Contemporary World," in *China's Foreign Relations in the 1980s*, ed. Harry Harding (New Haven, CT: Yale University Press, 1985), pp. 177–79.

14. Dai Bingguo, "Adhere to the Path of Peace and Development," *Xinhua*, December 6, 2011, china.usc.edu/ShowArticle.aspx?articleID=2325 (accessed July 3, 2012).

15. Kim, "China's International Organizational Behaviour," p. 402.

16. Ezra Vogel, *Deng Xioaping and the Transformation of China* (Cambridge, MA: Harvard University Press, 2011), pp. 266–92.

17. Robert Sutter, *Historical Dictionary of Chinese Foreign Policy* (Lanham, MD: Scarecrow, 2011), pp. 117–18, 194.

18. Roy, *Chinese Foreign Relations*, p. 38.

19. In addition to works already cited, see among others, A. Doak Barnett, *China and the Major Powers in East Asia* (Washington, DC: Brookings Institution, 1977); Michael Yahuda, *China's Role in World Affairs* (New York: St. Martins, 1978); Allen Whiting, *The Chinese Calculus of Deterrence: India and Indochina* (Ann Arbor: University of Michigan Press, 1975); Robert Ross and Jiang Changbin, eds., *Reexamining the Cold War* (Cambridge, MA: Harvard University Press, 2001); Michael Hunt, *The Genesis of Chinese Communist Foreign Policy* (New York: Columbia University Press, 1996); Harold Hinton, *China's Turbulent Quest* (New York: Macmillan, 1972); Peter Van Ness, *Revolution and Chinese Foreign Policy* (Berkeley: University of California Press, 1970); Melvin Gurtov and Byong-Moo Hwang, *China under Threat* (Baltimore, MD: Johns Hopkins University Press, 1981); John Garver, *Foreign Relations of the People's Republic of China* (Englewood Cliffs, NJ: Prentice Hall 1993); Lowell Dittmer, *Sino-Soviet Normalization and Its International Implications, 1945–1990* (Seattle, WA: University of Washington Press, 1992); Yong Deng, *China's Struggle for Status: The Realignment of International Relations* (New York: Cambridge University Press, 2008); Hu Sheng, *Imperialism and Chinese Politics* (Beijing: Foreign Language Press, 1985); Jiang Changbin and Robert S. Ross, eds., *Cong Duizhi zouxiang Huanhe: Lengzhan Shiqi Zhong Mei Guanxi zai Tantao* [From confrontation toward détente: A reexamination of U.S.-China relations during the Cold War] (Beijing: Shijie Zhishi Chubanshe, 2000); Pei Jianzhang, *Yanjiu Zhou Enlai: Waijiao sixiang yu shijian* [Researching Zhou Enlai: Diplomatic thought and practice] (Beijing: Shijie Zhishi Chubanshe, 1989); Wang Taiping et al., *Zhonghua renmin gongheguo waijiao shi, 1957–1969* [A diplomatic history of the People's Republic of China, 1957–1969] (Beijing: Shijie Zhishi, 1998); Gong Li, *Kuayue: 1969–1979 nian Zhong Mei guanxi de yanbian* [Across the chasm: The evolution of China-US Relations, 1969–1979] (Henan: Henan People's Press, 1992); Lin Qing, *Zhou Enlai zaixiang shengya* [The career of Prime Minister Zhou Enlai] (Hong Kong: Changcheng Wenhua Chubanshe, 1991); Wang Shuzhong, ed., *Mei-Su zhengba zhanlue wenti* [The question of contention for hegemony

28   *Chapter 1*

between the United States and the Soviet Union] (Beijing: Guofang daxue chubanshe, 1988); Wang Yu-san, ed., *Foreign Policy of the Republic of China* (New York: Praeger, 1990); Xie Yixian, *Zhongguo Waijiao Shi: 1949–1979* [China's diplomatic history: 1949–1979] (Henan: Henan Renmin Chubanshe, 1988); Men Honghua, *China's Grand Strategy: A Framework Analysis* (Beijing: Beijing Daxue Chubanshe, 2005); Yan Xuetong, *Zhongguo guojia liyi fenxi* [The analysis of China's national interest] (Tianjin: Tianjin Renmin Chubanshe, 1996).

20. Chen Jian, *Mao's China and the Cold War* (Chapel Hill: University of North Carolina Press, 2001); Thomas Christensen, *Useful Adversaries: Grand Strategy, Domestic Mobilization, and Sino-American Conflicts, 1949–1958* (Princeton, NJ: Princeton University Press, 1996).

21. Vogel, *Deng Xiaoping*, pp. 83–87.

22. Vogel, *Deng Xiaoping*, pp. 266–92.

23. Michael Chambers, "China and Southeast Asia: Creating a 'Win-Win' Neighborhood," in *China's "Good Neighbor" Diplomacy : A Wolf in Sheep's Clothing?* Special Report 126, ed. Gang Lin (Washington, DC: Woodrow Wilson Center for Scholars Asia Program, January 2005); "Wen Rolls Out 'Win-Win' Strategy in Africa," IPS News, June 21, 2006, ipsnews.net/news.asp?idnews=33702 (accessed July 16, 2010).

24. Yan Xuetong, "The Instability of China-US Relations," *Chinese Journal of International Politics* 3, no. 3 (2010): pp. 1–30; Zhang Liping, "A Rising China and a Lonely Superpower America," in *Making New Partnership: A Rising China and Its Neighbors*, ed. Zhang Yunlin (Beijing: Social Sciences Academic Press, 2008), pp. 324–55; Wu Xinbo, "The End of the Silver Lining: A Chinese View of the U.S.-Japanese Alliance," *Washington Quarterly* 29, no. 1 (Winter 2006): pp. 119–30.

25. Suisheng Zhao, *A Nation-State by Construction: Dynamics of Modern Chinese Nationalism* (Stanford, CA: Stanford University Press, 2004); Peter Gries, *China's New Nationalism* (Berkeley: University of California Press, 2004); Anne-Marie Brady, *Marketing Dictatorship: Propaganda and Thought Work in Contemporary China* (Lanham, MD: Rowman & Littlefield, 2008), pp. 151–74; John Garver, *Foreign Relations of the People's Republic of China* (Englewood Cliffs, NJ: Prentice Hall, 1993), pp. 1–28.

26. David M. Lampton, *Same Bed, Different Dreams* (Berkeley: University of California Press, 2001), p. 60.

27. Martin Indyk, Kenneth Lieberthal, and Michael O'Hanlon, *Bending History: Barack Obama's Foreign Policy* (Washington, DC: Brookings Institution, 2012), pp. 61–62.

28. Evelyn Goh, "Southeast Asia: Strategic Diversification in the 'Asian Century,'" in *Strategic Asia 2008–2009*, ed. Ashley Tellis, Mercy Kuo, and Andrew Marble (Seattle: National Bureau of Asian Research, 2008), pp. 261–96.

29. Vogel, *Deng Xiaoping*, pp. 266–92.

30. Robert Sutter, *U.S.-Chinese Relations: Perilous Past, Pragmatic Present* (Lanham, MD: Rowman & Littlefield, 2010).

31. Ming Wan, *Sino-Japanese Relations: Interaction, Logic and Transformation* (Stanford, CA: Stanford University Press, 2006); Richard Bush, *The Perils of Proximity* (Washington, DC: Brookings Institution, 2010).

Chapter Two

Mao's Changing Course in Foreign Affairs, 1949–1969

The foreign relations of the People's Republic of China (PRC) have experienced dramatic changes since 1949. Mao Zedong's rise in the 1930s and 1940s as the undisputed leader of the Chinese Communist Party (CCP) heralded the strong-man rule and Mao's dominance of Chinese foreign policy decision making for three decades, until his death in 1976. Under Mao's rule, the period of 1949–1976 witnessed dramatic swings in alignment, repeated and strong commitments to revolutionary goals and ideals along with more pragmatic emphasis on fostering China's national interests, and spasms of destructive mass campaigns within China that spilled over to impact Chinese foreign relations.

Chinese relations with the Soviet Union went from close alignment to the brink of war from 1950 to 1969. Under the pressure of Soviet military–backed coercion and intimidation, Mao in the early 1970s shifted course and aligned pragmatically with the United States, heretofore his main international adversary and the target of animus in a pervasive worldview fostered throughout China by Mao and the Communist government.

Coming after the disastrous results of the radical Great Leap Forward (1958–1961), fostered and perpetuated by Mao and which resulted in the deaths of thirty million Chinese, Mao initiated in 1966 a massive purge of Chinese government and party officials that destroyed the lives of hundreds of thousands of Chinese elites and their families while ending conventional Chinese relations with most of the world for several years. The resulting searing experiences for the leaders and people of China occurred in an international atmosphere of repeated episodes of tense Cold War confrontation and competition between two superpowers, the United States and the Soviet Union, which alternatively viewed China as a major adversary or as an asset in their ongoing contests with one another.

China reached the nadir of its international relationships and influence during the early years of the Cultural Revolution (1966–1976) when conventional diplomacy and experienced diplomats were put aside and dismissed in favor of strident ideological fervor bordering on xenophobia. China became alienated from all but a handful of remaining international friends. The road back to more conventional diplomacy and international interchange was slow and difficult amid stark differences over domestic and foreign policy issues among Chinese leaders engaged in what turned out to be life-or-death struggles for power. The process toward more conventional diplomacy and international interchange was expedited because Sino-Soviet frictions reached a point in 1969 where the Soviet Union, backed by its large military buildup along the Chinese border, warned it would invade China and destroy China's nuclear facilities. The Soviet threat forced China to put aside the rigidities of the recent past and seek common ground with international forces helpful in countering the Soviet threat, leading to China's opening to many countries, especially the United States.

Security and strategic interests continued to dominate Chinese foreign relations in the last two decades of the Cold War. China maneuvered between the two superpowers. In general, China's leaders, at first Mao and later Deng Xiaoping, who emerged as China's dominant leader in the late 1970s and remained in that position until the early 1990s, judged that their interests were best served by working cooperatively with the United States, its allies and associates, and other world powers. In doing so, they endeavored to block and curb the expansion of the power and influence of the Soviet Union, seen by China as its main security danger and concern. Notably, China under Deng Xiaoping undertook a major commitment against perceived Soviet expansion by launching a large military attack against Soviet-backed Vietnam, on account of Vietnam's invasion of Cambodia and toppling of the Chinese-supported Khmer Rouge regime in 1978–1979. At the same time, China registered frequent disappointment in U.S. resolve in the face of the Soviet Union's expansion. Its differences with the United States over Taiwan and other bilateral issues also flared repeatedly.

By the early 1980s, China saw Soviet power more encumbered at home and abroad. The new situation allowed China to announce and pursue an ostensibly more evenhanded policy toward the Soviet Union and the United States. Senior Chinese diplomats engaged in regular talks with Soviet counterparts on international issues and bilateral relations. In practice, however, China found the Soviets inflexible and the United States more beneficial for Chinese concerns.

The United States and its allies and associates not only were helpful in Chinese calculations of security and strategic interests. They also rose in importance in regard to what would emerge as the defining goal of post-Mao foreign relations—promoting Chinese economic development. After Mao died in September 1976 and his radical associates were removed from power the following month, Chinese leaders gradually came to a general consensus that continued rule of the Chinese Communist Party depended ultimately on successful economic development, which in turn required reaching out to foreign countries that had the capital, technology, and markets China needed in order to promote economic development. This consensus would be sustained and reinforced in the aftermath of domestic Chinese turmoil brought about by the mass demonstrations in Beijing and other cities in 1989, leading to the harsh crackdown by Chinese authorities against demonstrators in Tiananmen Square and other parts of China in June of that year. Chinese leaders endeavored to keep open advantageous economic ties with Western countries, even as many of them, led by the United States, tried to punish and isolate China on account of the Tiananmen crackdown.

China's successful economic development was accompanied by a large military buildup that added to growing Chinese influence and power in Asian and world affairs. A series of major military exercises in the Taiwan Strait in 1995 and 1996 served as a graphic warning to Taiwan and the United States of the consequences of perceived efforts to promote Taiwan independence from China.

As China emerged in the twenty-first century as an economic and military power second only to the United States, the new generations of Chinese leaders seemed determined to continue on the post-Mao course of foreign policy that had proven so effective in Chinese development. They had put aside the decisive and often erratic strong-man rule of Mao Zedong. They no longer had to deal with Soviet pressure, which had dominated the foreign policy maneuvers of Deng Xiaoping, who commanded foreign policy decision making for the two decades after Mao's death. They followed collaborative and consultative patterns of foreign policy making at home and abroad, seeking to sustain into the coming decades the generally favorable recent international circumstances seen as providing a prolonged period of "strate-gic opportunity" for China's economic and broader national development, which continued to be the top priority of the Chinese government. After considerable and prolonged domestic debate and discussion, China made the adjustments necessary to join the World Trade Organization (WTO) in 2001 as China integrated effectively with the global economy in seeking rapid modernization for China. Nevertheless, the Chinese pursuit of foreign poli-cies and practices supportive of development and nation building remained complicated. Strong patriotism led to nationalistic opinion in China that pushed for more assertive policies and behavior in defense of Chinese inter-ests abroad. Actions of various powers abroad, including the United States, Japan, India, Taiwan, North Korea, and others, challenged key Chinese inter-ests. New issues emerged as a result of unexpected developments including international economic crises, competition for international energy resources, and worldwide pressure for conformity to norms regarding terrorism, nuclear nonproliferation, and climate change.

CONFLICT AND CONTAINMENT

Mao Zedong and his Communist Party–led fighters faced daunting chal-lenges as they endeavored to consolidate their rule after defeating Chiang Kai-shek's Nationalist Party (Kuomintang—KMT) forces in the Chinese Civil War and established the People's Republic of China on the Chinese mainland in 1949. Chiang and his remaining forces retreated to Taiwan. The Communist armies prepared to attack Taiwan and finish the civil war. Pros-pects for Communist success in the assault improved as U.S. President Harry Truman decided that the United States should end support for Chiang's Na-tionalists.

China had been war ravaged for decades and arguably had been without effective governance for over a century. The collapse of the decaying Chi-nese empire in 1911 was followed by decades of warlord violence throughout the country. The interlude of Chinese Nationalist rule in the late 1920s and early 1930s ended with Japan's war against China. With one million Japa-nese troops and the support of Chinese collaborators, Japan controlled the most productive eastern half of China. Chinese deaths in the war with Japan (1937–1945) were about twenty million.

The Chinese Communists were a rural-based movement with over two decades of experience in guerrilla war and supporting administrative efforts in the Chinese countryside, but with little experience in managing the complicated affairs of China's cities, its urban economy, or its national administration. Seeking needed technical and economic backing as well as guarantees and support for China's national security, the Maoist leadership endeavored to consolidate relations with the Soviet Union in an international environment heavily influenced by the United States, the main international supporter of its Chinese Nationalist adversary, and American associated states influential in Asian and world politics. Mao made his first trip abroad and traveled to Moscow. He waited for weeks before Soviet leader Joseph Stalin, calculating Communist advances in Europe and Asia and uncertain of Mao's reliability, was ready to conclude an agreement on February 14, 1950, establishing the Sino-Soviet alliance.

These circumstances and determinants led to a strong current in analyses of Chinese relations, which emphasized Chinese imperatives of consolidation and development domestically and reactions internationally to perceived threats and occasional opportunities posed by circumstances involving notably the United States and the Soviet Union. In particular, as the Cold War spread from Europe and came to dominate international dynamics in Asia for several decades beginning in the late 1940s, Chinese foreign relations were seen as dominated in the 1950s and 1960s by Chinese efforts to deal with what emerged as a massive US-led military, economic, and political containment of China. Chinese interactions with the United States and Chinese foreign relations more broadly in this period often were assessed in terms of Chinese reactions to perceived threats posed by the power and actions of the United States and associated countries.[1]

Heading the list of strengths that the Maoist leaders brought to bear as they began national leadership in China were the Chinese Communist Party's broad experience in political organization and related social and economic mobilization, and a strong revolutionary ideology.[2] Mao Zedong and supporting leaders were committed to seeking revolutionary changes in China and in international affairs affecting China, and they had the determination and ability to move Chinese people along these paths. This set of determinants and circumstances led to another strong current in analyses of Chinese relations, which emphasized the importance of the Chinese leadership's resolve to challenge and confront the United States and its allies and associates in Asia as the Communist Chinese leadership sought to promote revolutionary change in Asian and world affairs. The analyses also showed a related tendency of the Chinese leadership to exploit episodes of confrontation with

America as means to mobilize greater support within China for the often revolutionary changes sought there by the Maoist leadership.[3]

Assessments of the record of the Maoist period show a complicated mix of revolutionary imperatives and more conventional imperatives of security and nation building driving Chinese decision making. Adding to the mix was the emergence of the dominant role of Mao Zedong and how his strong-man rule came to determine Chinese decision making regarding Chinese foreign relations in particular, notably relations with the United States and the Soviet Union. One consequence was the ability and the actual tendency of the PRC to shift direction dramatically in foreign affairs. China's strong alignment with the Soviet Union in 1950 and break with Moscow ten years later exemplify the kinds of major shifts in China's foreign policy during this period.[4]

EARLY EXPERIENCES IN FOREIGN AFFAIRS

The roots of Chinese Communist calculus and shifts in foreign affairs lay heavily with the protracted experience of Mao Zedong and his associates as leaders of a guerilla revolutionary movement struggling for success against great odds in the two decades prior to the establishment of the People's Republic of China in 1949. Chiefly concerned with the survival of their movement against Chiang Kai-shek's Nationalist Party–led administration, the Communist leaders devoted only secondary attention to events outside China.

Chiang's armies forced Mao and his cohort to retreat from base areas in southern China, embarking on the so-called Long March, which ended after great hardship with the remnants of the group arriving in northwestern China in 1936, where they developed new base areas. A mutiny among troops ostensibly under his command forced Chiang in late 1936 to agree to a united front with the Communists against Japan and its expansionist moves in China. Japan's launch of full-scale war against China in 1937 focused mainly against Chiang's forces, which were compelled after strong resistance to retreat from coastal China into the interior. The Nationalist-Communist united front eroded. The Japanese assault on Chiang's armies provided opportunity for Mao and the Communists to consolidate their bases in northwestern China, in particular.

Reflecting their isolation and apparent lack of information about foreign affairs, the CCP leaders showed little evidence of a sophisticated view of world events. In particular, they relied heavily on guidelines set by the Soviet

Union–dominated international communist movement (the Communist International, or Comintern) in assessing the policies of capitalist states such as the United States. Thus, when the USSR opposed the foreign policies of the United States and other Western powers in the early 1930s, Chinese party representatives carefully followed suit. A few years later, the CCP promptly echoed the Comintern's "united front" line, which drew a distinction between the "principal" enemy—that is, the fascist states—as opposed to the capitalist democracies, calling for alliance with the latter against the former. This line conformed to the CCP interests inside China, allowing the Communists to exploit an anti-Japanese approach in order to broaden their appeal within the country.[5]

The CCP also followed the Comintern line in foreign affairs even when it proved damaging to the Communists' position in China, as during the period of erratic shifts in Soviet foreign policy in 1939–1941. Mao Zedong personally supported the Comintern position on the most notorious example of expedient Soviet policy—the German-Soviet pact of August 1939—even though it seriously tarnished the CCP image in China. The Soviet move notably disappointed a prevailing Chinese hope that the USSR would unite with the capitalist democracies against the Axis powers, which came to include imperial Japan along with Adolf Hitler's Germany and Benito Mussolini's Italy, and accordingly would assist China, which was bearing the brunt of Japanese military might.[6]

The significance of the Chinese Communists' subservience to Moscow's line in foreign affairs remains unclear. It may be, as some have argued, that the CCP was in fact demonstrating an intense desire to win favor with Moscow as well as a genuine, ideologically based determination to follow the Soviet lead.[7] On the other hand, the CCP leaders may have been demonstrating little more than *pro forma* backing for the Comintern line, in a relatively unimportant sphere of foreign affairs, in order to keep on good terms with the Soviet-led international communist movement—the source of foreign support that the Chinese Communists had at this time.

At the same time, the Chinese Communists judged the United States and associated Western powers negatively on the basis of their ideological training in Marxism-Leninism and their particular belief in Vladimir Lenin's theory of imperialism. Prior to World War II, the Communists generally assessed the policies of the "imperialist" powers in China, including the United States, as motivated chiefly by economic gain; the desire for financial return was seen to cause the powers to intervene actively in China's internal affairs, militarily dominate the Chinese treaty ports, patrol rivers and coastal waterways, and supply warlords and other perceived nonprogressive power holders in China with arms and loans to suppress the CCP-supported, anti-imperialist movement.[8]

The twists and turns of the CCP's shifting emphasis in foreign affairs were reflected in on-again off-again initiatives toward the United States in the 1930s and 1940s. The termination of the Nationalist blockade and military campaigns against the Communists following the start of the CCP-KMT united front in late 1936 prompted the Communist leaders to try to break out of their isolated position. Overlooking past disputes and negative feelings toward the United States, they endeavored to win favor with American news reporters and other Westerners who visited their base in northwestern China. This opening to the West, highlighted by Mao's meetings with journalist Edgar Snow, was short lived. Nationalist forces reimposed a tight blockade around the Communist base while American interest was diverted to Japan's expansion in East Asia.[9]

Following the Japanese attack on Pearl Harbor and American entrance into the Pacific war, the Chinese Communist leadership initiated a more serious effort to win U.S. support. In China's wartime capital, Chongqing, CCP representatives led by Zhou Enlai made concerted efforts in private conversations with American officials to explain the Communists' positions that were at odds with those of the ruling Nationalist government. They also encouraged the Americans to send official representatives to the Communist-held areas in northern China for liaison work with the CCP officials in the war against Japan. The Communists' accommodating approach toward the United States came in spite of their past ill feeling toward Washington and their ideologically based antagonism toward the capitalist American government. It no doubt was in part prompted by the general line of the Communist International at this time, which emphasized the need for world Communists to unite with the capitalist democracies in order to defeat the fascist powers. However, the intensity of Communists' effort to woo American favor also appeared to be closely tied to the situation in China and to the CCP's competition for power with the Kuomintang.[10]

America emerged during World War II as the predominant foreign power in East Asia, and in China it brought its power, influence, and aid to bear solely on the side of Chiang Kai-shek's Nationalists. Facing this adverse trend, the Communists sought closer association with the United States. Their efforts resulted in the establishment of military and political connections, notably through a U.S. liaison office in the Communist headquarters at Yenan. U.S. mediation between the Communists and Nationalists beginning in 1944 failed to bridge the gap between the two and failed to end one-sided American support for Chiang Kai-shek's Nationalists. In the Chinese civil war following Japan's defeat the Americans sided strongly with the Nationalists, reinforcing the CCP's leaders' view of the United States as an enemy of the newly founded People's Republic of China. [11]

CONTAINMENT AND CHINA'S RESPONSE

The foreign policy plans of the newly established People's Republic of China (PRC) were confronted at the outset by miscalculations over Korea, which resulted in Sino-American war and the establishment of a massive U.S. military–led effort to surround and check Chinese Communism. The American deployments, alliances, and related economic embargo under the rubric of the policy of containment came to dominate the foreign policy calculations of the PRC for two decades. How China chose to deal with the American threat and other salient concerns in foreign affairs varied greatly, reinforcing a pattern of swings in Chinese foreign policy behavior that were hard to foresee. [12]

Neither the government of Mao Zedong nor the administration of President Harry S. Truman in the United States sought or foresaw a U.S.-China war in early 1950. The Americans were surprised when North Korean forces, with the support of Soviet and Chinese leaders, launched an all-out military attack against South Korean forces in June 1950. The Chinese Communist leaders and their Korean and Soviet Communist allies apparently calculated that the better-organized and better-armed North Koreans would attain victory quickly without provoking a major or effective U.S. military response. Thus, it was their turn to be surprised when the United States promptly intervened militarily in the Korean War and also sent the U.S. Seventh Fleet to prevent a Chinese Communist attack on Taiwan, where Chiang Kai-shek and his remaining forces had retreated after their defeat on the Chinese mainland. U.S. forces and their South Korean allies halted the North Korean advance and carried out an amphibious landing at Inchon in September 1950 that effectively cut off the North Korean armies in the South, leading to their destruction. [13]

The string of miscalculations continued. With the support of the United Nations, U.S. and South Korean forces proceeded into North Korea. The

Chinese warned and prepared to resist them, but U.S. leaders thought the warnings were a bluff. By November hundreds of thousands of Chinese Communist forces were driving the U.S. and South Korean forces south in full retreat. Eventually, the Americans and their allies were able to sustain a line of combat roughly in the middle of the peninsula, as the two armies faced off for over two more years of combat, casualties, and destruction. [14]

Chinese Communist leaders also launched domestic mass campaigns to root out pro-American and other Western influence and seize control of U.S. and Western cultural, religious, and business organizations that remained in China. The United States began wide-ranging strategic efforts to contain the expansion of Chinese power and Chinese-backed Communist expansion in Asia. A strict U.S. economic and political embargo against China, large U.S. force deployments, eventually numbering between one half and one million troops, massive foreign aid allocations to U.S. Asian allies and supporters, and a ring of U.S. defense alliances around China were used to block Chinese expansion and to drive a wedge between the PRC and its Soviet ally. [15]

President Dwight D. Eisenhower's administration used threats and negotiations in reaching an armistice agreement that stopped the fighting in Korea in 1953. But American efforts to strengthen military alliances and deployments to contain Chinese Communist–backed expansion continued unabated. The U.S.-led efforts faced off against enhanced Chinese efforts in the wake of the Korean armistice to strengthen support for Communist insurgents working against American-backed forces in French Indochina and direct Chinese military probes and challenges against the United States and their Chinese Nationalist allies in the Taiwan Strait.

Mao Zedong and his Communist Party–led government continued their consolidation of control inside China, notably through mass campaigns led by Communist activists targeting landlords, leading urban political and economic elites, and others deemed abusive or uncooperative with Communist goals. They prepared for major nation-building efforts with the support of their Soviet and Soviet bloc supporters to establish an administrative structure, often along the lines of that of the Soviet Union, to govern Chinese civil administration, economic planning, military modernization, intelligence collection, and other endeavors. They pursued efforts to tap into the surplus wealth being created in China's rural sector for investment in their planned expansion of China's industrial economy. After a brief period where peasants held land as a result of the mass campaign for land reform in rural China in the early 1950s, Chinese leaders saw the need to emulate the Soviet model and began to collectivize the land under government administration so as to better control the surplus rural wealth and to maximize its utility to the state's interests in promoting industrial development. The Soviet Union was providing over one hundred major projects to assist Chinese industrialization and modernization, but they had to be paid for. The Chinese saw collectivization in the rural areas and concurrent establishment of greater state control of the urban economy along Soviet lines as the appropriate way forward.

These dramatic and massive shifts in domestic policy and direction occurred frequently in conjunction with crises and confrontations with the United States and its allies and associates around China's periphery in Asia. At one level, the Chinese determination to work against and confront the U.S.-backed French forces in Indochina and the U.S.-supported forces of Chiang Kai-shek in the Taiwan Strait reflected a deeply held determination to confound and wear down the American-fostered containment system. The Chinese Communist leadership held a strong revolutionary commitment to change the international order dominated by the United States and its allies and to support Communist-led forces struggling against what they saw as foreign imperialism.[16]

The U.S. effort also directly threatened China's national security and sovereignty, often in graphic and severe ways. The Eisenhower administration threatened China with nuclear attack in order to push it toward an armistice in Korea, and the U.S. government used the threat of nuclear attack at other times in the face of perceived Chinese provocations in the 1950s. Mao Zedong's China had no viable defense against U.S. nuclear weapons and put top priority on developing Chinese nuclear weapons to deal with such repeated U.S. efforts at intimidation. At the same time, the Chinese Communist leaders also were seen to continue to use the crisis atmosphere caused by confrontations with outside threats posed by the United States and its allies as a means to strengthen their domestic control and their mobilization of resources for advancement of nation building and administrative competence.[17]

Defeat of U.S.-backed French forces in Indochina led to the 1954 Geneva Conference and accords that formalized French withdrawal. China backed the Communist-led Viet Minh victors with supplies and advisors, while the United States provided supplies to forces of France that ultimately were defeated at their Indochina stronghold, Dien Bien Phu, on May 7, 1954. France sought peace at the Geneva Conference in 1954, while the United States deepened involvement in Vietnam and elsewhere in Southeast Asia to check Chinese-backed Communist advances in Southeast Asia. After the conference, U.S. policy worked to support a non-Communist regime in South Vietnam, backing the regime when it resisted steps toward reunification set forth in the Geneva Accords. The United States also deepened and broadened defense and other links with powers in Southeast Asia in order to check Chinese-backed Communist gains in the region.

President Eisenhower and Secretary of State John Foster Dulles were wary of Chiang Kai-shek's maneuvers that might drag the United States into a war with the Chinese Communists over Taiwan. Using the fortuitous turn of events caused by the Korean War, Chiang Kai-shek's Nationalists consolidated their rule in Taiwan and with American support rapidly built up Taiwan's military forces with the objective of eventually taking the battle to mainland China. The political atmosphere inside the United States was supportive of Chiang and his harsh anti-Communist stance. The so-called China Lobby supporting Chiang and his Nationalist administration included liberals as well as conservatives in a variety of respected organizations. Thus, U.S. military and economic assistance to Chiang Kai-shek and the Nationalist forces on Taiwan expanded dramatically. [18]

Though Dulles and other leaders of the U.S. government were privately unsure of the wisdom of such close and formal U.S. ties to Chiang's Nationalists, Washington eventually brought Taiwan into the web of formal military alliances that provided the foundation of the U.S. containment system against Chinese-backed Communist expansion in Asia. The United States and Nationalist China signed a bilateral defense treaty on December 2, 1954.

The PRC reacted with harsh rhetoric and military assaults against Nationalist Chinese–controlled islands off the coast of the Chinese mainland. Great Britain and other U.S. allies, as well as some U.S. congressional leaders and other elites, did not welcome this new and potentially very dangerous military crisis between the United States and China so soon after the bloody conflict in Korea. But the U.S. administration firmly backed the Chinese Nationalists and their Republic of China (ROC). U.S. forces helped Nationalist forces on some exposed islands to withdraw as the Taiwan Strait crisis of 1955 continued, raising fears of a renewed U.S.-China war.

PEACEFUL COEXISTENCE

Against this background, the Chinese Communist government's stance against the United States moderated. The reasoning appeared related to a shift in Soviet policy toward the West following Stalin's death in 1953. The incoming Soviet leaders were more interested than Stalin had been in arranging an advantageous modus vivendi with Western powers in Europe. While they continued to give some public support to their Chinese ally in its dispute with the Chinese Nationalists and the United States, they also signaled Soviet wariness about getting involved in Asian conflicts. They played down the applicability to Asia of the Sino-Soviet alliance; Soviet official commentary implied that China was to bear the major responsibility for dealing with the United States and its allies and associates in Asia. The Chinese government also began at this time to endeavor to broaden productive economic and diplomatic ties with countries in Asia, Africa, and Europe, and Chinese leaders found that their hard line and confrontational behavior in the Taiwan Strait were counterproductive for this effort. Washington, for its part, had not sought to escalate military tensions with China, as this would complicate U.S. efforts to work with European and Asian allies to explore Soviet moderation and to build lasting alliance relationships to contain Asian Communist expansion.[19]

Thus, Beijing by early 1955 was faced with an increasingly counterproductive campaign over Taiwan, a potentially dangerous military confrontation with Washington, lukewarm support from its primary international ally, and increased alienation from world powers. In this context, Chinese leaders understandably chose to move to a more moderate stance when presented with the American offer in mid-January 1955 of a cease-fire in the armed conflict in the Taiwan Strait. Beijing responded to the U.S. proposal with criticism but indirectly signaled interest in the offer by gradually reducing Chinese demands concerning Taiwan.

Chinese Premier Zhou Enlai used the venue of the Afro-Asian Conference in Bandung, Indonesia, in April 1955 to ease tensions and call for talks with the United States. How serious the Chinese were in pursuing their avowed interest in such engagement with the United States was never shown, as the Chinese overtures met with a nuanced but firm rebuff from Washington. Secretary of State Dulles was wary that direct talks with the PRC would undermine Chiang Kai-shek's Nationalist government on Taiwan. Dulles's private strategy of vigorously pursuing a containment policy against China favored a tougher U.S. policy toward China than toward the Soviet Union. He endeavored thereby to force Beijing to rely on Moscow for economic and other needs, which the Soviet Union could not meet. In this and other ways, he hoped to drive a wedge between China and the USSR. On the other hand,

Dulles faced congressional and allied pressures to meet with the Chinese, so he agreed to low-level ambassadorial talks that began in Geneva in 1955. The talks met frequently for a time but little progress was made, as the United States repeatedly rejected Chinese initiatives and accused China of perfidy regarding the agreements that were reached. [20]

Zhou's overtures at Bandung also included Chinese efforts to improve relations with growing numbers of newly independent governments in the developing world by reassuring them with Chinese pledges to follow moderate foreign policies consistent with what became known as the Five Principles of Peaceful Coexistence. China established relations and improved ties with various governments and notably advanced Chinese relations with governments of such key large developing countries as Egypt, India, and Indonesia. Over time, those advances flagged as China pursued more radical and confrontational policies directed against the United States and eventually the Soviet Union in the late 1950s and 1960s. Nonetheless, Beijing's diplomatic relations broadened with a number of developing and some developed countries during this period.

In 1958, China moved into a more radical phase of foreign as well as domestic policy, and its resolve against the United States remained firm and deepened over the next decade. Beijing's public break with the Soviet Union by 1960 brought on stronger Chinese competition with the Soviet Union in the international communist movement and especially among developing nations. China's strident antagonism regarding both superpowers exacerbated differences with the wide range of countries and world leaders who maintained or sought amicable ties with either Washington or Moscow.

China sustained strong interest in ties with Egypt following the coming to power of Gamal Abdel Nasser in the 1950s. Nasser gave a strongly anti-Western cast to the prevailing ideas in the Afro-Asian and nonaligned movements. He also was a proponent of pan-Arabism and sought to reduce Western influence in Egypt, notably by nationalizing the Suez Canal. Egypt's confrontation with Great Britain and France over this move led it to establish diplomatic relations with China in 1956. It became the first country in Africa or the Middle East to do so. Egypt's militant anticolonialist stance and its role as the largest and most influential Arab state reinforced Chinese interest in maintaining close relations. The two governments differed, however, notably over China's strident opposition to the Soviet Union, which caused a major split with Egypt and others in the Afro-Asian People's Solidarity Organization in the 1960s. After the Egyptians' defeat to U.S.-backed Israel in

1967, China's advice to Nasser was to engage in protracted guerrilla war with Israel; this advice was deemed unhelpful and naïve among the Arab leaders.[21]

Other features of Chinese diplomacy in the 1950s included efforts to reach out to Japan, which was interested in trade and other conventional relations despite the American-led international embargo against China. Several European countries improved relations with China, as did some South and Southeast Asian nations interested in taking advantage of China's emphasis on peaceful coexistence.

Greater Chinese international activism in the mid-1950s also saw the PRC take a leading position on two major crises in the international communist movement, perhaps the most important arena of Chinese foreign policy activity in the 1950s. In 1956, China reacted differently to anti-Soviet trends in Poland and Hungary. As dedicated Marxist-Leninists, Chinese leaders supported the intervention of Soviet troops in Hungary in November 1956, as the existing Communist regime was seen as unable to contain a burgeoning mass movement that was increasingly taking outright anti-Communist forms. By contrast, Chinese officials that same year supported the leadership of Poland where the Communist Party resisted Soviet pressure to curb what was deemed by Moscow as excessive nationalism and defiance of Soviet instructions.[22] The lesson of these concurrent episodes was that China supported Communist regimes and forceful Soviet actions in support of Communist regimes against anti-Communist challenge, but China favored resistance to the Soviet Union's efforts to intimidate and coerce neighboring Communist regimes for the sake of Moscow's stature as leader of the international communist movement. In both cases, China's actions showed willingness to undertake a greater role regarding international communist matters following the death of Stalin and in emerging Chinese disagreements with Stalin's successors.

REVIVED RADICALISM

With the shift back to a more radical posture in foreign affairs in 1958, Mao Zedong's Communist forces used artillery barrages in an effort to challenge and halt resupply of the Nationalist Chinese forces holding the fortress island Quemoy and other Nationalist-controlled islands located only a few miles off the coast of the Chinese mainland. The military attacks predictably created another major crisis and war scare, with the United States firmly supporting

Chiang Kai-shek's forces and threatening nuclear attack. Chiang Kai-shek refused to consider withdrawal from the Quemoy fortress, where a large portion of his best troops were deployed as part of his broader military preparations to attack mainland China and reverse Communist rule.

The absence of landing craft and other preparations for an invasion suggested that Mao was testing Nationalist and U.S. resolve regarding the offshore island and did not intend to invade Taiwan itself. The crisis atmosphere played into Mao's efforts at the time to mobilize national resources for a massive "Great Leap Forward" in Chinese development. Later, foreign analysts argued persuasively that the domestic mobilization was a major Chinese objective in launching the military aggression on the offshore islands held by the Chinese Nationalists. [23]

Another line of analysis argued that the Chinese leader also used the confrontation with the United States to test Soviet resolve in supporting China in what was seen in China as a weakening Sino-Soviet alliance. The Chinese-Soviet alliance indeed began to unravel by the late 1950s. Ideological debates emblematic of the Sino-Soviet split came into public view by 1960, and Soviet leader Nikita Khrushchev ended assistance to China that year. The dispute broadened to include intense Sino-Soviet competition for influence in the international communist movement and among developing countries in world affairs. The Sino-Soviet border became an issue of public dispute in 1964. By that time, Leonid Brezhnev and Alexei Kosygin had replaced the deposed Khrushchev; they undertook a major buildup of Soviet forces along the Sino-Soviet border and in Mongolia. Escalating border clashes in 1969 foreshadowed full-scale Soviet military attack. [24]

The Soviet withdrawal of assistance to China in 1960 came at a time of acute economic crisis in China caused by the collapse and abject failure of the Great Leap Forward campaign. The staggering damage to China from the three-year effort included the premature deaths of thirty million people from starvation and nutrition deficits. During this period of weakness China became more concerned about border security in the face of Chiang Kai-shek's avowed plans to attack and India's perceived encroachments along its border with China. China prepared to use force against Chiang's armies, and in 1962 it launched a major assault destroying India's border defenses. [25]

As the first prime minister of independent India until his death in 1964, Jawaharlal Nehru presided over, and in many cases directed, the tortuous turns of Sino-Indian relations during this formative period of relations. Nehru chartered a course for India independent of the United States and the Soviet

Union. He pioneered a policy on nonalignment and became a leader of the Nonaligned Movement composed mainly of newly emerging and developing countries. He quickly established diplomatic relations with China, argued in favor of China's entry into the United Nations, and refused to condemn China as the aggressor in the Korean War. In the mid-1950s, Nehru built a relationship with Chinese premier Zhou Enlai, who was then emphasizing Chinese moderation consistent with the Five Principles of Peaceful Coexistence. He seemed surprised by revelations in 1958 of Chinese road building across Indian-claimed territory along the border with China known as the Aksai Chin. In 1959, he allowed the Dalai Lama and many thousands of his followers, escaping a Chinese crackdown in Tibet, to reside in India. Chinese-Indian border tensions worsened, though Nehru again seemed surprised by the Chinese military action overrunning Indian defenses along the eastern boundary in 1962, the nadir of Sino-Indian relations in the modern period.[26]

Elsewhere, China used diplomacy, established relations, and employed other conventional means to stabilize sensitive issues. In neighboring Laos, China fully supported the armed struggle against the rule by France in Indochina that resulted in the 1954 Geneva Accords and the creation of an independent Laos. The unstable Laotian government was subjected to pressures from rightist forces and forces associated with a Communist insurgency, which China supported. China established diplomatic relations with Laos in 1961. In 1961–1962 a second Geneva Conference, attended by U.S. and Chinese officials, eventually reached an understanding on the Communist vs. non-Communist armed struggle in Laos. The understanding temporarily defused this flash point of U.S.-Chinese conflicting interests, although the United States and China subsequently deepened military involvement in the country, as did the Chinese-backed forces from North Vietnam. The escalation of fighting in the Vietnam War involving Vietnamese Communist forces and forces of the United States in the 1960s dominated developments in the country. China fully backed the Vietnamese Communists and their Communist-led allies in Laos.[27]

China also advanced relations with Nepal. The Himalayan mountain state had deepened economic and security ties with India in the aftermath of China's military occupation of Tibet in 1950, and a Nepal-India Peace and Friendship Treaty was signed that year. Nepal improved relations with China in the mid-1950s in tandem with improvement in India's relations with China; subsequently, relations with Nepal continued to improve while Indian-Chinese relations declined. Nepal and China established diplomatic relations in 1955; Nepal recognized Tibet as part of China; and the two countries exchanged resident ambassadors by 1960. That year, Nepal and China signed a boundary settlement agreement and a treaty of peace and friendship. Nepal also began supporting China's entry into the United Nations. In 1961, Nepal and China agreed to build an all-weather road connecting the Nepalese capital, Kathmandu, with Tibet. During the Sino-Indian War of 1962, Nepal maintained neutrality.[28]

China's early involvement with Africa featured sometimes visionary efforts to help African countries throw off the influence of colonial or other foreign powers and to foster rapid development and social progress. China supported Gamal Abdel Nasser's leading Egypt against Western powers in the 1950s. In the 1960s, it supported newly emerging nations and armed resistance groups targeting colonial and white-ruled African regimes. It favored nations and groups that opposed or remained independent of the Soviet Union, the United States, and colonial powers of Europe. Major assistance projects included the TanZam Railway linking Zambia and Tanzania, representing a high point in Chinese assistance to Africa, and support for the pro-China leaders of the countries, Zambia's Kenneth Kaunda and Tanzania's Julius Nyerere.[29]

Among developed countries, China reached out to Japan in the 1960s for trade, technology, and other economic support following the end of Soviet assistance to China. The Japanese government and businesses found ways around the U.S.-led international embargo against China in order to reach understandings with Beijing that made Japan China's most important international economic partner in the 1960s. France, under the leadership of independent-minded President Charles de Gaulle, also broke with American-led efforts to isolate China and established diplomatic relations with the PRC in 1964.

TURMOIL IN THE CULTURAL REVOLUTION

During the 1960s, a disastrous result of the twists and turns in Chinese domestic and foreign policy following the widespread starvation and other calamities caused by the collapse of the Great Leap Forward were years of violence and life-or-death political struggle. Elites and other groups, mainly in Chinese cities, maneuvered and fought during the Cultural Revolution that began in 1966 and did not end until Mao's death in 1976.[30] At first, the sharply deteriorating domestic situation in the early 1960s caused Mao to retreat from regular involvement in administrative matters. His subordinates pursued more moderate and pragmatic policies designed to revive agricultural and industrial production on a sustainable basis without reliance on the highly disruptive and wasteful mass campaigns and excessive collectivization of recent years. The economy began to revive, but the progress was marred in Mao's eyes by a reliance on the kinds of incentives prevalent in the "revisionist" practices of the Soviet Union and its allied states and the controlling bureaucratic elites in those states, who were seen as restoring the kind of unequal and exploitative practices typical of capitalism.

Mao found that two of the three main pillars of power and control in China, the Communist Party and the Chinese government, continued to move in the wrong direction. The third pillar of power and control, the Chinese military, was under the leadership of Lin Biao following the purge of Defense Minister Peng Dehuai, who dared to resist Mao's Great Leap policies during a leadership meeting in 1959. Defense Minister Lin positioned his leadership in support of Maoist ideals of revolution, equality, and service to the people. Indoctrination and involvement in civil society and popular affairs often took precedence over professional military training. The distillation of Mao's wisdom from volumes of selected works was distributed throughout the Chinese military, the broader masses of China, and abroad in the form of a plastic covered "little red book," *Quotations from Chairman Mao Tsetung*, published with a preface by Lin Biao.

Mao was not prepared to break with his party and government colleagues until 1966. By that time he had become sufficiently opposed to prevailing administrative practices and tendencies. Also he had built up enough support outside normal administrative structures in order to challenge and reverse what was later portrayed as a drift toward revisionism and the restoration of capitalism. Relying on his personal charisma, organizational support from military leaders like Lin Biao, security forces controlled by radical leaders like Kang Sheng, and various political radicals and opportunists, Mao launched his unorthodox efforts, including the creation of legions of millions of young Red Guards leading the attack against established authority in urban China. The result was confusion, some resistance from political and government leaders often unaware of Mao's commitment to the radical Red Guards and their allies, and ultimately mass purges and persecution of senior and lesser authorities amid widespread violence and destruction carried out by Red Guard groups and others. By 1968, numerous neighborhoods in cities in China had burned during clashes between rival Red Guard groups, and the party and government structure had collapsed. The military was called into the cities to restore order. With Mao's support, they proceeded to transport the millions of Red Guards from the cities and to disperse them into various areas in the Chinese countryside where they were compelled to stay and work for the indefinite future.

The disaster and disruption in domestic affairs was duplicated in the shift toward radicalism in Chinese foreign relations. The Chinese split with the Soviet Union deepened and broadened in the 1960s. Beijing not only opposed the Soviet Union on ideological grounds but strongly attacked Moscow's willingness to cooperate with the United States in international affairs. Chinese leaders saw the newly independent Asian and African states as providing an important arena for struggle with Moscow as well as with the United States. Though weak economically and having little to spare following the depravations of the Great Leap Forward, China provided economic and military aid to left-leaning governments, and it provided training, military assistance, and financial support to armed insurgents struggling against colonial powers or right-leaning third world governments.

Chinese Premier Zhou Enlai visited Africa in 1964 and said it was "ripe for revolution." China endeavored to compete with the Soviet Union in support of various anticolonial insurgencies and to supply significant aid to African governments prepared to align closer to the PRC than to the Soviet Union or the West. In Asia, China strongly supported the Vietnamese Communist forces directed by the North Vietnamese government in Hanoi in the face of increased American military involvement in South Vietnam and other parts of Indochina. The Chinese government also organized and/or strengthened support for Communist-led insurgencies targeted against governments in Southeast Asia seen by China as pro-American or insufficiently accommodating to Chinese influence and interests. [31]

Although one of the first governments to recognize the People's Republic of China and despite its neutral stance during the Cold War, the government of Burma came under sometimes violent pressure from China. China was long involved with Communist insurgencies and dissident ethnic groups along the porous Sino-Burmese border. The border was finally settled in 1960. Relations deteriorated seriously in 1967 when clashes inspired by Cultural Revolution zealots led to full-scale anti-Chinese riots, leaving over one hundred Chinese dead. China subsequently organized, armed, and trained a large (20,000 fighters) insurgency against the Burmese government under the rubric of the Burmese Communist Party, which posed a major security threat to the Burmese government for the next twenty years.[32]

China followed two tracks in developing relations with Indonesia in the early 1960s. One track involved supporting President Sukarno in his radical nationalist policies of confrontation with Malaysia, which was backed by Great Britain, over whether Malaysia or Indonesia should control the disputed regions of Sarawak and Sabah. The other involved closer cooperation with the Indonesian Communist Party (PKI), the world's largest nonruling Communist party, which was growing rapidly in influence under Sukarno's regime. In 1965 the only organized opposition to the PKI was the army. In September, radical officers attempted a coup against the top-level, anti-Communist leadership of the army. Several army leaders were assassinated, but others escaped to organize a counterstrike. With much of the army's top leadership either dead or missing, General Suharto took control of the army and put down the abortive coup. The army quickly blamed the coup attempt on the PKI and instigated an Indonesia-wide anti-Communist propaganda campaign. An anti-Communist reign of terror developed; it was fed by popular Islamic and anti-Chinese prejudices. Hundreds of thousands of Communists, ethnic Chinese, and others were killed; the PKI was crushed. General Suharto outmaneuvered Sukarno politically and was appointed president in 1968, consolidating his influence over the military and government. The new order in Indonesia was led by military leaders among the most suspicious of China in the world. Relations between China and Indonesia were suspended in 1967.[33]

Following the poor record of Chinese advances among developing countries as it pursued a strong agenda against the United States and the Soviet Union in the 1960s, Maoist China during the early years of the Cultural Revolution that began in 1966 came to sacrifice conventional diplomacy in pursuing revolutionary fervor. The foreign minister and much of the senior foreign policy elite were purged. Ambassadors were recalled and forced to undergo extensive ideological retraining. Lower-level embassy officials often endeavored to show their loyalty to Mao and his revolutionary teaching by unauthorized demonstrations and proselytizing with often unreceptive and hostile foreign audiences. They and the staff of foreign policy organs in Beijing followed a radical line that alienated China from most foreign governments.[34]

The low point of Chinese diplomacy seemed evident in several developments in 1967. Huge Red Guard demonstrations were mobilized against the

Soviet embassy in Beijing, which was kept under siege in January and February. Later in 1967, Red Guards invaded the Soviet embassy's consular section and burned its files. When Moscow withdrew its diplomats' dependents
in February 1967, some were beaten or forced to crawl under pictures of Mao
Zedong on their way to planes to take them home. When Red Guard demonstrators in Hong Kong were arrested by British authorities for public disruption and disorder, a major crisis in Chinese-British relations ensued. A mob
of thousands of Chinese surrounded British diplomatic offices in Beijing and
set fires in the building. Escaping British diplomats ran into the hands of the
Chinese mob.

NOTES

1. A. Doak Barnett, *Communist China and Asia: Challenge to American Policy* (New
York: Harper and Brothers, 1960); A. Doak Barnett, *China and the Major Powers in East Asia*
(Washington, DC: Brookings Institution, 1977); Allen Whiting, *The Chinese Calculus of De-
terrence: India and Indochina* (Ann Arbor: University of Michigan Press, 1975).

2. Franz Schurman, *Ideology and Organization in Communist China* (Berkeley: University
of California Press, 1966).

3. Chen Jian, *Mao's China and the Cold War* (Chapel Hill: University of North Carolina
Press, 2001).

4. Odd Arne Westad, *Brothers in Arms: The Rise and Fall of the Sino-Soviet Alliance,
1945–1963* (Stanford, CA: Stanford University Press, 1998).

5. Warren Cohen, "The Development of Chinese Communist Policy toward the United
States, 1922–1933," *Orbis* 11 (1967): pp. 219–37; James Reardon-Anderson, *Yenan and the
Great Powers* (New York: Columbia University Press, 1980); Michael Hunt, *The Genesis of
Chinese Communist Foreign Policy* (New York: Columbia University Press, 1996); Robert
Sutter, *China-Watch* (Baltimore: Johns Hopkins University Press, 1978), pp. 10–18.

6. Sutter, *China-Watch*, p. 11.

7. Tang Tsou, *America's Failure in China* (Chicago: University of Chicago Press, 1963),
pp. 208–19.

8. Cohen, "The Development of Chinese Communist Policy toward the United States,
1922–1933"; Sutter, *China-Watch*, p. 11.

9. Kenneth Shewmaker, *Americans and Chinese Communists, 1927–1945: A Persuading
Encounter* (Ithaca, NY: Cornell University Press, 1971).

10. Reardon-Anderson, *Yenan and the Great Powers*; Sutter, *China-Watch*, pp. 14–15.

11. Tsou, *America's Failure in China*; Barbara Tuckman, *Stilwell and the American Experience in China* (New York: Macmillian, 1971).

12. Harold Hinton, *Communist China in World Politics* (Boston: Houghton Mifflin, 1966).

13. William Stueck, *The Korean War: An International History* (Princeton, NJ: Princeton
University Press, 1997); Bruce Cumings, *The Origins of the Korean War* (Princeton, NJ:
Princeton University Press, 1990); Chen Jian, *China's Road to the Korean War* (New York:
Columbia University Press, 1994).

14. Allen Whiting, *China Crosses the Yalu* (New York: Macmillan, 1960).

15. Robert Ross and Jiang Changbin, eds., *Reexamining the Cold War* (Cambridge, MA: Harvard University Press, 2001).

16. Hinton, *Communist China in World Politics*.

17. Barnett, *China and the Major Powers in East Asia*; Chen Jian, *Mao's China and the Cold War* (Chapel Hill: University of North Carolina Press, 2001); Thomas Christensen, *Useful Adversaries: Grand Strategy, Domestic Mobilization, and Sino-American Conflicts, 1949–1958* (Princeton, NJ: Princeton University Press, 1996).

18. Nancy Bernkopf Tucker, *Strait Talk* (Cambridge, MA: Harvard University Press, 2009).

19. Sutter, *China-Watch*, pp. 31–46.

20. Steven Goldstein, "Dialogue of the Deaf? Sino-American Ambassadorial-Level Talks, 1955–1970," in *Re-examining the Cold War: U.S.-China Diplomacy, 1954–1973*, ed. Robert Ross and Jiang Changbin (Cambridge, MA: Harvard University Press, 2001), pp. 200–37.

21. Robert Sutter, *Historical Dictionary of Chinese Foreign Policy* (Lanham, MD: Scarecrow, 2011), pp. 175–76.

22. John Garver, *Foreign Relations of the People's Republic of China* (Englewood Cliffs, NJ: Prentice Hall, 1993), pp. 125–27.

23. Chen, *Mao's China and the Cold War*, pp.163–204; Christensen, *Useful Adversaries.*

24. Alice Lyman Miller and Richard Wich, *Becoming Asia* (Stanford, CA: Stanford University Press, 2011), pp. 116–36, 182–93.

25. Allen Whiting, *The Chinese Calculus of Deterrence: India and Indochina* (Ann Arbor: University of Michigan Press, 1975).

26. Sutter, *Historical Dictionary of Chinese Foreign Policy*, p. 178.

27. Arthur Lall, *How Communist China Negotiates* (New York: Columbia University Press, 1968); Hinton, *Communist China in World Politics*, pp. 348–55.

28. Sutter, *Historical Dictionary of Chinese Foreign Policy*, pp.178–79.

29. Philip Snow, "China and Africa," in *Chinese Foreign Relations: Theory and Practice*, ed. Thomas Robinson and David Shambaugh (New York: Oxford University Press, 1994), pp. 283–89.

30. Roderick MacFarquhar and Michael Schoenhals, *Mao's Last Revolution* (Cambridge, MA: Harvard University Press, 2006); Joseph W. Esherick, Paul G. Pickowicz, and Andrew G. Walder, eds., *The Chinese Cultural Revolution as History* (Stanford, CA: Stanford University Press, 2006).

31. Peter Van Ness, *Revolution and Chinese Foreign Policy* (Berkeley: University of California Press, 1970).

32. Sutter, *Historical Dictionary of Chinese Foreign Policy*, p. 55.

33. Sutter, *Historical Dictionary of Chinese Foreign Policy*, p. 125.

34. David Mozingo, *China's Foreign Policy and the Cultural Revolution* (Ithaca, NY: Cornell University Press, 1970); Barbara Barnouin and Yu Changgen, *Chinese Foreign Policy during the Cultural Revolution* (New York: Columbia University Press, 1997).

Chapter Three

Maneuvering between the United States and USSR, 1969–1989

The middle decades of the foreign relations of the People's Republic of China (1969–1989) featured extraordinary changes. At the start of these two decades, the growing power of the Soviet Union supported Soviet Communist Party General Secretary Leonid Brezhnev's determination to use military and international pressure to compel China to come to terms favored by the USSR over border disputes, leadership in Asia, and a range of international and security differences. The danger of war with the Soviet Union rose in 1969 and compelled Mao and his often divided associates to curb the revolutionary excesses of the Cultural Revolution in developing an international approach that would protect China from Soviet coercion and the threat of war. The Chinese leaders found the United States weakened notably by the protracted and unsuccessful war in Vietnam and willing to end its containment of China and cooperate with Beijing, especially on common interests in dealing with the dangers both saw in Moscow's rising power. [1]

The development of China's approach in the U.S.-USSR-China triangular relationship, the so-called Geat Power Triangle, was anything but smooth. During the period from 1970 until the end of the Cold War in 1989, with the collapse of the Soviet Bloc and the dismantling of the Berlin Wall, changes in U.S. and Soviet policies and practices prompted shifts in the Chinese approaches. China also shifted course for its own reasons. Until his death in 1976, Mao worked carefully to sustain his influence and to preserve a positive legacy amid subordinates divided by political ambitions and glaring differences on how to deal with China's international and other priorities.

Mao's frequent interventions included, at first, policy moves to support an opening to the United States as a check against the USSR, and, later, policy moves reflecting disappointment with the results of the opening and criticism of senior leaders Zhou Enlai and Deng Xiaoping, who were charged at the time with managing the Chinese approaches toward the United States and the Soviet Union. [2]

After being purged for a second time under Mao's direction in 1976, Deng Xiaoping returned to a leading position in 1977 and established primacy among Chinese leaders by late 1978. He inherited the Maoist mantle of strong-man rule in Chinese foreign policy, and for much of the next fifteen years, Deng guided policies and practices that supported his top priority of fostering more efficient and effective economic development and nation building in China that would sustain the legitimacy of Communist Party rule. He reached out to Japan, other Western-aligned countries, and international financial institutions for economic and other support. As most developed countries and related international financial and economic institutions at this time were poised to cooperate more closely with China, the main challenges Deng faced in fostering greater international economic exchange came from inside China. After so many years of Maoist emphasis on self-reliance, ideological rigidity, and deeply rooted institutions and attitudes favoring state-directed economic development, Deng had to promote reforms that would allow for such pragmatic interchanges with other nations.

In this context, the focus in foreign affairs was on creating and sustaining a favorable international environment for the economic development and related economic and political reforms sought by Deng and his associates. The United States and other developed countries had the military power to balance and offset Soviet expansion, and they also supplied economic assistance, technology, and markets sought by China. Thus, these countries tended to receive high priority in China's foreign policy at this time. Nevertheless, volatile international circumstances and changing policies and practices of the Soviet Union and the United States prompted repeated recalibration and adjustments in China's approach toward the two superpowers and their allies and associates, as well as in other foreign affairs. China endeavored to maximize its advantage in an increasingly pragmatic pursuit of its interests in an international setting controlled more by others, notably the USSR and the United States, than by China. [3]

As will be discussed further in chapters 8 and 9, China's opening to conventional international exchange beginning in the late 1960s also dramatically broadened its foreign relations. Over the next few years, scores of countries established diplomatic relations with China, and China gained entry into the United Nations in 1971. Post-Mao leaders sought international assistance, and in the 1980s China advanced relations with the World Bank, the International Monetary Fund, the Asian Development Bank (ADB), and other assistance organizations. As a result, China became the leading or one of the leading recipients of foreign assistance by the late 1980s and early 1990s.

NORMALIZATION AND OPENING

The dramatic turnabout leading to China's opening to the United States and Western-aligned powers, and China's entry into the United Nations in the early 1970s began in what were very adverse circumstances. Maoist China had descended through phases of ideologically driven excess in foreign and domestic affairs, reaching a point of unprecedented international isolation. The United States had over 500,000 troops in Vietnam fighting a Communist-led adversary supported by China with supplies, financing, and the provision of many thousands of Chinese support troops. U.S. leaders were particularly fearful of an escalation of the prolonged and increasingly unpopular conflict that would somehow bring China more directly into a war that the American leaders were unsure how to win under existing conditions. The U.S. containment effort along China's periphery continued, as did the political isolation and economic embargo the United States brought to bear against the Beijing regime. Nascent U.S. efforts to consider greater flexibility in relations with the PRC ran up against Maoist hostility, disinterest, and contempt, and were overshadowed by the broad implications of the Vietnam quagmire.[4]

The turn toward normalization and opening in Chinese foreign relations at this time has been subject to different scholarly interpretations. One view sees a flagging of Mao's revolutionary drive and vigor, opening the way for the Chinese leader to consider and ultimately pursue pragmatic understanding with the United States and its allies and associates.[5] Another sees a reconfiguring in the U.S. calculus of China's position in world politics and its implications for the United States. This view highlights the importance of an apparent trend whereby U.S. leaders privately came to see China in the late 1960s as less threatening than in the past; eventually they came to view the Maoist regime as a potential asset in American strategy, which was focused increasingly on dealing with a rising and threatening Soviet Union.[6]

Despite these and other divergent views, assessments of this period and the opening in Sino-American relations and other aspects of Chinese foreign relations find it hard not to give priority to interpretations focused on the acute strategic necessities of both the United States and China amid circumstances of a regional and international order featuring a rising and powerful Soviet Union challenging their critical national interests. Only the threat of nuclear war with a domineering Soviet Union at a time of acute internal disruption and weakness in China appears sufficient to explain the remarkable turnabout in Beijing's foreign policy calculus and the approach to the United States and other foreign actors at this time. Given China's size and the preoccupation Chinese rulers have long evidenced with the tasks of managing the complicated internal affairs of this vast country, China historians and specialists of contemporary affairs often have given pride of place to Chinese domestic determinants in Chinese foreign policy. There was no better example during Maoist rule of how domestic Chinese policies and practices determined Chinese foreign policy than during the violent and disruptive early years of China's Cultural Revolution. Moving Chinese leaders out of their self-initiated isolation probably would have taken many years under more normal circumstances. But circumstances in the late 1960s were far from normal, giving rise to the real danger of the Soviet Union militarily invading China, destroying its nuclear and other strategic installations, and forcing China to conform to Soviet interests.[7]

Mao succeeded in removing political rivals in the early years of the Cultural Revolution, but at tremendous cost. Many burned urban areas testified to widespread violence and arson among competing groups. The party and government administration were severely disrupted. Experienced administrators were often purged, persecuted, or pushed aside by proponents of radical Maoist ideals or political opportunists. Expertise in economics, development, and other fields essential to nation building came to be seen as a liability in the politically charged atmosphere of repeated mass campaigns. Political indoctrination and adherence to Mao Zedong overshadowed education and training in practical tasks.[8]

Military forces called in to Chinese cities in order to restore order duly removed millions of disruptive Red Guards and began to lead the process of reconstituting a party and government infrastructure on the basis of military-led rule. Not surprisingly in this context, Defense Minister Lin Biao and his

People's Liberation Army (PLA) associates rose to new prominence in the Chinese hierarchy. Military representation in various party and government bodies was high. Not all military leaders were as supportive of the radical policies and practices of the Cultural Revolution as Lin Biao and his associates in the high command. Some experienced civilian and military cadres survived in office. But they appeared in the minority in a leadership featuring factional chieftains like the Gang of Four, involving Mao's wife and three other extremist party Politburo members; such luminaries as Mao's speechwriter and sometime confidant, Chen Boda; and security forces and intelligence operative Kang Sheng.[9]

Under these circumstances, the PRC was not prepared for a national security shock. Chinese troops were engaged in domestic peacekeeping and governance. They also for many years had followed Maoist dictates under the leadership of Defense Minister Lin Biao and eschewed professional military training in favor of ideological training and promoting popular welfare in China. Chinese military programs for developing nuclear weapons and ballistic missiles generally were excluded from the violence and disruption of the Cultural Revolution, but the PLA on the whole was poorly prepared to deal with conventional military challenges.[10]

In August 1968, the Soviet Union invaded Czechoslovakia and removed its leadership, putting in power a regime more compliant to Soviet interests. The Soviet Union also made clear that it reserved the right to take similar actions in other deviant Communist states, a view that came to be known as the Brezhnev doctrine, named after the Soviet party leader Leonid Brezhnev, who remained in control from the mid-1960s until the early 1980s. Of course, Chinese leaders well knew that, from the Soviet perspective, there was no Communist state more deviant than China. Moreover, since Brezhnev's takeover in 1964, the Soviet Union had backed political opposition to China with increasing military muscle, deploying ever-larger numbers of forces along the Manchurian border and, as a result of a new Soviet defense treaty with Mongolia, along the Sino-Mongolian border. The Soviet forces, mainly mechanized divisions designed to move rapidly in offensive operations, were configured in a pattern used by Soviet forces when they quickly overran Japanese forces in Manchuria and northern China in the last days of World War II.[11]

The Sino-Soviet dispute had emerged in the late 1950s as an ideological dispute with wide implications. The dispute broadened to include stark differences on international issues and how to deal with the United States.

Chinese accusations of Soviet weakness in the face of the firm U.S. stance against Soviet missiles during the Cuban missile crisis of 1962 were answered by the Soviets accusing China of accommodating colonial "outhouses" held by Great Britain and Portugal in Hong Kong and Macao respectively. Maoist China responded by reminding the world that imperialist Russia took by far the greatest tracts of Chinese territory by virtue of the so-called unequal treaties imposed on China by imperialist powers in the nineteenth and twentieth centuries.[12] The Sino-Soviet debate now focused on competing claims to disputed border territories, against the background of new uncertainty over the legitimacy of the boundaries established by the unequal treaties. Sino-Soviet negotiations soon after Brezhnev took power following the ouster of Nikita Khrushchev in 1964 failed to resolve border uncertainties, prompting the new Soviet leader to make the force deployments and arrangements noted above in order to deal with the Chinese disputes from a position of strength. With the declared Soviet ambitions under the terms of the Brezhnev doctrine and Moscow's military preparations, the stage was set for the border dispute to evolve into the most serious national security threat ever faced by the People's Republic of China.[13]

The combination of perceived greater threat and internal weakness caused a crisis and debate in the Chinese leadership that lasted into the early 1970s. Chinese leadership decision making in the Cultural Revolution was not at all transparent. Mao seemed to remain in overall command, but official Chinese media reflected competing views on how to deal with the new and apparently dangerous situation in relations with the Soviet Union.[14]

Some commentary presumably encouraged by some Chinese leaders favored reaching out to the United States as a means to offset the Soviet threat. In November 1968, the Chinese Foreign Ministry under Premier Zhou Enlai's direction called for renewed ambassadorial talks with the newly elected administration of Richard Nixon in a statement that was notable for the absence of the then usual Chinese invective critical of the United States. The argument used in media commentary proposing a reaching out to the United States was that the United States was in the process of being defeated in Indochina and was no longer the primary threat to China. It too faced a challenge from the expanding USSR, and China could take advantage of the differences between the competing superpowers in order to secure its position in the face of the newly emerging Soviet danger.[15]

Other commentary presumably backed by other Chinese leaders strongly opposed an opening to the United States. These commentaries were associated with Lin Biao and his lieutenants, along with the radically Maoist leadership faction, the Gang of Four. They argued in favor of continued strong Chinese opposition to both Washington and Moscow. Though weakened by the defeat in Vietnam, the United States could not be trusted in dealings with China. In particular, any sign of Chinese weakness toward either superpower likely would prompt them both to work together in seeking to pressure China and gain at its expense.[16]

The latter leaders held the upper hand in Chinese leadership councils during much of 1969. Chinese media rebuked and ridiculed the new U.S. president as he took office. At the last moment Chinese leaders canceled the slated ambassadorial talks in February. The Chinese authorities took the offensive in the face of Soviet military pressure along the border, ambushing a Soviet patrol on a disputed island in early March and publicizing the incident to the world. Far from being intimidated, Brezhnev's Soviet forces responded later in the month by annihilating a Chinese border guard unit, setting the stage for escalating rhetoric and military clashes throughout the spring and summer of 1969. The clashes were capped by an all-day battle along the western sector of the border in August that saw the Soviets inflict many casualties on the Chinese. Soviet officials followed with warnings to Americans, and other foreigners sure to relay the warnings to the Chinese, that the Soviet Union was in the process of consulting with foreign powers to assure they would stand aside as the Soviet Union prepared all-out attack on China, including the possible use of nuclear weapons.[17]

In the face of such threat and pressure, Chinese leaders were compelled to shift strategy. Zhou Enlai was brought forward to negotiate with Soviet leaders. It was clear that while negotiating with the USSR would temporarily ease tensions and the danger of war, China would not accept Soviet demands. Beijing now viewed the USSR as China's number one strategic threat. Seeking international leverage and support, it took measures to improve strained relations with neighboring countries and with more distant powers. It was nonetheless evident that while helpful, these improvements would not fundamentally alter China's strategic disadvantage in the face of Soviet intimidation and threat. Only one power, the United States, had that ability. Zhou and like-minded officials in the Chinese leadership were encouraged that the United States was weakened by the Vietnam War, and that it was also beginning to withdraw sizeable numbers of troops from Asia and dismantle the U.S. military containment against China. On this basis, Beijing could pursue relations with Washington as a means to deal with the Soviet threat. Howev-

er, Lin Biao and others continued to argue that both superpowers were enemies of China and in the end they would cooperate together to isolate and
control China. [18]

The debate seemed to get caught up with the broader struggle for power
in this period of the Cultural Revolution. Mao Zedong came to side with the
view associated with Zhou Enlai. Repeated initiatives by the Nixon administration to China ultimately succeeded in Sino-U.S. ambassadorial talks being
resumed in Warsaw in early 1970. China used the image of restored contacts
with the United States to offset and undermine Soviet efforts to intimidate
China. Chinese officials arranged for the meeting to be held in the secure
area of their embassy in Warsaw. The usual venue, a palace provided by the
Poles, was long suspected of being riddled with secret listening devices that
would give the USSR and Warsaw Pact allies the full transcript of the U.S.-
Chinese discussions. The Chinese diplomats also made a point of being
unusually positive to Western reporters during the photo opportunity as
American officials were welcomed to the Chinese embassy at the start of the
official talks. As Chinese officials presumably hoped, Soviet commentary on
the secret talks and improved atmosphere in U.S.-China relations viewed the
developments as complicating Soviet border negotiations with China and
nuclear armament limitation talks with the United States. Soviet commentators even charged that Beijing, fearful of Soviet intentions, was seeking to
come to terms with United States in order to play one nuclear power off
against the other. [19]

The Nixon administration's expansion of the Vietnam War by invading
Cambodia in spring 1970 caused China to cancel the talks and slowed forward movement. Mao highlighted a mass demonstration in Beijing on May
20, 1970, where he welcomed the Cambodian leader, Norodom Sihanouk,
who had been deposed by the U.S.-backed military leaders in Cambodia. The
Chinese chairman in his last major public statement denouncing the United
States called on the people of the world to rise up against U.S. imperialism
and their running dogs. Outwardly, it appeared that Mao was siding with the
Chinese advocates of a harder line against the United States. However, clandestine U.S.-China communication continued, as did the withdrawal of U.S.
forces from Vietnam and other parts of Asia, so that by October 1970 Mao
was prepared to tell visiting U.S. journalist Edgar Snow that Nixon could
visit China. [20]

The shift in Mao's stance was accompanied by other moves that appeared
to undermine the leadership standing of Lin Biao and his radical allies in the

Chinese leadership. A key radical leader, Chen Boda, dropped from public view in late 1970 in what later was shown to be intensified factional maneuvering leading up to the alleged coup plans by Lin and his allies.[21]

What role the differences over the opening to the United States played in the struggle in the Chinese leadership remains hidden by pervasive secrecy in Chinese leadership decision making. Emblematic of the significance of the opening to the United States in Chinese politics at the time was the unusual greeting of U.S. National Security Advisor Henry Kissinger on arrival in Beijing on his secret mission in July 1971 to open U.S.-China relations. The first Chinese official to greet Kissinger on arrival was not a protocol officer from the foreign ministry or some other appropriate official. It was Marshall Ye Jianying. Ye was one of the most senior Chinese military leaders. He had survived the Cultural Revolution, advised Mao to use connections with the United States in the face of the Soviet threat, later played a key role in the arrest of the Gang of Four following Mao's death in 1976, and became president of China. His approach was close to Zhou Enlai and at odds with Lin Biao.[22]

The announcement of Kissinger's successful secret trip appeared to represent a serious defeat for Lin Biao and his allies in their debate with opponents on how to deal with the Soviet Union and the United States. The setback came amid rising pressures and adverse developments affecting the military leader. The stakes apparently were very high. Two months later, Lin, his wife, son, and close aides were dead as a result of an air crash in Mongolia, as they were allegedly trying to escape China following a failed coup attempt against Mao and his opponents. The military high command in the PLA, who had risen to power under Lin's tenure as defense minister, were arrested, removed from power, and not seen again until they eventually were brought out for public trial along with the discredited radical leaders of the Gang of Four in the years after Mao's death.[23]

MANEUVERING BETWEEN THE SUPERPOWERS IN THE 1970S

The PRC's emerging openness to international interchange prompted many Western countries to establish relations with China. With the strong support of developing countries, China in 1971 gained entry into the United Nations, and Taiwan withdrew. China and the United States made progress in normalizing relations and established liaison offices directed by high-ranking officials in Washington and Beijing in 1973. Against this background and in the course of a few years, dozens of countries, many closely aligned with the United States, established diplomatic relations with China. China also seemed satisfied with the 1973 Paris Peace Agreement that ended major U.S. combat operations in Vietnam as U.S. forces continued to withdraw from Vietnam and from around the periphery of China. [24]

President Nixon's resignation over the Watergate scandal in 1974 precluded progress toward normalization with China. Mao signaled Chinese dissatisfaction with the slow progress in U.S. withdrawal from Taiwan and with perceived U.S. use of ties with China as a means to advance U.S. détente with the Soviet Union in ways seen as disadvantageous for China. He backed criticism of Zhou Enlai for being too accommodating in dealing with the Americans. He supported Deng Xiaoping's début as China's foreign policy spokesman in a speech to the United Nations in 1974 propounding the Three Worlds theory critical of the United States as well as the Soviet Union that was said to guide China's foreign policy in the new international situation. [25]

As Maoist China in the latter stages of the Cultural Revolution moved away from ideologically driven support for radical insurgent movements targeting established governments and sought to develop conventional relations with existing administrations beneficial to China, it employed the Three Worlds theory featured in the speech by Deng Xiaoping at the United Nations in 1974. The theory divided the world into three categories of governments: the first were the two superpowers, the United States and the Soviet Union, whose domineering policies and practices were seen as the main cause of international problems; the second were the other developed countries of Europe, North America, and the Asia-Pacific; the third were the vast majority of countries that made up the developing world, or the so-called third world. China saw the third world as the main source of resistance to the "hegemonism" of the superpowers, and it sought to align with them and, where possible, countries of the second world in order to resist the superpowers and create a more equitable and just international order. [26]

At a very general level, the framework of the Three Worlds theory helped to guide China's foreign approach, though in practice Chinese leaders repeatedly adjusted and changed course within the broad framework. Thus, the timing of the 1974 speech signaled a shift reflecting Mao's dissatisfaction with the results of the opening to the United States and U.S. détente with the USSR. In practice, however, China's approach in world affairs for the most part reflected strong preoccupation with the danger posed by growing Soviet power targeted against China and its interests, especially in Asia. China relied heavily on the United States and its allies and associates to deal with this danger. The third world played a very secondary role in helping China to secure the favorable environment it sought in order to carry out reforms fostering efficient and effective nation building in China.[27]

Chinese leaders came to be preoccupied with Mao's declining health and the most important leadership succession struggle in the history of the People's Republic of China. Zhou Enlai died in January 1976, followed by Mao in September of that year. Zhou's purported successor, recently rehabilitated veteran leader Deng Xiaoping, gave the eulogy at the memorial service for Zhou and then disappeared from public view, purged from the leadership for a second time. The radical Gang of Four seemed to exert more influence for a time, but demonstrations of support for Zhou and his relatively moderate policies by thousands of Beijing people placing flowers and wreaths in his memory at the monument for revolutionary martyrs in the capital in April appeared to underline that the days of radicalism were numbered. The death of senior military leader Zhu De in July preceded Mao's by two months, setting the stage for the struggle for succession.[28]

That China had far to go in creating a foreign policy that dealt with the United States and other countries in conventional and normal ways was underlined by the tragedy of an earthquake in July that demolished the industrial city of Tangshan, 105 miles southeast of Beijing, and did severe damage in nearby areas including the capital and the major port and industrial city of Tianjin. It later was disclosed that hundreds of thousands of Chinese died in the quake and that the needs for relief were enormous. Nevertheless, in a remarkable and extremely damaging demonstration of Maoist "self-reliance," the radical leadership in Beijing at the time refused to acknowledge these needs or to allow foreign countries and groups to assist in efforts to save lives and reduce misery.[29]

Deng Xiaoping, who was purged at the start of the Cultural Revolution and purged again in 1976, was brought back to power. By 1978, Deng was able to consolidate a leading position within the administration and to launch the economic and policy reforms that provided the foundation for China's recent approach to international affairs. Deng and his supporters were compelled to maneuver amid competing interests and preferences within the Chinese leadership and the broader polity in order to come up with changes that they felt would advance China's wealth and shore up the legitimacy of the Chinese Communist Party, which had been severely damaged by the excesses and poor performance of the past.[30]

While Chinese leaders were preoccupied internally, their priorities internationally focused on dealing with Soviet intimidation and threat. The United States was weakened by Nixon's resignation and the Gerald Ford government was hobbled by the president's pardon of Nixon. Ford was in a poor position to continue strong support for the struggling South Vietnamese government and the neighboring Cambodian government aligned with the United States. Strong Soviet assistance to Vietnamese Communist forces bolstered their efforts to take control of the South. The Cambodian regime collapsed and Chinese-backed Khmer Rouge insurgents entered Phnom Penh in April 1975. The new regime immediately began carrying out radical and brutal policies that would see the evacuation of the capital and the massive repression and deaths of over one million Cambodians. North Vietnamese forces launched an all-out assault in South Vietnam. The Saigon regime disintegrated; the Americans and what Vietnamese associates they could bring with them fled in ignominious defeat; and the Communist forces barged through the gates of the presidential palace and occupied Saigon in late April.[31]

Chinese officials showed considerable alarm at the turn of events around China's periphery. Stronger efforts by the Soviet Union to use military power and relations with allies around China like Vietnam and India to contain and pressure China, mimicked the U.S.-led containment effort against China earlier in the Cold War. Under these circumstances, Chinese leaders focused on shoring up U.S. resolve and the resolve of other governments and forces seen as important in what China depicted as a united front against expanding Soviet power and influence in Asian and world affairs.

Over the next few years, Chinese officials reached out to conservative world leaders seen as useful in the struggle against the USSR, including the Shah of Iran and Sese Mobutu in Zaire. They were less generous in foreign assistance to developing countries, seeking instead to focus Chinese resources on China's own modernization. They also endeavored to cut back support for insurgents they had long supported in the past directed against neighboring governments and governments in places like Africa and the Middle East. And they encouraged resistance to what they called Soviet "hegemonism" on the part of Japan, leading European powers, and countries in Southeast Asia, among others.[32]

With the support of President Jimmy Carter, National Security Adviser Zbigniew Brzezinski was in the lead in seeking rapid progress in normalizing U.S.-China relations in 1978, and in subsequent steps to advance U.S.-China relations as a means to counter Soviet power and expansion. Soviet and Soviet-backed forces had made gains and were making inroads that seemed at odds with common U.S. and Chinese interests in different parts of Africa, the Middle East, Central America, and Southwest and Southeast Asia. Chinese officials were prominent among international advocates in warning the United States to avoid the dangers of "appeasement" and to stand firm and work with China against the expanding Soviet power.[33]

U.S. and, especially, Chinese leaders used the signs of improved U.S.-China relations in a communiqué establishing relations on January 1, 1979, and during Chinese leader Deng Xiaoping's widely publicized visit to the United States in January 1979 to underline Sino-U.S. cooperation against "hegemony," notably a Soviet-backed Vietnamese military assault against Cambodia beginning in late December 1978. Returning from the United States, Deng launched a large-scale Chinese military offensive into Vietnam's northern region. Chinese forces withdrew after a few weeks, though they maintained strong artillery attacks and other military pressure against Vietnamese border positions until the Vietnamese eventually agreed to withdraw from Cambodia ten years later.[34]

President Carter and his aides were less successful than President Nixon in winning U.S. domestic support for their initiatives toward China. Many in Congress were satisfied with the stasis that had developed in U.S. relations with the PRC and with the Republic of China on Taiwan in the mid-1970s. They were unconvinced that the United States had any strategic or other need to formalize already existing relations with the PRC that was worth the price of breaking a defense treaty and other official ties with Taiwan. Bipartisan majorities in Congress resisted the president's initiatives and passed laws, notably the Taiwan Relations Act (TRA), that tried to tie the hands of the administration on Taiwan and other issues.

Nevertheless, the backlash from Congress and a variety of American interest groups failed to halt the forward movement in U.S. relations with China. Notably, the United States met Chinese conditions for normalization, broke all official relations with Taiwan, and ended the defense treaty with Taiwan. The TRA and other congressional initiatives, however, made clear the continuing strong opposition among important elements in the United

States to the rapid development of relations with China that appeared to them to come at the expense of American values and interests.[35]

MANEUVERING BETWEEN THE SUPERPOWERS IN THE 1980S

Throughout much of the 1970s, China was more vocal than the United States in warning of the dangers of the Soviet Union's expansion, which was seen as the greatest threat to China's security and integrity. Chinese officials saw the U.S. approach to Moscow as vacillating between a tough line and accommodation. In late 1979 the Soviet Union sent forces to invade and occupy Afghanistan in support of a pro-Soviet government there, resulting in an intense backlash by the United States and allied powers. The overall situation prompted the Chinese leaders to again begin to recalculate their respective approaches to the Soviet Union and the United States. The previous perceived danger, that the United States would appease the Soviet Union and thereby allow Moscow to direct its pressure against China, now appeared remote. Carter's last year in office and President Ronald Reagan's initial stance toward the USSR saw a large increase in U.S. defense spending and military preparations. Closely allied with the United States, European powers and Japan also were building forces and taking tough positions against the USSR. Meanwhile, the Soviet Union was experiencing increasing complications and weaknesses, including problems of leadership succession, economic sustainability, and tensions in Poland and elsewhere in the Warsaw Pact. Faced with such adverse circumstances, prior to his death in 1982, Brezhnev reached out with positive initiatives toward China, attempting to improve relations.[36]

Despite the continued political and rhetorical interest in ties with developing countries under the overall rubric of the Three Worlds theory, China's pragmatic leadership under Deng Xiaoping cut back sharply China's previously generous assistance to developing countries. China now became a major competitor with these countries in seeking international financial and other support from the World Bank, UN assistance agencies, and developed countries. China had few illusions that the developing countries could provide a suitable foundation for its efforts to secure an advantageous international position. Instead, it deepened domestic reforms designed in considerable measure to open opportunities for economic, technical, and other interchange with developed countries.[37]

Against this background of perceived Soviet decline and strong strategic resolve by the United States and its allies and associates, Chinese officials saw an opportunity to exert a freer hand in foreign affairs and to position China in a stance less aligned with the United States. The priority to stay close to the United States in order to encourage resolute U.S. positions against Soviet expansion was no longer as important as in the recent past. Also, there were salient Chinese differences with the Reagan administration over Taiwan and new opportunities to negotiate with Soviet leaders calling for talks. Thus, by 1981 China's new "independent foreign policy" featured a modest revival of Chinese interest in relations with the developing third world and in the international communist movement, which had been broadly neglected in favor of emphasis on the anti-Soviet front in the 1970s despite the stated framework of China's Three Worlds theory.[38]

China between the United States and the Soviet Union

A key turning point in China's "independent foreign policy" and maneuvering in favor of closer ties with the USSR and away from one-sided alignment with the United States came with the resignation in 1982 of U.S. Secretary of State Alexander Haig. Haig was widely known to favor a strong U.S. effort to meet Chinese demands on Taiwan and other issues in order to preserve a close Sino-American relationship directed against the Soviet Union. Amid continued strong Chinese pressure tactics on a wide range of U.S.-China disputes, American policy shifted with Haig's resignation in 1982 and the appointment of George Shultz as secretary of state. Reagan administration officers who were at odds with Haig's emphasis on the need for a solicitous U.S. approach to China came to the fore. They were led by Paul Wolfowitz, who was chosen by Shultz as assistant secretary of state for East Asian affairs; Richard Armitage, the senior Defense Department officer managing relations with China and East Asia; and the senior National Security Council staff aide on Asian affairs and later assistant secretary of state for East Asian affairs, Gaston Sigur. Officers who had backed Haig's pro-China slant were transferred from authority over China policy, and the new U.S. leadership contingent with responsibility for East Asian affairs moved U.S. policy toward a less solicitous and accommodating stance toward China, giving much higher priority to U.S. relations with Japan, as well as other U.S. allies and friends in East Asia. There was less emphasis on China's strategic importance to American competition with the Soviet Union, and there was less

concern among U.S. policy makers about China possibly downgrading relations over Taiwan and other disputes.[39]

The significance of this perceived change in U.S. policy and behavior
toward China can be better understood against the background of developments since the Nixon administration. As noted earlier, the scholarship on
the U.S. opening to China beginning in the Nixon administration focuses on
powerful strategic and domestic imperatives that drove the United States and
China to cooperate together in a pragmatic search for advantage for their
respective national and leadership interests. The scholarship also underlines
the primacy of China in American foreign policy in Asia while relations with
Japan and other East Asian allies and friends remained secondary and were
sometimes viewed as declining assets or liabilities.[40]

Some scholars discern an important adjustment in U.S. strategy toward
China and in East Asia more broadly beginning in 1982.[41] The reevaluation
of U.S. policy toward China under Secretary of State George Shultz is seen
to have brought to power officials who opposed China's high priority in U.S.
strategy toward East Asia and the world and who gave much greater importance to U.S. relations with Japan and other U.S. allies in securing American
interests amid prevailing conditions. The reevaluation on the whole is depicted as working to the advantage of the United States. Notably it is seen to
have worked with the changing balance of forces affecting Chinese security
and other interests in Asian and world affairs that prompted heretofore demanding Chinese leaders to reduce pressures on the United States for concessions on Taiwan and other disputed issues. The changes in Chinese policy
helped to open the way for several years of comparatively smooth U.S.-
China relations after a period of considerable discord in the late 1970s and
early 1980s.

Other scholars explain the improvement in U.S.-China relations with a
focus on the dynamics of the relations themselves.[42] They discern American
compromises and accommodations that assuaged Chinese demands and met
Chinese interests over Taiwan and other issues. They tend to shun analysis of
how any shift in emphasis in U.S. policy away from China toward Japan and
the East Asian region might have altered Chinese calculations and the overall
dynamic in U.S. interaction with China.

The analysis in this volume supports the former view. It shows that the
Chinese leaders, despite their emphasis on a new independent foreign policy,
grudgingly adjusted to the new U.S. stance, viewing their interests being best
served by less pressure and more positive initiatives directed to the Reagan

administration, as evidenced by their warm welcome for the American president on his visit to China in 1984. Cooperative Chinese relations with the United States were critically important to the Chinese leadership in maintaining Chinese security in the face of continuing pressure from the Soviet Union and in sustaining the flow of aid, investment, and trade essential to the economic development and modernization under way in China—the linchpin of the Communist leadership's plans for sustaining their rule in China. Meanwhile, the Reagan leadership learned not to provoke the Chinese over issues like military and other support for Taiwan with overt and heavy-handed action. Thus, the accommodations that characterized U.S.-China relations in Reagan's second term in office were mutual, but they involved significant Chinese adjustments and changes influenced by the firmer posture toward China undertaken by Secretary of State Shultz and his colleagues. U.S. firmness in the face of Chinese demands had the seemingly counterintuitive effect of improving U.S.-Chinese relations. Meanwhile, the actions of the Chinese and U.S. governments during the tenure of Secretary Shultz also reflected the primacy of relations with the United States in Chinese foreign policy calculations, despite China's rhetorical emphasis on developing countries, assertions of independence, and active maneuvering within the U.S.-Soviet-Chinese triangular relationship.

The scholarship that portrays the improvement in U.S.-China relations at this time as largely based on the dynamics of those relations seems too narrowly focused. The United States is seen to make compromises that accommodate Chinese interests and thus allow for smoother U.S.-Chinese relations. By limiting the focus to the dynamics of U.S.-China ties, this scholarship seems to miss the importance of the shift in American emphasis during the tenure of George Shultz. Yet, overall, that shift significantly enhanced U.S. influence over China in negotiations over Taiwan and other disputes, and it compelled China to make concessions of its own in order to insure a positive relationship with the United States. This changed dynamic, with the United States in a more commanding position vis-à-vis China, also was much more acceptable to congressional members, others in American politics, and the media, who had been alienated by the secrecy and perceived excessive U.S. deference to China in the previous decade. It made executive-congressional relations over China policy much smoother than in the previous six years.[43]

China's Changing Strategic Calculus and the Importance of the United States

The details of the adjustments in American policy toward China and Asia undertaken prior to and during the tenure of Secretary Shultz and under the direction of such influential U.S. officials as Wolfowitz, Armitage, and Sigur are shown here against the background of the much more solicitous U.S. approach to China in the previous decade. The U.S. adjustments are seen to impact significantly China's broader international calculations, influencing its approach toward the United States.

Chinese foreign policy throughout the period 1969–1989 was strongly influenced by Chinese assessments of the relative power and influence of the Soviet Union and the United States, and the effects these had on Chinese security and development. As noted earlier, throughout much of the 1970s, China had been more vocal than the United States in warning of the dangers of expansion by the Soviet Union, which China viewed as the greatest threat to its security and integrity. Chinese official commentary depicted the Soviet Union as aggressively seeking to contain China in Asia through its military buildup and advanced nuclear ballistic missile deployments along the Sino-Soviet border, its deployments of mobile mechanized divisions in Mongolia, its stepped-up naval activity in the western Pacific along the China coast, its military presence in Vietnam including active use of formerly American naval and air base facilities, its ever-closer military relationship with India, and its growing involvement with and eventual invasion of Afghanistan. These Soviet actions were seen as part of a wider expansion of Soviet power and influence that China wanted countered by a united international front including China and led by the United States. [44]

Chinese disappointment with perceived U.S. ambivalence toward the Soviet Union showed in criticism of Secretary of State Henry Kissinger for being too soft toward Moscow during the Ford administration. Beijing followed with strong criticism of Carter administration UN envoy Andrew Young, who took a moderate view toward Soviet-backed Cuban troop deployments and other Soviet expansion in Africa. More cautious official commentary registered reservations about Secretary of State Cyrus Vance's approach in seeking arms limitation talks with Moscow. [45]

As noted above, after the Soviet invasion of Afghanistan in late 1979, Chinese leaders recalculated. The previous perceived danger that the United States would "appease" the Soviet Union and thereby allow Moscow to direct its pressure against China now appeared remote. Brezhnev also was seen in a weaker position as he tried to improve ties with China.[46] Chinese officials moved to an "independent foreign policy" less aligned with the United States and ostensibly open to accommodation with the Soviet Union.[47]

However, the shift in Chinese policy away from the United States and somewhat closer to the Soviet Union did not work very well. Chinese leaders continued to speak of their new independent foreign policy approach, but they seemed to change their international calculations based largely on perceptions of shifts in the international balance of power affecting China. By 1983, Chinese leaders showed increasing concern about the stability of the nation's surroundings in Asia at a time of unrelenting buildup of Soviet military and political pressure along China's periphery, and of a serious and possibly prolonged decline in relations with the United States. Against this backdrop, they decided that the foreign policy tactics of the previous two years, designed to distance China from the policies of the United States and to moderate and improve Chinese relations with the Soviet Union, were less likely to safeguard the important Chinese security and development concerns affected by the stability of the Asian environment.[48]

The Chinese leaders appeared to recognize in particular that Beijing would have to stop its pullback from the United States for fear of jeopardizing this link so important for maintaining its security and development interests in the face of persistent Soviet pressure in Asia. Thus, in 1983, Beijing began to retreat from some of the tactical changes made the previous two years under the rubric of an independent approach to foreign affairs. The result was a substantial reduction in Chinese pressure on the United States over Taiwan and other issues; increased Chinese interest and flexibility in dealing with the Reagan administration and other Western countries across a broad range of economic, political, and security issues; and heightened Sino-Soviet antipathy. Beijing still attempted to nurture whenever possible the increased influence it had garnered by means of its independent posture in the developing third world and the international communist movement, but it increasingly sided with the West against the USSR in order to secure basic strategic and economic interests.[49]

A key element in China's decision to change tactics toward the United States was an altered view of the likely course of Sino-American-Soviet relations over the next several years. When China began its more independent approach to foreign affairs and its concurrent harder line toward the United States in 1981–1982, it had hoped to elicit a more forthcoming U.S.

attitude toward issues sensitive to Chinese interests, notably Taiwan. Beijing probably judged that there were serious risks of alienating the United States, which had provided an implicit but vital counterweight serving Chinese security interests against the USSR for over a decade and was assisting more recent Chinese economic development concerns. But the Chinese seemed to have assessed that their room for maneuver had been increased because:

- The United States had reasserted a balance in East-West relations likely to lead to a continued major check on possible Soviet expansion. Chinese worries about U.S. "appeasement" of the USSR seemed a thing of the past.
- The Soviet ability to pressure China appeared to be at least temporarily blocked by U.S. power, the determination of various U.S. allies to thwart Soviet expansion, and Soviet domestic and international problems. China added to Soviet difficulties by cooperating with the United States in clandestine operations, supporting fighters resisting the Soviet occupation of Afghanistan.
- At least some important American leaders, notably Secretary of State Alexander Haig and his subordinates in the East Asia Bureau of the State Department continued to consider preserving and developing good U.S. relations with China as a critically important element in U.S. efforts to confront and contain Soviet expansion.[50]

By mid-1983, China saw these calculations upset. In particular, the United States under Secretary of State George Shultz adopted a new posture that publicly downgraded China's strategic importance. The adjustment in the U.S. position occurred after the resignation of Haig, perhaps the strongest advocate in the Reagan administration of sustaining good relations with China as an important strategic means to counter the USSR. Secretary Shultz and such subordinates as Paul Wolfowitz were less identified with this approach. Shultz held a series of meetings with governmental and nongovernmental Asian specialists in Washington in early 1983, in order to review U.S. Asian policy in general and policy toward China in particular. The results of the reassessment—implicitly but clearly downgrading China's importance to the United States—were reflected in speeches by Shultz and Wolfowitz later in the year.[51]

U.S. planners now appeared to judge that efforts to improve relations with China were less important than in the recent past because:

- China seemed less likely to cooperate further with the United States (through military sales or security consultations, for instance) against the Soviet Union at a time when the PRC had publicly distanced itself from the United States and had reopened talks on normalization with the USSR.
- At the same time, China's continued preoccupation with pragmatic economic modernization and internal development made it appear unlikely that the PRC would revert to a highly disruptive position in East Asia that would adversely affect U.S. interests in the stability of the region.
- China's demands on Taiwan and a wide variety of other bilateral disputes, and the accompanying threats to downgrade U.S.-Chinese relations if its demands were not met, seemed open-ended and excessive.
- The U.S. ability to deal militarily and politically with the USSR from a position of greater strength had improved, particularly as a result of the Reagan administration's large-scale military budget increases and perceived serious internal and international difficulties of the USSR.
- U.S. allies, for the first time in years, were working more closely with Washington in dealing with the Soviet military threat. This was notably true in Asia, where Prime Minister Yasuhiro Nakasone took positions and initiatives underlining common Japanese-U.S. concerns against the Soviet danger, setting the foundation for the close "Ron-Yasu" relationship between the U.S. and Japanese leaders.
- Japan and U.S. allies and friends in Southeast Asia—unlike China—appeared to be more important to the United States in protecting against what was seen as the primary U.S. strategic concern in the region—safeguarding air and sea access to East Asia, the Indian Ocean, and the Persian Gulf from Soviet attack. China appeared less important in dealing with this perceived Soviet danger.[52]

Western press reports quoting authoritative sources in Washington alerted China to the implications of this shift in the U.S. approach for PRC interests. In effect, the shift seemed to mean that the ability to exploit U.S. interest in strategic relations with China against the Soviet Union and U.S. interest in avoiding disruptions or other negative consequences flowing from a downgrading of China's relations with the United States were reduced. The ability of China to compel the United States to meet its demands on Taiwan and other questions seemed less than in the recent past. Underlining these trends for China was the continued unwillingness of the United States to bend to high-level PRC pressure over Taiwan, the issue of asylum in the case of

Chinese tennis player Hu Na, Chinese representation in the Asian Development Bank, and other questions. The Reagan administration publicly averred that U.S. policy would remain constant whether or not Beijing decided to retaliate or threatened to downgrade relations by withdrawing its ambassador from Washington or some other action.[53]

Moreover, Chinese commentary and discussions with Chinese officials suggested that Beijing perceived its leverage in the United States to have diminished. Chinese media duly noted the strong revival in the U.S. economy in 1983 and the positive political implications this had for President Reagan's reelection campaign. China also had to be aware, through contacts with leading Democrats, notably House of Representatives Speaker Tip O'Neill who visited China at this time, that Beijing could expect little change in U.S. policy toward Taiwan under a Democratic administration. As 1983 wore on, the Chinese saw what for them was an alarming rise in the influence of U.S. advocates of self-determination for Taiwan among liberal Democrats. In particular, Senator Claiborne Pell took the lead in gaining passage of a controversial resolution in the Senate Foreign Relations Committee that endorsed, among other things, the principle of self-determination for Taiwan—anathema to Beijing.[54]

Meanwhile, although Sino-Soviet trade and cultural and technical contacts were increasing, Beijing saw few signs of Soviet willingness to compromise on basic political and security issues during vice ministerial talks on normalizing Sino-Soviet relations that began in October 1982. And the Soviet military buildup in Asia—including the deployment of highly accurate SS-20 intermediate-range ballistic missiles—continued.[55]

In short, if Beijing continued its demands and harder line of the previous two years against the United States, pressed the United States on various issues, and risked downgrading relations, it faced the prospect of a period of prolonged decline in Sino-American relations—possibly lasting until the end of Reagan's second presidential term. This decline brought the risk of cutting off China's implicit but vitally important strategic security understanding with the United States with regard to the threat of the USSR.

The Chinese also recognized that a substantial decline in Chinese relations with the United States would undercut their already limited leverage with Moscow; it probably would reduce Soviet interest in accommodating China in order to preclude closer U.S.-Chinese security ties or collaboration against the USSR. It also would possibly upset China's ability to gain greater access not only to American markets and financial and technical expertise, but also to those of other important capitalist countries. Now that the Chinese economy was successfully emerging from some retrenchments and adjustments undertaken in 1981–1982, the Western economic connection seemed more important to PRC planners. Yet many U.S. allies and friends, notably Japan, were more reluctant to undertake heavy economic involvement in China at a time of uncertain U.S.-China political relations. The United States also exerted strong influence in international financial institutions that were expected to be the source of several billion dollars of much needed aid for China in the 1980s.

China had to calculate as well that a serious decline in U.S.-Chinese relations would likely result in a concurrent increase in U.S.-Taiwanese relations. As a result, Beijing's chances of using Taiwan's isolation from the United States to prompt Taipei to move toward reunification in accord with PRC interests would be set back seriously.

The deliberations of Chinese policy makers regarding maneuvers between the United States and the Soviet Union during this period remain shrouded in secrecy. But, given the upswing in Chinese public as well as private pressure against the United States during the early years of the Reagan administration over Taiwan arms sales and many other areas of dispute, any backing away from a firm line toward the United States on such issues almost certainly represented a difficult compromise for those leaders who had pushed this approach in 1981–1982.

Unlike in the case of the United States, there was no major change at this time in China's foreign affairs leadership, which ultimately depended on the attentive direction of strong-man ruler Deng Xiaoping. Deng appeared to have a freer hand to shift policy in foreign affairs than in the complicated mix of domestic politics at the time. Thus, for example, he was able to decide to shelve the sensitive territorial dispute of the Diaoyu/Senkaku Islands during negotiations with Japan over a peace treaty in 1978, and he allowed the agreement on normalization of relations with the United States to go forward that year despite the U.S. intention to continue arms sales to Taiwan. Deng endorsed the most sensitive clandestine Chinese arms sale on record—the transfer of over thirty intermediate-range nuclear-capable ballistic missiles to Saudi Arabia in the early 1980s, at a time when China also was transferring nuclear weapons technology and assistance that allowed Pakistan to develop and test a credible nuclear deterrent in the 1990s. Against this background, Deng seemed to have the domestic political standing to carry out the adjustment and moderation in China's approach to the United States without serious negative implications. Whatever took place behind the scenes in Chinese decision making over policy toward the United States and the Soviet Union at this time, Chinese officials did in fact pull back from pressing American leaders. The routine harangues on Taiwan and other differences that greeted senior Reagan administration visitors on the initial meetings in Beijing dropped off. Chinese leaders worked harder to curry favor with President Reagan and his associates.

Moderation toward the United States

Appearing anxious to moderate past demands and improve relations with the United States, the Chinese responded positively to the latest in a series of Reagan administration efforts to ease technology transfer restrictions—announced by Commerce Secretary Malcolm Baldrige during a trip to China in May 1983. The Chinese followed up by agreeing to schedule the long-delayed visit by Secretary of Defense Caspar Weinberger in September and to exchange visits by Premier Zhao Ziyang and President Reagan at the turn of the year. In order to not appear too anxious to improve relations with China, Reagan administration officials were successful in getting Premier Zhao to visit Washington for a summit in January 1984, before the U.S. president would agree to go to China later that year. Beijing media attempted to portray these moves as Chinese responses to U.S. concessions and consistent with China's avowed "independent" approach in foreign affairs and its firm stance on U.S.-Chinese differences. But, as time went on, it became clear just how much Beijing was prepared to moderate past public demands and threats of retaliation over Taiwan and other issues for the sake of consolidating Sino-American political, economic, and security ties. [56]

- In 1981, Beijing had publicly disavowed any interest in military purchases from the United States until the United States satisfied China's position on the sale of arms to Taiwan. Beijing continued to note that China was dissatisfied with U.S. arms transfers to Taiwan after the August 1982 communiqué, which continued at a pace of over $700 million a year; but it now was willing to negotiate with the United States over Chinese purchases of U.S. military equipment. Defense Minister Zhang Aiping disclosed that negotiations on arms sales were revived during Secretary Weinberger's visit to China in September 1983.

- Chinese officials and official media moderated past demands, threats, and accusations that the United States was not fulfilling the 1979 and 1982 Sino-American communiqués.
- Beijing backed away from previous demands that the United States repeal or amend the Taiwan Relations Act or face a decline in relations.
- Beijing muffled previous demands that the United States alter its position regarding Taiwan's continued membership in the Asian Development Bank.
- China reduced criticism of official and unofficial U.S. contacts with counterparts in Taiwan. It notably avoided criticism of U.S. officials being present at Taipei-sponsored functions in Washington. Beijing was even willing to turn a blind eye to the almost thirty members of Congress who traveled to Taiwan in various delegations in January 1984—coincident with Zhao Ziyang's trip to Washington. It even welcomed some of the members who traveled on to the mainland after visiting Taiwan.
- Beijing allowed Northwest Airlines to open service to China in 1984, even though the airline still served Taiwan. This was in marked contrast with the authoritative and negative Chinese position adopted in 1983 in response to Pan American Airline's decision to reenter the Taiwan market while also serving the mainland.
- China reduced complaints about the slowness of U.S. transfers of technology to China and about the continued inability of the administration to successfully push through legislative changes that would have allowed the Chinese to receive American assistance.[57]

China's greatest compromise was to give a warm welcome to President Reagan, despite his continued avowed determination to maintain close U.S. ties with "old friends" on Taiwan. Visits by Speaker O'Neill and others had made clear to China the importance of the China visit in assisting the U.S. president's reelection bid in the fall. Chinese leaders also understood that the president was unlikely to accommodate China's interests over Taiwan and some other sensitive issues during the visit. Indeed, Chinese reportage made clear that there was no change in the president's position on the Taiwan issue during the visit. Thus, the best the Chinese appear to have hoped for was to try to consolidate U.S.-PRC relations in order to secure broader strategic and economic interests, while possibly expecting that such a closer relationship over time would reduce the president's firm position on Taiwan and other bilateral disputes.

The Reagan administration, meanwhile, attempted to add impetus to the relationship by accommodating Chinese concerns through the avoidance of strong rhetorical support for Taiwan that in the past had so inflamed U.S.-PRC tensions, and by moving ahead on military and technology transfers to the PRC. Nevertheless, when the U.S.-Chinese nuclear cooperation agreement, which had been initialed during the president's visit, became stalled because of opposition from nonproliferation advocates in the United States who were concerned about China's support for Pakistan's nuclear weapons program, China only managed a minor complaint and went along with the Reagan administration's explanations of their inability to overcome the opposition.[58]

In short, by mid-1984 it appeared that at a minimum Beijing was determined to further strengthen military and economic ties with the United States and to soft-pedal bilateral differences that had been stressed earlier in the decade. On the question of Taiwan, Beijing retreated to a position that asked for U.S. adherence to the joint communiqué and accelerated reductions of U.S. arms sales to Taiwan, but was not prepared at this time to make a significant issue of what they saw as U.S. noncompliance unless seriously provoked. This meant giving lower priority to Chinese complaints about President Reagan's interpretations of the communiqué at odds with China's position and lower priority to Chinese complaints over the U.S. president's continued strong determination to support U.S. interests in helping the defense of Taiwan. The new Chinese position also meant downplaying Chinese criticism of methods used by the United States to calculate the value of arms sales to Taiwan at high levels, thereby allowing over $500 million of U.S. sales to the island's armed forces for years to come. And it also meant that China chose not to contest vigorously the ultimately successful maneuvers used by Taiwan and U.S. defense manufacturers that allowed the United States to support, through commercial transfers of equipment, technology, and expertise, the development of a new group of over one hundred jet fighters, the so-called indigenous fighter aircraft, for Taiwan's air force.[59]

Continued Sino-Soviet Differences

China's incentive to accommodate the United States was reinforced by Beijing's somber view of Sino-Soviet relations. China appeared disappointed with its inability to elicit substantial Soviet concessions—or even a slowing in the pace of Soviet military expansion in Asia—during the brief administration of Yuri Andropov (d. 1984). Beijing saw the succeeding government of Konstantin Chernenko (d. 1985) as even more rigid and uncompromising. In response, China hardened its line and highlighted public complaints against Soviet pressure and intimidation—an approach that had the added benefit of broadening common ground between China and the West, especially the strongly anti-Soviet Reagan administration.[60]

The Sino-Soviet vice ministerial talks on normalizing relations were revived in October 1982 following their cancellation as a result of the Soviet invasion of Afghanistan in late 1979. They met semiannually, alternating between Moscow and Beijing. The chief Chinese negotiator was Vice Foreign Minister Qian Qichen; his Soviet counterpart was Vice Foreign Minister Leonid Ilichev, a veteran of the Sino-Soviet border talks of the 1970s. Technically, the talks were not considered formal negotiations, which had been suspended by the Chinese after the Soviet invasion of Afghanistan. Although progress was made on some secondary issues, these talks were unable to bridge a major gap between the positions of the two sides on basic security and political issues. Beijing stuck to its preconditions for improved Sino-Soviet relations involving withdrawal of Soviet forces from along the Sino-Soviet border and from Mongolia (later China added specific reference to Soviet SS-20 missiles targeted against China); an end to Soviet support for Vietnam's military occupation of Cambodia; and withdrawal of Soviet forces from Afghanistan.[61]

Beijing sometimes said that Soviet movement on only one of these questions would open the way to substantially improved Sino-Soviet relations. But Moscow remained unwilling to compromise, stating that the USSR would not discuss matters affecting third countries.

In part to get around this roadblock, a second forum of vice ministerial discussions began in September 1983, during the visit of Soviet Vice Foreign Minister Mikhail Kapitsa to China. This was the fourth visit to China by Kapitsa, a leading Soviet China expert, in as many years, but it was the first time he came at the invitation of the Chinese government. The other times he came at the request of the Soviet embassy in Beijing.

Kapitsa held two sessions of talks with his Chinese counterpart, Vice Foreign Minister Qian Qichen, and he met with Foreign Minister Wu Xueqian. The discussions covered each side's views of recent developments in the Middle East, Central America, the Indian Ocean, Afghanistan, and Indochina; concerns over arms control, including the deployment of SS-20 missiles in Asia; and other questions. No agreement was noted.

Progress in both sets of talks came only in secondary areas of trade, technology transfers, and educational and cultural exchanges:

- They agreed to substantially increase Sino-Soviet trade over the minimal levels in recent years.
- They agreed to exchange language students and teachers.
- China agreed to consider Soviet offers to rehabilitate some of the Soviet-supplied factories in China.
- They were in accord on exchanges of tourist, friendship, technical, and other delegations.

Both sides attempted to give added impetus to progress in these areas coincident with the exchange of high-level Sino-American visits in early 1984. In particular, Moscow proposed and Beijing accepted a visit to China by Soviet First Deputy Prime Minister Ivan Arkhipov, reportedly to discuss longer-term economic and technical assistance to China. Arkhipov, who had been a senior Soviet economic adviser in China in the 1950s, would have been the highest-level Soviet official to visit China since 1969. The visit was timed to occur just after President Reagan's departure from China in early May 1984. Moscow presumably judged that the visit provided the USSR with a certain amount of influence over China—Arkhipov could be forth-coming or not with economic assistance for China, depending on how close Sino-American relations became during President Reagan's visit. For Bei-jing, improved contacts with Moscow allowed it to preserve a semblance of balance in its relations with the two superpowers and thereby enhance its independent image in foreign affairs.

Nevertheless, both sides proved to be willing to disrupt these contacts when more important strategic and political issues were at stake. Beijing saw meager results from its initial overture to the new Chernenko regime. China had sent its ranking vice premier, Wan Li, as its representative to the funeral of Andropov in February 1984—marking a substantial upgrading from Bei-jing's dispatch of Foreign Minister Huang Hua to Brezhnev's funeral in 1982. But Wan received a cool welcome in Moscow. Moreover, the Soviets then appeared to go out of their way to publicize strong support for Mongolia and Vietnam against China, and they underlined Soviet unwillingness to make compromises with China at the expense of third countries.

Beijing also saw Moscow resorting to stronger military means in both Europe and Asia in order to assert Soviet power and determination at a time of leadership transition in the Kremlin. Official Chinese media portrayed Moscow as on the defensive on a whole range of international issues, particularly its failure to halt the deployment of U.S. Pershing and cruise missiles in Western Europe, or to exploit the peace movement in Europe as a way to disrupt the Western alliance over the deployments and other issues. The Chinese media now saw Moscow—faced with growing Western military power and solidarity in the face of the Soviet threat—as lashing out with new demonstrations of its own military power. In Asia, the perceived Soviet approach directly and negatively affected Chinese security and appeared designed ultimately to bring China to heel. In February and March, the Soviet Union deployed two of its three aircraft carriers to the western Pacific; one passed near China in late February, on its way to Vladivostok. And in March, the USSR used an aircraft carrier task force to support its first joint amphibious exercise with Vietnam, which was conducted fairly close to China and near the Vietnamese port city of Haiphong. This followed the reported stationing of several Soviet medium bombers at Cam Ranh Bay, Vietnam, in late 1983—the first time Soviet forces were reported to be stationed outside areas contiguous with the USSR.[62]

Meanwhile, the Chinese escalated their military pressure against the Vietnamese—taking their strongest action precisely at the time of President Reagan's visit to China in late April and early May 1984. As it had done in 1978 and again in 1979, Beijing presumably felt more secure in confronting Moscow's Asian ally after it had consolidated Chinese relations with the United States. China's actions also underlined an area of important strategic common ground between Beijing and the strongly anti-Soviet Reagan administration. Beijing at the same time escalated charges regarding the Soviet threat to Chinese security, especially via Vietnam, and attempted to establish publicly an identity of interests with both Japanese Prime Minister Nakasone, during a visit to China in March, and President Reagan in April–May, on the basis of opposition to Soviet expansion in Asia.[63]

The result was the most serious downturn in Sino-Soviet relations since the Soviet invasion of Afghanistan in late 1979:

• Both Moscow and Beijing revived polemical exchanges, trading particular charges over sensitive security issues in Asia, East-West arms control efforts in Europe, and the international communist movement. There still were limits on the polemics, however. They did not exchange charges against each other's internal political-economic-social systems, nor did they engage in personal invective directed at individual leaders.

- The bilateral diplomatic dialogue was disrupted for a time, as the USSR—presumably concerned about and irritated by China's closer relations with the United States and its tougher posture toward Vietnam—postponed for an indefinite time the visit of First Deputy Prime Minister Arkhipov to China.
- Sino-Vietnamese military confrontation along their common border continued into the summer of 1984, well beyond the usual period of fighting coincident with the annual Vietnamese dry season campaigns against Chinese-supported resistance forces in Cambodia. This heightened fighting prompted the USSR leaders, and Chernenko in particular, to publicly condemn China by name—the first such occurrence since before Brezhnev's death in 1982.
- Sino-Soviet political competition heated up in Korea as both sides maneuvered to improve relations with Kim Il Song and his successors. In particular, Moscow welcomed Kim Il Song in May—the Korean leader's first visit to the USSR since 1961.
- Beijing continued to move ahead in establishing closer economic and military ties with the United States, despite the absence of ostensibly balancing progress in Sino-Soviet relations. An article in the Chinese journal *Liaowang* on July 16, 1984, rationalized the now clear Chinese tilt in favor of the United States. It asserted that even though China continued to pursue an "independent" foreign policy, current international circumstances dictated that it would make greater progress with the United States than in relations with the USSR.[64]

China was still anxious to manage the Soviet threat without recourse to force, however. It notably held out the option of resumed Sino-Soviet border talks, with party leader Hu Yaobang reportedly telling visitors that a border agreement could be reached relatively easily. In addition, China agreed to redraw frontier lines with the Soviet satellite Mongolia and agreed to set up joint commissions to discuss economic exchanges with Moscow's close East European allies. Moscow had long proposed renewed border delineation agreements and the establishment of similar joint economic commissions in Sino-Soviet relations. Beijing also said that it was willing to receive Arkhipov whenever the USSR would send him, and that China was willing to conduct foreign ministerial consultations with the Soviets during the UN General Assembly session in September.

Moscow moved to respond to the Chinese gestures and to resume forward movement in the less sensitive economic and technical areas of Sino-Soviet relations. The Soviets timed Arkhipov's visit for late December, only two weeks prior to Foreign Minister Andrei Gromyko's meetings with Secretary of State Shultz regarding U.S.-Soviet arms limitations. The timing suggested that Moscow had some interest to induce uncertainty in the minds of U.S. leaders about possible future progress in Sino-Soviet relations, and also re-duce the perceived influence the United States had gained in regard to the USSR as a result of growing Sino-American relations.

Arkhipov was warmly received as "an old friend of China" by high-level Chinese officials headed by Premier Zhao Ziyang and economic overseer Chun Yun. The visit saw the signing of three agreements that would provide for a broad array of economic cooperation, including the exchange of pro-duction technology, the construction and revamping of industrial enterprises, and technical training and exchange of experts and scientific data under the supervision of a new Sino-Soviet economic, trade, scientific, and technologi-cal committee. It was announced that the two countries had agreed to sign a five-year trade agreement in 1985 and that their trade level in 1985 would be 60 percent greater than the value of their trade in 1984.

The visit and agreement brought China's economic relationship with Moscow into line with the expanding Chinese economic relations with other Soviet bloc countries. It apparently did little to ease the differences between the two sides on major political and security issues. Indeed, such differences were exacerbated by Soviet-backed Vietnam's strong military attacks against Chinese-supported insurgents in Cambodia near the Thai border, actions that coincided with Arkhipov's stay in China.

In sum, the record of developments in China's approach toward and rela-tions with the United States and the Soviet Union in the 1980s shows that the approach adopted by Secretary of State George Shultz and the senior officials responsible for Asian affairs during this period of the Reagan administration worked effectively in support of American interests in policy toward China in several important ways. The approach was firmer than in the past on various U.S.-China differences. The new U.S. stance notably played into an array of concerns and uncertainties in Chinese foreign policy calculations and interests, causing the Chinese leaders to move to a more accommodating posture toward the United States that played down issues that in the recent past Chinese officials had said threatened to force China to take steps to downgrade the U.S.-China relationship. U.S. officials made sure that their Chinese counterparts understood that the United States was no longer as anxious as evident in the first decade of Sino-American rapprochement and normalization to seek China's favor as a source of influence against Moscow. The United States was increasingly confident in its strategic position vis-à-vis the Soviet Union, and had begun a process to roll back the gains the Soviets had made in the previous decade in various parts of the developing world. It was China that appeared to face greater difficulties posed by Soviet military buildup and expansion. China needed the U.S. relationship as a counterweight to this Soviet posture, and it increasingly needed a good relationship with the United States to allow for smooth economic interchange with the developed countries of the West and Japan and the international financial institutions they controlled. [65]

In the mid-1980s, with the rise to power of Mikhail Gorbachev and his reform-mined colleagues in the Soviet Union, China and the Soviet Union slowly moderated past differences and appeared determined to improve political, economic, and other bilateral concerns. Chinese and Soviet leaders focused on internal economic and political reforms, and expressed interest in fostering a stable, peaceful international environment conducive to such domestic change. Ideological, territorial, and leadership differences between Beijing and Moscow were deemed less important. However, the two sides remained divided largely over competing security interests in Asia. Gorbachev gradually began to accommodate China's interests in this area by starting to pull back Soviet forces from Afghanistan, Mongolia, and other places around China's periphery. Concurrently, Chinese military planners began to revise substantially China's strategic plans. They downgraded the danger of Soviet attack and allowed for a major demobilization of Chinese ground forces. [66]

The Soviet initiatives also reduced Chinese interest in cooperating closely with the United States and its allies and associates in Asia in order to check possible Soviet expansion. But China's growing need for close economic and technical ties with these countries compensated to some degree for its decreased interest in closer security ties with them. Chinese officials also wished to improve relations with the Soviets in order to keep pace with the rapid improvement in Gorbachev's relations with the United States and Western Europe. Otherwise, Chinese leaders ran the risk of not being consulted when world powers debated international issues important to China.

The agreement marking the Soviet withdrawal from Afghanistan was reached without China playing an active role in the negotiations, for example.

During this period, the United States and its allies found the Soviet Union more accommodating than China on matters of interest to the West. At the same time, the changes in U.S.-Soviet relations and in China's policy to the Soviet Union reduced the perceived American need to sustain and develop close strategic cooperation with China against the Soviet Union. Meanwhile, some specialists judged that the United States did not consider economic interchange with China important enough to compensate for the reduced anti-Soviet strategic cooperation, even though China remained important for Asian security and international arms control. Reflecting this slow change in U.S.-China relations, long-standing bilateral and other irritants in China-U.S. relations over human rights, treatment of intellectuals, and Tibet appeared to take on more prominence in Sino-American relations.[67]

RELATIONS APART FROM THE "GREAT POWER TRIANGLE"

As noted at the outset of this chapter and discussed in chapters 8 and 9, China changed during this two-decade period from an inward-looking and myopic international approach characterized by Maoist ideological rigidity and self-reliance to an approach that increasingly integrated China with neighboring countries, international economic organizations, and countries farther from China. In addition to the security concerns related to dealing with the danger posed by the Soviet Union and the opportunities and disputes associated with the United States, discussed in detail above, Chinese motivation for burgeoning international relationships focused on how they assisted China's economic development and how they added to the prestige and standing of China in world affairs.

As highlighted earlier in the chapter, Chinese leaders gave a much higher profile to being a recipient of foreign assistance, technology, and trade than they did to China's unique role under Mao as an impoverished country spreading influence through generous provision of foreign assistance to a range of states and movements seen deserving of support. China now actively competed with developing states for the foreign assistance provided by developed countries and international economic institutions, and it competed with developing countries for access to advanced foreign technology and markets for Chinese manufactured and other products.

Chinese officials endeavored to get along with countries and groups that they had in the past shunned or opposed for ideological, strategic, or other reasons. Efforts continued to improve China relations with non-Communist governments along China's periphery, including notably Japan and the governments that were members of the Association of Southeast Asian Nations (ASEAN). Economic ties grew with the advancing South Korean economy, though political ties were to wait until after the end of the Cold War. By the end of the period, China was reciprocating efforts by countries that were aligned with the now rapidly declining Soviet Union, notably India and Vietnam, to begin the process of normalizing their heretofore very strained relations with China.

Chinese friendships and mutually advantageous relationships with developing countries in Africa, the Middle East, and to a degree Latin America remained active, though China generally avoided costly assistance projects of the past. China's willingness to provide nuclear weapons technology and ballistic missiles to Pakistan headed the list of egregious Chinese weapons proliferation practices that served to solidify Chinese relations with key countries like Pakistan and Saudi Arabia; and China rose to prominence as a leading provider of conventional arms to both Iran and Iraq in their protracted war during the 1980s. China further distanced itself from the terrorist practices of the Palestine Liberation Organization (PLO) and other such groups, while it moved pragmatically to develop closer relations with Israel involving intelligence exchanges; arms sales; and in the early 1990s, official diplomatic relations.

Chinese interest in developed countries like Japan and West European countries centered on their role in working with the United States in dealing with the expansion of the Soviet Union and in their economic prowess, the source of assistance, technology, and markets important to Chinese development. In international organizations and governance, China tended to avoid controversy, endeavoring to remain on good terms with most states and eschewing costs or commitments that might hamper the nascent growth of China's economy as it integrated more closely with the world economy. China was glad to keep its UN dues and payments to UN peacekeeping very low. For the most part, it avoided using its Security Council veto, preferring to abstain on issues it did not approve of.

NOTES

1. Alice Lyman Miller and Richard Wich, *Becoming Asia* (Stanford CA: Stanford University Press, 2011), pp. 161–93.

2. Ezra Vogel, *Deng Xiaoping and the Transformation of China* (Cambridge, MA: Harvard University Press, 2011), pp. 91–183.

3. John Garver, *Foreign Relations of the People's Republic of China* (Englewood Cliffs, NJ: Prentice Hall, 1993), pp. 70–112.

4. A. Doak Barnett, *A New U.S. Policy toward China* (Washington, DC: Brookings Institution, 1971); Rosemary Foot, *The Practice of Power: U.S. Relations with China since 1949* (New York: Oxford University Press, 1997); Evelyn Goh, *Constructing the U.S. Rapprochement with China, 1961–1974* (New York: Cambridge University Press, 2005); Gong Li, *Kuayue: 1969–1979 nian Zhong-Mei guanxi de yanbian* [Across the chasm: The evolution of relations between China and the United States, 1969–1979] (Zhengzhou: Henan renmin chubanshe, 1992); Pei Jianzhang, ed., *Zhonghua renmin gongheguo waijiaoshi* [Diplomatic history of the People's Republic of China] (Beijing: Shijie zhishi chubanshe, 1994); Xie Yixian, *Zhongguo Waijiao Shi: 1949–1979* [China's diplomatic history: 1949–1979] (Henan: Henan Renmin Chubanshe, 1988); Wang Taiping et al., *Zhonghua renmin gongheguo waijiao shi, 1957–1969* [A diplomatic history of the People's Republic of China, 1957–1969] (Beijing: Shijie Zhishi, 1998); Xie Xide and Ni Shixiong, *Quzhe de licheng: Zhong Mei jianji ershi nian* [From normalization to renormalization: twenty years of Sino-US relations] (Shanghai: Fudan Daxue Chubanshe, 1999).

5. Chen Jian, *Mao's China and the Cold War* (Chapel Hill: University of North Carolina Press, 2001).

6. Foot, *The Practice of Power*; Goh, *Constructing the U.S. Rapprochement with China*.

7. A. Doak Barnett, *China and the Major Powers in East Asia* (Washington, DC: Brookings Institution, 1977); Robert Ross, *Negotiating Cooperation: The United States and China, 1969–1989* (Stanford, CA: Stanford University Press, 1995); Robert Sutter, *China-Watch: Toward Sino-American Reconciliation* (Baltimore: Johns Hopkins University Press, 1978), pp. 83–102; Thomas Gottlieb, *Chinese Foreign Policy Factionalism and the Origins of the Strategic Triangle* (Santa Monica, CA: RAND, 1977); John Garver, *China's Decision for Rapprochement with the United States, 1968–1971* (Boulder, CO: Westview, 1982). Wang Zhongchun, "The Soviet Factor in Sino-American Normalization, 1969–1979," in *Normalization of U.S.-China Relations*, ed. William Kirby, Robert Ross, and Gong Li (Cambridge, MA: Harvard University Press, 2005).

8. Li Jie, "China's Domestic Politics and the Normalization of Sino-U.S. Relations, 1969–1979," in Kirby, Ross, and Li, eds., *Normalization of U.S.-China Relations*, pp. 56–89; Philip Bridgham, "Mao's Cultural Revolution: The Struggle to Seize Power," *China Quarterly* 41 (1970): pp. 1–25.

9. Gottlieb, *Chinese Foreign Policy Factionalism and the Origins of the Strategic Triangle*; Roderick MacFarquhar and Michael Schoenhals, *Mao's Last Revolution* (Cambridge, MA: Harvard University Press, 2006).

10. Harlan Jencks, *From Muskets to Missiles: Politics and Professionalism in the Chinese Army, 1945–1981* (Boulder, CO: Westview, 1982).

11. Miller and Wich, *Becoming Asia*, pp. 161–93; Allen Whiting, "The Sino-American Détente: Genesis and Prospects," in *China and the World Community*, ed. Ian Wilson (Sydney: Australian Institute of International Affairs, 1973), pp. 70–89; Thomas Robinson, "The Sino-Soviet Border Dispute: Background, Development and the March 1969 Clashes," *American*

Political Science Review 66, no. 4 (December 1972): pp. 1175–78; Harold Hinton, *Bear at the Gate: Chinese Policymaking under Soviet Pressure* (Stanford, CA: Hoover Institute, 1971).

12. For Mao's statements, see Ministry of Foreign Affairs of the People's Republic of China and Document Research Office of the CCP Central Committee, *Mao Zedong Waijiao Wenxuan* [Selected works of Mao Zedong on diplomacy] (Beijing: Zhongyang Wenxian Chubanshe and Shijie Chubanshe, 1994).

13. Garver, *Foreign Relations of the People's Republic of China*, pp. 304–20.

14. David Bachman, "Mobilizing for War: China's Limited Ability to Cope with the Soviet Threat," *Issues and Studies* 43, no. 4 (December 2007): pp. 1–38; Gottlieb, *Chinese Foreign Policy Factionalism*; Roger Brown, "Chinese Politics and American Policy: A New Look at the Triangle," *Foreign Policy* 23 (Summer 1976): pp. 3–23.

15. Sutter, *China-Watch*, pp. 72–75.

16. Sutter, *China-Watch*, pp. 75–78; for background see among others Wang Shuzhong, ed., *Mei-Su zhengba zhanlue wenti* [The question of contention for hegemony between the United States and the Soviet Union] (Beijing: Guofang daxue chubanshe, 1988).

17. Miller and Wich, *Becoming Asia*, pp. 166–70; Garver, *Foreign Relations of the People's Republic of China*, pp. 306–10.

18. Sutter, *China-Watch*, pp. 78–102.

19. Michael Schaller, *The United States and China: Into the Twenty-First Century* (New York: Oxford University Press, 2002), p. 170; Garver, *Foreign Relations of the People's Republic of China*, pp. 74–83; Ross, *Negotiating Cooperation*, pp. 33–34.

20. Ross, *Negotiating Cooperation*, pp. 28, 34–35.

21. Garver, *Foreign Relations of the People's Republic of China*, pp. 74–83; Ross, *Negotiating Cooperation*, p. 34; Immanuel C. Y. Hsu, *The Rise of Modern China* (New York: Oxford University Press, 2000), pp. 711–14, 822.

22. Robert Sutter, *Historical Dictionary of United States-China Relations* (Lanham, MD: Scarecrow, 2006), pp. 190–91.

23. Hsu, *The Rise of Modern China*, pp. 710–14, 820–23.

24. Sutter, *China-Watch*, pp. 109–12.

25. Vogel, *Deng Xiaoping and the Transformation of China*, pp. 76–119.

26. Sutter, *Historical Dictionary of Chinese Foreign Policy*, pp. 240–41.

27. Vogel, *Deng Xiaoping and the Transformation of China*, pp. 76–88.

28. Hsu, *The Rise of Modern China*, pp. 763–73; for background see among others Wang Taiping, ed., *Zhonghua renmin gongheguo waijiaoshi* [History of the diplomacy of the People's Republic of China], vol. 3 (*1970–1978*) (Beijing: Shijie Zhishi chubanshe, 1999).

29. Wang Wenlan, "Tangshan Earthquake: Unforgotten History," *China Daily*, July 26, 2006, www.chinadaily.com (accessed September 14, 2009); John K. Fairbank and Merle Goldman, *China: A New History* (Cambridge, MA: Harvard University Press, 1999), pp. 404–5.

30. Vogel, *Deng Xiaoping and the Transformation of China*, pp. 217–48.

31. Nayan Chanda, *Brother Enemy: The War after the War* (New York: Harcourt Brace Jovanovich, 1986).

32. Garver, *Foreign Relations of the People's Republic of China*, pp. 166–77, 310–11.

33. Robert Sutter, *U.S.-Chinese Relations* (Lanham, MD: Rowman & Littlefield, 2010), pp. 76–80.

34. Ross, *Negotiating Cooperation*, pp. 125–26; James Mann, *About Face* (New York, Knopf, 1999), pp. 98–100.

35. House Committee on Foreign Affairs, *Executive-Legislative Consultations over China Policy, 1978–1979* (Washington, DC: U.S. Government Printing Office, 1980).

36. Robert Sutter, *Chinese Foreign Relations: Developments after Mao* (New York: Praeger 1986), pp. 18–96; Garver, *Foreign Relations of the People's Republic of China*, pp. 98–103, 317–19.

37. Sutter, *Chinese Foreign Relations*, pp. 104–7.

38. Ross, *Negotiating Cooperation*, pp. 164–74.

39. Nancy Bernkopf Tucker, *Strait Talk* (Cambridge, MA: Harvard University Press, 2009), pp. 153–60.

40. Harry Harding, *A Fragile Relationship* (Washington, DC: Brookings Institution, 1992); Ross, *Negotiating Cooperation*; Mann, *About Face*; David M. Lampton, *Same Bed Different Dreams* (Berkeley: University of California Press, 2001); Robert Suettinger, *Beyond Tiananmen* (Washington, DC: Brookings Institution, 2003); Jean Garrison, *Making China Policy: From Nixon to G. W. Bush* (Boulder, CO: Lynne Rienner, 2005). Garrison's analysis (pp. 80–85) identifies two competing groups of U.S. decision makers regarding China policy in the early 1980s as the "China-first" group and the "pan-Asian" group. The analysis in this chapter builds on the Garrison analysis.

41. Ross, *Negotiating Cooperation*, pp. 170–245; Mann, *About Face*, pp. 119–36; Garrison, *Making China Policy*, pp. 79–106; Tucker, *Strait Talk*, pp. 153–60.

42. Harding, *Fragile Relationship*, pp. 131–45; David Shambaugh, "Patterns of Interaction in Sino-American Relations," in *Chinese Foreign Policy: Theory and Practice*, ed. Thomas Robinson and David Shambaugh (New York: Oxford University Press, 1994), pp. 203–5.

43. Sutter, *U.S.-Chinese Relations*, pp. 82–84.

44. Garver, *Foreign Relations of the People's Republic of China*, pp. 310–19.

45. Sutter, *Chinese Foreign Relations*, pp. 18–96.

46. Garver, *Foreign Relations of the People's Republic of China*, pp. 98–103, 317–19.

47. Ross, *Negotiating Cooperation*, pp. 164–74.

48. Sutter, *Chinese Foreign Relations*, p. 182.

49. Sutter, *Chinese Foreign Relations*, p.178.

50. Garver, *Foreign Relations of the People's Republic of China*, pp. 98–103; Ross, *Negotiating Cooperation*, pp. 170–200.

51. Tucker, *Strait Talk*, pp. 153–60; Mann, *About Face*, pp. 128–33.

52. Sutter, *Chinese Foreign Relations*, p. 178.

53. Richard Nations, "A Tilt Towards Tokyo," *Far Eastern Economic Review*, April 21, 1983, p. 36; Ross, *Negotiating Cooperation*, pp. 228–33.

54. Sutter, *Chinese Foreign Relations*, pp. 178–79.

55. Sutter, *Chinese Foreign Relations*, pp. 178–79.

56. Ross, *Negotiating Cooperation*, pp. 233–45; Tucker, *Strait Talk*, pp. 160–61.

57. Sutter, *Chinese Foreign Relations*, pp. 180–81.

58. Ross, *Negotiating Cooperation*, pp. 233–44; Sutter, *Chinese Foreign Relations*, pp. 181–82.

59. Tucker, *Strait Talk*, pp. 155–60.

60. Gerald Segal, *Sino-Soviet Relations after Mao*, Adelphi Papers, no. 202 (London: International Institute for Strategic Studies, 1985); Michael Yahuda, *The International Politics of the Asia-Pacific* (London: RoutledgeCurzon, 2004), pp. 85–94; Lowell Dittmer, *Sino-Soviet Normalization and its International Implications, 1945–1990* (Seattle: University of Washington Press, 1992); Miller and Wich, *Becoming Asia*, pp. 194–202.

61. The review of Sino-Soviet relations in the remainder of this section is adapted from Sutter, *Chinese Foreign Relations*, pp. 182–86. For specific meetings and developments in Sino-Soviet relations, see *China Quarterly* "Chronology" (issued each March, June, September, and December during these years). See also Chi Su, "Sino-Soviet Relations of the 1980s:

From Confrontation to Conciliation," in *China and the World*, ed. Samuel S. Kim, 2nd ed. (Boulder, CO: Westview, 1989), pp. 148–78; Segal, *Sino-Soviet Relations after Mao*; and Miller and Wich, *Becoming Asia*, pp. 194–202.

62. Official Chinese media published U.S. and Japanese references to these Soviet actions during March–May 1984.

63. See discussion of Chinese leaders' remarks to visiting Prime Minister Nakasone and visiting President Reagan in Sutter, *Chinese Foreign Relations*, pp. 181–83, 186–89.

64. Sutter, *Chinese Foreign Relations*, pp. 184–85.

65. Sutter, *U.S.-Chinese Relations*, pp. 93–94.

66. Miller and Wich, *Becoming Asia*, pp. 194–202.

67. Harding, *Fragile Relationship*, pp. 173–214.

Chapter Four

Chinese Foreign Relations after the Cold War

This chapter deals with the evolution of Chinese foreign relations in the post–Cold War period in two ways. First, important developments in Chinese foreign relations and relevant domestic Chinese events in the 1990s are discussed in chronological order. Second, there follows a more detailed assessment of the internal and external factors, providing an overall context of developments in Chinese foreign relations in the twenty-first century that are featured in more detail in later chapters of this book. The assessment of the policies and priorities of the Chinese government relevant to China's approach to foreign affairs concludes with discernment of clear goals motivating Chinese policy and practice in contemporary international affairs. As noted earlier and discussed in later chapters, the goals often conflict with one another, precluding a clear and predictable strategy in foreign affairs.

DEVELOPMENTS IN THE 1990S

The weakening and collapse of the Soviet threat to China improved China's overall security situation. For the first time, the People's Republic of China was not facing an immediate foreign threat to its national security. However, the sharp international reaction to China's harsh crackdown on dissent after the June 1989 Tiananmen incident caught Chinese leaders by surprise. They reportedly had expected industrialized nations to restore stable relations with China after a few months. They had not counted on the rapid collapse of Communism in Eastern Europe, the subsequent march toward self-determination and democratization throughout the Soviet republics, and ultimately the end of the Soviet Union in 1991. These unexpected events for several years diverted industrialized nations' return to China with advantageous investment, assistance, and economic exchanges, called into question China's strategic importance as a counterweight to the Soviet Union, and posed the most serious challenge to the legitimacy of the Chinese Communist regime since the Cultural Revolution. Taiwan's concurrent moves toward greater democracy and self-determination received greater positive attention in the United States and the West, adding to China's concerns about broad international trends and what to do about them.[1]

The United States was seen as both the greatest threat and most important partner in Chinese foreign policy. In response to U.S.-led sanctions and criticisms in the late 1980s and early 1990s, the Chinese government endeavored to use foreign affairs to demonstrate the legitimacy and prestige of its Communist leaders. High-level visits to Asian capitals and elsewhere in the non-Western world were used along with trade and security arrangements in order to strengthen China's image before skeptical audiences at home and abroad. To reestablish internal political stability, Chinese leaders also gave high priority to the resource needs of the military and public security forces. Thus began a long series of double-digit annual increases in China's defense budget that has persisted up to now and has made China a more formidable military competitor of the United States and Asia's leading military power.[2]

Recognizing that communist ideology was not popular enough to support their continued monopoly of power, leaders in Beijing played up more traditional themes of Chinese patriotism and nationalism to support their rule. U.S. and other foreign criticisms of the communist system in China were portrayed not as attacks against unjust arbitrary rule but as assaults on the national integrity of China. These attacks were equated with earlier "imperialist" pressures on China in the nineteenth century and the first half of the twentieth century.[3]

Meanwhile, statements and initiatives by Deng Xiaoping spurring economic reform and opening during a tour of southern China in 1992 pushed other Chinese senior leaders away from their hesitant approach to economic modernization and reform after the Tiananmen crackdown. Deng called for faster growth and increased economic interchange with the outside world, especially the developed economies of Asia and the West. This call coincided with the start of an economic boom on the mainland that continued for several years of double-digit growth and then declined a bit to the still rapid pace of 7–8 percent annual growth. The consequences of such rapid growth initially included serious inflation as well as broader economic dislocation and many social problems, but the growth also caught the attention of foreign business and government leaders. Many of China's well-to-do neighbors such as Hong Kong and Taiwan already had become well positioned to take advantage of the mainland's rapid growth. They were followed rapidly by West European, Japanese, Southeast Asian, and Korean entrepreneurs. American business interest in the China market grew markedly from 1992, and was credited with playing an important role in convincing the Clinton administration in 1994 to stop linking U.S. most-favored-nation trade treatment to improvements in China's still poor human rights conditions.[4]

Deng Xiaoping and the new third generation of leaders headed by president and party leader Jiang Zemin continued the post-Mao policies, emphasizing fostering a better economic life for the people of China in order to justify their continued monopoly of political power. As the prestige of Mao and Communism had faded rapidly, Chinese leaders found themselves depending heavily on foreign trade, and related foreign investment and assistance, for China's needed economic development. China depended particularly on its Asian neighbors for aid, investment, and trade benefits, and on the United States and other major consumer markets to absorb its exports, which were growing at double the rate of the fast-developing Chinese economy. To insure their political survival, China's leaders continued to emphasize the maintenance of a peaceful international environment, especially in nearby Asia, which would facilitate the continued trade, investment, and assistance flows so important to Chinese economic well-being.[5]

The leadership followed earlier steps to put aside self-reliance and to broaden international contacts by increasing efforts to meet the requirements of the United States and others regarding market access, intellectual property rights, and other economic issues, and to become a member of the World Trade Organization (WTO). Chinese leaders accepted more commitments and responsibilities stemming from their participation in such international economic organizations as the World Bank, the Asian Development Bank, and the Asia-Pacific Economic Cooperation (APEC) forum.[6]

Chinese leaders remained sensitive on matters of national sovereignty and international security issues close to home. But they adjusted to world pressure when resistance appeared detrimental to broader Chinese concerns. Examples of this adjustment included Chinese cooperation with the international peace settlement in Cambodia in 1991, willingness to join the 1968 Treaty

on Non-proliferation of Nuclear Weapons and to halt nuclear tests by the end
of 1996 under an international agreement, willingness to abide by terms of
the Missile Technology Control Regime (MTCR), and efforts to help the
United States reach an agreement with North Korea in October 1994 over the
latter's nuclear weapons development program. Beijing also endeavored to
meet international expectations on other transnational issues, such as polic-
ing drug traffic, curbing international terrorism, and working to avoid further
degradation of the global environment.[7]

China's consistent hard line against outside criticism of its political authoritarianism and poor human rights record continued to illustrate limits of
China's accommodation to international norms. China continued to transfer
sensitive military technology or dual-use equipment to Pakistan, Iran, North
Korea, and other potential flash points, despite criticism from Western countries. Furthermore, Chinese political and military leaders were not reluctant
to use rhetorical threats or demonstrations of military force to intimidate
those they believed were challenging China's traditional territorial or nationalistic claims in sensitive areas such as Taiwan, the South China Sea, and
Hong Kong.[8]

As a general rule, Chinese leaders tended to approach each foreign policy
issue on a case-by-case basis, each time calculating the costs and benefits of
adherence to international norms. This kind of approach applied especially to
security and political issues, while Chinese leaders came to view economic
norms differently, seeing China generally well served by embracing economic globalization and the norms associated with it. By 1991, Chinese officials
saw that maintaining past support for the Khmer Rouge in Cambodia would
counter broader Chinese interests in achieving a favorable peace settlement
in Cambodia and solidifying closer Chinese relations with Association of
Southeast Asian Nations (ASEAN) members, Japan, and the West—all of
whom saw continued Chinese aid to the Khmer Rouge as a serious obstacle
to peace. Similarly, in 1994, China had to announce its decision to stop
nuclear testing by the end of 1996 and to join the comprehensive nuclear test
ban, or it would have risked major friction in its relations with the United
States, Japan, Western Europe, and Russia.[9]

Influencing the case-by-case approach was a rising sense of nationalism
among Chinese leaders and the Chinese people more broadly. Tending to
view the world as a highly competitive, state-centered system, Chinese leaders were slow to embrace multilateralism and interdependence, though they
came to accept these trends regarding economic issues. In security and politi-

cal affairs, however, they were inclined to see the world in fairly traditional balance-of-power terms. They stressed that the world was becoming more multipolar (that is, having a number of competing nation states), though in the face of undiminished U.S. dominance, they came to play down multipolarity for the time being in favor of multilateralism. The latter required the United States to sacrifice some freedom of maneuver for the sake of an interdependent international order, thereby constraining U.S. power that could be used against Chinese interests. [10]

Chinese suspicions of the prevailing Asian and international order centered on the dominant role of the United States and its allies and associates. These nations were seen as setting the agenda of many international regimes in order to serve their own particular national interests, in the process giving short shrift to the interests and concerns of newly emerging powers like China. For example, many leaders in China during the 1990s saw foreign efforts to encourage or pressure China to conform to standards on international security, human rights, and economic policies and practices as motivated by the foreign powers' fear of China's rising power, their unwillingness to share power fairly with China, and their desire to "hold down" China—that is, to keep it weak for as long as possible. [11]

Chinese leaders recognized that the United States exerted predominant strategic influence in East Asia and the western Pacific, was a leading economic power in the region, and was one of only two powers (along with Russia) capable of exerting sufficient power around China's periphery to pose a tangible danger to Chinese security and development. As the world's remaining superpower, the United States was seen by Chinese officials in the 1990s as exerting strong influence in international financial and political institutions, such as the World Bank and the United Nations, that were particularly important to Beijing. The United States also played a key role in areas of great sensitivity to China's leaders, notably regarding Taiwan and international human rights. [12]

While Chinese leaders tried hard to work constructively with U.S. leaders in areas of mutual interest, more often than not, U.S. policy in Asian and world affairs was seen as adverse to Chinese interests. Chinese leaders were preoccupied with maneuvering carefully and sometimes forcefully to defend and protect important interests while accommodating American concerns in other areas. A military face-off with two U.S. aircraft carrier battle groups in the Taiwan area in 1996 and the trashing of U.S. diplomatic properties in China by Chinese demonstrators after the U.S. bombing of the Chinese embassy in Belgrade in 1999 illustrated how far Chinese leaders were prepared to go in fending off perceived American pressure. Chinese media in these years were full of affirmations of Chinese determination to make necessary sacrifices to defend important interests against U.S. "hegemonism."[13]

As party leader and president, Jiang Zemin exerted increasing influence in Chinese policy making during the 1990s. Jiang was successful in maneuvers against formidable leadership competition, notably from the likes of former president Yang Shangkun and his nephew Yang Baiping. He initiated a more flexible position that became a central tenet in the Chinese stance toward Taiwan, even though it was temporarily upset by Taiwan President Lee Teng-hui's visit to Cornell University in 1995 and the subsequent crisis and military standoff in cross-strait relations leading to the deployment of U.S. aircraft carriers to the Taiwan area in 1996. Jiang also worked with Vice Premier Zhu Rongji and other senior government leaders to bring inflation under control while sustaining strong economic growth. Jiang pursued and advanced policies generally consistent with those set forth by Deng Xiaoping, whose health declined in the several years before his death in February 1997.[14]

Deng's passing allowed Jiang to assume the mantle and actual position of China's paramount leader. His overall standing, of course, was much weaker than that of Deng, whose prestige and leadership credentials traced back to the legendary Long March during the 1930s. But Jiang was especially active in foreign affairs, leading Chinese efforts to sustain an effective approach toward the United States, adjusting the mix of incentives and sanctions in Chinese policy toward Taiwan, and creating a more coherent and active Chinese policy toward its periphery in Asia.[15]

With Deng gone, Chinese leaders in 1997 were anxious to minimize problems with the United States and other countries in order to avoid complications in their efforts to appear successful in completing three major tasks for the year:

- The July 1, 1997, transition of Hong Kong to Chinese rule
- The reconfiguration of Chinese leadership and policy at the Fifteenth CCP Congress in September 1997, the first major party meeting since the death of senior leader Deng Xiaoping in February 1997
- The Sino-U.S. summit of October 1997, which China hoped would show people in China and abroad that its leaders were now fully accepted as

respectable world leaders following a period of protracted isolation after the 1989 Tiananmen crackdown. [16]

Generally pleased with the results of these three endeavors, Chinese leaders headed by President Jiang Zemin began implementing policy priorities for 1998. At the top of the list was an ambitious multiyear effort, begun in earnest after the National People's Congress (NPC) meeting in March 1998, to transform tens of thousands of China's money-losing state-owned enterprises (SOEs) into more efficient businesses by reforming them (for example, selling them to private concerns, forming large conglomerates, or other actions). Beijing embarked on major programs to promote economic and administrative efficiency and protect China's potentially vulnerable financial systems from any negative fallout from the 1997–1998 Asian economic crisis and subsequent uncertainties. Thus, at the NPC meeting in March 1998, it was announced that government rolls would be drastically cut in an effort to reduce inefficient government interference in day-to-day business management. China's new premier, Zhu Rongji, initiated sweeping changes in China's banking and other financial systems designed to reduce or eliminate the vulnerabilities seen elsewhere in Asia. [17]

As a result of the September 1997 Party Congress and the March 1998 NPC meeting, a new team was in place, managing policy without such powerful leaders of the past as Mao Zedong and Deng Xiaoping. There were problems reaching consensus on the power-holding arrangements made at the Party and People's Congresses, but on the whole, top-level leaders seemed to be working smoothly together pursuing Chinese policy interests. [18]

Making collective leadership work was an ongoing challenge for China's top leaders. Traditionally one senior decision maker dominated the People's Republic of China. Periods of collective leadership, notably after Mao's death in 1976, were short and unstable. President Jiang Zemin gained in stature and influence in the 1990s, but his power still did not compare to that exerted by Mao and Deng. Also, in the background lay the scenario that when it came time for Jiang and his senior colleagues to retire, some struggle for power and influential positions by up-and-coming leaders remained a distinct possibility. All were aware that if a major economic, political, or foreign policy crisis were to emerge, leadership conflict over what to do, how to do it, and who to do it could be intense. [19]

There were few signs of disagreement among senior leaders over the broad recent policy emphasis on economic reform, though sectors affected

by reform often resisted strenuously. The ambitious plans for economic reform, especially reform of the SOEs, were needed if China's economy was to
become efficient enough to sustain the growth rates viewed as needed to
justify continued Communist rule and to develop China's wealth and power.
China anticipated joining the World Trade Organization (WTO) in 2001 or
2002, strengthening the need for greater economic efficiency and reform.
The reforms also exacerbated social and economic uncertainties, which reinforced the government's determination to maintain a firm grip on political
power and levers of social control. By late 1998, instability caused by economic change and growing political dissent prompted the PRC leadership to
initiate significant suppression of political dissidents and related activities.
The repression continued into the twenty-first century. [20]

Against this background, foreign affairs generally remained an area of
less urgent policy priority. Broad international trends, notably improved relations with the United States and an upswing in China's relations throughout
its periphery, supported the efforts by the Chinese authorities to pursue policies intended to minimize disruptions and to assist their domestic reform
endeavors. The government remained wary of the real or potential challenges
posed by a possible renewed Asian economic crisis, by Taiwan, by efforts by
Japan and the United States to increase their international influence in ways
contrary to Beijing's interests, by India's great power aspirations and nuclear
capability, and by other concerns. The PRC at this time voiced special concern over the implications of U.S. plans to develop and deploy theater ballistic missile defense systems in East Asia, and a national missile defense
(NMD) for the United States. Chinese officials also voiced concern over the
downturn in U.S.-China relations at the outset of the George W. Bush administration, but appeared determined to cooperate with the U.S.-led antiterrorism campaign begun in September 2001. [21]

TWENTY-FIRST CENTURY POLICIES AND PRIORITIES

In the first decades of the twenty-first century, the policies and priorities of
the Chinese leadership have depended on key internal and external variables
that will determine the future of the Communist regime and its role in Asian
and world affairs. A mainstream view among American officials and nongovernment China specialists holds that the Chinese government appears
resilient enough to deal with most anticipated problems internally, at least for
a number of years. China is wary of the United States and is steadily building

military power. But unless Beijing is challenged by circumstances, China is seen as reluctant to confront the United States or to engage in military expansion. Alternative views include those who see Chinese leaders ready and able to confront the United States and Asian neighbors, by military means if necessary, over such key issues as Taiwan and territorial claims along China's periphery. [22]

Political Leaders and Institutions

China's "third-generation" leadership under Jiang Zemin (with Mao's being the first generation and Deng's the second) and its successors in the "fourth generation" (led by president and party leader Hu Jintao—in power 2002–2012) and the fifth generation (led by incoming leaders Xi Jinping and Li Keqiang) were thought likely to continue the process of political regularity and institutionalization that made China's political behavior much more predictable than it had been during the Maoist period (1949–1976). The more recent political leaders have lacked charisma but have been more technically competent and less ideologically rigid than past leaders. They have been aware of the problems they have faced and prepared to deal with at least some of the most important ones. [23]

Some experts note that fourth-generation leaders headed by Hu Jintao, who was selected as party leader at the Sixteenth Party Congress in November 2002, president at the Tenth National People's Congress in March 2003, and chairman of the Central Military Commission in 2004, often had diverse political views and lacked the binding solidarity of experiences that the previous generations of leaders had gained on the Long March and during the war against Japan, for example. For many years, there was a split between top officials close to Jiang Zemin and those close to Hu Jintao. The level of political skills of the fourth generation also is questioned, but Hu Jintao and his colleagues handled more or less effectively a number of difficult domestic and foreign policy concerns ranging from sustaining economic growth during the global recession of 2008–2010 to repeated crises caused by North Korea's nuclear weapons development and other provocations. [24]

Similar concerns surrounded the transfer of power to fifth-generation leaders beginning in 2012. That transfer was notably disrupted by the removal from power in March 2012 of Politburo member Bo Xilai amid a major scandal involving Bo's wife and the murder of a British businessman long associated with Bo and his family, the arrest of Bo's lieutenant after he sought refuge in the U.S. consulate in Chengdu, and Bo's reported ambitions to seek a position on the Politburo Standing Committee at the Eighteenth CCP Congress in late 2012.[25]

Composed of technocrats, economists, managers, and other professionals, the fourth and the fifth generations are seen as capable and pragmatic when confronted with economic and social problems, but having limited experience with and understanding of the West. In practice, the leadership has attempted to adhere to existing policies promoting rapid economic development, but with more attention to the disadvantaged and others left behind as a result of the sweeping economic changes. They remain strict in enforcing laws and regulations against those who would seek to challenge one-party rule in China, resulting in a wide range of human rights violations according to international observers.[26]

The institutionalization of China's politics was the result of a proliferation of institutions from the top down. Accompanying the growth in the number of institutions was a distinct break with the Maoist past in the growing regularization and routine procedures. Beginning in the late 1970s, Chinese Communist Party and NPC sessions and plenums were regularly held, and planning and budgetary cycles were adhered to. The principles of class struggle were replaced by budgets geared to a socialist market economy and political constituencies. Socialist laws continued to be promulgated, although enforcement remained problematic.[27]

Some experts argued that however important institutionalization was, one of the most significant changes in China's political landscape was occurring outside the state: the growth of civil society amid the increasing wealth and influence of businesspeople and academics. On July 1, 2001, China's then party leader, Jiang Zemin, made a major speech advocating the recruitment of such wealthy and influential people into the party's ranks. His injunction was followed at the Sixteenth Party Congress in November 2002. Increasing incorporation of elites amid party institutionalization was a stabilizing factor; it meant less arbitrary decision making. A disadvantage was that China's current and future leaders might not be as decisive as Mao Zedong or Deng Xiaoping because they were hemmed in by diverse interests, growing bureaucracy, and procedures.[28]

The military had less representation than in the past at the top-level CCP Politburo. An urban, educated elite, the leadership was civilian based: only two of the twenty-plus members of the Fifteenth Communist Party Congress Central Committee Politburo and the Sixteenth Communist Party Congress Central Committee Politburo had military experience or could be considered "military politicians"; the Seventeenth CCP Politburo had three military leaders. Some observers wondered if the military would be able to muster sufficient support for its modernization programs, though evidence of China's steady military buildup showed strong leadership support behind military modernization.[29]

Leadership succession, nepotism, favoritism, and corruption continue to be serious problems, as evidenced notably by the scandal associated with the removal from power of Politburo member Bo Xilai in March 2012. Although China's politics are becoming more stable and predictable, with the battles being fought on the institutional level, personal rivalries and relations remain important. Jiang Zemin used his influence to retain the chairmanship of the party's Central Military Commission until 2004, two years beyond the established retirement date. In the maneuvering to succeed Hu Jintao two candidates, Xi Jinping and Li Keqiang, each backed by different leadership groups, emerged at the Seventeenth CCP Congress in 2007. Corruption was seen by some experts to pave the way for the weakening and end of Communist rule, though others viewed the growth of corruption as having stabilized in recent years.[30]

Economic and Social Trends

Economic growth sustained the overall rise in the standard of living that characterizes Chinese development during the previous two decades. The relatively young, well-trained labor force with modern technical skills increased in numbers. The rapidly improving infrastructure of rail, roads, and electronic communications greatly reduced perceived distance and helped link the poorly developed interior to the booming coastal regions.

Chinese development remains heavily dependent on foreign trade, investments, and scientific/technical exchange. The government faces daunting problems—notably ailing or inefficient State Owned Enterprises (SOEs) and a weak banking/financial system. The massive and often wasteful use of energy and other resources and a widespread shortage of uncontaminated water heads the list of major environmental problems that appear hard to resolve without large production cutbacks or expensive technology. China's foreign-invested manufacturing and infrastructure development seems at odds with the goal of the Hu Jintao government to move China from dependence on foreign trade to an economy driven by domestic consumption. Chinese household consumption remains low. Government support for social services improved from a low base, but Chinese families continue to rely on personal savings to cover education, health care, and retirement expenses that in other countries are met with government funds. The interest payments on massive domestic savings are held artificially low, providing plenty of funding from banks to SOEs but disadvantaging savers; thus people have less money to devote to consumer spending.[31]

The global economic uncertainties beginning with the crisis and recession of 2008–2010 brought sometimes sharp cutbacks in Western consumption of Chinese and other imports. In 2009 Chinese trade figures and the overall Chinese economy turned sharply downward. Unemployment rose dramatically, especially among the millions of rural migrants who had moved to coastal and urban areas to engage in construction and manufacturing driven by foreign demand. The leadership took concrete steps to promote large-scale infrastructure and other domestic development and spending. In 2010 the Chinese economy resumed double-digit growth, but faced new uncertainties with continued stagnation in major markets in Europe and Japan, and weak growth in the United States.[32]

Leadership differences reflecting diverging policy preferences and bureaucratic and institutional interests continue to influence the Chinese policy process. One result of China's external outreach is the growing importance of ministries with responsibility in foreign affairs, such as the Ministry of Foreign Affairs (MOFA) and the Ministry of Foreign Trade and Economic Cooperation (MOFTEC). The latter, especially, became more important when Beijing joined the WTO. (In 2003, MOFTEC changed its name and became China's Commerce Ministry.) The National Development and Reform Commission of the PRC has sustained broad and strong powers dealing with economic policies. Central regulatory bodies such as the State Economic and Trade Commission (SETC) also became more important for a time. The old bureaucracies and their stakeholders associated with the planning system, such as the State Planning Commission (SPC), have become less important and have had to reorganize themselves for alternative functions. As China instituted a more market-oriented economy, the changes this approach created in society clashed with communist ideology and the authoritarian political system favored by many Chinese officials and other opinion leaders and interests.[33]

As leading officials in the central administration agreed on a course of action, they often found their plans thwarted by poor implementation further down the bureaucratic chain of command or in the provinces. The decentralization of economic authority that had proven so effective in promoting growth in the post-Mao period meant that the Hu Jintao administration and earlier ones often were unable to see their priorities implemented. This was especially the case when the central authorities pushed for cutbacks in local economic growth that was environmentally damaging, focused on heavily resource-consuming industries, or otherwise contrary to national develop-ment goals. It was also the case when the Hu administration pushed local officials to spend more of their limited resources on helping those disadvan-taged or left behind by China's rapid modernization rather than continuing the pace of economic development. Lower-level and local officials depended on economic growth for employment and social stability. For them, follow-ing such central guidelines risked disorder and their personal career advance-ment, and they often found loopholes and other weaknesses in the economic administrative structure to follow paths that sustain economic growth at the expense of following central guidelines.[34]

The commercial officials of developed countries have long been well aware of the weaknesses of the implementation of central Chinese adminis-tration guidelines on such sensitive economic issues as Chinese infringement of intellectual property rights (IPR). American and other governments' IPR disputes with China have a history spanning more than two decades, yet the issues have continued to fester despite repeated agreements, in large measure because of poor implementation. Much more damaging for China's interna-tional economic reputation and its longer-term economic competitiveness was the series of scandals beginning in 2007 caused by Chinese exports of poisoned pet food and toothpaste, tainted medicines, and toxic children's toys. Lax Chinese administrative control hit home in 2008 when it was discovered that the Chinese supply of milk was widely tainted and had caused deaths and widespread illness among babies and small children.[35]

Manifestations of social discontent have been widespread in recent years. A variety of sources of social tension and conflict in China have presented opportunities for expressions of discontent. Groups that have exploited such tensions include people living in the poorer interior provinces (versus the richer coastal regions), ethnic minorities, farmers, members of the unem-ployed or underemployed so-called floating population (that is, the rural migrants seeking work in urban areas), laid-off SOE workers and other laid-off workers, students and intellectuals, and members of sects such as the Falun Gong. There also were mass demonstrations of broadly middle-class people who had advanced economically in recent years but opposed particu-lar government policies.[36]

Available Chinese government figures show the number and frequency of these demonstrations grew to seventy-four thousand reported in 2004 and more than eighty thousand in 2005. Official Chinese reporting for later years shows roughly ninety to one hundred thousand "mass protests" have been reported annually in the past several years. The importance of these demonstrations and protests grew with the strong advance of Internet communication in China. The Internet provides a means of rapid dissemination of information regarding salient disputes and conflicts that are hard for the legions of Chinese Internet monitors to control. Coordinated and uncontrolled demonstrations are seen as a clear danger to continued one-party rule in China.

Although certainly worrisome for Chinese leaders concerned with preserving stability and continued CCP rule, these developments seem to have a way to go before they pose a major or direct threat to the government. Notably, the discontented need to establish communications across broad areas, groups need to establish alliances with other disaffected groups, and the alliances need to put forth leaders prepared to challenge the regime and gain popular support with credible moral claims. Success also requires a lax or maladroit regime response. The attentiveness of the government to dissidence and the ruthless crackdown on the Falun Gong beginning in 1999 strongly suggest that Beijing remains keenly alert to the implications of social discontent and prepared to use its substantial coercive and persuasive powers to keep it from growing to threatening levels.[37]

Security and Foreign Policies

In the twenty-first century, China remains dependent on its economic connections with the developed countries of the West, Japan, and China's other Asian neighbors. Nonetheless, Chinese nationalism has been one of the leading forces pushing Chinese policy in directions that resist U.S. international leadership, the power of the United States, and U.S. allies in eastern Asia, notably Japan and Taiwan. Chinese leaders on the one hand have attempted to stay on good terms with their neighbors and to keep economic and other channels with the United States open. On the other hand, they have endeavored over time to weaken overall U.S. power and influence in a long-term attempt to create a more "multipolar" world. Military modernization continues the rapid pace begun in the 1990s. This poses an increasingly serious challenge to the already modern and advancing militaries of the United States and its allies and associates in eastern Asia, especially in areas such as Taiwan, where the Chinese development of ballistic and cruise missiles and acquisition of advanced Russian weaponry pose notable dangers.[38] Balancing the successes in military modernization, the People's Liberation Army (PLA) remains limited in its ability to quickly absorb sophisticated weapons systems and to develop the joint operations doctrine necessary in order to use these weapons effectively.[39]

A challenging international security environment and several international security trends have caused concern in China, notably the perceived U.S. "containment" and military "encirclement" of China seen in the Obama administration's emphasis on security and other reengagement with Asia. In recent years it has also worried over U.S. national and theater missile defense (TMD) programs, and the potential for Japan and India to improve their regional force projection capabilities with the support of the United States. A drawback for China of the U.S.-led antiterrorism campaign is that it increased U.S. influence and presence along China's western periphery—adding to Beijing's overall sense of being surrounded by U.S. power and influence. American control of sea-lanes from oil-producing countries of the Middle East and Africa to China is an added worry in China's growing concern over energy security.[40]

Taiwan, however, remains China's main security focus, and it is the biggest problem both politically and militarily in U.S.-China relations. The issues of continuing U.S. arms sales and defense deployments in the region remain problematic for the future. China and the United States attempted to find common ground and interest in rebuilding relations in the wake of the 1999 Belgrade embassy bombing, and they did so again following the downturn in relations resulting from the so-called EP-3 incident involving a crash between a Chinese jet fighter and a U.S. reconnaissance plane off the Chinese coast in 2001. They reached some common ground in opposition to the pro-independence initiatives of Taiwan's President Chen Shui-bian (2000–2008), and both registered support for the moderate policies of President Ma Ying-jeou beginning in 2008, but the buildup of Chinese and U.S. forces targeted at one another continues.[41]

The Outlook for Regime Survival

Regime survival remains the central concern of China's leaders. The balance sheet of challenges versus strengths of the Communist regime argues for its continuing in power, though there is considerable debate among specialists about the future direction of China's governance. The array of political, social, and economic pressures facing China's authoritarian rulers seriously challenges the government's legitimacy and survival. However, the Communist Party's residual power, coercive capabilities, and other strengths still outweigh its weaknesses. [42]

The sweeping structural changes necessitated by China's WTO entry and the broader demands of economic globalization and the information revolution generated significant new levels and types of social and economic disruption that have added to an already wide range of domestic and international problems. As noted above, the Internet and the various related means of rapid communications among disaffected groups support the instability caused by the many thousands of mass protests in China each year. The cumulative impact of these steep challenges seriously tests the capacity of China's system and the competence and unity of a leadership facing repeated cycles of leadership change in the now-routine CCP and National People's Congresses every five years. Developing succession arrangements and policies that sustain leadership unity, advantageous economic growth, and a modicum of popular support is essential to regime continuity. [43]

The Communist government has been able to manage this increasingly complex and growing set of challenges as evidenced in the following:

- Generally pragmatic leaders under Jiang Zemin passed power more or less smoothly to equally pragmatic and technologically knowledgeable successors headed by Hu Jintao. While leadership differences clouded the succession arrangements made at the Seventeenth Party Congress in 2007, they remained behind the scenes. Plans developed for a smooth leadership transition at the Eighteenth Party Congress in 2012 were disrupted but not derailed by the removal of Politburo member Bo Xilai amid charges of power abuse and corruption in March 2012.
- The Communist leadership maintains the command of strong military, police, and other security forces and has used them against dissident political and social movements; the Falun Gong; Tibetan, Uighur, and other ethnic separatists; and other perceived opponents.
- There is no clear alternative to Communist rule, and there remains strong popular and elite aversion to the fragmentation and chaos that could accompany regime change. Popular acquiescence also comes from the positive performance of the economy. The government's economic management seems sufficiently sound so as to provide a degree of legitimacy. Chinese achievements like the successful holding of the 2008 summer Olympic Games add to popular support for the regime. [44]

These strengths, however, are arrayed against the party's often growing weaknesses and challenges:

- Jiang Zemin's remaining in a senior leadership position while seeking the retirement of many of his Politburo Standing Committee colleagues headed the list of succession issues at the Sixteenth Party Congress in 2002. Thus far succession issues have been handled in a businesslike fashion as Hu Jintao retired after his ten-year tenure as party and state leader at the Eighteenth Party Congress in 2012.

- Decisions on economic opening and reform have benefited some Chinese groups while disadvantaging others, increasing the risk of leadership divisions. Other economic problems include massive debt; lagging reforms of SOEs; financial sector weaknesses; rising inequalities; large-scale unemployment; unsustainable levels of pollution; energy shortages; and the inadequacy of the national welfare, health, education, and pension systems. These problems remain interlocked, with reforms helping development in one area and having negative consequences in others, thus offering no easy solutions.

- The CCP has been able to recruit some talented newcomers, but ideological commitment remains weak despite recent efforts to reinvigorate training and propaganda. Rampant corruption at all levels of party and state authority add to widespread disaffection among elite and popular opinion.

- Economic change has gone hand in hand with social changes, producing increasing pressure on the government to adjust its policies. The flexibility of the leadership in adapting to new trends continues to be tested, with high potential for further dissonance between citizens and government and greater instability in both urban and rural areas. Aggrieved and disaffected groups present in all parts of society continue demonstrations and work stoppages.[45]

- Seeking continued economic engagement with the rest of the world, PRC leaders try—with limited success—to control entry of perceived adverse outside information and other sources of pressure that come with greater economic openness and information exchange. Taiwan's separate status and democratic example challenges regime legitimacy and adds to leadership debate, as to a lesser degree does the example of Hong Kong's greater freedoms. Pressure from the United States and other countries in support of principles championed by ethnic and democratic activists in China combine with the strong U.S. strategic posture to appear to Beijing as a

challenge to the Chinese government's goals. China reacted defensively
with internal security forces on alert in response to the Arab Spring popular protests that threatened and brought down long-standing autocratic
rulers in northern Africa and the Middle East.[46]

Thus, certain factors appear poised to cause China to become more stable
or less stable. Any one factor by itself probably is insufficient to produce
significant regime change, but a combination could.[47]

Leadership Priorities and Preoccupations

Leadership unity probably is the most important factor affecting China's
stability. Tests of the leadership were particularly acute in 2002–2003, as
many top leaders retired and passed power to the next generation. A similarly
large leadership transition is occurring in 2012–2013, as the leadership contingent headed by Hu Jintao passes responsibility to the younger "fifth generation." A failure to accomplish this transition smoothly—or to choose a
competent core of new leaders who inspire some level of popular confidence—would increase greatly the prospects for political crisis.[48]

Civil-military tensions could rise. Despite the civilian party leaders' efforts to win loyalty with appointments and growing budgets, their personal
lack of military experience has limited their authority. Potential also exists
for serious policy differences, particularly if military leaders believe that the
civilian leadership is risking sovereignty over Taiwan or other nationalistic
issues by reluctance to turn to military options. In recent years, foreign specialists and many in China tend to see considerable debate among elements
in China's "fractured" leadership decision-making structure on sensitive issues, including those involving issues of sovereignty and security around
China's rim. The PLA and various civilian security agencies play important
roles in these decisions, and their input adds weight to those arguing for a
more assertive and forceful Chinese approach regarding territorial disputes
along China's periphery.[49]

Many Western specialists also anticipate leadership differences based on
organizational perspective. The membership of the CCP, around seventy-five
million, is larger than the population of France, yet it is a small elite (around
3 percent) when compared with China's total population. The party is responsible for making decisions and for overseeing their implementation, but
over the years, the large bureaucracies that administer the party and the
government have acquired institutional interests and positions that frequently

conflict with one another. Policy debates in the party have emerged and reflect the struggles over turf and primacy. Struggles over budgets, for example, lead to winners and losers, as do struggles over reform and reorganization. These lead to bureaucratic rivalry and leadership dissension. [50]

A problem characteristic of single-party authoritarian regimes also prevails in China: personal factionalism. Personal loyalty networks (guanxi) are pervasive in the CCP and often supplant organizational hierarchy. Jiang Zemin exerted extraordinary influence to safeguard his continuation in power and the ascendancy of his key protégés at the Sixteenth Party Congress in 2002. Unconfirmed but widespread reporting of the opaque leadership selection process at the Seventeenth Party Congress showed factional division over which member of the upcoming fifth generation should be placed on track to lead the party at the Eighteenth Congress in 2012.

Based on these factors, various questions and forms of divergence continue to challenge and preoccupy China's leadership, including the following: [51]

- Deciding how power will be shared among the fifth-generation leaders was uncertain and became a priority concern of Chinese leaders in the period before and after the Eighteenth Party Congress in 2012.
- It remains unclear to what degree the PLA should be involved in formulating policy and participating in personnel appointments.
- Leaders are divided about a long list of difficult domestic economic issues focused on how to manage economic growth and development and their uneven effects; how to move toward less polluting, more technologically advanced, more sustainable, and more domestic-driven growth benefiting Chinese consumers more equitably without sapping the pace of economic development needed to sustain adequate employment and social stability; how to adjust internal economic policies to accommodate the WTO; how to obtain energy and other resources needed for development; and how to meet international demands on pollution and climate change.
- Social ferment and mass disturbances require continued attention of Chinese leaders from the top to the bottom of the administrative structure. The officials have been constantly forced by circumstances to address the question of how to use an array of positive and negative incentives and coercive means to deal with the multifaceted challenges posed by ethnic separatists, disaffected rural and urban workers, middle-class protesters, and others. The challenges center on issues caused by malfeasance or nonfeasance by inept or corrupt Chinese administrators and unintended,

intended, or unavoidable consequences of the rapid social, economic, and other changes caused by China's dramatic modernization.

• Leaders face difficult decisions and show some differences about the degree of force or persuasion to use in dealing with Taiwan and an array of disputed territorial claims along China's eastern and southern periphery. Some Chinese officials have participated in extensive debates among nongovernment elites and public opinion over whether or not China should sustain the moderate foreign policy approach that focuses on the "peace and development" evident in the past decade; some urge that China take more initiatives in defense of Chinese territorial, security, economic, and other interests, even at the expense of smooth Chinese relations with the United States, Chinese neighbors, and others.

The External Environment

Changes in the external environment continue to cause shifts in Chinese domestic policy and Chinese leaders' overall priorities and preoccupations. Particularly important is how China perceives the threat from abroad. Although they no longer see a major military threat to China's national security, Chinese leaders continue to see influence from the outside world—notably the United States and Western-aligned countries—as constituting a major threat to China's stability; many of their comments about this threat appear to be exaggerated rhetoric designed in part to justify a firm party grip. China also is concerned about the influence of Islamic countries on ethnic minorities in Xinjiang and other parts of northwest and southwest China, and this in part led China to support the U.S.-led antiterrorist campaign after September 11, 2001.[52]

Tensions across the Taiwan Strait, in the territorial disputes with Japan or India, in the South China Sea and the Yellow Sea, or in other areas near China increase China's perception of threat and result in more assertive security policies at home and abroad. Stronger disputes with the United States probably would have a similar effect. The recent record shows Chinese leaders have been relatively unconstrained by foreign criticism in using force to crack down on internal dissidents or suppressing public discussion of foreign policy issues. In circumstances of growing tensions with the United States or nearby powers, it seems likely that the use of nationalistic propaganda would become more evident.[53]

Other external developments also could have a significant effect on China's internal stability:

- Foreign economic developments have often helped or hindered China's economic growth. An increased ability to absorb China's exports has fostered growth, but recessions among China's key trading partners or a significant drop-off in foreign direct investment hurts growth and contributes to social problems in China.
- Cultural change abroad has spilled over into China. China's opening to outside cultural influence, including foreign television, music, and other media, could amplify dissent, notably among youth—especially if the administration does not permit greater openness and pluralism.
- Chinese efforts to host international events such as the 2008 Olympics are a source of pride, but also risk further opening to outside influence. Beijing's failed bid for the 2000 Olympics became a source of political tension with the United States and other Western countries; the controversy over China's repression of violence in Tibet in March 2008 prompted large demonstrations in Western cities against China's hosting of the 2008 Olympic Games and a series of Chinese counterprotests directed mainly against European countries. [54]

CHINA'S GOALS IN FOREIGN AFFAIRS

Regime survival remains the leaders' top priority, and continues to drive Chinese leadership preoccupations with the myriad domestic issues noted previously. Against this background, Chinese government policies and practices in international affairs on the whole are of somewhat less immediate importance and lower priority. They reflect goals and objectives in world affairs that have existed in China for decades. In general, they are far from being achieved and seem likely to continue well into the twenty-first century. Chinese leaders appear to have reached consensus on these objectives, although they frequently do not agree on which ones should have priority and the means by which to achieve them. [55]

To recap, Chinese leaders have continued to share certain overarching objectives:

- They have sought to perpetuate their power and avoid the fate of the Soviet Union and other East European communist regimes.
- They have pursued territorial unification and integrity, especially with Taiwan and, to a lesser degree, claims in the East China, South China, and Yellow seas and claims regarding India.

- They have also sought to modernize China's economic, technological, and military capabilities and improve social conditions while maintaining stability.

In addition, China has strategic objectives that have reflected its status as a rising power:

- *Regional preeminence:* Although U.S. and other foreign specialists have offered differing opinions on China's long-term regional and world goals, a middle-range view sees China's leaders wanting to be in a position of sufficient strength (with both positive and negative incentives—carrots and sticks) so that other countries in the region and Asian regional organizations will routinely take China's interests and equities into account in determining their own policies. Beijing wishes to be seen as the leading power in Asia and not as lower in prestige or regional influence than its neighbors. It also wishes to be able to project power sufficient to counter hostile naval power and airpower.
- *Global influence:* A permanent member of the UN Security Council, China desires status and prestige among the community of nations. It intends to be a more important and major player in the International Monetary Fund, the World Bank, the WTO, and other key international institutions. China's leaders have sought to assert influence on issues deemed important to China, not only to protect and defend Chinese interests but also to bolster China's standing as a major power. Chinese leaders believe that international power and prestige are an extension of national economic and technological prowess, which they intend to develop.

China's officials have approached the broad strategic objectives listed here in an international environment where Chinese leaders tend to view China's influence as growing at an impressive rate but far from dominant and where external and internal factors limit China's freedom of action and possible assertiveness in world affairs. At the start of the twenty-first century, Chinese perceptions of global trends appeared to be in flux and a matter of considerable internal debate. As previously noted, Chinese leaders, as reflected in official comments, had believed in the early 1990s that the world was becoming multipolar, with the United States as the single superpower but increasingly less able to exert its will as other countries and regions opposed U.S. initiatives. This view changed sharply beginning in the mid- to late 1990s because of the striking disparities between U.S. economic performance and that of other major powers and also because of U.S. leadership in the Balkan crisis, U.S. policy on missile defense, the U.S. war on terrorism, and other issues.[56]

The Chinese apparently concluded in the late 1990s that the world would be unipolar in the near term, with the United States exerting greater influence than Chinese commentators had originally calculated. Chinese leaders often perceived that this influence might not be benign regarding China's key interests, notably Taiwan and around China's periphery.[57] Chinese commentary expressed concern about the expansion and strengthening of the U.S. alliance structure and the ability of U.S.-led alliances to intervene globally. Chinese officials worried that the Kosovo intervention had implications for China; they particularly were concerned that the United States could use this precedent to justify intervention in Tibet or Taiwan. Chinese officials judged that China therefore had to be on guard to counter actions by the United States or its expanded alliance structure that were detrimental to Chinese interests. Chinese officials also were particularly anxious about what was perceived as a strengthening U.S.–Japanese military relationship and the potential for revived Japanese militarism. The acceleration of either trend was seen as likely to alarm China.[58]

Developments in the past decade appear to have altered Chinese perspectives of China's power and that of the United States. China's quick rebound and America's slow recovery from the global economic crisis and recession of 2008–2010 added to renewed perceptions in China that a multipolar world—with China as a leading power and America in decline—was emerging. The perceptions fed into the ongoing Chinese foreign policy debate, with some officials and other commentators urging China to take more initiatives to enhance and secure its interests, even at the expense of smooth relations with the United States and its allies and associates. The result was episodes of tension in China's relations with the United States, Japan, South Korea, India, and several Southeast Asian nations.

On the whole, the episodes did not appear to work well for Chinese interests. Notably, the United States launched a wide-ranging and widely publicized "reengagement" with the Asia-Pacific that highlighted U.S. security, economic, and political initiatives that were broadly welcomed by regional governments anxious to encourage U.S. stabilizing measures and in some cases to be seen to collaborate with the United States during a period of perceived Chinese assertiveness and coercive tactics over claims in disputed territory along its eastern and southern periphery.

Beginning in late 2010, senior Chinese foreign policy officials strongly reaffirmed China's heretofore more moderate and accommodating approach emphasizing "peace and development," though Chinese commentary also reflected resentment and suspicion over the U.S. reengagement initiatives in the Asia-Pacific region. In practice, Chinese behavior toward the United States and its Asian neighbors became muddled in 2011. On the one hand, there were authoritative reaffirmations emphasizing peace and development and pledges of international behavior in line with established world norms; and on the other hand, there were remarkable demonstrations of Chinese efforts to intimidate, coerce, and threaten Chinese neighbors with threats, sanctions, and sometimes violent actions grossly out of line with the established international norms. The muddle reinforced foreign and some Chinese specialists' view of "fractured" rule involving disputing groups in Chinese foreign policy making.[59]

Meanwhile, despite China's turn from traditional Marxist-Leninist-Maoist ideology, components of this tradition continued to influence the thinking of some leaders. Some Chinese officials see themselves locked in a struggle of values with the West and particularly the United States, which they see as bent on dividing or "Westernizing" China. Also common is the long-standing Chinese tendency to focus on a primary adversary in world affairs, to exaggerate its threat to China, and to seek domestic and foreign power to offset and counter this threat. Patterns of behavior reflecting this tendency can be seen repeatedly in Chinese leaders' policies and behavior toward the United States and its interests in Asia in the post–Cold War period.[60]

Preoccupied with domestic issues of modernization and stability, Chinese leaders have tended to be reactive to international developments. Deng Xiaoping stated that China should not get out in front on world issues but should take advantage of opportunities, bide its time, and gradually build Chinese power and influence; his successors generally held to this view. The Hu Jintao administration reportedly saw the period until about 2020 as a "strategic opportunity" for China's leadership to modernize and develop national wealth and power in an international atmosphere that, if managed appropriately, would support Chinese domestic development goals.

However, Chinese leaders also have become more active in bilateral and multilateral diplomacy. In international forums (the United Nations, the WTO, arms control discussions, and other arenas), China increasingly has tried to ensure that it is one of the rule makers for the global environment of the twenty-first century.[61] Beijing has also perceived that it needs to continue to build its military capabilities to be able eventually to back up its diplomacy, especially over the status of Taiwan, other territorial claims, and a widening range of important interests regarding energy security and the security of sea lines of communications, space, and other global commons. In particular, China has shown that it is willing to use military-backed actions by an array of Chinese security forces, trade sanctions, violent and destructive demonstrations in China, and other means in pursuit of its goals regarding sensitive security, sovereignty, and other contested issues involving the United States and governments along China's rim in nearby Asia.[62]

NOTES

1. Robert Sutter, *Shaping China's Future in World Affairs* (Boulder, CO: Westview, 1996), pp. 32–33.

2. Harry Harding, *A Fragile Relationship* (Washington, DC: Brookings Institution, 1992), pp. 235–39; Ashley J. Tellis and Travis Tanner, eds., *Strategic Asia, 2012–13: China's Military Challenge* (Seattle, WA: National Bureau of Asian Research, 2012).

3. Joseph Fewsmith, *China since Tiananmen* (New York: Cambridge University Press, 2001), pp. 21–43, 75–158.

4. Robert Suettinger, *Beyond Tiananmen: The Politics of U.S.-China Relations, 1989–2000* (Washington, DC: Brookings Institution, 2003), pp. 194–99.

5. Sutter, *Shaping China's Future in World Affairs*, pp. 33–34.

6. Andrew Nathan and Robert Ross, *The Great Wall and Empty Fortress* (New York: Norton, 1997), pp. 158–77.

7. Sutter, *Shaping China's Future in World Affairs*, pp. 33–34.

8. Shirley Kan, *China as a Security Concern in Asia*, Report 95-465 (Washington, DC: The Library of Congress, Congressional Research Service, December 22, 1994).

9. David M. Lampton, ed., *The Making of Chinese Foreign and Security Policy in the Era of Reform* (Stanford, CA: Stanford University Press, 2001), pp. 34–36.

10. Evan Medeiros and Taylor Fravel, "China's New Diplomacy," *Foreign Affairs* 82, no. 6 (November–December 2003): pp. 22–35; Zhang Yunling and Tang Shiping, "More Self-Confident China Will Be a Responsible Power," *Straits Times*, October 2, 2002, www.Taiwansecurity.org (accessed October 4, 2002); Denny Roy, "Rising China and U.S. Interests: Inevitable vs. Contingent Hazards," *Orbis* 47, no. 1 (2003).

11. Sutter, *Shaping China's Future in World Affairs*, p. 35.

12. Chinese Academy of Social Sciences, *Trends of Future Sino-US Relations and Policy Proposals* (Beijing: Institute for International Studies of the Academy of Social Sciences, September 1994).

13. David M. Lampton, *Same Bed, Different Dreams* (Berkeley: University of California Press, 2001), pp. 59–60.

14. Fewsmith, *China since Tiananmen*, pp. 159–89.

15. H. Lyman Miller and Liu Xiaohong, "The Foreign Policy Outlook of China's 'Third Generation' Elite," in *The Making of Chinese Foreign and Security Policy*, ed. David M. Lampton (Stanford, CA: Stanford University Press, 2001), pp. 143–50.

116   *Chapter 4*

16. Robert Sutter, *Chinese Policy Priorities and Their Implications for the United States* (Lanham, MD: Rowman & Littlefield, 2000), p. 18.

17. Barry Naughton, "China's Economy: Buffeted from Within and Without," *Current History*, September 1998, pp. 273–78.

18. Joseph Fewsmith, "China in 1998," *Asian Survey* 39, no.1 (January–February 1999): pp. 99–113.

19. Cheng Li, "Fourth Generation Leadership in the PRC," in *China's Future: Implications for U.S. Interests*, Conference Report CR99-02 (Washington, DC: U.S. National Intelligence Council, September 1999), pp. 13–36.

20. Jean-Pierre Cabestan, "The Tenth National People's Congress and After," *China Perspectives* 47 (May–June 2003): pp. 4–20.

21. Thomas Christensen, "China," in *Strategic Asia: Power and Purpose, 2001–2002*, ed. Richard Ellings and Aaron Friedberg (Seattle, WA: National Bureau of Asian Research, 2001), pp. 27–70; Thomas Christensen, "China," in *Strategic Asia: Power and Purpose, 2002–2003*, ed. Richard Ellings and Aaron Friedberg (Seattle, WA: National Bureau of Asian Research, 2002), pp. 51–94.

22. C. Fred Bergsten, Charles Freeman, Nicholas Lardy, and Derek Mitchell, *China's Rise: Challenges and Opportunities* (Washington, DC: Peterson Institute for International Economics and Center for Strategic and International Studies, 2008); *2010 Report to Congress of US-China Economic and Security Review Commission,* www.uscc.gov/ (accessed February 19, 2011).

23. Cheng Li, ed., *China's Emerging Middle Class* (Washington, DC: Brookings Institution, 2010).

24. Li, *China's Emerging Middle Class.*

25. Susan Shirk, "Power Shift in China—Part III," *Yaleglobal Online*, April 20, 2012, yaleglobal.yale.edu.

26. Cheng Li, *China's Leaders: The New Generation* (Lanham, MD: Rowman & Littlefield, 2001); Cheng Li, "Power Shift in China—Part I," *Yaleglobal Online*, April 16, 2012, yaleglobal.yale.edu.

27. Alice L. Miller, "Institutionalization and the Changing Dynamics of Chinese Leadership Politics," in *China's Changing Political Landscape: Prospects for Democracy*, edited by Cheng Li, pp. 61–79 (Washington, DC: Brookings Institution, 2008).

28. Jing Huang, "Institutionalization of Political Succession in China," in Li, *China's Changing Political Landscape*, pp. 80–98.

29. Dennis Blasko, *The Chinese Army Today* (London: Routledge, 2012).

30. David Shambaugh, "China's 17th Party Congress: Maintaining Delicate Balances," *Brookings Northeast Asia Commentary*, November 11, 2007; Bergsten et al., *China's Rise*, pp. 92–94; Li, "Power Shift in China—Part I."

31. Bergsten et al., *China's Rise*, pp. 105–30; Wayne Morrison, *China's Economic Conditions*, Report RL33534 (Washington, DC: Library of Congress, Congressional Research Service, 2012).

32. Morrison, *China's Economic Conditions.*

33. Tony Saich, *Governance and Politics of China* (London: Palgrave, 2004), pp. 135, 233–67; Bruce Dickson, "Updating the China Model," *Washington Quarterly* 34, no. 4 (Fall 2011).

34. Bergsten et al., *China's Rise*, pp. 75–90.

35. Morrison, *China's Economic Conditions*, pp. 17–18.

36. Minxin Pei, *China's Trapped Transition* (Cambridge, MA: Harvard University Press, 2006), pp. 83–84, 189, 200–204; Thomas Lum, *Human Rights in China and U.S. Policy,*

Report RL 34729 (Washington, DC: Library of Congress, Congressional Research Service, July 18, 2011), pp. 28–29.

37. Lum, *Human Rights in China and U.S. Policy*, p. 6; Martin King Whyte, "Chinese Social Trends: Stability or Chaos," in *China's Future: Implications for U.S. Interests*, pp. 67–84; Bergsten et al., *China's Rise*, pp. 96–97, 103.

38. U.S. Department of Defense, *Annual Report to Congress: Military and Security Developments Involving the People's Republic of China 2012* (Washington, DC: U.S. Department of Defense, May 2012).

39. "Friend or Foe? A Special Report on China's Place in the World," *Economist*, December 4, 2010, pp. 6–8.

40. David M. Lampton, *Three Faces of Chinese Power* (Berkeley: University of California Press, 2008), pp. 40–42; Mark Manyin, coord., *Pivot to the Pacific? The Obama Administration's "Rebalancing" toward Asia*, Report R42448 (Washington, DC: Library of Congress, Congressional Research Service, March 28, 2012).

41. Shirley Kan and Wayne Morrison, *U.S.-Taiwan Relationship: Overview of Policy Issues*, Report R41952 (Washington, DC: Library of Congress, Congressional Research Service, June 15, 2012), pp. 1–10.

42. David Shambaugh, *China's Communist Party: Atrophy and Adaptation* (Washington, DC: Woodrow Wilson Center, 2008), pp. 161–82; Dickson, "Updating the China Model."

43. Lampton, *The Three Faces of Chinese Power*, p. 208; Stapleton Roy, "Power Shift in China—Part II," *Yaleglobal Online*, April 18, 2012, yaleglobal.yale.edu.

44. Morrison, *China's Economic Conditions* (2012); Susan Lawrence and Thomas Lum, *U.S.-China Relations: Policy Issues*, Report R41108 (Washington, DC: Library of Congress, Congressional Research Service, March 11, 2011).

45. Yongnian Zheng, "China in 2011," *Asian Survey* 52, no. 1 (January–February 2012): pp. 28–41.

46. Richard Baum, "Political Implications of China's Information Revolution: The Media, the Minders, and Their Message," in Li, *China's Changing Political Landscape*, pp. 161–84; Peter Mattis, "Executive Summary for 'China in 2012,'" *China Brief* 12, no. 2 (January 20, 2012): pp. 1–3.

47. Mattis, "Executive Summary"; Li, "Power Shift in China—Part I."

48. Susan Lawrence and Michael Martin, *Understanding China's Political System*, Report R41007 (Washington, DC: Library of Congress, Congressional Research Service, May 12, 2012).

49. "Friend or Foe?" pp. 6–8.

50. Lawrence and Martin, *Understanding China's Political System*, pp. 10–16.

51. Zheng, "China in 2011"; Li, "Power Shift in China—Part I"; Linda Jacobson and Dean Knox, *New Foreign Policy Actors in China*, SIPRI Policy Paper 26 (September 2010); David Shambaugh, "Coping with a Conflicted China," *Washington Quarterly* 34, no.1 (Winter 2011): pp. 7–27.

52. Michael Swaine, "China's Regional Security Posture," in *Power Shift: China and Asia's New Dynamics*, ed. David Shambaugh (Berkeley: University of California Press, 2005), pp. 266–88. Manyin, "Pivot to the Pacific?" pp. 8–9, 15–16, 18–19, 23–24.

53. Suisheng Zhao, "China's Pragmatic Nationalism: Is It manageable?" *Washington Quarterly* 29, no. 1 (2005): 131–44; Lum, *Human Rights in China and U.S. Policy*, p. 1.

54. Peter Gries refers to this kind of sensibility as "face nationalism." Peter Hayes Gries, "A China Threat? Power and Passion in Chinese 'Face Nationalism,'" *World Affairs* 162, no. 2 (Fall 1999): p. 67.

55. On Chinese leaders' goals, especially as they relate to world affairs, see the discussion in subsequent chapters and in the selected bibliography in this book.

56. Avery Goldstein, *Rising to the Challenge: China's Grand Strategy and International Security* (Stanford, CA: Stanford University Press, 2005); Yong Deng, "Hegemon on the Offensive: Chinese Perspectives on U.S. Global Strategy," *Political Science Quarterly* 116, no. 3 (Fall 2001): pp. 343–65; Qian Qichen, "The International Situation and Sino-U.S. Relations since the 11 September Incident," *Waijiao Xueyuan Xuebao* (Beijing) 3 (September 25, 2002): pp. 1–6.

57. Jacobson and Knox, *New Foreign Policy Actors in China*; Shambaugh, "Coping with a Conflicted China."

58. David Shambaugh, "China's Military Views the World," *International Security* 24, no. 3 (Winter 1999–2000): pp. 52–79.

59. "Friend or Foe?" 8–15; Dai Bingguo, "Stick to the Path of Peaceful Development," *Beijing Review* 51, December 23, 2010, www.bjreview.com.cn; Shambaugh, "Coping with a Conflicted China."

60. Robert Sutter, *Chinese Policy Priorities and Their Implications for the United States* (Lanham, MD: Rowman & Littlefield, 2000), pp. 46–53; Shambaugh, "Coping with a Conflicted China."

61. Evan Medeiros, *China's International Behavior* (Santa Monica, CA: RAND Corporation, 2009).

62. Lampton, *The Three Faces of Chinese Power*, pp. 25–36; Stephanie Kleine-Ahlbrandt, "Dangerous Waters," *Foreign Policy*, September 17, 2012, www.foreignpolicy.com/articles/2012/09/17/dangerous_waters (accessed October 7, 2012).

Chapter Five

Patterns in Decision Making and International Outlook

The foreign policy and behavior of the People's Republic of China (PRC) is determined by leaders who make the decisions on the basis of what they think about the issues being decided. The patterns of decision making and the international outlook of Chinese leaders have changed in the post–Cold War period:[1]

- China's greater opening to the outside world since the death of Mao and China's remarkable integration with international economic, security, political, and other multilateral organizations have accompanied greater transparency and openness in Chinese foreign policy decision making.
- The number of people in and outside the Chinese government with an interest and influence in Chinese foreign policy decision making has grown enormously from the Maoist period. At that time, the Chinese Communist Party (CCP) chairman made most of the key decisions, often changing policy in radical directions, with the assistance of a few advisers.
- The Chinese decision makers today also represent a much broader set of Chinese interests in international affairs, notably in international economics and overall global stability and welfare. This trend contrasts with the predominantly security-oriented interests that dominated Chinese leadership concerns over foreign affairs during much of the Cold War. These security-oriented interests were focused on narrower concerns about preserving national sovereignty and security against superpower opposition.

- The outlook of Chinese decision makers on international affairs at times appears more cosmopolitan and compatible with prevailing international trends and norms, with less emphasis than in the past on the need for China to be on guard and prepared to take assertive and forceful action against dangerous and predatory powers seeking to exploit, oppress, and constrain China. At other times, guarded suspicion seems more salient.

This chapter reviews highlights of what is known of the evolving structure and processes in the Chinese government's decision making on foreign policy and important features of the international outlook of Chinese decision makers. The assessment shows that in the Chinese government, the CCP, and the People's Liberation Army (PLA), the three key administrative groups governing China, the structure and processes in Chinese decision making on foreign policy have become more regularized and institutionalized than in the past. Also in contrast to past practice, Chinese leaders often are more accommodating to international trends and more in conformity with prevailing international norms.

However, the assessment also shows significant areas of secrecy; long-standing suspicion of other world powers, especially in nearby Asia; nationalistic and military ambitions; and other trends that seem at odds with or contradict cosmopolitan and accommodating Chinese foreign policy and behavior. The net result reinforces a finding in this book that while much of the recent orientation of China's foreign policy should be encouraged and welcomed by the international community, world leaders should not assume that these Chinese policy trends will uniformly prevail or that Chinese policy and behavior will invariably continue in directions of peace and development. Leaders in China long have held conflicting views over how far to go in accommodating other countries and in conforming to international norms.

Foreign policy decision making at the top levels of the Chinese leadership, notably in the past and at times in the present, can lead to arbitrary and abrupt decisions that can prompt the Chinese leadership to shift course under certain circumstances in directions that could be adverse to other international interests in peace, stability, and prosperity. Several examples from recent Chinese foreign relations illustrate why uncertainty and caution seem to be appropriate in predicting continuation of recent trends toward a Chinese foreign policy that does not threaten others and is in the broad international interest.

For instance, Chinese foreign policy in recent years repeatedly has shown abrupt shifts toward confrontation during international crises involving China. The accidental U.S. bombing of the Chinese embassy in Belgrade in May 1999 prompted an abrupt shift toward the negative in China's approach toward the United States.[2] The danger of abrupt reversal in Chinese policy toward the United States surfaced again in 2001 as a result of the April 1 clash between a Chinese jet fighter and a U.S. reconnaissance aircraft in international airspace near China's southern coast.[3] In contrast with China's accommodating approach toward neighboring countries, labeled China's "good-neighbor" policy, mass demonstrations against Japanese diplomatic and business installations in China in 2005 resulted in damage and destruction. Contrary to international norms, Chinese government officials allowed demonstrators to carry out violent actions for several days before using coercive measures to stop the destruction.[4] Repeated assertive actions beginning in 2008 and continuing into 2010 by the PLA Navy, maritime surveillance forces, and Chinese foreign policy organizations employed intimidation, coercion, harassment, and other forceful actions along with often extraordinary rhetorical attacks against fishing, energy prospecting, maritime surveillance, and military and diplomatic actions by foreigners involving Chinese-claimed territorial and other rights in waters along China's rim. Efforts by Japan, South Korea, and several Southeast Asian nations to support their claimed rights and interests, along with complaints from the United States, met with truculent Chinese charges featuring authoritative accusations of foreign "attacks" against and "containment" of China.

The Chinese assertiveness appeared to subside as President Hu Jintao reaffirmed China's focus on moderation and negotiation during a summit with President Obama in January 2011 and during later meetings with Asian leaders, but observers inside and outside of China were unsure whether or not the trend toward moderation would hold. Their uncertainty was justified, as 2012 featured extraordinary demonstrations of Chinese use of a wide-ranging means of power and force short of direct military action to coerce, intimidate, and compel neighbors with claims to territory in the South China Sea and the East China Sea to give way to China's demands. The means involved repeated shows of force by Chinese civilian-controlled maritime security forces, diplomatic threats, economic sanctions at odds with established international norms, and in the case of Japanese claims in the East China Sea, mass demonstrations in over one hundred Chinese cities for a weeklong period in

September 2012 that resulted in widespread violence including burning and looting of Japanese properties and beatings of Japanese citizens in China.[5]

Adding to the uncertainty among Chinese and foreign observers regarding how and why Chinese foreign policy decisions are made is the prevailing secrecy that continues to surround Chinese policy on key foreign policy questions. To this day, Chinese and foreign specialists remain in the dark about how senior Chinese leaders deliberated in the weeks following the crises with the United States in May 1999 and April 2001.[6] Similar uncertainty pervades reviews of what is known of Chinese decision making during the April 2005 demonstrations against Japan and in the repeated episodes of coercion, intimidation, and extralegal actions including trade sanctions and periodic violence beginning in 2008 that impacted China's neighbors and the United States.[7] Even key Chinese decisions in international economics, such as the considerations that top leaders focused on in making the final decision for China to accept significant compromises in 1999 to reach agreement in order to join the World Trade Organization (WTO), are not clearly known.[8] One of the most important international security issues facing Chinese decision makers involves the international crisis brought about by North Korea's development of nuclear weapons and North Korea's concurrent leadership transition. Yet Chinese officials and specialists are frank in acknowledging that they remain in the dark and uncertain about the emphasis top Chinese decision makers give to these and other concerns in the secret deliberations they have with the reclusive North Korean regime.[9]

KEY DECISION MAKERS IN CHINESE FOREIGN POLICY

There is general agreement among Chinese and foreign specialists regarding the continued decisive role of the "paramount" leader at the top of the hierarchy of central administration actors influencing Chinese foreign policy decision making. Mao Zedong, Deng Xiaoping, Jiang Zemin, and, until very recently, Hu Jintao played that role in past years up to the present. Xi Jinping became Communist Party general secretary, government president, and chairman of the Central Military Commission in late 2012 and early 2013; he is in this key final decision-maker role. It is generally held that Mao and Deng were strong and decisive in guiding Chinese foreign policy, where Jiang and Hu were much more consultative and cautious in their foreign policy roles. While it remains to be seen what role Vice President Xi Jinping will play in foreign policy once he emerges as China's senior leader in 2013, it is widely assumed that he will adhere to the more consultative and cautious approach of recent years.[10]

Supporting the paramount leader and influencing his decisions are his top-level colleagues in the CCP's Politburo Standing Committee. Under Hu Jintao's leadership, there were nine members of the Standing Committee and many had experience and played important roles in foreign policy. In the lead was Prime Minister Wen Jiabao, who was more active than President Hu in dealing with foreign affairs.

During the leadership of Jiang Zemin, who left his last official leadership post in 2004, specialists assessed that the broader CCP Politburo and the CCP secretariat under the Politburo played supporting roles as the paramount leader made decisions. Also of importance was the so-called Leading Small Group for Foreign Affairs. During Jiang's tenure as party leader and president, this decision-making and deliberative body on foreign affairs was at first chaired by Premier Li Peng (until sometime in the 1990s) and then by Jiang himself. Also a member was Vice Premier Qian Qichen, a former foreign minister, who played a key decision-making and advisory role on foreign affairs throughout Jiang Zemin's rule. Also represented were the top-level officials of the Foreign Affairs, Defense, and State Security ministries.[11]

The Financial and Economic Affairs Leading Small Group was the most important organ in economic decision making. Premier Zhu Rongji was the leader of this group during his five-year tenure (1998–2003), and Premier Wen Jiabao chaired the group beginning in 2003. As the Chinese authorities increasingly integrated the Chinese economy into the world economy, this body made decisions on these matters.

National security matters influencing foreign policy have been dealt with routinely by the party's Central Military Commission, which has been headed in recent years by Jiang Zemin and more recently Hu Jintao and is now directed by Xi Jinping. The commission is made up of key representatives from PLA departments and services. There have been some reports of a Leading Small Group on National Security, which would appear to overlap with the Central Military Commission. Meanwhile, policy toward Taiwan has been dealt with by the Leading Group on Taiwan Affairs, which Jiang and then Hu have headed.[12]

One purpose of these leading groups is to allow key government, party, and military components to have input into important foreign policy decisions. A second purpose is to allow the paramount leader and his close advisers to benefit from these contributions as they seek to formulate effective policies that reflect the expertise and interests of relevant parts of the Chinese administration. Among administrative actors consulted in such decision making are the Ministry of Foreign Affairs, the Commerce Ministry, the *Xinhua* news agency, the International Liaison Department of the CCP, and components of the PLA dealing with intelligence, military exchanges, and arms transfers.

The importance of leading small groups and other organizational structures in the making of Chinese foreign policy has depended heavily on the leadership and decision-making approach of the paramount leader. What is known about usually secret foreign policy decision making under Mao Zedong indicates that Mao at times consulted with other senior leaders about key decisions and used the expertise of China's foreign policy and national security bureaucracies. Senior leaders concerned with particular issues also would deliberate prior to offering policy recommendations. In the end, Mao would decide on the path China would take, with varying and sometimes little consideration of the views of foreign policy professionals and other leaders with a stake in the decision. [13]

Such strong-man rule was reinforced by Chinese leaders' deference to Mao's wishes in most policy areas, especially national security and foreign affairs. The danger of challenging Mao's authority was enormous, as shown in Mao's harsh reaction to criticism of Defense Minister Peng Dehuai and other senior leaders in 1959 regarding Mao's push for development in the disastrous Great Leap Forward. Though the collapse of the Chinese economy eventually allowed more pragmatic Chinese leaders to nudge Mao to the sidelines and move domestic policies to less radical development policies in the early 1960s, Mao remained predominant in foreign affairs. The Cultural Revolution disrupted and destroyed much of China's foreign policy apparatus, resulting in Mao making decisions with the advice of senior leaders like Zhou Enlai and a small circle of other advisors. [14]

The abrupt changes in Chinese foreign policy in the Maoist period cannot be explained without reference to Mao's dominant leadership role. He was in a position to steer China toward closer ties with the Soviet Union and then change course after a few years toward ever-greater hostility to Moscow. It appears that only such a paramount leader as Mao could support China's position in the early 1960s of opposition to both nuclear weapons–wielding superpowers at a time when China seemed very weak and vulnerable because of internal economic collapse. Mao subsequently led China from decades of violent opposition to the United States to the surprising opening to the Nixon administration and other developed countries.

Even as his health declined, Mao's leadership in foreign affairs remained supreme. Available scholarship shows successful efforts by Mao after the opening to the United States to check the rising stature of Premier Zhou Enlai in foreign affairs and to push Chinese policy toward the United States in directions more assertive than the moderate approaches favored by Zhou. Deng Xiaoping is seen to have been well aware of Mao's dominance, as he made his debut as Zhou's replacement as China's top foreign policy representative with a speech at the United Nations in 1974 propounding China's Three Worlds theory. As noted in chapter 3, the speech underlined Maoist resolve to remain tough toward the United States while seeking support from Washington in China's ongoing search for security and support against the Soviet Union. [15]

Upon Deng Xiaoping's ascendance as China's top leader following his return to top levels of power in 1978, the Chinese reformer began to exert a dominant influence in Chinese foreign relations that lasted until the end of the Cold War and the decline in his health in the 1990s. Unlike Mao, whose drive toward visionary goals led China to repeated domestic disasters and wide swings in China's foreign approach, Deng was more focused and consistent in domestic and international affairs. In general, he saw foreign relations as secondary to promoting economic development in China, which provided the basis for the continued legitimacy of Communist Party rule in the country. Effective nation building on the one hand required a stable international environment that at the time was challenged by perceived dangers to China from the expanding power of the Soviet Union. On the other hand, also required was China's opening to increased interchange with developed countries, led by the United States, which had the capital, technology, and markets needed for advancing Chinese economic development.

Deng favored patterns of leadership decision making more regularized and predictable than the often idiosyncratic means used by Mao. Nevertheless, he kept decision making on foreign and national security matters firmly in his own hands. Thus, he relied on the expertise of professionals and leaders dealing with foreign and national security matters, but he made and took responsibility for final decisions. [16]

The consequences of these decisions were often dramatic and far reaching. Thus, Deng was at the center of the Chinese decisions in late 1978 and early 1979 to invade Vietnam over its invasion of Cambodia and toppling of the Chinese-backed Khmer Rouge regime. Vietnam had recently aligned formally with the Soviet Union, which backed the Vietnamese invasion of Cambodia and had many divisions poised in offensive configurations along the northern border of China. Despite the clear danger of Soviet military action against China if China attacked Moscow's new ally in Vietnam, Deng decided to invade Vietnam in February 1979. At the time he also endeavored to use his leading role as the final arbiter of China's normalization agreement with the United States in December 1978 and China's peace agreement with Japan earlier in the year with his trips to the United States and Japan in 1979 in order to align China closely with these powers in directions that opposed Soviet expansion and dominance. [17]

Subsequently, Deng was in charge of charting China's course in dealing with the Soviet invasion of Afghanistan in late 1979, cooperating clandestinely with the United States in supporting Afghan resistance and allowing U.S. monitoring stations in China to assess advances in Soviet missile developments. He led efforts to deal with Ronald Reagan's backsliding on U.S. agreements with China over Taiwan and to move China toward a more "independent" and evenhanded public posture in dealing with the two superpowers, eventually seeing the wisdom of consolidation of China's relations with the United States in the face of uncompromising Soviet positions. Deng faced off with Britain's Margaret Thatcher, compelling the "iron lady" to back down and meet China's requirements in an agreement returning Hong Kong to China. Deng's vision of how China should deal with the international isolation faced following the Tiananmen crackdown of 1989 and the end of the Cold War has remained the foundation of Chinese foreign policy calculus up to the present. [18]

THE FOREIGN POLICY CONCERNS AND WORLDVIEWS OF CHINESE LEADERS

Assessments of Chinese foreign policy thinking at the start of this century made the case that Chinese foreign policy and behavior were changing markedly in directions more in line with international norms, especially regarding economic and cultural matters and constructive participation in multilateral organizations. These changes in Chinese policy were seen as influenced by a more pluralistic range of Chinese decision makers, whose diverse interests were reflected in foreign policy and behavior. These decision makers represented a variety of government, party, and military bureaucracies, government-affiliated and nongovernment think tanks, and provincial and local governments, as well as broad segments of Chinese people, reflecting aroused public opinion, especially on nationalistic issues. According to the assessments, the broad range of those influencing Chinese foreign policy meant that the Chinese foreign policy process needed to be more consultative and attentive to wide-ranging inputs. As a result, the decision-making process often was slower and more cumbersome than in the past, when the top leader could decide changes in policy on his own authority.[19]

As Chinese policy and practice became increasingly engaged in international relations, better-educated and younger officials and nongovernment specialists played a more important role in informing and guiding the decision-making process. They contributed on such complicated issues as economic regulations, intellectual property rights, environmental compliance, arms control regulations, human rights, and international law. Another feature of the recent foreign policy–making process in China was that foreign governments, businesses, and other nongovernment groups had more entry points that allowed them to influence some or all of the diverse range of Chinese actors that have influence in determining Chinese foreign policy and behavior. These outside influences tended to push China toward behavior more in line with international norms.

The assessments acknowledged the still secretive and hierarchic structure of Chinese foreign policy decision making, with the top-level party, government, and military leaders exerting dominant influence on final decisions, especially on national security questions.[20] They also highlighted a prevailing worldview among this elite that emphasized seeing international affairs in terms of competing states, with China required to maintain its guard against exploitation and oppression as it seeks to develop national wealth and power and greater influence in Asian and world affairs. Nonetheless, the assessments pointed out that these leaders needed the expertise and broad inputs that came from consulting the wide range of bureaucratic and nongovernment specialists and interests noted previously. To do otherwise risked ineffective or mistaken policies that could have a direct impact on top Chinese leaders, whose legitimacy rested heavily on demonstrating an ability to advance Chinese power and influence without major international complications or confrontation. In sum, there was some optimism that the recent trend of increasing Chinese foreign policy conformity with and adherence to international norms, along with continued emphasis on promoting general trends toward world peace and development, were likely to continue.[21]

On assuming the leading CCP position in 2002, Hu Jintao appeared to follow the pattern of generally cautious moves toward moderation in Chinese foreign affairs seen in the latter years of Jiang Zemin. Hu's leadership featured emphasis on "peaceful development" and supporting a "harmonious" world.[22] However, beginning in 2008, repeated episodes of Chinese assertiveness and truculence over sensitive issues with the United States, Japan, South Korea, India, several Southeast Asian states, and other countries seemed at odds with Hu's stated policy goals. They raised questions regarding whether or not the Chinese leader had the will and the ability to control China's interagency foreign policy coordination process and its various stakeholders, as well as influential elements outside the formal process, including public opinion fanned by sometimes sensational media coverage of sensitive foreign policy issues. As noted above, Hu strongly reaffirmed a moderate line in foreign affairs during 2011, but impressive demonstrations of coercive and truculent Chinese behavior toward neighboring states in 2012 assured that questions about the durability of Chinese moderation and other longer-term trends would remain unresolved. An authoritative study of Chinese foreign policy actors in 2010 concluded that foreign policy decision making has become more "fractured"; the Chinese military and other conservative forces have become more prominent, a development that is strengthened by widespread Chinese opinion that China should be "less submissive" and defend more strongly its interests in disputes with other countries. Subsequently, a leading American specialist on China, David Shambaugh, warned of the implications of the "current consensus among the more conservative and nationalist elements to toughen its policies and selectively throw China's weight around."[23]

A review of the various worldviews propounded by leaders of the People's Republic of China since 1949 indicates how difficult it remains for China to fully accept existing international norms and an accommodating posture to the Western countries and other leaders and large stakeholders in the prevailing international mechanisms. As specialists in China have repeatedly emphasized in recent years, China's rising international prominence has brought to the fore nationalistic and zero-sum realist foreign policy calculations on the part of a variety of influential foreign policy actors in China that have put those Chinese leaders arguing for progressive accommodation to existing international norms in a more defensive and increasingly less influential position. These nationalistic and realist calculations tap into deeply rooted Chinese views of world affairs.

There is little disagreement among Chinese and foreign specialists that Chinese officials and the rest of the Chinese people have long been conditioned through the education system and government-sponsored media coverage to think of China as having been victimized by international powers since the early nineteenth century. Emphasis on this historical conditioning was strengthened after the CCP crisis at the time of the Tiananmen demonstrations and bloody crackdown in 1989 and continues up to the present. Sensing that communism no longer provided adequate ideological support for continued CCP rule, the authorities instituted a patriotic education campaign with related media coverage. The campaign was designed to encourage regime-supporting patriotism in China by recalling the more than one hundred years of foreign affronts to Chinese national dignity. With this focus, foreign complaints about human rights and other abuses in China after the Tiananmen crackdown were depicted as the latest in a long series of foreign efforts to abuse and victimize China. As such, they were likely to elicit negative responses from Chinese people directed at foreign governments rather than result in Chinese people agreeing with the foreign criticism of the abuses of Chinese Communist rule.[24]

The historic record since the first Opium War (1839–1842), featured in Chinese indoctrination, education, and media efforts, provides a rich legacy for those seeking to view China as an aggrieved party in international affairs.[25] For example, foreign powers, mainly Great Britain but including the United States, used opium trade as a way to balance their purchases of tea and other commodities from China in the early nineteenth century. Backed by superior military power, British, and later joint British-French, military expeditions defeated Chinese forces and compelled the opening of several so-called treaty ports along Chinese rivers and coastal areas, where foreigners lived under their own jurisdiction, not Chinese law, and foreign missionaries were free to spread religious beliefs seen as heterodox by Chinese officials. Foreign military power coerced the Chinese government to give large swaths of territory to foreign rule. After Japan unexpectedly defeated China in a war over dominance in Korea and took Taiwan from China in 1895, the foreign powers seemed poised to divide up China into their respective colonies or spheres of influence.[26]

China probably would have been divided by the foreign imperialists had not the tensions leading to World War I caused the European powers to withdraw forces from China in order to prepare for war in Europe. The field was then open for Japan to dominate China, which it did. Other foreign powers did little other than object to Japan's expansion and eventual take-over of Manchuria.

In 1937, as full-scale war broke out between China and much stronger and technologically superior Japanese forces, China stood basically alone. Through brutal and rapacious attacks, one million Japanese soldiers occupied the most productive parts of China. With Japan's defeat in 1945, the United States sided with Chiang Kai-shek against the Chinese Communists in three years of Chinese civil war, ending with the Communist victory on the Chinese mainland in 1949 and Chiang Kai-shek's retreat to Taiwan.

The Chinese Communists then confronted the United States following the June 1950 U.S. intervention into the Korean War as well as the U.S. intervention into the Taiwan Strait that prevented the Communists from reunifying Taiwan with the mainland. In the Chinese view, twenty years of hostility, confrontation, and abuse of China at the hands of American leaders were followed by twenty years of similar treatment of China by the Soviet Union, which emerged as China's main security threat in the late 1960s. Finally, at the end of the Cold War, the PRC experienced an international situation where for the first time it did not face immediate danger of war with one or two nuclear-armed superpowers.

The lessons of this sordid experience, which continues to be strongly emphasized by Chinese education, media, and propaganda organs, heavily influence the world outlook of Chinese leaders and people:[27]

- The world is viewed darkly. It is full of highly competitive, unscrupulous, and duplicitous governments that are seeking their selfish interests at the expense of China and others.
- To survive and develop, China needs power—military power backed by economic power and political unity. If there is disunity at home, foreign powers will use Chinese differences to exploit China, just as they did in the past.
- China is an aggrieved party. It has suffered greatly at foreign hands for almost two centuries. It needs to build its power and influence to protect what it has and to get back what is rightfully China's. This means restoration of Taiwan to Chinese sovereignty and securing other Chinese territorial claims.
- China does not dominate the world order; other powers do—during the Cold War, the United States and Soviet Union; after the Cold War, the United States. China needs to work toward an international balance that

helps Chinese interests and avoids outside dominance. In this vein, Chinese leaders in recent years have emphasized the benefits of a multipolar world order where China would have greater freedom of maneuver and security than in an international order dominated by the United States.

Complementing this historical discourse showing China as the victim of predatory outsiders are other features influencing China's worldview to various degrees:

- The ideological and revolutionary drive of Mao Zedong and his colleagues to foster revolution in China and abroad has largely ended, though as noted in the previous chapter, China's leaders remain determined to preserve Communist Party rule in the face of perceived political challenges and values supported by the West.
- Chinese self-reliance, so important in the latter Maoist period discussed in chapters 2 and 3, has been put aside with China's ever-growing interdependence with the world, especially in economics and trade. Nevertheless, with the exception of North Korea, China scrupulously avoids alliances with or formal dependence on other states as it seeks ties with other countries based on the "win-win" formula that determines Chinese foreign relations recently. Chinese cooperation with others is contingent on a "win" for China that is within the scope of a win-set defined narrowly in terms of tangible benefit for the Chinese state.
- Chinese officials recently have fostered an idealized depiction of benevolent Chinese imperial interaction with China's neighbors. The hierarchic order of international relations with China at the center seen during much of the Ming and Qing dynasties from the fourteenth to nineteenth centuries is depicted showing Chinese naval expeditions and other foreign interchange that reflects China's unwillingness to be expansionist.[28]
- As discussed in chapter 1, Chinese official discourse and related scholarship tend to play down foreign depictions of Chinese leaders changing foreign policies and even overall alignments as Chinese interests shift with changing circumstances at home and abroad. Rather, they portray Chinese policies and practices as consistent, based on appropriate principles in line with broad moral goals, and aligning China's approach with the "progressive" forces in international affairs.
- China's "peculiar" operational code of conduct—"firmness in principle and flexibility in application," as Samuel Kim labels it—is another aspect

foreign observers find troubling. For Kim and others there is a gap between principle and practice, with China repeatedly attempting to show
through sometimes adroit and sometimes awkward use of a wide range of
old and new sets of principles that interest-based changes in Chinese
foreign relations remain consistent with righteous principles.
• And, as discussed in chapter 1, one result of such Chinese reasoning is an
  acute sense of Chinese exceptionalism. Many Chinese truly believe that
  the People's Republic of China has always followed morally correct
  foreign policies in the interest of progressive world forces. They believe
  China has done nothing wrong in world affairs; if difficulties arise with
  other states over foreign policy concerns, the fault naturally lies with the
  other party.

The overall implications of China's acute sense of grievance against past
international victimization of China on the one hand and the strong sense of
righteousness in the foreign policy and practice of the PRC on the other hand
support a Chinese popular and elite worldview of poor self-awareness of
Chinese international shortcomings and sharp sensitivity to international
pressure.

Meanwhile, although some foreign and Chinese specialists look on the
bright side and see China conforming more to international norms, more
sober views see China adjusting to circumstances. They see that adjustments
could shift in ways at odds with international stability if the circumstances
were to change, say, for example, with a rise in Chinese power and decline of
the power of the United States.

CHINESE ELITE AND POPULAR VIEWS OF THE UNITED STATES

This section of the chapter focuses on Chinese elite and popular views of the
United States. It gives special attention to this topic because in the post–Cold
War period, the United States has been widely seen in China as the leading
international power, a superpower determined to maintain dominance and
hegemony in world affairs.[29] The conditioning of Chinese elite and popular
opinion for many years by government-controlled education and media has
reinforced a strong sense of patriotism and suspicion of the United States.
The conditioning often stresses the need to speed China's drive for comprehensive national power in order to ensure China's rightful interests in the
face of U.S. and other foreign pressures. At times of cooperative China-U.S.

relations, Chinese government authorities play down the anti-U.S. stance, but it emerges often and with surprising vehemence at times of Sino-U.S. friction.[30]

Assessments by U.S., Chinese, and other specialists have continued to find that Chinese officials and the experts who advise them view U.S. policy and behavior with a great deal of suspicion. Wang Jisi, one of the most prominent Chinese specialists on U.S.-China relations and a frequent adviser to President Hu Jintao and key Chinese leaders, wrote in 2005 that despite some ups and downs in Chinese views of the United States since the end of the Cold War, "the official line continues to point to the United States as the mainstay of the 'hostile forces' that try to destabilize China and refers to the United States as the hegemonic power that threatens global security." He added, "To most Chinese observers, . . . the United States is an insatiable domineering country that believes only in its own absolute power, one that would never allow any other country to catch up with it." Given their perception of American intentions and hegemony, these Chinese elites tend not to trust U.S. motives. Although they see China benefiting from and heavily dependent on economic and other ties with the United States, they continue to fear American manipulation of China in international strategic terms, exploitation in economic terms, and subversion in political and ideological terms. As Wang advised Chinese readers in an interview in October 2008, "Pax Americana" is an unjust international order "under power politics," and "China cannot accept being led by the United States" even as Beijing pursues cooperation with Washington for pragmatic reasons. Professor Wang teamed with a prominent American China specialist, Kenneth Lieberthal, to publish an important study in 2012 that reaffirmed the deep suspicions of Chinese and U.S. official elites toward one another.[31]

At the start of the twenty-first century, the list of Chinese charges and grievances against U.S. hegemonism was long and involved many issues of direct concern to China and nearby Asia. They included the large and growing U.S. defense budget; a strong tendency to use coercive measures in U.S. foreign policy; allegedly wanton disregard of international institutions and rules when deemed inconvenient; an aggressive agenda in promoting Western values; unilateral decisions to build missile defenses; endeavoring to restrict high-technology information to China and others; arrogant violations of other countries' sovereignty; unjustified expansion of U.S. alliances in Europe and Asia; and determination to contain emerging powers, notably China.[32]

To American policy makers and others interested in better U.S. relations with China, the clear tendency of Chinese leaders to exaggerate the negatives in the U.S. approach to China and to highlight the threat the United States posed to the key interests of the CCP leadership were major obstacles to improved relations. Remedying these tendencies was difficult. Part of the problem was how deeply rooted the inclination was for leaders in China (and the United States) to exaggerate the power and influence—usually seen as negative—posed by the other side.[33]

Chinese strategists throughout the Cold War tended to focus on how the United States and/or the Soviet Union could or did use "power politics" and outright coercion to force China to compromise over key interests. The exaggerated Chinese claims that the United States was seeking to split up, hold back, and contain China in the 1990s and later echoed this approach. Adding to the tendency was the long-standing Chinese leadership practice of analyzing world politics in terms of "contradictions" derived from Marxism-Leninism and developed by Mao Zedong. As discussed in chapter 1, the Chinese international approach and worldview thus had a clear focus on the "main enemy" or danger to China and its interests. The United States played this role in the 1950s and 1960s; the Soviet Union was the main enemy in the 1970s and much of the 1980s. Beginning in the 1990s, despite China's strong need to promote advantageous economic and other relations with the United States, Chinese elite thinking and behavior showed that the United States again became the main target of Chinese international concern—that is, China's main "enemy."[34]

In order to mobilize domestic and international forces to deal with the main danger, Chinese leaders tended to portray the adversary in starkly negative terms. Often associated with this kind of international outlook was a "united front" policy. This involved Chinese efforts to win over other powers to assist in the focused attempts to counter the danger posed by the main adversary. Of course, China's dealings with the United States in the 1990s were not as clear-cut as its dealings with the Americans and the Soviets in the Cold War. The United States was not seen only as an adversary; it also was a competitor and a partner whose cooperation was essential to Chinese modernization. Thus, Chinese leaders endeavored to sustain a balanced approach to the United States that preserved a working relationship—especially economic relations—while continuing to view U.S. power as threatening many important Chinese interests.[35]

The episodes of greater Chinese assertiveness against the United States, its Asian partners, and others in nearby Asia beginning in 2008 included a revival of exaggerated claims that the United States, now under the Obama administration, was using its avowed efforts to reengage with Asia-Pacific countries as a thinly veiled effort to contain and hold back China's rising influence in the region and throughout the world. Slow U.S. recovery from the global economic crisis that started in 2008 and other perceived American weaknesses, contrasting with economic, military, and other Chinese advances, led many Chinese elite and popular observers to recalculate the international balance of power in China's favor. A weakened U.S. superpower and the rise of China and other nations meant that a multipolar world was not far off, allowing, in the calculations of these Chinese opinion leaders, for a more assertive Chinese policy regarding a range of differences with the United States.[36]

CHINESE OPPOSITION TO SUPERPOWER DOMINANCE IN ASIA

Another legacy of the past that influences Chinese officials' contemporary worldview is the long record of Chinese policy and behavior in Asia, which shows repeated maneuvering to keep China's periphery as free as possible from hostile or potentially hostile great-power pressure. As noted earlier, Asia, especially the countries around China's periphery, has been the main arena of Chinese foreign relations. Efforts to keep this periphery free of potentially hostile great-power presence and pressure are seen as central to Chinese security, and China has long used both offensive and defensive measures to thwart perceived great-power ambitions in the region. This trend has persisted, along with the growing Chinese economic integration, increasing political and security cooperation, and active engagement with various multilateral organizations in the region.[37]

Available scholarship[38] shows a growing acceptance by PRC leaders of interdependence in international economic relations but continued wariness regarding close interaction with and dependence on others regarding political, security, environmental, and other concerns. It indicates that it is still too early to know if Chinese leaders are genuinely internalizing and embracing global norms and values that would argue for greater stability and moderation in Asian and world affairs. Alternatively, they may be merely adapting to global norms to derive tactical benefits, biding their time to exert greater pressure and force to achieve Chinese goals when future circumstances are more advantageous. While Chinese leaders have moved over time to see their interests best served by full engagement with international economic norms, Chinese leaders generally seem to follow a case-by-case approach, doing cost-benefit analysis in making key foreign policy decisions. Interdependence with and moderation and accommodation toward powers involved in Asian and world affairs appear to prevail when the costs of a more assertive posture—one more consistent with Chinese nationalistic attitudes and evidenced in periodic recent assertive behavior toward Japan, India, Southeast Asian claimants to disputed territories in the South China Sea, and South Korea, as well as the United States, Taiwan, and others—outweigh the benefits. When the assessed cost-benefit calculus allows, China has appeared ready and willing to use coercion, intimidation, and violence to have its way in disputes in nearby areas.

Chinese foreign policy in the Maoist period strongly opposed U.S. and Soviet power and pressure, especially along China's periphery. As reviewed in chapter 3, Moscow's persisting military buildup and search for greater political and military influence around China's periphery became the strategic focus of Chinese foreign policy in Asia and China's overall approach to world affairs in the late 1960s. After serious leadership disagreements were resolved by the deaths and imprisonment of much of the Chinese military high command and other involved leaders, China developed a fairly consistent approach, at first under the leadership of Premier Zhou Enlai and Chairman Mao Zedong and later under Deng Xiaoping. It attempted to use U.S.-Soviet differences pragmatically to China's advantage. The Chinese leaders recognized that only at tremendous cost and great risk could China confront the Soviet Union on its own. It relied heavily on international counterweights to Soviet power, provided mainly by the United States and its allies and associates in Asia and elsewhere. As the United States reevaluated its former containment policy directed against China and no longer posed a serious military threat to Chinese national security, Chinese leaders maintained a collaborative relationship with the United States and the West as a key link in its security policy against the Soviet Union.[39]

For post-Mao Chinese leaders, the highest priority was to accomplish modernization as well as to maintain national security and internal order. Chinese leaders recognized the fundamental prerequisite of establishing a relatively stable strategic environment, especially around China's periphery in Asia. The alternative would be a highly disruptive situation requiring much greater Chinese expenditures on national defense and posing greater danger to domestic order and tranquility. China did not control this environment. It influenced it, but the environment remained controlled more by others, especially the superpowers and their allies and associates. As a result, China's leaders were required repeatedly to assess their surroundings for changes that affected Chinese security and development interests. The result was repeated Chinese adjustments to take account of such changes. [40]

At the same time, Chinese leaders had nationalistic and ideological objectives regarding irredentist claims (such as Taiwan) and a desire to stand independently in foreign affairs as a leading power among "progressive" developing nations of what was called the third world. These goals struck a responsive chord politically inside China. Occasional leadership discussion and debate over these and other questions regarding foreign affairs sometimes had an effect on the course of Chinese foreign policy. However, following Deng Xiaoping's rise to power in the late 1970s, the debates became less serious—at least until the leadership impasse in the late 1980s, which set the stage for the Tiananmen crisis and crackdown of 1989. Of course, that leadership crisis focused mainly on domestic issues, and China's foreign policy orientation toward strengthening national security and development was not altered fundamentally. [41]

Thus, in the two decades after the most violent phase of the Cultural Revolution ended in 1969, China's top foreign policy priority remained the pragmatic quest for a stable environment needed for effective modernization and development. Chinese leaders since the late 1960s saw the main danger of negative change in the surrounding environment posed by the Soviet Union. At first, Chinese leaders perceived Soviet power as an immediate threat to its national security. Over time, it came to see the Soviet Union as more of a long-term threat, determined to use its growing military power and other sources of influence to encircle and pressure China into accepting its dominance in the balance of influence in Asia. [42]

As discussed in chapter 3, the Soviet Union was seen as having a strategy of expansion that used military power relentlessly but cautiously in order to achieve political influence and dominance throughout the periphery of the Soviet Union. China long held that the focus of Soviet attention was in Europe but that NATO's strength required Moscow to work in other areas, notably the Middle East, southwestern Asia, Africa, and eastern Asia, in order to outflank the Western defenses. China was seen as relatively low on Moscow's list of military priorities, although Chinese leaders clearly appreciated the dire consequences if the Soviet Union were able to consolidate its position elsewhere and then focus its strength to intimidate China.

China's strategy of deterrence and defense, therefore, aimed basically to exacerbate Soviet defense problems by enhancing the worldwide opposition to Soviet expansion in general and by raising the possibility of the Soviet Union confronting a multifront conflict in the event it attempted to attack or intimidate China in particular. Chinese leaders saw their nation's cooperation with the United States as especially important in strengthening deterrence of the Soviet Union and in aggravating Soviet strategic vulnerabilities. Chinese leaders also encouraged anti-Soviet efforts by the so-called second world, developed countries—most of whom were formal allies of the United States—and by developing countries of the third world. At the same time, Chinese leaders used a mix of political talks, bilateral exchanges, and other forms of dialogue to help manage the danger posed by the Soviet Union.

Within this overall effort to establish a stable environment in Asia, Chinese leaders employed a varying mix of tactics to secure their interests, depending on international variables, such as the perceived strength and intentions of the superpowers, and Chinese domestic variables, such as leadership cohesion or disarray. For example, when Chinese leaders judged that their strategic surroundings were at least temporarily stable, they had less immediate need for close ties with the United States and thus felt freer to adopt more insistent policies on Taiwan and other nationalistic issues that appealed to domestic constituencies but offended the United States. This type of calculus was in part responsible for China's tougher approach to the United States over Taiwan and other issues in 1981–1983. But when the Chinese leaders judged that such tactics risked seriously alienating the United Stares and thereby endangered the stability of China's environment, they put them aside in the interest of preserving peaceful surroundings. Such reasoning undergirded China's moderation in approach toward the United States in 1983 and 1984, discussed in chapter 3.[43]

Chinese maneuvers to free China's periphery as much as possible from the potentially hostile and debilitating presence of great powers continue in the post–Cold War period and focus on Chinese concerns over the United States. For the first decade after the Cold War, Chinese officials adopted a rhetorically confrontational approach, attacking the U.S. alliance system in Asia and other reflections of what they saw as "Cold War thinking," "power politics," and "hegemonism" in U.S. policies and behavior. The Chinese approach failed in the face of Asian states' unwillingness to side with China against the United States and in the face of strong U.S. power and influence determined to confront if necessary Chinese assertiveness over Taiwan and other issues.[44]

Adjusting to the adverse balance of costs and benefits for Chinese interests, Chinese leaders changed policy. By 2003, they articulated a new policy that emphasized China's peaceful rise and peaceful development in Asian and world affairs. This policy continues up to the present, though the episodes of Chinese assertive actions and strident rhetoric against the United States, its Asian partners, and other nearby states beginning in 2008 have raised questions about the policy's durability. Unlike previous Chinese policy and behavior, the policy approach since 2003 seeks not to confront publicly the United States on most issues. Chinese leaders still register strong differences with U.S. dominance in Asian and world affairs and remain concerned about how that U.S. power hurts Chinese interests regarding Taiwan and other sensitive issues. They openly demonstrate this opposition when the costs and benefits of doing so are seen to favor Chinese interests. The mix of stated moderation and periodic forceful actions and rhetoric confuse the situation. In the main, top-level Chinese leaders still emphasize a policy that plays down differences, striving to keep U.S.–Chinese relations as well as Chinese relations with most Asian and world governments on the generally positive footing that is seen as needed for Chinese stability and economic development.[45]

UNCERTAIN OUTLOOK: CHINA, THE UNITED STATES, AND NEARBY ASIA

The Chinese assertiveness and truculence beginning in 2008 presumably was prompted by calculations of at least some Chinese leaders who perceived American decline and Chinese ascendance opening the way for China to adopt tougher public actions and positions on long-standing differences with the United States and a variety of Asian countries with important security and sovereignty disputes with China. Although top-level Chinese leaders in 2011 toned down differences and reaffirmed interest in peace, harmony, and development, the assertive Chinese behavior in 2012 reviewed at the start of this chapter shows that the future course of Chinese policy remains uncertain. Other reasons to remain uncertain about China's peaceful approach to world affairs include long-standing viewpoints among the Chinese leadership registering deep suspicions of U.S. policy and behavior and other potential or actual world conditions adverse to Chinese interests.

Given the salience of the United States in Chinese foreign policy calculations over the years, it is important to assess the implications of Chinese wariness that appeared deepened by the American government's emphasis starting in 2011 on U.S. reengagement with the Asia-Pacific region as the focus of American foreign policy following the end and wind-down of the wars in Iraq and Afghanistan. President Obama, Secretary of State Hillary Clinton, Secretary of Defense Leon Panetta, and other administration leaders traveled to the region and made numerous speeches and pronouncements underlining U.S. determination to remain Asia's leading power and to fulfill assignments long seen as at odds with Chinese ambitions. The comments were accompanied by agreements with regional governments, U.S. announcements of strategy, troop movements, trade initiatives, and other measures designed to strengthen the U.S. position in the region.

Meanwhile, the fact remains that optimistic projections about U.S.-China relations have been made at various times during the post–Cold War period when those relations seemed to be improving, but then deteriorated into confrontation and acrimony as a result of a crisis or persisting differences.[46] Indeed, the record of U.S.-China relations since 1989 seems to favor a less rosy perspective, which available evidence and testimony by Chinese specialists indicate is the prevailing view among senior Chinese leaders. The less optimistic perspective takes account of the many deeply rooted differences that Chinese and U.S. leaders will continue to grapple with in the years ahead. As there is no guarantee that the conditions that came to hold those differences in check and gave rise to a more positive path at the beginning of this century will continue or that third parties (e.g., North Korea, Taiwan, Japan, Vietnam, the Philippines, India, and others) might not intervene in ways that disrupt U.S.-China relations, it is advisable to be cautious in predicting any long-term or fundamental change in Chinese policies involving the United States and related developments especially in nearby Asia.[47]

The most important differences in U.S.-China relations that appear likely to remain relevant determinants of Chinese foreign policy include the following:[48]

- *Taiwan:* Taking office in May 2008, Taiwan President Ma Ying-jeou reversed the provocative pro-independence stance of the previous government of President Chen Shui-bian and reached out to China for progress in cross-strait relations. Economic and social contacts advanced, but progress was slower regarding China's ongoing isolation of Taiwan internationally and its buildup of military forces to intimidate Taiwan and its U.S. supporters. Strategists in the United States welcomed the increased dialogue and exchanges in cross-strait relations, but they saw the military buildup as a threat to the United States as well as Taiwan and responded by strengthening Taiwan and U.S. forces in the region, prompting China to threaten cutoff of U.S. military contacts and publicly campaign against U.S. initiatives to reengage with Asian-Pacific countries.[49]

- *Asia:* China's leaders have long viewed China's rise in power and influence as eventually displacing U.S. military power around China's periphery, but at the start of the twenty-first century, U.S. superpower influence and military deployments grew around China's periphery to the point where the United States appeared more powerful in Asian affairs than at any time since before the Vietnam War. The wars in Iraq and Afghanistan and the global economic crisis beginning in 2008 weakened overall U.S. power and appeared to prompt some in China to become more assertive in dealing with long-standing differences with the United States over Asian and other matters, causing uncertainty at home and abroad about China's future course. That President Obama and his administration have stressed American military, economic, and political reengagement with the Asia-Pacific region as the centerpiece of U.S. foreign strategy could presage U.S.-Chinese tensions over the region.[50]

- *CCP legitimacy:* Although the George W. Bush administration and the Barack Obama administration appeared to accept the legitimacy of CCP rule in China, strong forces in the U.S. government, Congress, media, and various nongovernment interest groups continued to work to change China's political system.[51]

- *U.S. world leadership:* Although generally reluctant to confront U.S. world leadership, particularly when other world powers often were unwilling to do so, China remained opposed to U.S. "hegemonism" and sought to use international organizations and multilateral groups to constrain U.S. power. Chinese officials hoped that this will lead over time to a diminution of U.S. power and a multipolar world.

Regarding important bilateral U.S.-Chinese differences, which are reviewed in chapter 7, they involve clusters of issues in security, political, and economic categories. Apart from Taiwan, bilateral security disputes involved

U.S. complaints over China's proliferation of weapons of mass destruction (WMD), China's large defense budget increases, and Chinese use of cyber attacks and espionage against the United States; China's complaints and concerns over U.S. military actions and pressure, including the negative implications for China of U.S. missile defense programs; expanded U.S.-Japanese security cooperation; NATO expansion; and stepped-up U.S. military deployment throughout China's periphery.[52]

A key security flash point is North Korea. China has worked with the United States to seek to curb North Korea's nuclear weapons program. At the same time, Beijing is reluctant to follow the U.S. lead and apply significant pressure on North Korea. Many specialists argue that China would work against any U.S. effort to use force or serious economic pressure against North Korea because China has a much stronger interest than the United States in preserving North Korea as a viable state and avoiding the disruption that greater pressure on Pyongyang would cause.[53]

The interface of U.S. and Chinese military forces along China's periphery is not without significant incident, even as the two powers endeavored to resume more normal ties after the April 1, 2001, crash of a Chinese jet fighter and a U.S. surveillance plane, the EP-3. An unarmed U.S. Navy surveillance ship was harassed and rammed by Chinese boats in waters off the Chinese coast in 2002. American surveillance aircraft along China's periphery routinely encounter Chinese fighters, sometimes at close quarters. A Chinese submarine was detected following a U.S. aircraft carrier in the western Pacific in 2006. U.S. surveillance ships encountered harassing Chinese boats in the South China Sea in 2008 and 2009. Support by the United States for the Dalai Lama and continued criticism of Chinese policies in Tibet are seen by Beijing as challenging China's territorial integrity. When combined with U.S. support for Taiwan and criticism of Chinese repression of dissent in Xinjiang, U.S. actions regarding Tibet appear to some in China as part of a broader longer-term U.S. effort to break up China.[54]

Political concerns focus on powerful forces in the United States and China that incline toward harder-line policies that would exacerbate the differences. The wide range of U.S. interest groups that favor a tougher U.S. stance to China was well demonstrated during congressional and media debates over U.S. China policy in the 1990s. The U.S. preoccupation with the war on terrorism and major crises dealing with Iraq and North Korea curbed the attention these groups gained after 2001. The victory of the Democratic Party in the 2006 congressional elections foreshadowed stronger U.S. government criticism of China over trade and other differences, though it was muted by a U.S. need to cooperate with China on salient security issues like North Korean nuclear weapons and on the massive consequences of the global economic crisis beginning in 2008. The generally moderate and cooperative posture toward China of the Obama administration failed to hide continued differences between the two countries over a long list of issues highlighted by trade and economic disputes, conflicting strategies in the Asia-Pacific, and human rights.[55] In China, the prevailing nationalistic emphasis in leadership discourse and popular opinion reinforced suspicions of American intentions as debate continued on whether or not conditions justified a more demanding and "less submissive" posture toward the United States and its Asian and other international associates.

Economic issues center on the friction arising from asymmetrical growth in trade and commercial relations. American businesses are sometimes frustrated with conditions in China or lack of Chinese openness to their products. U.S. labor and other groups see the burgeoning trade deficit with China—the largest U.S. trade deficit with any country—as a threat to U.S. jobs and economic well-being. China resents strong U.S. pressures for greater market opening, Chinese currency revaluation, and other measures. Chinese officials chafe at U.S. restrictions on high-technology transfers to China, while U.S. officials warn that such transfers increase China's ability to pose a national security threat to the United States. Meanwhile, debate continues in the United States and China over the wisdom of China's large purchases of U.S. government securities as part of China's massive holdings of foreign exchange reserves.[56]

NOTES

1. David M. Lampton, ed., *The Making of Chinese Foreign and Security Policy in the Era of Reform* (Stanford, CA: Stanford University Press, 2001); Evan Medeiros and Taylor Fravel, "China's New Diplomacy," *Foreign Affairs* 82, no. 6 (November–December 2003): pp. 22–35; People's Republic of China State Council Information Office, "China's Peaceful Development Road," *People's Daily Online*, December 22, 2005; Linda Jakobson and Dean Knox, *New Foreign Policy Actors in China* (Stockholm: SIPRI Policy Paper No. 26, September 2010).

2. David M. Lampton, *Same Bed, Different Dreams* (Berkeley: University of California Press, 2001), pp. 59–61; Robert Sutter, *China's Rise in Asia: Promises and Perils* (Lanham, MD: Rowman & Littlefield, 2005), p. 29.

3. John Keefe, *Anatomy of the EP-3 Incident* (Alexandria, VA: Center for Naval Analysis, 2002); Michael Swaine and Zhang Tuosheng, eds., *Managing Sino-American Crises: Case Studies and Analysis* (Washington, DC: Carnegie Endowment 2006).

4. James Przystup, "Japan-China Relations: No End to History," *Comparative Connections* 7, no. 2 (2005): pp. 119–32.

5. "China Placates Foes Abroad, Nationalists at Home," *Economist*, June 4, 2008; Wang Jisi, "China's Search for a Grand Strategy," *Foreign Affairs* 90, no. 2 (March/April 2011): pp. 68–79; "China-Southeast Asia Relations," *Comparative Connections* 13, no. 1 (May 2011), www.csis.org/pacfor; James Przystup, "Japan-China Relations," *Comparative Connections* 13, no. 3 (January 2013), www.csis.org/pacfor.

6. Personal consultations with U.S. government officials, Washington, DC, 1999–2001; Swaine and Zhang, *Managing Sino-American Crises*.

7. "Friend or Foe? A Special Report on China's Place in the World," *Economist*, December 4, 2010, pp. 3–16.

8. Personal consultations with U.S. government officials, Washington, DC, November 1999.

9. Personal interviews and consultations with Chinese officials and foreign policy specialists, Beijing and Shanghai, May–June 2006, Beijing, June 2010.

10. Lu Ning, "The Central Leadership, Supraministry Coordinating Bodies, State Council Ministries, and Party Departments," in *The Making of Chinese Foreign and Security Policy in the Era of Reform*, ed. David M. Lampton (Stanford, CA: Stanford University Press, 2001), pp. 39–60; Fei-Ling Wang, "Beijing's Incentive Structure: The Pursuit of Preservation, Prosperity, and Power," in *China Rising: Power and Motivation in Chinese Foreign Policy*, ed. Yong Deng and Fei-Ling Wang (Lanham, MD: Rowman & Littlefield, 2005), pp. 19–50.

11. Alice Miller, "The CCP's Central Committee's Leading Small Groups," *China Leadership Monitor* 26 (Fall 2008), www.chinaleadershipmonitor.org.

12. Miller, "The CCP's Central Committee's Leading Small Groups."

13. See among others Chen Jian, *Mao's China and the Cold War* (Chapel Hill: University of North Carolina Press, 2001).

14. Barbara Barnouin and Yu Changgen, *Chinese Foreign Policy during the Cultural Revolution* (New York: Columbia University Press, 1997).

15. Ezra Vogel, *Deng Xiaoping and the Transformation of China* (Cambridge, MA: Harvard University Press, 2012), pp. 91–119.

16. Vogel, *Deng Xiaoping and the Transformation of China*, pp. 266–348, 640–63.

17. Vogel, *Deng Xiaoping and the Transformation of China*, pp. 266–348.

18. Immanuel Hsu, *The Rise of Modern China* (New York: Oxford University Press, 2000), pp. 763–980.

19. Lampton, *The Making of Chinese Foreign and Security Policy in the Era of Reform*, pp. 1–38.

20. Lu Ning, "The Central Leadership, Supraministry Coordinating Bodies, State Council Ministries, and Party Departments," in Lampton, ed., *The Making of Chinese Foreign and Security Policy in the Era of Reform*, pp. 39–60; Fei-Ling Wang, "Beijing's Incentive Structure: The Pursuit of Preservation, Prosperity, and Power," in *China Rising: Power and Motivation in Chinese Foreign Policy*, ed. Yong Deng and Fei-Ling Wang (Lanham, MD: Rowman & Littlefield, 2005), pp. 19–50.

21. Lampton, *The Making of Chinese Foreign and Security Policy in the Era of Reform*; Evan Medeiros and Taylor Fravel, "China's New Diplomacy," *Foreign Affairs* 82, no.6 (November–December 2003): pp. 22–35.

22. "Priorities Set for Handling Foreign Affairs," *China Daily*, August 24, 2006, p. 1.

23. Jakobson and Knox, *New Foreign Policy Actors in China*; David Shambaugh, "Coping with a Conflicted China," *Washington Quarterly* 34, no. 1 (Winter 2011): pp. 7–27.

24. Suisheng Zhao, *A Nation-State by Construction: Dynamics of Modern Chinese Nationalism* (Stanford, CA: Stanford University Press, 2004); Peter Gries, *China's New Nationalism* (Berkeley: University of California Press, 2004); Anne-Marie Brady, *Marketing Dictatorship: Propaganda and Thought Work in Contemporary China* (Lanham, MD: Rowman & Littlefield, 2008), pp. 151–74.

25. John Garver, *Foreign Relations of the People's Republic of China* (Englewood Cliffs, NJ: Prentice Hall, 1993), pp. 1–28.

26. Sources for this historical review include Warren I. Cohen, *America's Response to China: A History of Sino-American Relations* (New York: Columbia University Press, 2010).

27. Yan Xuetong, "The Instability of China-US Relations," *Chinese Journal of International Politics* 3, no. 3 (2010): pp. 1–30; Suisheng Zhao, "China's Pragmatic Nationalism: Is It Manageable?" *Washington Quarterly* 29, no. 1 (Winter 2005–2006): pp. 131–44.

28. Among foreign studies on this subject, see David Kang, *China's Rising: Peace, Power and Order in East Asia* (New York: Columbia University Press, 2007).

29. Hu Guocheng, "Chinese Images of the United States: A Historical Review," in *Chinese Images of the United States*, ed. Carola McGiffert (Washington, DC: CSIS, 2006), pp. 3–8.

30. Lampton, *Same Bed, Different Dreams*, p. 60.

31. Wang Jisi, "From Paper Tiger to Real Leviathan: China's Images of the United States since 1949," in McGiffert, ed., *Chinese Images of the United States*, pp. 12–18; Zhao Lingmin, "Optimistic View of Sino-US Relations—Exclusive Interview with Professor Wang Jisi," *Nanfeng Chuang* (Guangzhou), October 8, 2008, pp. 50–53; Kenneth Lieberthal and Wang Jisi, *Assessing U.S.-China Strategic Mistrust* (Washington, DC: Brookings Institution John Thornton China Center, 2012).

32. Rosalie Chen, "China Perceives America," *Journal of Contemporary China* 12, no. 35 (2003): pp. 288–92.

33. Robert Ross and Jiang Changbin, *Re-Examining the Cold War: U.S.-China Diplomacy 1954–1973* (Cambridge, MA: Harvard University Press, 2001), pp. 19–21; Lieberthal and Wang, *Assessing U.S.-China Strategic Mistrust.*

34. Wang, "From Paper Tiger to Real Leviathan"; Gong Li, "The Official Perspective: What Chinese Government Officials Think of America," in McGiffert, ed., *Chinese Images of the United States*, pp. 9–32.

35. The mix of challenge and opportunity posed by the United States for Chinese interests and policies in Asian and world affairs prompted differing assessments by Chinese and foreign specialists. Some emphasize positive and cooperative aspects of U.S.-China relations. See Medeiros and Fravel, "China's New Diplomacy"; Jia Qingguo, "Learning to Live with the Hegemon: Evolution of China's Policy toward the United States," *Journal of Contemporary China* 14, no. 44 (August 2005): pp. 395–407; and Stephanie Kleine-Ahlbrandt and Andrew Small, "China's New Dictatorship Diplomacy," *Foreign Affairs* 87, no. 1 (January–February 2008): pp. 38–56; Others emphasize more negative and competitive aspects. See Joshua Kurlantzick, *Charm Offensive: How China's Soft Power Is Transforming the World* (New Haven, CT: Yale University Press, 2007); U.S.-China Economic and Security Review Commission, *Report to Congress*, 2008, www.uscc.gov; U.S. Department of State, *China's Strategic Modernization: Report from the Secretary's International Security Advisory Board (ISAB) Task Force*, 2008, video1.washingtontimes.com/video/ChinaStrategicPlan.pdf (accessed December 27, 2008); People's Republic of China State Council Information Office, "China's National Defense in 2006," Beijing, December 29, 2006.

36. Thomas Christensen, "The Advantages of an Assertive China," *Foreign Affairs* 90, no. 2 (March–April 2011): pp. 54–67.

37. Yan , " The Instability of China-US Relations"; Lampton, *The Three Faces of Chinese Power*, 164–74; Zhang Liping, "A Rising China and a Lonely Superpower America," in *Making New Partnership: A Rising China and Its Neighbors*, ed. Zhang Yunlin (Beijing: Social Sciences Academic Press, 2008), pp. 324–55; Wu Xinbo, "The End of the Silver Lining: A Chinese View of the U.S.-Japanese Alliance," *Washington Quarterly* 29, no. 1 (Winter 2006): pp. 119–30.

38. Robert Sutter, *China's Rise in Asia: Promises and Perils* (Lanham, MD: Rowman & Littlefield, 2005), p. 35. Among differing perspectives, see Lampton, *The Three Faces of Chinese Power*; Alastair Iain Johnston, "Is China a Status Quo Power?" *International Security* 24, no. 4 (Spring 2003): pp. 5–56; and Yong Deng and Thomas Moore, "China Views Globalization: Toward a New Great-Power Politics," *Washington Quarterly* 27, no. 3 (Summer 2004): pp. 117–36.

39. Robert Sutter, *Chinese Foreign Policy: Developments after Mao* (New York: Praeger, 1986), p. 5.

40. Sutter, *Chinese Foreign Policy*, p. 9.

41. Garver, *Foreign Relations of the People's Republic of China*, pp. 70–109.

42. Sutter, *Chinese Foreign Policy*, pp. 10–12.

43. James Mann, *About Face* (New York: Knopf, 1999), 128–54.

44. Sutter, *China's Rise in Asia*, pp. 10–17.

45. Martin Indyk, Kenneth Lieberthal, and Michael O'Hanlon, *Bending History* (Washington, DC: Brookings Institution, 2012), pp. 24–69.

46. Robert Suettinger, *Beyond Tiananmen* (Washington, DC: Brookings Institution, 2003); Lampton, *Same Bed, Different Dreams*; Mark Manyin, coord., *Pivot to the Pacific? The Obama Administration's " Rebalancing " Toward Asia*, Report R42448 (Washington, DC: Library of Congress, Congressional Research Service, March 28, 2012).

47. Lieberthal and Wang, *Assessing U.S.-China Strategic Mistrust.*

48. Robert Sutter, *U.S.-Chinese Relations: Perilous Past, Pragmatic Present* (Lanham MD: Roman and Littlefield, 2010).

49. Christensen, "The Advantages of an Assertive China"; *Economist*, "Friend or Foe?"; Ralph Cossa and Brad Glosserman, "Regional Overview," *Comparative Connections* 12, no. 4 (January 2011), www.csis.org/pacfor.

50. David Finkelstein, *China Reconsiders Its National Security: The Great Peace and Development Debate of 1999* (Alexandria, VA: CNA, December 2000); Qian Qichen, "The International Situation and Sino-U.S. Relations since the 11 September Incident," *Waijiao Xueyuan Xuebao* (Beijing) 3 (September 25, 2002); Wang, "China's Search for a Grand Strategy."

51. Susan Lawrence and Thomas Lum, *China-U.S. Relations: Policy Issues*, Report RL 41108 (Washington, DC: Library of Congress, Congressional Research Service, March 11, 2011).

52. Lawrence and Lum, *China-U.S. Relations*, pp. 6–16.

53. Scott Snyder, "DPRK Provocations Test China's Regional Role," *Comparative Connections* 12, no. 4 (January 2011), www.csis.org/pacfor.

54. Li Heng, "What Is U.S. Vessel Up To in Chinese Waters?" *People's Daily*, September 30, 2002, english.people.com.cn (accessed October 2, 2002); Bill Gertz, "Chinese Jet Fighters Fly Near U.S. Spy Planes," *Washington Times*, June 27, 2002, p. 1; Bonnie Glaser, "U.S.-China Relations: Bilateral Stability, but Challenges on China's Borders," *Comparative Connections* 10, no. 1 (April 2008): pp. 25–31; Bonnie Glaser, "Friction and Cooperation in the Run-up to Hu's US Visit," *Comparative Connections* 12, no. 4 (January 2011), www.csis.org/pacfor.

55. Sutter, *U.S.-Chinese Relations*, pp. 147–68.

56. Wayne Morrison, *China-U.S. Trade Issues*, Report RL33536 (Washington, DC: Library of Congress, Congressional Research Service, May 21, 2012).

Chapter Six

China's Changing Importance in World Affairs

The review of Chinese foreign policies and behavior in chapters 2 through 4 shows enormous change. Not surprisingly, the People's Republic of China's impact on and role in world affairs has changed dramatically as well. The introductory pages in chapter 1 show how China's contemporary rise as a world power second only to the United States is based on China's rapidly growing economic importance, advancing military power, and increasing prominence in bilateral and multilateral diplomacy and global governance. These important changes support the widespread assessments that China has advanced to the point of challenging the existing international order in the Asia-Pacific region and more broadly. When combined with recent judgments of economic and international decline on the part of the United States and other developed countries on account of economic weaknesses and various external and internal failings and constraints, China's rise is commonly viewed to represent a fundamental power shift in regional and world politics.

As noted in chapter 1, this book judges that such forecasts of a power shift resulting in Chinese primacy and leadership in the Asia-Pacific and broader world affairs are premature and probably wrong. This chapter provides two areas of assessment that assist readers in understanding the more balanced and realistic examination of China's actual influence in regional and world affairs presented in the three following chapters.

The first area of assessment highlights instances of the People's Republic of China's past impact on regional and world affairs to show that China's strategic and political importance was often seen by major powers and states in Asia as intensely important. The perceived importance of China and its international influence loomed especially large in the Asia-Pacific region and as part of the competition for international leadership by the United States and the Soviet Union during the Cold War. At several junctures during this period, China's actual impact in the calculus of U.S., Soviet, and Asian leaders appeared more salient to their important interests than does the impact of rising China in recent years.

The second area of assessment involves examination in some detail of the key elements in China's contemporary regional and world influence: economic development, diplomacy and other involvement in global governance, and military power. Showing China's constraints and limitations as well as advances in these three areas provides a foundation for the more nuanced and sober view of Chinese influence in world relationships detailed in the three following chapters.

Today's China's greatest importance is as the world's second-largest and fastest-growing economy. China's modernization and economic advance spread and deepen throughout the vast country and into all corners of the world. They support active diplomacy in multilateral and bilateral relations. They also provide the basis for the fastest-growing military modernization of any country in the post–Cold War period, and thereby change the security calculus of China's neighbors and other concerned powers, notably the United States.

China's role in today's world has depended fundamentally on the success of the economic reforms and international outreach begun in the post-Mao period by Deng Xiaoping and his colleagues and their successors. China's growing international economic footprint has increased its heretofore limited importance to a wide range of countries in the developed and developing world as a trading partner, a recipient and source of investment, and a creditor.

Prior to that time, China exerted important influence in world affairs in different ways and for different reasons. As discussed in chapters 2 and 3, China's vast size, strategic location, revolutionary and nationalistic zeal, and broad popular mobilization made China a formidable opponent for both the United States and the Soviet Union and an important determinant in the foreign policy calculations of neighboring Asian countries. China's importance grew as it developed nuclear weapons and the ballistic missiles to deliver them to targets as far away as Washington, D.C. Ironically, China's prevailing backwardness in economic development for much of this period made China more difficult for the U.S. and Soviet superpowers to deter and to counter adverse Chinese moves, thereby increasing China's importance in their calculations.

Thus, one can argue that the Truman and early Eisenhower administrations' focus on China's importance in the Korean War, and President Lyndon Johnson's preoccupation with the protracted war in Vietnam, where hundreds of thousands of Chinese soldiers served in North Vietnam and Laos, gave more importance to managing relations with China than any U.S. president in the post–Cold War period. Subsequently, with the establishment of a rough balance of power and influence between the United States and the Soviet Union after two decades of Cold War, China came to be seen by both superpowers as the most important independent source of international influence in world affairs. Beginning with the Nixon administration, the United States assiduously sought China's support, giving relations with China very high importance in U.S. strategic calculations. The record seems to show that the importance U.S. policy gave to relations with China during the late 1960s until the early 1980s was even more than the relatively high importance U.S. policy has given to China in the contemporary period. For its part, the leadership in Moscow under the Soviet Union during this period clearly devoted more attention to relations with China than post-Soviet Russia has ever devoted to China. Details showing China's actual and often remarkable international impact during the forty years of the Cold War follow.

CHINA'S INITIAL COLD WAR INFLUENCE

U.S. and Soviet competition for influence in Asia in the early years of the Cold War at first appeared secondary to their competition in Europe and the Middle East. The American support for Chiang Kai-shek against the Communist-led forces of Mao Zedong in the Chinese Civil War ended with Chiang's defeat and retreat to Taiwan in 1949. The failure of U.S. policy in China, the so-called "loss" of China, fed into often partisan debates in American public opinion on how the United States should be positioned in dealing with Mao's government and new realities in China. Mao's leaning to the Soviet Union in the Cold War and the signing of the Sino-Soviet alliance in February 1950 added to growing concerns in America that the Soviet Union and its partners were posing direct threats to the United States. [1]

The North Korean attack on South Korea in June 1950, which had the backing of Moscow and Beijing, represented a tipping point in American calculations and behavior. The U.S.-led ring of containment against Soviet-backed expansion in Europe and the Middle East was now expanded to Asia and concentrated on China. The upshot included two and a half years of hard combat with Chinese forces in Korea. Despite American advanced weaponry and control of air and sea access, China resorted to manpower-intensive battlefield and logistical measures that allowed their forces to fight the Americans to a standstill. The American commitment to protect Taiwan against China grew into a formal defense alliance as part of the various treaties, military deployments, and foreign assistance arrangements featured in the strong U.S. presence along China's eastern flank.[2]

The United States countered two major episodes of military confrontation in the Taiwan Strait—in 1954 and again in 1958—with strong military measures and threats to use nuclear weapons against China. The Americans also supported the French against Communist forces backed by China in Indochina, and became more actively involved in the region following the French withdrawal in 1954. In the 1959 uprising against Chinese rule in Tibet the United States clandestinely supported the Tibetan resistance with training and weapons. The hidden American strategy in this period was for the United States to differentiate between the Soviet Union and China, seeking to exert heavy pressure on China while showing some moderation toward, and engaging in some pragmatic interchange with, post-Stalin Soviet leaders. The intent was to exacerbate differences between the Sino-Soviet partners on how to deal with the United States.[3]

While Stalin was in a position to dictate terms in the Sino-Soviet alliance, post-Stalin leaders headed by Nikita Khrushchev at various times sought Chinese support or sought to offset Chinese initiatives in policy areas of importance to the USSR. Khrushchev seemed confident enough in his struggle for top power in the post-Stalin leadership to spend two weeks in China on the occasion of the PRC's fifth anniversary in October 1954. He endeavored to appeal to China by lauding China's role in leading revolutionary forces in Asia, agreeing to return Soviet-held territory to China, and supporting China in an emerging military confrontation with Chiang Kai-shek's U.S.-backed forces in the Taiwan Strait.[4]

After Khrushchev rose to undisputed leadership with the demotion of Georgy Malenkov in 1955, he found that China often complicated his policies and reforms. Mao opposed Khrushchev's denunciation of Stalin's excesses in his secret speech to the Soviet Party Congress in February 1956. The Chinese supported the leadership of Poland, where the Communist Party in October 1956 resisted pressure from Khrushchev to avoid what was deemed by Moscow as excessive nationalism and defiance of Soviet instructions. In contrast, Chinese leaders supported the intervention of Soviet troops into Hungary in November 1956 because the existing Communist regime was seen to be unable to contain burgeoning mass movements that were increasingly taking outright anti-Communist forms.[5]

Mao opposed Khrushchev's moderate approach to Yugoslavia's Josip Tito and his periodic pragmatic relations with the United States. And, at the international gathering of Communist leaders in Moscow in 1957, Mao's call for a tougher stance against the United States stood in contrast to Khrushchev's policies. Mao later rebuffed Khrushchev's efforts to coordinate Sino-Soviet military operations, and his launching of the Great Leap Forward and the Taiwan Strait crisis in 1958 were seen by Khrushchev as reckless and involving gross misuse of massive Soviet material support to China. By 1960 aid relations were ended and polemics intensified over differences within the international communist movement, relations with the United States, and appropriate paths to development. China sided with dissidents in the international communist movement, notably Enver Hoxa of Albania, and took a high profile in support of newly formed nations and liberation movements in Africa and elsewhere in the developing world. As such, China competed with the Soviet Union as well as with the West for international influence.[6]

As discussed in chapter 2, China's Communist-led neighbors North Korea and North Vietnam maneuvered between Moscow and Beijing in order to support their interests in opposition to the United States and its allies and associates. Many other Chinese neighbors saw their interests best served by close alignment with the United States in opposition to China, though the most important U.S. Asian ally, Japan, endeavored to reach out to China and became its major international trading partner after the collapse of the Sino-Soviet alliance. Leading nonaligned Asian countries, notably India and Indonesia, moved to establish closer ties with China before adverse developments in the 1960s caused them to reverse course and become deeply suspicious of China and its intentions.

THE "GREAT POWER TRIANGLE"

The opening of Chinese relations with the United States and many other countries beginning during a period of violent Chinese conflict with the Soviet Union in the late 1960s reflected contrasting views of China's international importance and influence. Scholarship shows that American strategists and other international observers saw China weakened by the massive economic disaster of the Great Leap Forward (1958–1961) followed by years of violent and disruptive governance during the Cultural Revolution begun in 1966. China was isolated in international affairs. Its strident emphasis on economic self-reliance sharply limited foreign trade, and technology transfer, educational exchanges, and other interaction conducive to economic modernization were minimal, pushing China and its self-righteous and self-reliant leadership further behind in economic development compared with many of its neighbors in Asia. Most Chinese initiatives in support of newly emerging states in the developing world collapsed as a result of territorial and political differences, Chinese excesses during the so-called Red Guard diplomacy years of the Cultural Revolution, and Soviet and Western competition. By 1968 only a small handful of developing countries had workable foreign relations with China.[7]

Nevertheless, the prevailing perception of China during this period was one of great international influence. The reasons were predominantly strategic. A rough balance of influence emerged between the rising Soviet Union and the United States. America's failure in the massive and protracted war effort in Vietnam headed the list of its economic, social, and strategic problems. While the United States appeared in decline with no good answer to its predicament in Vietnam, the Soviet Union appeared to reach parity with U.S. strategic weaponry. The more confident and assertive leadership of Leonid Brezhnev was expanding Soviet commitments and involvement into Asia and other parts of the world that further complicated U.S. interests and was seen to pose a direct threat to Maoist China.[8]

As explained in chapter 3, the Soviet expansion and various U.S. and Chinese weaknesses and vulnerabilities provided the foundation for the opening of China's relationship with the Nixon administration and a variety of other countries as well as the United Nations. For much of the next twenty years, U.S. officials sought closer ties with China as a means to right the balance in Cold War competition with the USSR. American interest in the so-called U.S.-Soviet-Chinese Great Power Triangle gave China high priority in U.S. foreign policy calculations. The American interest was shared by many of its allies and associates, who also were anxious to work closely with China as a means to counter perceived dangers posed by Soviet expansion. Thus, U.S.-aligned countries in Europe, the Asia-Pacific region, and the Western Hemisphere moved quickly to establish formal diplomatic relations with newly welcoming China. Companies in these countries and the international economic institutions supported by these countries prepared for what turned out to be an enormous increase in economic interchange once the post-Mao economic reforms took hold in China in the late 1970s.[9]

Moscow for its part endeavored to deal with an emerging international united front with the United States, its allies, and China at the center. On the one hand, it employed a thinly disguised containment effort directed against China in Asia, involving Soviet treaties and strategic agreements with Mongolia, Vietnam, and India, large Soviet military deployments in Mongolia and along the disputed Sino-Soviet border, close military cooperation and bases in Vietnam, active air and naval patrols along China's maritime periphery, and arms sales and military cooperation with India. On the other hand, Soviet leaders endeavored to seek common ground in détente efforts with the United States and Western countries as a means to reduce East-West tensions and undermine the Western-Chinese united front effort. The Soviet Union also periodically made efforts to ease tensions with China in ways that seemed to threaten U.S. and Western interests.[10]

The overlap of U.S.-Soviet and Sino-Soviet rivalry complicated the foreign policy calculations of China's Communist-ruled neighbors, North Korea and Vietnam. Vietnam decided to align with Moscow as it invaded Cambodia and expelled the Chinese-backed Khmer Rouge regime in 1978, setting the stage for China's limited invasion of Vietnam and ten years of confrontation and conflict in Sino-Vietnamese relations.[11] North Korea's Kim Il Sung was more flexible, as he continued to maneuver between China and the Soviet Union for assistance and other benefits that would strengthen North Korea against South Korea and its backer, the United States.[12]

America's non-Communist allies and associates in Southeast Asia were alarmed by the U.S. decline and pullback from the region after the defeat in Vietnam in 1975. They shored up their security by reaching out to China, which was reaching out to them in order to deal with the common danger posed by the expansion of Soviet-backed Vietnam into Cambodia. With its interest in a common front against the USSR, China welcomed Japan's improvements of its military capabilities within the framework of the U.S.-Japan alliance and the coordination of its foreign policies with both Washington and Beijing against perceived Soviet expansion. South Korea's closer ties with China developed slowly, focusing at first on mutually beneficial economic exchanges between dynamic South Korean enterprises and the newly opening Chinese economy. China was reluctant to develop closer political and security ties out of concern for its relations with North Korea. [13]

As discussed in chapter 3, the importance of China among the developing countries in Africa, the Middle East, and elsewhere in the so-called third world was more muted during this period. China's siding with the United States and its allies, including various right-wing regimes (e.g., the Shah of Iran; Chile's Augusto Pinochet; Zaire's Sese Mobutu) in the developing world alienated elite and public opinion in developing countries that remained friendly to Moscow and suspicious of the West. China's call for developing countries to resist the expansion of the Soviet Union into Africa, Southwest and Southeast Asia, and Latin America was not backed by much concrete Chinese support for these states. Beijing began to cut back its aid efforts and began directly competing with developing countries for international assistance provided by UN and regional financial and economic organizations.

CHINA'S RECENT ROLE IN THE WORLD ECONOMY, GOVERNANCE, AND DEFENSE

China's importance and engagement in the world economy and in international governance have grown dramatically in the post–Cold War period. Measuring the actual importance of China to the international economy and assessing the actual significance of Chinese involvement in international governing bodies remain difficult, however. Some specialists in China and abroad view Chinese leaders as increasingly confident as they use China's large economic power to exert influence in line with China's long-standing ambitions of greater regional and global power. Others, myself included, view the Chinese leaders as continuing to follow contingent policies based on changing assessments of the costs and benefits for China that in turn depend on international and domestic circumstances. The amount of influence China exerts on the world economy is growing, but so is China's dependence on key variables in the world economy that the Chinese leadership does not control, including scarcity of energy and other resources, protectionist tendencies among developed countries, and international disapproval of China's impact on climate change and the broader environment. Such dependence limits the amount of influence China actually exerts in international affairs.

Meanwhile, China's leaders use greater engagement in multilateral organizations defensively, notably to protect Chinese interests from unwanted U.S. interventions, as much as they use such involvement to enhance China's international prominence and importance. At the start of the second decade of the twenty-first century, the reality seems to be that China remains an emerging power with a large and growing economy that is heavily dependent on important international and internal variables. Against this background, China's leaders generally continue to eschew major risks, costs, or commitments involved in providing regional or international common goods or asserting international leadership except in cases with direct bearing on carefully and usually narrowly defined Chinese national interests. Such practices limit the amount of influence China actually exerts in international affairs. [14]

Thus, while China has a large footprint in world affairs and often seeks the limelight in international meetings and the councils of international governance, China also is widely seen as a "free rider" or at least a "cheap rider" in undertaking costs and commitments for common regional and global goods. In general terms, China is strongly wedded to the "win-win" approach in international relations. If China is going to extend effort and resources for a common good, it has to be shown that such actions will result in tangible benefits for China defined in a fairly narrow Chinese win-set. For example, China repeatedly publicizes its role as the largest participant in UN peacekeeping efforts among the permanent members of the UN Security Council. It rarely points out that its contributions are noncombatants, and thus generally its personnel are positioned out of harm's way. It avoids highlighting the fact that the Chinese participants, like those from Bangladesh and other large contributors to UN peacekeeping missions, get paid from the UN peacekeeping budget. And China rarely notes the size of its peacekeeping budget contribution, which has risen from a very low base and recently has been at the same low level as that of Italy. Meanwhile, though China strongly supports the United Nations as the ultimate arbiter of international issues, it is reluctant to see its allotment to the UN budget rise from its recent remarkably low level, which is about the same as that of Spain. [15]

Evidence of self-serving Chinese behavior carefully nurturing tangible benefits for China and eschewing risks and costs for regional and global goods include China's continued receiving over $6 billion of foreign assistance annually from UN programs, the World Bank, the Asian Development Bank and a variety of OECD (Organization for Economic Cooperation and Development) countries. For example, China in 2008 renewed long-term agreements with the World Bank for providing continued loans to China for several years into the future, and in 2010 it renewed for five more years the generous contributions to Chinese development of the UN Development Program (UNDP) and over twenty other UN-affiliated agencies offering assistance in China. Such reception comes at a time when China's economic condition is so flush with cash that it has over $3 trillion in foreign exchange reserves. A more generous China might be inclined to encourage some of this foreign assistance to go to more needy nations in a less advantageous economic position than China. [16]

The reasons for China's continued reception of large amounts of foreign assistance and its reluctance to spend abroad in the interests of regional and global governance appear related to Chinese domestic requirements. The range of obligations inside China requiring resources seems wide and deep. Chinese leaders appear disinclined to turn away foreign assistance that benefits these domestic requirements or to extend efforts and expenses abroad that could be employed for domestic Chinese concerns. [17]

When one contrasts the Chinese cheap riding of today with Chinese actions abroad in previous decades, one sees episodes of remarkable leadership by Mao Zedong and Deng Xiaoping that obviously added to Chinese influence in world affairs. Mao undertook enormous commitments and risks in confronting the United States in Korea, in supporting the Communist insurgents in Indochina against the French and against the United States, and in probing and wearing down the U.S. containment. His commitment to the international struggle against Soviet hegemonism showed a willingness to endure great sacrifice while encouraging the United States and its allies and associates to hold the line against the USSR. As explained earlier, Deng Xiaoping followed in Mao's path in undertaking great costs and risking Chinese national security in order to teach Vietnam a "lesson" over its invasion of Cambodia in 1978. The Chinese lesson also applied to the United States and its allies and associates, showing them that China was prepared to stand up to Soviet expansion and that they should do the same.

There are few instances in the post–Cold War period that compare to such episodes demonstrating international influence and leadership under Mao and Deng. This gap helps to explain why China's recent big international footprint often does not translate into international influence.

China's Economic Importance

Since the beginning of economic reforms following the death of Mao Zedong in 1976, China has been the world's fastest-growing major economy. As noted in chapter 1, from 1979 to 2011, the average annual growth rate of China's gross domestic product (GDP) was about 10 percent. China became the world's second-largest economy, after the United States. It was the world's largest exporter, largest manufacturer, and second-largest trader. China also was the second-largest destination of foreign investment, the largest holder of foreign exchange reserves and the largest creditor nation. Though some observers forecast trouble ahead, expert opinion tends to see China on track to surpass the United States probably within ten years as the world's largest economy. The massive growth of Chinese trade and of foreign investment in China continued while China's own investment abroad grew very rapidly beginning in the past ten years.[18]

Trade continues to play a major role in China's rapid economic growth. In 2004, China surpassed Japan as the world's third-largest trading economy, after the European Union and the United States, and in 2007 it was reported to have surpassed the United States as the world's largest exporter. In 2011, total trade was valued at $3.6 trillion, with China, as usual, running a trade surplus, valued in that year at $159.9 billion.[19]

China's trade boom was dependent on large inflows of foreign direct investment (FDI) into China. Annual utilized FDI in China (excluding the financial sector) grew from $636 million in 1983 to $105.7 billion in 2010. The cumulative level of FDI in China at the end of 2010 was over $1 trillion, making China one of the world's largest destinations of FDI. Based on cumulative FDI since1979, about 40 percent of FDI in China came from Hong Kong, 10 percent from the British Virgin Islands (a well-known tax haven), 8 percent from Japan, and 7 percent from the United States. The largest sector for FDI flows in China in recent years was manufacturing, which often accounted for over half of total annual FDI in China. Over half of China's foreign trade is accounted for by foreign-invested firms in China. The combination of trade surpluses and FDI added to China's foreign exchange reserves, the largest in the world, valued at $3 trillion in 2011. Against this background, China's outbound direct investment increased rapidly in recent years. It amounted to $67.6 billion in 2011. These economic trends provided the foundation for China's increasingly important role in international economic relations.[20]

There are differing views among Chinese officials and international specialists about how important China is in international economic affairs. The views differ as well about what this means for overall Chinese foreign relations, especially China's expanding role in regional and global international organizations that deal with economic as well as political, security, environmental, and other matters of importance to the world community in the post–Cold War period.

According to many Chinese officials and international observers, China's growing economy and its burgeoning international trade and investment relationships provide a solid foundation for China to play an ever more important role in influencing and managing world affairs. In 2011, a debate emerged in mainstream Chinese media over whether or not China's economic success had reached a point where it provided a model to be followed by other countries. Many in the West in recent years saw the emergence of a "Beijing consensus" encompassing the main features of China's development approach; they judged that the Chinese government was in the process of spreading this development model throughout the world—a trend they viewed as adverse to Western values and goals, summed up as what they called the "Washington consensus."[21]

On the other hand, senior Chinese officials tended to eschew association with a Beijing consensus or a China model that would oppose Western norms. The Chinese leaders duly criticized Western efforts to impose their values and development norms on other countries through conditions on foreign assistance, sanctions, and other means of interfering in other states' internal affairs. In their assessment foreign countries should be free to choose their desired development path, and should not feel obliged to follow one model or another. Some Chinese economic specialists were frank in highlighting the many shortcomings of the Chinese development model, suggesting that China had a long way to go before its economic development experience could provide a model for others to emulate.[22]

Based on its status as the largest trading partner with Africa, Brazil, and most of its Asian neighbors; the top producer of steel and other metals, cement, ships, cars, electronic goods, and textiles; the leading consumer of many categories of international raw materials; and the world's largest creditor nation,[23] China is looked to increasingly as a leader in Asian and world affairs. A wide range of developing and developed countries that didn't consider China very important in the past, now give high priority to relations with China. As discussed in later chapters of this book, government leaders throughout the world often consult closely with Chinese leaders in bilateral exchanges and in international organizations, endeavoring to influence and govern international affairs to their mutual benefit.

Conforming to norms of economic globalization, Chinese leaders notably put aside past Chinese government suspicion of Asian and international multilateral organizations.[24] They have embraced burgeoning Asian and international economic groupings, and they have shown sometimes more guarded cooperation with other international organizations dealing with political, security, and other issues. On balance, Chinese engagement has met with the general satisfaction of other regional and international participants.

Against this background, a number of foreign specialists and commentators in recent years have portrayed China as a leader in international economic affairs, surpassing Japan, India, and the European powers, as it closes the gap with the United States.[25] Thus, they commonly assert that China has become an economic superpower whose continuing rise will require perhaps painful and difficult adjustments on the part of the United States and other heretofore leading powers in the international economy. The latter will need to give way to China and its rising influence.

A contrasting view of China's international economic importance comes from some Chinese officials who are diffident about Chinese economic power and influence in world affairs. They frequently emphasize important limitations and preoccupations at home and abroad that act as a brake on China's adopting a strong leadership role anytime soon in international economic and other world affairs. Indeed, a fundamental premise of the Chinese government's recent stress on China's adherence to the goals of peace and development is the argument that Chinese authorities face many obstacles and problems at home and a variety of actual or potential obstacles abroad. Chinese leaders need to encourage and sustain a peaceful and harmonious world order as they deal with these concerns and pursue a longer-term goal of developing China's "comprehensive national power." I, along with some other foreign specialists, agree with this line of Chinese thinking. We also see significant obstacles in the path of China becoming an economic superpower or taking on the obligations of world leadership in the next decade.[26]

The arguments of the Chinese and foreign observers who are diffident about China's emerging power and influence in international economics and global governance start with the judgment that both China's future international role and the stability of the administration led by the Chinese Communist Party (CCP) depend heavily on healthy growth of the Chinese economy.

This in turn depends on the overall health of the world economy and on the Chinese government's effective implementation of reforms conducive to economic growth. The targets of economic and related reform in China are many, posing ongoing challenges for China's future economic growth and stability.[27]

The weaknesses and challenges include:

- *State-owned enterprises:* Accounting for about one-third of Chinese industrial production and employing a large part of China's urban workers, SOEs put a heavy strain on China's economy. Over half are believed to lose money and must be supported by subsidies, mainly through state banks.
- *Uneven economic growth:* The global economic crisis since 2008 has demonstrated to the Chinese government the dangers of relying too heavily on foreign trade and investment for economic growth.
- *An inflexible currency policy:* China does not allow its currency to float and therefore must make large-scale purchases of dollars to keep the exchange rate within certain target levels.
- *The banking system:* Banking in China faces several major difficulties because of its financial support of SOEs and its failure to operate solely on market-based principles.
- *The agricultural system:* This system has been highly inefficient because of government policies that have sought to maintain a high degree of self-sufficiency in grains.
- *Rule of law:* The lack of the rule of law in China has led to widespread government corruption, financial speculation, and misallocation of investment funds.
- *Poor government regulatory environment:* China maintains a weak and relatively decentralized government structure to regulate economic activity in China.
- *Social issues:* A number of social problems have arisen from China's rapid economic growth and extensive reforms. These include a widening of income disparities between coastal and interior regions and between urban and rural parts of China and a growing number of bankruptcies and worker layoffs.
- *Growing pollution:* The level of pollution in China continues to worsen, posing serious health risks for the population.

Internationally, economic growth and increased trade and investment enhance China's prominence, but increased trade and investment with neighbors in Asia do not automatically place China in a leadership position in Asia, much less in other areas farther from China's borders. Looking at China's profile in neighboring Asian areas, the growth in trade and South Korean investment in China provided the lead elements in improving China–South Korean relations, arguably one of the areas of greatest success in China's recent foreign policy, at least until recent years.[28] A similar pattern of Chinese trade and Southeast Asian investment in China has seen China advance markedly in relations with the countries of ASEAN, at least until very recently. Burgeoning Asian trade networks of processing trade involving Southeast Asia and China pushed China ahead of the United States as ASEAN's top trading partner. The Chinese government also set the pace in economic and other relations with the group of ten Southeast Asian states with initiatives involving a China-ASEAN free trade agreement.[29]

Nevertheless, the strong economic links were not sufficient to prevent a serious downturn in China's relations with South Korea and with several Southeast Asian governments in recent years over disputed territorial claims and approaches to regional problems. That better economic ties sometimes do not automatically translate into good overall relations also showed graphically in China's relations with Japan. As discussed in chapter 8, booming trade with Japan and strong investment in China by Japanese businesses have helped to moderate political and security tensions between China and the neighboring government. Yet the Chinese government more often than not has had difficulty in improving strained relations with Japan, which feature periodic and hard-to-predict outbursts of intense Chinese pressure, including extralegal trade sanctions and violence directed at Japan and Japanese properties and people in China over sensitive issues of sovereignty and security between the two powers.

International Governance: Increasing but Still Selective Involvement

China's growing involvement with and dependence on the world economy heads the list of reasons explaining China's broadening and deepening involvement with various multilateral organizations. As noted in chapter 1, scholars and specialists have seen remarkable changes and increased Chinese activism in Asian regional multilateral organizations, with China in recent years taking a leading role in creating such structures as the China-ASEAN

Free Trade Agreement and a regional security body that includes Russia and four central Asian states known as the Shanghai Cooperation Organization (SCO). The Chinese approach in these endeavors strives to meet the interests of the other participants while ensuring that Chinese interests of development and stability are well served. China also has participated actively in recent years in loosely structured global groups, notably the G-20, involving the world's twenty leading powers, and the BRICS, involving Brazil, Russia, India, China, and South Africa.[30]

China's approach to multilateralism has changed markedly since it became an active participant in such endeavors on entry into the United Nations in 1971. At one level of analysis, there has been a steady trend since then toward closer Chinese government cooperation with the United Nations and an ever wider range of multilateral organizations and the international norms they support. The record of Chinese adherence to multilateral guidelines and norms remains somewhat mixed, however.[31]

Chinese engagement with international economic organizations has been the most active and positive. These organizations provide numerous material benefits for China's development, and China's active participation ensures that China will play an important role in decisions affecting the world economy, on which Chinese development depends. There are some limits on Chinese cooperation with international economic institutions. For example, China does not cooperate closely with international organizations that seek to regulate scarcities in the global oil market. Rather than rely on the global energy market and international groups that seek to facilitate its smooth operation, China pursues an independent approach to ensure that it has the energy it needs for economic growth. China gives little attention to international complaints of rising energy prices and other negative results for the world oil market that result, for example, when China purchases foreign oil rights at high prices.[32]

China's recently more active and positive approach in Asian regional economic, security, and political organizations seems to reflect the Chinese leadership's goal not to be seen as a danger by its neighbors and the region's dominant outside power, the United States. As noted in chapter 4 and chapter 7, China's emphasis on its "peaceful rise," following the road of "peaceful development," and seeking of a "harmonious world" are part of its efforts to avoid actions that could prompt foreign measures that would work against the continuing rise of Chinese power. China's attentive diplomacy and periodic deference to the interests of its neighbors have helped to reassure most of them about its intentions, giving rise to significant improvement in Chinese relations throughout its periphery. On the other hand, some see the recent rise of Chinese military power and international assertiveness over territorial claims and other issues, along with China's economic power and positive multilateral diplomacy, as inconsistent with China's avowed peaceful intentions and posing a possibly serious threat to the security of Asian states and regional stability.[33]

China is reluctant to commit to international norms regarding regulation of environmental practices if they infringe on Chinese efforts to expand economic growth. As a result, media reports in late 2012 cited studies showing that China emits twice the carbon dioxide of the United States just three years after it overtook the United States as the world's largest greenhouse gas emitter.[34] The Chinese government's approach to international human rights regimes has long focused on engaging in protracted dialogue and cooperating where possible or needed in order to avoid international sanction while nonetheless consistently avoiding significant commitments that would impede its ability to coerce those who are seen as challenging the Communist administration.[35] Likewise with international arms control measures, China's cooperation has grown steadily in the past two decades, though it continues to avoid commitments that would impede its independence in certain areas sensitive to important Chinese interests.[36]

Specialists differed in assessing what this record of greater involvement actually meant for the Chinese government's attitude to international norms supported by the multilateral groups. A prevailing view held that Beijing at the start of the post–Cold War period was particularly reluctant to allow such participation to curb its freedom of action regarding key issues of security and sovereignty or to require costly economic or other commitments. Its participation involved maneuvering to pursue narrow national interests without great concern for international norms, primarily burnishing China's global image, deflecting international opprobrium, and securing Chinese interests more effectively.[37]

Over time, the Chinese government appeared truly to have accepted cooperative multilateralism as a means to take advantage of its strengths as an attractive economic and trading opportunity.[38] A more mixed picture has continued to prevail on human rights, environmental, energy, and international security questions, including arms control. While more cooperative in several instances, China remains concerned to defend narrow Chinese national interests, and it is particularly on guard in the face of possible U.S.-led efforts to constrain Chinese power.[39]

China's Growing Military Power: Mixed Implications for China's Foreign Influence

There is probably no more important reason for continuing international uncertainty about China's approach to world affairs than the apparent disconnect between China's national development policy and China's national security policy. Chinese officials are the first to highlight that China in recent years has crafted a relatively clear national development policy. That Chinese approach was laid out authoritatively in the December 2005 Chinese government document "China's Peaceful Development Road," and has been repeated in similar documents, most recently in late 2010. This approach is consistent with the thrust of Chinese leadership pronouncements since 2003, emphasizing Chinese leaders' determination to avoid trouble abroad and to seek international cooperation and a harmonious world order as China develops and rises peacefully in importance in Asian and world affairs in the twenty-first century.[40]

Unfortunately, the December 2005 document and the follow-on documents make little or no reference to military conflict, the role of the rapidly modernizing People's Liberation Army (PLA), and other key national security questions. When asked about this, one senior Chinese Foreign Ministry official said in May 2006 that China's national security policy is less clearly developed than China's national development policy.[41] In fact, however, the broad outlines of Chinese national security policy are fairly clearly laid out in official Chinese documents and briefings.[42] They—and the remarkable recent advances in China's military modernization in the post–Cold War period—are in the lead among Chinese statements and behaviors that have called into question just how peaceful and cooperative China's approach to Asia and the world actually will be.

Foreign specialists on the Chinese military pointed out seeming contrasts and contradictions in recent Chinese official pronouncements and actions dealing with trends in international security. Authoritative Chinese foreign policy pronouncements emphasized China's view of an emerging harmonious world order in which China was rising peacefully in national strength and international influence. China often was seen as occupying its most influential position in world affairs in the modern era. In contrast, white papers on national security,[43] recent public presentations by authoritative

Chinese military representatives, and the continuation of an impressive buildup and modernization of the Chinese military forces in recent years have revealed the Chinese leadership's strong concern about China's security in the prevailing regional and international order. This concern has continued despite almost twenty years of double-digit-percentage increases in China's defense budgets and despite the view of many foreign specialists that China was becoming Asia's undisputed leading military power and an increasingly serious concern to American security planners as they sought to preserve stability and U.S. leadership in Asia. [44]

Chinese military modernization programs have been under way for thirty years. They have reached the point where they strongly suggest that the objective of the Chinese leadership is to build Asia's most powerful defense force. [45] China's military growth complicated China's relations with the United States and some Asian neighbors, notably Taiwan, Japan, India, Vietnam, and South Korea, as well as such countries as Indonesia, the Philippines, Australia, and New Zealand. Leaders from the United States and some Asian countries were not persuaded by Chinese leadership pledges to pursue the road of peace and development. They saw Chinese national security policies and programs as real or potential threats to their security interests. [46]

Chinese national security pronouncements duly acknowledged that with the end of the Cold War, the danger of global war—a staple in Chinese warning statements in the 1970s and 1980s—ended. However, recent Chinese national security statements rarely highlighted the fact that Chinese defense policy was being formulated in an environment that was less threatening to China than at any time in the past 200 years. Typically, in the 2010 white paper on national defense, the international system was represented as stable, but "international strategic competition" was "intensifying," "security threats" were "increasingly" volatile, and "world peace" was "elusive." The carefully measured Chinese response to the Obama government's recent emphasis since 2011 on military as well as economic and political reengagement with Asia reflected thinly disguised Chinese suspicion of a revival of American efforts to constrain and contain China's spreading influence. [47]

PLA pronouncements and Western scholarship made clear that the United States remained at the center of the national security concerns of Chinese leaders. [48] The 2004 white paper presented a widening military imbalance of grave concern to China caused by U.S. military technological advances and doctrinal changes referred to as the "World Wide Revolution in Military Affairs (RMA)." Authoritative PLA briefings in 2008 presented growing

U.S. military power as the most serious complication for China's international interests, China's main security concern in the Asian region, and the key
military force behind Chinese security concerns over Taiwan, Japan, and
other neighbors. Explaining China's concerns in the Asia-Pacific region, the
2010 white paper warned that "the United States is reinforcing its regional
military alliances, and increasing its involvement in regional security affairs."

Chinese statements and the PLA buildup opposite Taiwan underlined that
Taiwan was the most likely area of military conflict. And the United States
and its military allies were portrayed as the principal sources of potential
regional instability in Asia. China responded harshly to indications of closer
U.S.-Japanese strategic cooperation over Taiwan, notably a statement supporting a peaceful resolution of the Taiwan issue that was released following
the U.S.-Japan Security Consultative Committee meeting in February 2005.
The Chinese Foreign Ministry claimed that U.S. Secretary of State Hillary
Clinton's intervention concerning disputes in the South China Sea at the
ASEAN Regional Forum (ARM) meeting in Hanoi in July 2010 represented
an "attack on China."[49]

The PLA and other Chinese officials registered strong determination to
protect Chinese territory and territorial claims, including areas having strategic resources such as oil and gas. As Chinese-Japanese and other territorial
conflicts involving energy resources in the East and South China seas grew
in scope and intensity, they intruded ever more directly on these PLA priorities. Chinese concerns increased over U.S. and allied forces controlling sea
lines of communication, which were essential for increasing oil flows to
China. The Chinese government appeared uncertain as to the seriousness of
the strategic danger posed by the vulnerability of China's energy flows from
the Middle East and Africa through the Malacca Strait and other choke points
in Southeast Asia and what should be done about it. Chinese national security
officials openly debated these issues.[50] The solutions pursued included overland oil and gas pipelines that would bypass the Malacca Strait and the
steady buildup of Chinese naval capabilities, including the development of
Chinese aircraft carriers that would provide more military capability to protect Chinese trade, energy flows, and other maritime communications.[51]

Given the recent record of U.S. policies and behavior regarding China,
the concern Chinese leaders had over the strategic intentions of the United
States concerning Taiwan, Japan, Asia, and world affairs was not unwar-
ranted. The George W. Bush administration worked more closely with Tai-

wan's government in efforts to support Taiwan's defense against China than any U.S. administration since the break in official U.S. relations with Taiwan in 1979. It also worked more closely in defense collaboration with Japan, which focused on Taiwan and other possible contingencies regarding China, than at any time since the normalization of U.S. and Japanese relations with China in the 1970s. Policy statements such as the National Security Strategy of the United States of 2002 and the Quadrennial Defense Report of 2006 made clear that the U.S. military was able and willing to take steps to sustain Asian stability in the face of possible adverse consequences of China's rising military strength. Bush administration leaders emphasized U.S. uncertainty over China's longer-term strategic intentions; they affirmed that they were not fully persuaded by Chinese pronouncements on peace and development and remained unsure if China would be a friend or a foe of the United States. They built up U.S. forces in Asia and collaborated with Japan and other allies and partners, including India, in part to ensure that U.S. interests and Asian stability would be sustained in the face of possible disruptive or negative actions by Chinese military forces.

The Barack Obama administration continued American resolve in the face of China's military buildup as it carried out the most significant U.S. reengagement with the Asia-Pacific region in many years. Speaking to reporters on the way to Beijing in January 2011, Secretary of Defense Robert Gates publicly affirmed U.S. determination to deal effectively with Chinese advancing military capabilities.[52]

In this context, it appeared reasonable for Chinese leaders to carry out the acquisition, development, and advancement of military capabilities specifically designed to defeat U.S. forces, especially if they were to intrude in a confrontation regarding China's avowed top priority: restoring Taiwan to Chinese sovereignty. And as the Chinese leaders devoted ever greater effort to this military buildup, the U.S. advancement of its military deployments and defense cooperation with Taiwan, Japan, Australia, India, and others also seemed logical in order to deter Chinese attack and preserve stability. Of course, the result was an escalating arms race and defense preparations that seemed very much at odds with the harmonious international environment Chinese leaders sought to nurture and sustain. In effect, the respective Chinese and U.S. defense buildups and preparations regarding Taiwan demonstrated that Chinese leaders were not prepared to pursue uniformly "the road to peace and development" set forth in the document "China's Peaceful Development Road." The emphasis on peace and development and a harmonious international environment clearly were goals of Chinese foreign policy, but Chinese leaders at the same time were hedging their bets, notably with an impressive array of military acquisitions that provided capabilities they judged necessary.[53]

Overall, Chinese defense acquisition and advancement showed broad ambitions for Chinese military power. While they appeared focused recently on dealing with U.S. forces in the event of a Taiwan contingency, these forces can be used by Chinese leaders as deemed appropriate in a variety of circumstances.[54] Salient Chinese defense acquisitions and modernization efforts include the following:[55]

- Research and development in space systems to provide wide-area intelligence, surveillance, and reconnaissance and the development of antisatellite systems to counter the surveillance and related efforts of potential adversaries
- Cruise missile acquisitions and programs that improve the range, speed, and accuracy of Chinese land-, air-, and sea-launched weapons
- Ballistic missile programs that improve the range, survivability (through mobile systems in particular), reliability, accuracy, and response times of tactical, regional, and intercontinental-range weapons to augment or replace current systems
- Development of ballistic missiles capable of targeting U.S. or other naval combatants
- Construction and acquisition of advanced conventional-powered submarines with subsurface-launched cruise missiles and guided torpedoes and nuclear-powered attack and ballistic missile submarines to augment or replace older vessels in service
- Development and acquisition of more capable naval surface ships armed with advanced antiship, antisubmarine, and air defense weapons
- Air force advances, including hundreds of modern multirole fighters, advanced air-to-air missiles, airborne early warning and control system aircraft, aerial refueling capabilities, and unmanned aerial vehicles
- Air defense systems involving modern surface-to-air missiles and air defense fighters
- Improved power projection for ground forces, including more sea- and airlift capabilities, special operations forces, and amphibious warfare capabilities

- Research and development of defense information systems and improved command, control, communications, and computer systems
- Development of cyber warfare capabilities
- Increasing the tempo and complexity of exercises in order to make the PLA capable in joint interservice operations involving power projections, including amphibious operations

As noted in chapter 1, the Chinese advances mean that no single Asian power can match China's military power on continental Asia. With the possible exception of Japan, no Asian country will be capable of challenging China's naval power and airpower in maritime eastern Asia. Should Beijing choose to deploy naval and air forces to patrol the sea lines of communications in the Indian Ocean, only India conceivably would be capable of countering China's power.[56]

Looking to the future, it is possible to limit the scope of China's military buildup. Available evidence shows that it is focused on nearby Asia. The major possible exceptions include the long-range nuclear weapons systems that target outside Asia and cyber warfare and space warfare capabilities. China has used its long-range nuclear weapons to deter the United States and other potential adversaries by demonstrating a retaliatory, second-strike capability against them.[57]

The objectives of the Chinese military buildup seem focused first on Taiwan, preventing its move toward independence and ensuring that China's sovereignty will be protected and restored. More generally, Chinese forces can be deployed to defeat possible threats or attacks on China, especially China's economically important eastern coastline. Apart from conflict over Taiwan, they are designed to deal with a range of so-called local war possibilities. These could involve territorial disputes with Japan, Southeast Asian countries, or India or instability requiring military intervention in Korea. Meanwhile, the Chinese military plays a direct role in Chinese foreign policy, which seeks to spread Chinese international influence, reassure neighboring countries and others of Chinese intentions, and nurture an international environment that will allow China to rise in power and influence without major disruption. This role likely will involve continued active diplomacy by Chinese military officials, increasing numbers of military exercises with Asian and other countries, some Chinese arms sales to and training of foreign military forces, and more active participation by Chinese national security officials in regional and other multilateral security organizations and agreements.[58]

The Chinese military is on course to continue a transformation from its past strategic outlook, that of a large continental power requiring large land forces for defense against threats to borders. The end of the threat from the Soviet Union and the improvement of China's relations with India, Vietnam, and others have eased this concern. China is likely to move further away from a continental orientation requiring large land forces to a combined continental/maritime orientation requiring smaller, more mobile, and more sophisticated forces capable of protecting China's inland and coastal periphery. Unlike the doctrine of protracted land war against an invading enemy prevalent until the latter years of the Cold War, Chinese doctrine probably will continue its more recent emphasis on the need to demonstrate an ability to attack first in order to deter potential adversaries and to carry out first strikes in order to gain the initiative in the battlefield and secure Chinese objectives.

To fulfill these objectives, Chinese forces will need and will further develop the ability to respond rapidly, to take and maintain the initiative in the battlefield, to prevent escalation, and to resolve the conflict quickly and on favorable terms. Chinese military options will include preemptive attacks and the use of conventional and nuclear forces to deter and coerce adversaries. Chinese forces will expand power-projection capabilities, giving Chinese forces a solid ability to deny critical land and sea access (e.g., Taiwan Strait) to adversaries and providing options for force projection farther from Chinese borders.[59]

To achieve these objectives, Chinese conventional ground forces will evolve, consistent with recent emphasis, toward smaller, more flexible, highly trained, and well-equipped rapid reaction forces with more versatile and well-developed assault, airborne, and amphibious power-projection capabilities. Special operations forces will play an important role in these efforts. Navy forces will build on recent advances with more advanced surface combatants and submarines having better air defense, antisubmarine warfare, and antiship capabilities. Their improved weaponry of cruise missiles and torpedoes, an improved naval air force, and greater replenishment-at-sea capabilities will broaden the scope of their activities and pose greater challenges to potential adversaries. Air forces will grow with more versatile and modern fighters, longer-range interceptor/strike aircraft, improved early warning and air defense, and longer-range transport, lift, and midair refueling capabilities.

These forces will be used increasingly in an integrated way consistent with an emphasis on joint operations that involve more sophisticated command, control, communications, computers, intelligence, and strategic reconnaissance (C4ISR) early warning and battlefield management systems. Improved airborne and satellite-based systems will improve detection, tracking, targeting, and strike capabilities and enhanced operational coordination of the various forces.

Chinese strategic planners are sure to build on the advantages that Chinese strategic missile systems provide. Estimates vary, but it appears likely that Chinese plans call for over 1,500 short-, medium-, and intermediate-range solid-fueled, mobile ballistic missiles (with a range under 4,000 miles) and short-range cruise missiles with increased accuracy and some with both nuclear and conventional capabilities. China is also modernizing a small number of longer-range nuclear missiles capable of hitting the continental United States and seems likely to develop a viable submarine-launched nuclear missile that would broaden Chinese nuclear options. Chinese nuclear missiles will have smaller and more powerful warheads with potential multiple independently targeted reentry vehicles or multiple reentry vehicle capabilities. The emphasis on modern surveillance, early warning, and battle management systems with advanced C4ISR assets seen in Chinese planning regarding conventional forces also applies to nuclear forces.

These advances pose concerns for the United States, Taiwan, Japan, and many other neighbors of China, and they will build on China's existing military abilities. Those abilities include the following:

- The ability to conduct intensive, short-duration air and naval attacks on Taiwan as well as prolonged air, naval, and possibly ground attacks. China's ability to prevail against Taiwan is seen as increasing steadily, especially given less than robust defense preparedness and political division in Taiwan. Massive U.S. military intervention is viewed as capable of defeating a Chinese invasion, but Chinese area denial capabilities could substantially impede and slow the U.S. intervention.
- Power-projection abilities to dislodge smaller regional powers from nearby disputed land and maritime territories and the ability to conduct air and sea denial operations for 200 miles along China's coasts.
- Strong abilities to protect Chinese territory from invasion, to conduct ground-based power projection along land borders against smaller regional powers, and to strike civilian and military targets with a large and

growing inventory of ballistic missiles and medium-range bombers armed with cruise missiles.

- A limited ability to project force against the territory of militarily capable neighboring states, notably Russia, India, and Japan.
- Continued ability to deter nuclear and other attacks from the United States and Russia by means of modernized and survivable Chinese nuclear missile forces capable of striking at these powers.

As China's military capabilities continue to grow more rapidly than those of any of its neighbors and as China solidifies its position as Asia's leading military power, the situation clearly poses serious implications for and some complications in China's foreign policy. As I have discussed, Chinese officials have worked hard and with some success to persuade skeptical neighbors, the United States, and other concerned governments that China's rising power and influence will be peaceful and of benefit to all. However, many neighboring officials and those in the United States and elsewhere, sometimes publicly and more often privately, remain concerned.

The history of the use of force in Chinese foreign policy provides little assurance that China's current peaceful emphasis will be sustained. The Chinese government has resorted to the use of force in international affairs more than most governments in the modern period. People's Republic of China security forces have at various times crossed the borders of most of China's neighboring countries. The reasons have varied and include Chinese determination to deter perceived superpower aggression, defend Chinese territory and territorial claims, recover lost territory, and enhance China's regional and global stature. Studies of Chinese leaders' strategic thinking have led to the conclusion that modern Chinese leaders, like those in the past, have been more inclined than not to see the use of military force as an effective instrument of statecraft.[60]

Although facing superpower adversaries with much greater military might, Mao Zedong frequently initiated the use of military force to keep the more powerful adversary off balance and to keep the initiative in Chinese hands. Deng Xiaoping was much more focused than Mao on conventional Chinese nation building and sought to foster a peaceful environment around China's periphery in order to pursue Chinese economic modernization. However, Deng also undertook in 1979 strong Chinese military action against Soviet-backed Vietnam, and he continued for several years to confront Soviet power throughout China's periphery despite China's military weakness relative to the Soviet superpower. In the post–Cold War period, Chinese officials judged that the Taiwan president's visit to the United States in 1995 so challenged Chinese interests that it warranted nine months of military tensions in the Taiwan Strait. These tensions included live-fire military exercises, ballistic missile tests near Taiwan ports, and a private warning from a senior Chinese military leader of China's determination to use nuclear weapons to deter U.S. intervention in a Taiwan confrontation.[61]

China's growing stake in the international status quo and its dependence on smooth international economic interchange are seen to argue against Chinese leaders' resorting to military force to achieve international objectives. At the same time, the rapid development of Chinese military capabilities to project power and the change in Chinese doctrine to emphasize striking first to achieve Chinese objectives are seen to increase the likelihood of Chinese use of force to achieve the ambitions and objectives of the Chinese government. Against this background, it is not surprising that an active debate continues about Chinese national security intentions and whether they will override the Chinese government's public emphasis on promoting peace and development in Chinese foreign affairs.

Overall, the ongoing debate over how and why China will use its advancing international economic and military power adds to uncertainty about China's future course. Despite the growing sinews of Chinese economic and military power, Chinese leaders may remain preoccupied at home, pursuing "win-win" policies that avoid significant risk and cost for China and avoiding disruption of the strategic opportunity posed by an international environment supported by the United States and others that serves Chinese priority concerns with advancing domestic development. Such a posture appears to restrict China's importance in world affairs, and contrasts notably with the decisive actions in foreign policy undertaken by Mao Zedong and Deng Xiaoping, which greatly influenced past international calculations of China's regional and global importance.

On the other hand, episodes in recent years of Chinese assertiveness against the United States and Chinese neighbors over important sovereignty and security issues in particular demonstrate that Chinese leaders may soon reach a point where China's rising capabilities and continued dissatisfaction with prevailing international conditions may lead to a stronger and more forceful approach to regional and other issues. China's international importance under those circumstances would rise accordingly, in ways probably not in the interests of China's neighbors, the United States, and other concerned powers.

NOTES

1. Tang Tsou, *America's Failure in China, 1941–1950* (Chicago: University of Chicago Press, 1963); Zi Zhongyun, *No Exit? The Origin and Evolution of US Policy toward China, 1945–1950* (Norwalk, CT: Eastbridge, 2004).

2. William Stueck, *The Road to Confrontation: American Policy toward China and Korea, 1947–1950* (Chapel Hill: University of North Carolina Press, 1981).

3. Gordon Chang, *Friends and Enemies: The United States, China, and the Soviet Union, 1948–1972* (Stanford, CA: Stanford University Press, 1990); Su Ge, *Meiguo: Dui hua Zhengce yu Taiwan wenti* [America: China policy and the Taiwan issue] (Beijing: Shijie Zhishi Chubanshe, 1998).

4. Robert Sutter, *China-Watch* (Baltimore: Johns Hopkins University Press, 1978), pp. 40–42.

5. John Garver, *Foreign Relations of the People's Republic of China* (Englewood Cliffs, NJ: Prentice Hall, 1993), pp. 125–27.

6. Alice Lyman Miller and Richard Wich, *Becoming Asia* (Stanford, CA: Stanford University Press, 2011), pp. 122–36; Robert Sutter, *Historical Dictionary of Chinese Foreign Policy* (Lanham, MD: Scarecrow, 2011), pp. 117–18, 242.

7. Evelyn Goh, *Constructing the U.S. Rapprochement with China* (New York: Cambridge University Press, 2005).

8. Luella Christopher, *United States–Soviet Union–China: The Great Power Triangle* (Summary of hearings conducted by the Subcommittee on Future Foreign Policy Research and Development of the Committee on International Relations, October–December 1975, March–June 1976) (Washington, DC: U.S. Government Printing Office, 95th Congress, 1st session, Committee print, 1997).

9. Robert S. Ross, ed., *China, The United States and the Soviet Union: Tri-polarity and Policy Making in the Cold War* (Armonk, NY: M. E. Sharpe, 1993).

10. Miller and Wich, *Becoming Asia*, pp. 174–202.

11. David W. P. Elliott, ed., *The Third Indochina Conflict* (Boulder, CO: Westview, 1981); Miller and Wich, *Becoming Asia*, pp. 191–93.

12. Robert Sutter, *Chinese Foreign Policy: Developments after Mao* (New York: Praeger, 1986), pp. 162–64, 189–91.

13. Ezra Vogel, *Deng Xiaoping and the Transformation of China* (Cambridge, MA: Harvard University Press, 2011), pp. 266–93.

14. See debates and differing views of China's international economic importance in "'China Model' 30 Years on: From Home and Abroad," *People's Daily online*, April 21, 2011, www.english.peopledaily.com.cn; Evan Medeiros, "Is Beijing Ready for Global Leadership?" *Current History* 108, no. 719 (September 2009): pp. 250–56; Qu Xing, "China's Real Responsibilities," *China Daily*, February 18–20, 2011, p.12; Stephan Halper, *The Beijing Consensus* (New York: Basic Books, 2010); Martin Jacques, *When China Rules the World* (London: Penguin, 2009); C. Fred Bergsten et al., *China's Rise: Challenges and Opportunities* (Washington, DC: Peterson Institute/CSIS 2008); David M. Lampton, *The Three Faces of Chinese Power* (Berkeley: University of California Press, 2008); U.S. Senate, Committee on Foreign

Relations, *China's Foreign Policy and "Soft Power" in South America, Asia, and Africa* (Washington, DC: U.S. Government Printing Office, 2008).

15. "Nation to Chip In More for UN Kitty," *China Daily*, December 31, 2009, p. 2.

16. Xin Zhiming, "Government Clears $5.4b World Bank Loan," *China Daily*, July 25, 2008, p. 13; Asian Development Bank, *Asian Development Bank and the People's Republic of China: 2008 A Fact Sheet*, www.adb.org; Fu Jing and Hu Haiyan, "China, UN Jointly Unveil Five-Year Aid Framework," *China Daily*, April 2, 2010; Gillian Wong, "China Rises and Rises, Yet Still Gets Foreign Aid," Associated Press, September 27, 2010, www.ap.com; Antoine Dechezlepretre, et al., "Technology Transfer by CDM Projects," *Energy Policy* 37, no. 2 (2009): p. 1; Keith Bradsher, "China Leading Global Race to Make Clean Energy," *New York Times*, January 31, 2010, www.nytimes.com (accessed February 2, 2010); The World Bank, "Global Environmental Facility (GEF) Projects in China," July 2009; The World Bank, "World Bank, GEF-Backed Energy Efficiency Program Expands in China," January 2008; Asian Development Bank, *Asian Development Bank and People's Republic of China: Fact Sheet*, December 2008, p. 3.

17. Qu Xing, "China's Real Responsibilities."

18. Wayne Morrison, *China's Economic Conditions*, Report 33534 (Washington, DC: Library of Congress, Congressional Research Service, June 26, 2012), pp. 10–25.

19. Morrison, *China's Economic Conditions*, p. 17; trade figures used in this section are from the UN COMTRADE database atcomtrade.un.org/db.

20. Morrison, *China's Economic Conditions*, p. 15; "Foreign Investment in China Hits Record in 2010," Agence France Presse, January 18, 2011, www.afp.com; Ding Qingfen, "ODI Set to Overtake FDI 'within Three Years,'" *China Daily*, May 6, 2011, p. 1; Xin Zhiming, "Trade Surplus Reaches New Peak," *China Daily*, September 11, 2008, p. 13; Morrison, *China's Economic Conditions* (2009), pp. 4–9; Diao Ying, "Firms Urged to Diversify Export Markets," *China Daily*, December 24, 2008, p. 1.

21. "'China Model' 30 Years on"; Halper, *The Beijing Consensus*.

22. Yu Yongding, "A Different Road Forward," *China Daily*, December 23, 2010, p. 9.

23. Morrison, *China's Economic Conditions*, 1; David M. Lampton, *The Three Faces of Chinese Power* (Berkeley: University of California Press, 2008), pp. 78–116.

24. Zhang Yunling, "China and Its Neighbors: Relations in a New Context," in *Making New Partnership: A Rising China and Its Neighbors*, ed. Zhang Yunling (Beijing: Social Science Academic Press, 2008), pp. 1–18.

25. See varying perspectives on these points in Arvind Subramanian, "The Inevitable Superpower: Why China's Rise Is a Sure Thing," *Foreign Affairs* 90, no. 5 (September–October 2011): pp. 66–78; Carl Dahlman, *The World under Pressure: How China and India Are Influencing the Global Economy and Environment* (Stanford, CA: Stanford University Press, 2011); Bates Gill, *Rising Star: China's New Security Diplomacy* (Washington, DC: Brookings Institution, 2007); Joshua Kurlantzick, *Charm Offensive* (New Haven, CT: Yale University Press, 2007); David Kang, *China Rising: Peace, Power and Order in East Asia* (New York: Columbia University Press, 2007); and David Shambaugh, "China Engages Asia: Reshaping the Regional Order," *International Security* 29, no. 3 (Winter 2004–2005): pp. 64–99.

26. Zheng Bijian, "China's 'Peaceful Rise' to Great-Power Status," *Foreign Affairs* 84, no. 5 (2005): pp. 18–24; People's Republic of China State Council Information Office, "China's Peaceful Development Road," *People's Daily Online*, December 22, 2005, english.peopledaily.com.cn (accessed July 7, 2006); Rosemary Foot, "Chinese Strategies in a U.S.-Hegemonic Global Order: Accommodating and Hedging," *International Affairs* 82, no. 1 (2006): pp. 77–94; Susan Shirk, *China: Fragile Superpower* (New York: Oxford University Press, 2007); Yu, "A Different Road Forward"; Qu, "China's Real Responsibilities."

27. Morrison, *China's Economic Conditions*, 26–32.

28. Samuel Kim, *The Two Koreas and the Great Powers* (New York: Cambridge University Press, 2006).

29. Michael Glosny, "Heading toward a Win-Win Future? Recent Developments in China's Policy toward Southeast Asia," *Asian Security* 2, no. 1 (2006): pp. 24–57.

30. Michael Yahuda, *The International Politics of the Asia-Pacific* (London: RoutledgeCurzon, 2004) 298–305; Jing-Dong Yuan, "China's Role in Establishing and Building the Shanghai Cooperation Organization (SCO)," *Journal of Contemporary China* 19, no. 67 (November 2010): pp. 855–70; Wu Xinbo, "Chinese Perspectives on Building an East Asian Community in the Twenty-First Century," in *Asia's New Multilateralism*, ed. Michael Green and Bates Gill (New York: Columbia University Press, 2009), pp. 55–77; Robert Sutter, *Historical Dictionary of Chinese Foreign Policy* (Lanham, MD: Scarecrow, 2011), pp. 54, 111.

31. Jianwei Wang, "China's Multilateral Diplomacy in the New Millennium," in *China Rising: Power and Motivation in Chinese Foreign Policy*, ed. Yong Deng and Fei-Ling Wang (Lanham, MD: Rowman & Littlefield, 2005), pp. 159–66.

32. David Zweig and Bi Jianhai, "China's Global Hunt for Energy," *Foreign Affairs* 84, no. 5 (September–October 2005): 25–38.

33. Jianwei Wang, "China's Multilateral Diplomacy," pp. 166–77; Yahuda, *The International Politics of the Asia-Pacific*, pp. 298–305.

34. Shi Jiangtao, "China's Carbon Pollution Could Match US on Per Capita Basis by 2017," *South China Morning Post*, September 20, 2012, www.scmp.com (accessed October 9, 2012).

35. Ming Wan, "Democracy and Human Rights in Chinese Foreign Policy," in Deng and Wang, eds., *China Rising*, pp. 279–304.

36. Evan Medeiros, *Reluctant Restraint: The Evolution of China's Nonproliferation Policies and Practices, 1980–2004* (Stanford, CA: Stanford University Press, 2007).

37. Bates Gill, "Two Steps Forward, One Step Back: The Dynamics of Chinese Nonproliferation and Arms Control Policy-Making in an Era of Reform," in *The Making of Chinese Foreign and Security Policy in the Era of Reform*, ed. David M. Lampton (Stanford, CA: Stanford University Press, 2001), pp. 257–88; Alastair Iain Johnston and Paul Evans, "China's Engagement," in *Engaging China*, ed. Alastair Iain Johnston and Robert Ross (New York: Routledge, 1999), p. 253.

38. Margaret Pearson, "China in Geneva: Lessons from China's Early Years in the World Trade Organization," in *New Directions in the Study of China's Foreign Policy*, ed. Alastair Iain Johnston and Robert S. Ross (Stanford, CA: Stanford University Press, 2006), pp. 242–75.

39. Samuel Kim, "Chinese Foreign Policy Faces Globalization Challenges," in Johnston and Ross, eds., *New Directions in the Study of China's Foreign Policy*, pp. 276–308.

40. People's Republic of China State Council Information Office, "China's Peaceful Development Road," *People's Daily Online*, December 22, 2005, english.peopledaily.com.cn (accessed July 7, 2006); "Full Text of Chinese President Hu Jintao's Speech at Opening Session of Boao Forum," *China Daily*, April 15, 2011, www.chinadaily.com.cn.

41. Interview, Chinese Foreign Ministry, Beijing, May 30, 2006.

42. I benefited notably from comprehensive briefings on China's national security policy given by leaders of the PLA's Academy of Military Science in Beijing in June 2008 and June 2011 and briefings by senior representatives of the academy at a public meeting at Georgetown University, Washington, D.C., in October 2008.

43. People's Republic of China State Council Information Office, "China's National Defense in 2004" (Beijing, December 27, 2004); People's Republic of China State Council Information Office, "China's National Defense in 2006" (Beijing, December 29, 2006); People's Republic of China State Council Information Office, "China's National Defense in 2008"

(Beijing, January 2009); People's Republic of China State Council Information Office, "China's National Defense in 2010" (Beijing, March 2011).

44. Paul Godwin, "China as a Major Asian Power: The Implications of Its Military Modernization (A View from the United States)," in *China, the United States, and Southeast Asia: Contending Perspectives on Politics, Security, and Economics*, ed. Evelyn Goh and Sheldon Simon (New York: Routledge, 2008), pp. 145–66.

45. Chu Shulong and Lin Xinzhu, "It Is Not the Objective of Chinese Military Power to Catch Up and Overtake the United States," *Huanqiu Shibao* (Beijing), June 26, 2008, p. 11.

46. U.S. Department of Defense, *Annual Report to Congress: Military and Security Developments Involving the People's Republic of China 2012* (Washington, DC: U.S. Department of Defense, May 2012).

47. People's Republic of China State Council Information Office, "China's National Defense in 2010," p. 4; Martin Indyk, Kenneth Lieberthal, Michael O'Hanlon, *Bending History: Barack Obama's Foreign Policy* (Washington, DC: Brookings Institution, 2012), pp. 61–62.

48. David Shambaugh, "Coping with a Conflicted China," *Washington Quarterly* 34, no. 1 (Winter 2011): pp. 7–27; M. Taylor Fravel, "China's Search for Military Power," *Washington Quarterly* 33, no. 3 (Summer 2008): pp. 125–141; briefings by Major General Luo Yuan and Senior Colonel Fan Gaoyue of the Academy of Military Science, Georgetown University, Washington, DC, October 2, 2008; People's Republic of China State Council Information Office, "China's National Defense in 2010," p. 4.

49. Hu Xiao, "Japan and U.S. Told, Hands Off Taiwan," *China Daily*, March 7, 2005, p. 1; Academy of Military Science briefings, June 2008, October 2008; People's Republic of China State Council Information Office, "China's National Defense in 2004"; "Chinese FM Refutes Fallacies on the South China Sea Issue," *China Daily*, July 25, 2010, p. 1.

50. "China-Southeast Asia Relations," *Comparative Connections* 9, no. 3 (October 2007): p. 75, www.csis.org/pacfor.

51. "China-Southeast Asia Relations," *Comparative Connections* 10, no. 4 (January 2009), www.csis.org/pacfor.

52. Evan Medeiros, "Strategic Hedging and the Future of Asia-Pacific Stability," *Washington Quarterly* 29, no. 1 (2005–2006): pp. 145–67; Elizabeth Bumiller, "U.S. Will Counter Chinese Arms Buildup," *New York Times*, January 8, 2011, www.nytimes.com.

53. Richard Bush and Michael O'Hanlon, *A War Like No Other: The Truth about China's Challenge to America* (Hoboken, NJ: Wiley, 2007).

54. Dan Blumenthal, "Fear and Loathing in Asia," *Journal of International Security Affairs* (Spring 2006): pp. 81–88.

55. Paul Godwin, "China as a Major Asian Power"; U.S. Department of Defense, *Annual Report to Congress: Military and Security Developments Involving the People's Republic of China 2012*; Andrew Erickson and David Yang, "On the Verge of a Game-Changer," *Proceedings* (May 2009), pp. 26–32.

56. Ashley J. Tellis and Travis Tanner, eds., *Strategic Asia 2012–13: China's Military Challenge* (Seattle, WA: National Bureau of Asian Research, 2012).

57. Michael Swaine, "China's Regional Military Posture," in *Power Shift: China and Asia's New Dynamics*, ed. David Shambaugh (Berkeley: University of California Press, 2005), p. 266; David M. Lampton, *The Three Faces of Chinese Power* (Berkeley: University of California Press, 2008), pp. 40–42.

58. David Shambaugh, "China's Military Modernization: Making Steady and Surprising Progress," in *Strategic Asia 2005–2006*, ed. Ashley Tellis and Michael Wills (Seattle, WA: National Bureau of Asian Research, 2005), pp. 67–104; Bates Gill, *Rising Star: China's New Security Diplomacy* (Washington, DC: Brookings Institution, 2007).

59. The discussion here and in the following several paragraphs is adapted from Swaine, "China's Regional Military Posture," pp. 268–72; see also U.S. Department of Defense, *Annual Report to Congress: Military and Security Developments Involving the People's Republic of China 2012.*

60. John Garver, *Foreign Relations of the People's Republic of China* (Englewood Cliffs, NJ: Prentice Hall, 1993), pp. 249–64; Thomas Christensen, "Windows and War: Trend Analysis and Beijing's Use of Force," in *New Directions in the Study of China's Foreign Policy*, ed. Alastair Iain Johnston and Robert Ross (Stanford, CA: Stanford University Press, 2006), pp. 50–85.

61. Robert Suettinger, *Beyond Tiananmen* (Washington, DC: Brookings Institution, 2003), pp. 200–263.

Chapter Seven

Relations with the United States

The record of Sino-American relations discussed in this chapter shows the continued central role of the United States in the foreign policy of the People's Republic of China. The discussion acknowledges that there have been periods of intense Chinese preoccupation with domestic matters, as during the early years of the Cultural Revolution, when foreign policy in general and China's relations with the United States seemed secondary. It demonstrates that there have been periods when China's leaders saw others, notably the Soviet Union, as more threatening and thereby more important to China's interests than the United States. And it shows that there have been periods, as during the Ford and Carter administrations and in recent years, when China saw U.S. power and influence in decline.

Nevertheless, the overall record makes clear the sustained central role of the United States in the changing foreign policy calculations of Chinese leaders. Since the radical phase of the Cultural Revolution, Chinese leaders have viewed appropriate management of relations with the United States as a top priority in order to sustain China's security, preserve and enhance China's sovereignty, and advance China's economy. For its part, the United States focused on the PRC as a danger and gave a high priority to trying to isolate and contain it for twenty years in the 1950s and 1960s. With Nixon's opening, American officials for the next two decades devoted often extraordinary efforts to developing closer ties with China, initially for security reasons having to do with the threat seen posed by the Soviet Union. The 1989 Tiananmen crackdown and the end of the Cold War initiated several years when U.S. leaders, with some notable exceptions, viewed American interests in China as best served by restricting contacts and isolating China. That phase ended with the ascendance of the Chinese economy in American international calculations and the Taiwan Strait crisis of 1995–1996, which provided a wake-up call to U.S. officials who thought they could infringe on important Chinese interests without serious consequence. Since then, U.S. administrations have given a high priority to managing increasingly multifaceted and complicated relations with China.

CONFLICT AND CONTAINMENT

As noted in chapter 2, Mao Zedong and his Communist Party–led fighters faced serious challenges as they endeavored to consolidate their rule after defeating Chiang Kai-shek's Nationalist forces in the Chinese Civil War and establishing the People's Republic of China on the Chinese mainland in 1949. China had been war ravaged for decades and arguably had been without effective governance for over a century. The Communists were a rural-based movement with decades of experience in guerrilla war and supporting administrative efforts in the countryside, but with little experience in managing the complicated affairs of China's cities, its urban economy, or its national administration. Seeking needed technical and economic backing as well as guarantees and support for China's national security, the Maoist leadership endeavored to consolidate relations with the Soviet Union in an international environment heavily influenced by the United States, the main international supporter of its Chinese Nationalist adversary, and American-associated states influential in Asian and world politics. Communist China's approach toward American power also demonstrated determination to challenge the United States and its allies and associates in Asia as the Maoist leadership sought to promote revolutionary changes at home and abroad. A related tendency was to exploit episodes of confrontation with America as a means of mobilizing greater national support for those revolutionary changes. [1]

Chairman Mao Zedong and President Harry Truman did not foresee war between the United States and China in early 1950. The Americans were surprised when North Korean forces, with the support of Soviet and Chinese leaders, launched an all-out military attack against South Korean forces in June of that year. Likewise, the Chinese Communist leaders and their Korean and Soviet Communist allies were surprised when the United States quickly intervened militarily, and also sent the U.S. Seventh Fleet to prevent a Chinese Communist attack on Taiwan. By early fall, U.S. and South Korean forces with growing international support had destroyed the North Korean armies, setting the stage for new miscalculations and a wider war.[2] Ignoring Chinese warnings, U.S. and South Korean forces proceeded into North Korea, and by November hundreds of thousands of Chinese Communist forces were driving them south in full retreat. Eventually, the Americans and their allies were able to sustain a line of combat roughly in the middle of the peninsula, as the two armies faced off for over two more years of warfare.[3]

Chinese Communist leaders took the opportunity to initiate campaigns to root out domestic pro-American influence and seize control of U.S. cultural, religious, and business organizations that remained in China. For its part, the United States began a wide-ranging strategic effort to contain the expansion of Chinese power and Chinese-backed Communist expansion in Asia. A strict U.S. economic and political embargo against China, large U.S. force deployments eventually numbering between five hundred thousand and one million troops, massive aid allocations to Asian allies and supporters, and a ring of U.S. defense alliances around China were used to block Chinese expansion and to drive a wedge between China and its Soviet ally.

Employing the advantage of possessing nuclear weapons, the Eisenhower administration used threats and negotiations to reach an armistice agreement that stopped the fighting in Korea in 1953. Meanwhile, it advanced American efforts to strengthen military alliances and deployments to contain Chinese Communist–backed expansion in the region. Defeat of U.S.-backed French forces in Indochina led to the 1954 Geneva Conference and Accords that formalized French withdrawal. U.S. policy worked to support a non-Communist regime in South Vietnam, backing the regime when it resisted steps toward reunification set forth in the Geneva Accords.[4]

Although President Eisenhower and Secretary of State John Foster Dulles were wary of Chiang Kai-shek and Chinese Nationalist maneuvers that might drag the United States into a war with the Chinese Communists, they dramatically expanded U.S. military and economic assistance to Taiwan, and Washington signed a bilateral defense treaty with Taipei in December 1954.[5] Mao reacted with harsh rhetoric and military assaults against Nationalist-controlled islands off the coast of the Chinese mainland. U.S. forces helped Nationalist forces on some exposed islands to withdraw. This Taiwan Strait crisis of 1955 raised fears of renewed war between the United States and China.[6]

Chinese Premier Zhou Enlai used the Afro-Asian Conference in Bandung, Indonesia, in 1955 to ease tensions and call for high-level talks with the United States. Secretary of State Dulles was wary that direct talks with the PRC would undermine Chiang Kai-shek's Nationalist government on Taiwan, but facing congressional and allied pressures to meet with the Chinese, Dulles agreed to low-level ambassadorial talks that began in Geneva in 1955. The two sides reached an agreement on repatriating detained personnel, but the agreement was soon disputed. The U.S. side also pressed hard for a Chinese renunciation of force regarding Taiwan, effectively stopping all progress in the talks, which were suspended for a time before resuming in Warsaw in 1958. There the two sides met periodically without much result. The talks did at least provide a useful line of U.S.-PRC communication during times of crisis, as both sides strove to avoid direct military conflict.[7]

Dulles vigorously pursued a U.S. containment policy against China, favoring a tougher policy toward China than toward the Soviet Union. He endeavored thereby to force Beijing to rely on Moscow for economic and other needs that the Soviet Union could not meet. In this and other ways, he hoped to drive a wedge between China and the USSR.[8]

The Chinese-Soviet alliance in fact began to unravel by the late 1950s, and 1960 saw a clear public break, with the withdrawal of Soviet economic aid and advisers. U.S. policy makers were slow to capitalize on the situation, however, as China remained more hostile than the Soviet Union to the United States and deepening U.S. military involvement in Vietnam exacerbated U.S.-China frictions.[9]

During the 1960 presidential election campaign, Senator John F. Kennedy criticized the "tired thinking" of the outgoing administration on issues regarding China, but said little about China once he assumed office in 1961. U.S. domestic opposition, Chinese nuclear weapons development, Chinese aggression against India, and Chinese expansion into Southeast Asia were among factors that blocked meaningful U.S. initiatives toward China. Kennedy took firm action in 1962 to stop plans by Chiang Kai-shek to attack the Chinese mainland at a time of acute economic crisis in China, but continued strong U.S. backing of Chiang in the United Nations.[10]

During the administration of Lyndon Johnson, 1963–1969, escalating American military commitment and related difficulties in Vietnam dominated U.S. Asian policy. There was some movement within the U.S. government for a more flexible approach to China, consistent with growing signs of congressional and U.S. interest-group advocacy in favor of a U.S. policy of containment without isolation toward China. But it came to little, as China entered the throes of the violent and often xenophobic practices of the Cul-

tural Revolution, and American forces in Vietnam faced hundreds of thousands of Chinese support troops sent to Vietnam and Laos. Johnson was
anxious to avoid prompting a full-scale military involvement of China in the
Vietnam conflict, and American diplomats signaled these intentions using
the otherwise moribund ambassadorial talks in Warsaw. Chinese officials
made it clear that China would restrain its intervention accordingly. [11]

By early 1968, the bitter impasse in U.S.-Chinese relations had lasted two
decades and seemed unlikely to change soon. Chinese leaders were in the
midst of life-or-death struggles for power and attendant violent mass campaigns that brought conventional Chinese diplomacy to a halt and required
martial law to restore order in Chinese cities. Militant Chinese policies in
support of the Vietnamese and other Communist insurgencies in Southeast
Asia complemented a rigid Chinese stance on Taiwan, Korea, and other
issues that had divided China and the United States. U.S. leaders saw little
prospect for any significant movement in relations with the PRC as they
grappled with consuming preoccupations associated with the failing
American effort against Communist insurgents in Vietnam. [12]

RAPPROCHEMENT AND NORMALIZATION

Despite deeply rooted differences between the U.S. government and Chinese
Communist leaders on ideological, economic, and international issues, their
relations since the start of World War II witnessed a few instances where one
side or the other saw their interests served by reaching out and seeking
reconciliation and better ties with the other party. The Chinese Communists
in particular tried a moderate and accommodating approach to the United
States in greeting the American Military Observer Group to Yenan in 1944,
and in the initial ambassadorial talks following Zhou Enlai's moderate overture at Bandung in 1955. The Americans tried more tentative overtures to
Beijing in 1949, and showed interest in more flexibility toward China by the
1960s. Unfortunately, these initiatives and overtures failed, as there were
never occasions when both sides sought improved relations at the same time,
until internal and international weaknesses in 1968 and 1969 drove the United States and China closer together in a pragmatic search for ways to deal
with difficult circumstances. [13]

Difficulties in the United States in 1968 began in January when the Communist Tet offensive throughout South Vietnamese cities shattered the Johnson administration's predictions of progress in the Vietnam War and

prompted American commanders to call for 200,000 more troops in addition to the over half a million already in the country. Antiwar demonstrations in the United States grew in size and frequency. President Johnson's mandate collapsed when he did poorly in the March 12 New Hampshire primary, running against an otherwise unexceptional opponent who emphasized an antiwar platform. Johnson pulled out of the race and redoubled peace efforts in talks with the Vietnamese Communists in Paris.[14]

The assassination of Martin Luther King on April 4 set off a rampage of urban looting and burning that afflicted several American cities and notably closed Washington, D.C., for days as the city burned and fire fighting was prevented by snipers and mob violence. Order was restored only after the imposition of martial law by U.S. Army combat troops. The contentious Democratic primaries reached a conclusion in California, where Senator Robert Kennedy won, only to be assassinated on June 5 just after the victory was secured.

With Kennedy dead, antiwar advocates gathered in Chicago in August to protest the likely selection of Johnson's vice president, Hubert Humphrey, as the Democratic standard bearer. Chicago's Mayor Richard Daley and his police officers promised tough measures to deal with unauthorized demonstrations. They delivered on their promise as American television audiences watched in shock as police officers clubbed and beat demonstrators, reporters, and others they deemed obstructing the smooth flow of the convention and nearby hotel receptions.

The Republicans at their convention in August nominated Richard Nixon. On a political comeback after retreating from public life in the early 1960s, Nixon said he had a plan to deal with the Vietnam morass. He did not speak very much about an opening to China. Upon entering office, Nixon moved quickly to begin what would turn out to be the withdrawal of over 600,000 U.S. troops from around China's periphery in Asia. In his first year in office, he announced a broad framework for Asia's future without massive American troop deployments. He also made several mainly symbolic gestures to the Chinese government while pursuing vigorous efforts in secret to develop communications with the Mao Zedong leadership.

As explained in chapter 3, China was in turmoil. Mao succeeded in removing political rivals in the early years of the Cultural Revolution, but at tremendous cost. Two of the three pillars of control in the PRC, the Communist Party and the government administration, were seriously disrupted. The third pillar, the army, was called in to rule the cities with de facto martial law. Under these circumstances, China was not prepared for a national security shock.

The Soviet Union invaded Czechoslovakia in August 1968 and removed its leadership, putting in power a regime more compatible with Soviet interests. Under the so-called Brezhnev doctrine, the Soviet Union made clear that it reserved the right to take similar actions in other deviant Communist states. Chinese leaders well knew that, from the Soviet perspective, there was no Communist state more deviant than China. Some in China also were alarmed over Moscow's deploying ever-larger numbers of modern and mobile forces along the Manchurian and Sino-Mongolian borders.

The crisis and debate in the Chinese leadership saw some reaching out to the United States as a means to offset the Soviet threat. The Chinese Foreign Ministry under Zhou Enlai's direction called for renewed ambassadorial talks with the newly elected Nixon administration. Others strongly opposed an opening to the United States, with Lin Biao and his lieutenants, along with the radically Maoist leadership faction, the Gang of Four, arguing in favor of continued strong Chinese opposition to both the United States and the Soviet Union.[15]

The latter leaders held the upper hand in Chinese leadership councils during much of 1969. Chinese media rebuked and ridiculed the new U.S. president and at the last moment Chinese leaders canceled the slated ambassadorial talks in February. The Chinese authorities took the offensive in the face of Soviet military pressure along the border, ambushing a Soviet patrol on a disputed island in early March and publicizing the incident to the world. The Soviets responded with greater force, resulting in a series of escalating military clashes along the frontier. By late summer, Soviet officials were warning Americans and others abroad that the Soviet Union was in the process of consulting with foreign powers to be assured they would stand aside as the Soviet Union prepared an all-out attack on China, including the possible use of nuclear weapons.[16]

Zhou Enlai eased the tension in negotiations with Soviet leaders. China was buying time as it refused to accept Soviet demands and prepared for protracted confrontation with its new number one enemy. Zhou and others in the Chinese leadership argued for an opening to the United States to assist China against the Soviet Union, but Lin Biao and others argued that both superpowers were enemies of China and in the end they would cooperate together to isolate and control China.[17]

Mao Zedong came to side with the view associated with Zhou Enlai. Repeated initiatives by the Nixon administration ultimately succeeded and Sino-U.S. ambassadorial talks were resumed in Warsaw in early 1970. The Nixon administration's expansion of the Vietnam War by invading Cambodia in 1970 caused China to cancel the talks, however, and slowed forward movement. Nonetheless, clandestine U.S.-China communication continued, as did the withdrawal of U.S forces from Vietnam and other parts of Asia. [18]

The July 1971 announcement of Nixon's trip to China came as a surprise to most Americans, who watched with general approval and interest the president's visit to China in February 1972. Nixon privately indicated to Chinese leaders he would break U.S. ties with Taiwan and establish diplomatic relations with China in his second term. In the Shanghai Communiqué signed at the end of President Nixon's historic visit to China, both sides registered opposition to "hegemony," a code word for Soviet expansion; laid out differences on a variety of Asian and other issues; and set forth the U.S. intention to pull back militarily from Taiwan and to support a "peaceful settlement of the Taiwan question by the Chinese themselves." Subsequently, both sides agreed to establish U.S.-Chinese liaison offices staffed with senior diplomats in Beijing and Washington in 1973, despite the fact that the United States still maintained official relations with the Chinese Nationalist government in Taipei. [19]

Progress toward establishing formal U.S.-Chinese relations, the so-called normalization of relations, was delayed in the mid-1970s on account of circumstances mainly involving the United States. A politically motivated break-in at the Watergate office complex in Washington, D.C., and cover-up of the crime involved President Nixon in criminal activity. As the congressional investigation led toward impeachment, Nixon resigned in August 1974. His promise to normalize relations with China in his second term ended with his resignation. President Gerald Ford privately reaffirmed Nixon's pledge to shift diplomatic recognition from Taiwan to China, but then he backtracked in the face of U.S. domestic opposition and international circumstances. [20]

Chinese leaders did not register great dissatisfaction in the delay, as they were preoccupied with Mao's death and the most important leadership succession struggle in the history of the People's Republic of China. The struggle involved the arrest and detention of the four radical senior leaders known as the Gang of Four a few weeks after Mao's death in September 1976. The radicals were held until they were put on public trial and sentenced to prison

terms in 1980. In 1977, senior leader Deng Xiaoping—who had been removed from power at the start of the Cultural Revolution, restored to a
leadership position in 1973, and then removed again in 1976—resumed a
leadership position; Deng began a rapid comeback to power that would make
him China's most important leader by 1978. While interested in establishing
official diplomatic relations with the United States, Chinese leaders at this
time also were preoccupied with efforts to counter strong moves by the
Soviet Union to use military power and relations with allies around China's
periphery like Vietnam and India to contain and pressure China, mimicking
the U.S.-led containment effort against China earlier in the Cold War. Under
these circumstances, Chinese leaders were prepared to wait for the United
States to meet their conditions on breaking all official ties with Taiwan,
including the U.S.-Taiwan defense treaty, before moving ahead with full
normalization of PRC relations with the United States. [21]

Desiring to complete the normalization of U.S.-China relations begun by
President Nixon, President Jimmy Carter felt compelled to wait until after his
success in spring 1978 in gaining Senate passage of a controversial treaty
transferring control of the Panama Canal to Panama. A visit by Secretary of
State Cyrus Vance to China in 1977 showed that Chinese leaders were not
prepared for significant compromise on Taiwan. President Carter was aware
that a complete ending of U.S. official relations with Taiwan would alienate
many in the U.S. Senate, and he needed the support of many of these senators
for the two-thirds Senate vote of ratification on the Panama Canal treaty.
Once the Senate approved the Panama treaty in spring 1978, Carter moved
forward expeditiously with normalization with China. [22]

National Security Adviser Zbigniew Brzezinski was in the lead in seeking
rapid progress in normalizing U.S.-China relations in 1978, and in subsequent steps, as a means to counter Soviet power and expansion. Carter followed Brzezinski's advice against that of Secretary of State Cyrus Vance,
who gave a higher priority to U.S.-Soviet arms control agreements. The
United States–China communiqué announced in December 1978 established
official U.S. relations with the People's Republic of China under conditions
whereby the United States recognized the PRC as the government of China,
acknowledged that Taiwan was part of China, ended official U.S. relations
with the Republic of China (ROC) government on Taiwan, and terminated
the U.S. defense treaty with the ROC on Taiwan. Official U.S. statements
underlined American interest that Taiwan's future be settled peacefully and
that the United States would continue sales of defensive arms to Taipei. [23]

U.S. and especially Chinese leaders used the signs of their improved relations in the communiqué and during Chinese leader Deng Xiaoping's widely publicized visit to the United States in January 1979 to underline Sino-U.S. cooperation against "hegemony," notably a Soviet-backed Vietnamese military assault against Cambodia beginning in late December 1978. In February 1979, Deng launched a large-scale Chinese military offensive into Vietnam's northern region. Chinese forces withdrew after a few weeks; however, they maintained strong artillery attacks and other military pressure against Vietnamese border positions until the Vietnamese eventually agreed to withdraw from Cambodia ten years later. Carter administration officials voiced some reservations about Deng's confrontational tactics against Soviet and Vietnamese expansionism, but Sino-U.S. cooperation against the USSR and its allies increased.[24]

In pursuing normalization of relations with China, President Carter and National Security Adviser Brzezinski followed the pattern of secret diplomacy used successfully by President Nixon and National Security Adviser Henry Kissinger in early interaction with China. Thus, there was very little consultation with Congress, key U.S. allies, or the Taiwan government regarding the conditions and timing of the 1978 normalization agreement. In contrast to general U.S. congressional, media, and popular support for the surprise Nixon opening to China, President Carter and his aides notably were less successful in winning U.S. domestic support for their initiatives. Many in Congress were satisfied with the stasis that had developed in U.S.-PRC-ROC relations in the mid-1970s and were unconvinced that the United States needed to end defense and other official ties with Taiwan. They resisted the president's initiatives and passed the Taiwan Relations Act (TRA) and other laws that blocked a full break in American defense and other sensitive relations with Taiwan.[25]

The Taiwan Relations Act was passed by Congress in March 1979 and signed by President Carter on April 10, 1979. The initial draft of the legislation was proposed by the Carter administration to govern U.S. relations with Taiwan once official American ties were ended in 1979. Congress rewrote the legislation, notably adding or strengthening provisions on U.S. arms sales, opposition to threats and use of force, economic relations, human rights, and congressional oversight. Treating Taiwan as a separate entity that would continue to receive U.S. military and other support, the law appeared to contradict the American stance in the U.S.-PRC communiqué of 1978 establishing official U.S.-PRC relations. Subsequently, Chinese and Taiwan officials and their supporters in the United States competed to incline American policy toward the commitments in the U.S.-PRC communiqué or the commitments in the TRA. U.S. policy usually supported both, though it sometimes seemed more supportive of one set of commitments than the other.[26]

Running against President Carter in 1980, California Governor Ronald Reagan criticized Carter's handling of Taiwan. Asserting for a time that he would restore official relations with Taipei, Reagan later backed away from this stance but still claimed he would base his policy on the Taiwan Relations Act. The Chinese government put heavy pressure on the Reagan administration. It threatened serious deterioration in relations over various issues, but especially continuing U.S. arms sales to Taiwan. Viewing close relations with China as a key element in American strategy against the Soviet Union, Secretary of State Alexander Haig led those in the Reagan administration who favored maintaining those relations and opposed American arms sales to Taiwan that might provoke China. For a year and a half, Haig and his supporters were successful in leading U.S. efforts to accommodate PRC concerns over Taiwan, especially arms sales to the ROC, in the interest of fostering closer American-Chinese cooperation against the Soviet Union. The United States ultimately signed the August 17, 1982, communiqué with China. In the communiqué, the United States agreed gradually to diminish arms sales and China agreed it would seek peaceful reunification of Taiwan with the mainland. Subsequent developments showed that the vague agreement was subject to varying interpretations. President Reagan registered private reservations about this arrangement, and his administration also took steps to reassure Taiwan's leader of continued U.S. support.[27]

As explained in chapter 3, American policy shifted with Haig's resignation in 1982 and the appointment of George Shultz as secretary of state. American policy moved toward a less solicitous and accommodating stance toward China, while giving much higher priority to U.S. relations with Japan. There was less emphasis on China's strategic importance to the United States in American competition with the Soviet Union, and there was less concern among U.S. policy makers about China possibly downgrading relations over Taiwan and other disputes.

The Chinese leaders grudgingly adjusted to the new U.S. stance, viewing their interests best served by less pressure and more positive initiatives to the Reagan administration, seen notably in their warm welcome for the U.S. president on his visit to China in 1984. Cooperative relations with the United

States were critically important to the Chinese leadership in maintaining the flow of aid, investment, and trade essential to the economic development and modernization under way in China—the linchpin of the Communist leadership's plans for sustaining their rule in China. Meanwhile, the Reagan leadership learned not to confront the Chinese over issues like Taiwan overtly, seeking to continue U.S. military and other support for Taiwan in ways less likely to provoke strong Chinese reaction. As shown in chapter 3, Reagan's second term in office did not see repetition of the controversies that had marked Reagan's relations with China in his first term.

TIANANMEN, TAIWAN, AND POST–COLD WAR REALITIES

Unexpected mass demonstrations centered in Beijing's Tiananmen Square and other Chinese cities in spring 1989 represented the most serious challenge to China's post-Mao leadership. Deng Xiaoping was decisive in resolving Chinese leadership differences in favor of hard-liners who sought a crackdown on the demonstrators and a broader suppression of political dissent. The crackdown began with the bloody attack on Tiananmen Square on June 4, 1989. Reform-minded leaders were purged and punished. [28]

Anticipating shock and disapproval of the Tiananmen crackdown from the United States and the West, Deng nonetheless argued that the negative reaction would have few prolonged negative consequences for China. The Chinese leader failed to anticipate the breadth and depth of U.S. disapproval, which would profoundly influence American policy into the twenty-first century. The influence was compounded by the unanticipated and dramatic collapse of Communist regimes in the Soviet bloc and other areas, leading to the demise of the Soviet Union by the early 1990s. These developments undermined the perceived need for the United States to cooperate pragmatically with China against the Soviet Union. Meanwhile, Taiwan's authoritarian government was moving steadily at this time to promote democratic policies and practices, marking a sharp contrast to the harsh political authoritarianism in mainland China and greatly enhancing Taiwan's popularity and support in the United States. [29]

Taken together, these circumstances generally placed the initiative in U.S.-Chinese relations with American leaders. Chinese leaders at first focused on maintaining internal stability as they maneuvered to sustain workable economic relations with the United States while rebuffing major U.S. initiatives that infringed on Chinese internal political control or territorial and sovereignty issues involving Taiwan and Tibet. As the Chinese government presided over strong economic growth beginning in 1993, Chinese leaders reflected more confidence as they dealt with American pressures for change. However, they generally eschewed direct confrontation that would endanger the critically important economic relations with the United States. [30]

Effective U.S. policy toward China proved elusive amid contentious American domestic debate over China policy during the 1990s. That debate was not stilled until the September 11, 2001, terrorist attacks on America muffled continued U.S. concerns over China amid an overwhelming American concern to deal with the immediate and broad consequences of the global war on terrorism. [31]

RELATIONS DURING THE
GEORGE H. W. BUSH ADMINISTRATION

President George H. W. Bush, with strong personal conviction in the importance of cooperative American relations with China, at first tried to preserve cooperative ties amid widespread American outrage and pressure for retribution after the Tiananmen Square crackdown. President Bush was the most experienced U.S. chief executive in dealing with China. He had served as the head of the American liaison office in China in the mid-1970s. Bush took the lead in his own administration, 1989–1993, in dealing with the severe problems in China-U.S. relations and the decline in U.S. strategic interest in China as a result of the collapse of the Soviet bloc.

The U.S. Congress, most American media, and broad public opinion favored sanctions and other pressures on China's rulers. They focused particularly on the annual requirement for the president to notify Congress of his decision to renew "most favored nation" (MFN) tariff treatment for China's trade with the United States. As with other presidents since the normalization of relations with China, President Bush favored the renewed trade status for China; without the renewal, tariffs on Chinese imports would rise dramatically and halt most Sino-American trade. Congress annually considered legislation to disapprove or strongly condition the continuing MFN trade status for China. Bush rejected such congressional moves, and Congress, in often heated debate, was unable to muster the two-thirds vote in each house of Congress needed to overcome the actual or threatened presidential veto of such legislation.

   Although Bush told Congress that he had cut off senior contacts with
China after the Tiananmen crackdown, in following months he resorted to
secret diplomacy and sent his national security adviser and the deputy secretary of state on two clandestine missions for talks in Beijing. When the
missions were publicly disclosed in late 1989, an uproar in Congress and
among U.S. media soured the president's already poor standing with the U.S.
Congress, media, and interest groups.

   Senior Chinese leaders remained fairly rigid against Bush's efforts to
maintain constructive communication. Uncertain of their ability to maintain
control and promote economic and other development inside China, as well
as facing strong negative reactions from most developed countries, the Chinese leaders were unable or unwilling to make many gestures to help Bush
justify a continued moderate stance toward China.[32]

   Bush eventually became frustrated with the Chinese leadership's intransi-
gence and took a tough stance on trade and other issues, though he made
special efforts to ensure that the United States continued MFN tariff status
for China, despite opposition by a majority of the U.S. Congress and much of
the American media. Reflecting more positive U.S. views of Taiwan, the
Bush administration upgraded American interchange with the ROC by sending a cabinet-level official to Taipei in 1992, the first such visit since official
relations were ended in 1979. He also seemed to abandon the limits on U.S.
arms sales set in accord with the August 17, 1982, U.S. communiqué with
China by agreeing in 1992 to a sale of 150 advanced F-16 jet fighters to
Taiwan worth over $5 billion.[33]

RELATIONS DURING THE BILL CLINTON ADMINISTRATION

Presidential candidate Bill Clinton used sharp attacks against Chinese
government behavior, notably the Tiananmen crackdown, and President
Bush's moderate approach to China to win support in the 1992 election. The
presidential candidate's attacks, though probably reflecting sincere anger and
concern over Chinese behavior, also reflected a tendency in the American
China debate in the 1990s to use China issues, particularly criticism of China
and U.S. policy toward China, for partisan and other ulterior purposes. The
president-elect, and U.S. politicians in following years, found that criticizing
China and U.S. policy toward China provided a convenient means to pursue
political and other ends. For candidate Clinton and his aides, using China
issues to discredit the record of the Republican candidate, George H. W.

Bush, proved to be an effective way to take votes from the incumbent. Once he won the election and was in office, President Clinton showed little interest in China policy, leaving the responsibility to subordinates. [34]

In particular, Assistant Secretary of State for East Asia Affairs Winston Lord in 1993 played the lead administration role in working with congressional leaders—notably Senate Majority Leader George Mitchell and a House of Representatives leader on China and human rights issues, Representative Nancy Pelosi—and others to establish the human rights conditions the Clinton administration would require before renewing MFN tariff status for China. The terms he worked out were widely welcomed in the United States at the time. However, the Chinese government leaders were determined not to give in on several of the U.S. demands, and they appeared to calculate that U.S. business interests in a burgeoning Chinese economy would be sufficient to prevent the United States from taking the drastic step of cutting MFN tariff treatment for China and risking the likely retaliation of the PRC against American trade interests. U.S. business pressures pushed Clinton to intervene in May 1994 to reverse existing policy and allow for unimpeded U.S. renewal of MFN status for China. [35]

Pro-Taiwan interests in the United States, backed by American public relations firms in the pay of entities and organizations in Taiwan, took the opportunity of congressional elections in 1995 giving control of the Congress to pro-Taiwan Republican leaders to push for greater U.S. support for Taiwan, notably a visit by ROC President Lee Teng-hui to his alma mater Cornell University. President Clinton was privately urged by his administration's China policy advisors not to depart from understandings with China that required restricting access by the Taiwan president to the United States. Nevertheless, Clinton allowed Taiwan's president to visit, as he was under heavy domestic political pressure from Congress, which was almost uniform in supporting the administration granting a visa to the Taiwan president. The congressional view also was reflected strongly in American media. [36]

A military confrontation with China in the Taiwan Strait eventually involving two U.S. aircraft carrier battle groups resulted, and the Clinton administration moved to a much more coherent engagement policy toward China that received consistent and high-level attention from the president and his key aides. Marked by two U.S.-China summit meetings in 1997 and 1998, the administration's new and intense focus of developing positive engagement with China was premised in part on the high priority administration officials now gave to insuring no repetition of the dangerous confrontation between U.S. and Chinese military forces in the Taiwan area in 1996. The change in policy also reflected and relied on the growing interest of U.S. businesses that had an increasingly important stake in improving profitable economic relations with China. For their part, the Chinese leaders welcomed the summits with the American leader, which signaled to audiences at home and abroad that Chinese leaders were now accepted as legitimate among developed countries despite the bloody crackdown at Tiananmen and the now waning international sanctions against China.

Progress in the avowed process of building a "strategic partnership" between the United States and China was difficult. Negotiations between representatives of the two powers often were tense and acrimonious, reflecting in particular deep Chinese suspicions and the negative experiences in the years after Tiananmen. Apart from the summits, an agreement in 1999 led to China's entry into the World Trade Organization in 2001 and U.S. passage of legislation in 2000 agreeing to provide permanent normal trade status for China. The latter U.S. move ended the annual requirement to renew MFN tariff treatment for China, which had proven to be the focal point of congressional debate on China for ten years. However, the newly positive Clinton administration approach to China failed to still the vigorous U.S. debate against forward movement in U.S. relations with China on a wide range of strategic, economic, and political issues.[37]

As in the case of Clinton's attacks on George H. W. Bush, many of the attacks on Clinton's engagement policy with China after 1996 were not so much focused on China and China issues for their own sake as on partisan concerns. Most notably, as congressional Republican leaders sought to impeach President Clinton and tarnish the reputation of his administration, they endeavored to dredge up a wide range of charges regarding issues such as China's illegal involvement in U.S. political fund-raising; espionage; and deviations from international norms regarding human rights, nuclear weapons, and ballistic missile proliferation in order to discredit President Clinton's moderate engagement policy toward China, and in so doing cast doubt on the moral integrity and competence of the president and his aides.[38]

The Clinton policy of engagement with China also came under attack from organized labor interests within the Democratic Party, some of which used the attacks on the administration's China policy as a means to get the administration to pay more attention to broader labor interests within the Democratic Party. In a roughly similar fashion, social conservatives in the Republican Party used sharp attacks against continuation of U.S. MFN tariff status for China (a stance often supported by congressional Republican leaders) as a means to highlight Chinese coercive birth control policies and embarrass and pressure the Republican leaders to pay more attention to the various agenda issues of social conservatives.

During the 1990s, congressional criticism of China and the moderate U.S. policy toward China was easy to do and generally had benefits for those doing the criticism. The criticism generated positive coverage from U.S. media strongly critical of China. It generated support and perhaps some fund-raising for the congressional critics from the many interest groups in the United States that focused criticism on Chinese policies and practices. The Chinese government, anxious to keep the economic relationship with the United States on an even keel, was disinclined to take substantive action against such congressional critics. More likely were Chinese invitations to these members of Congress for all-expenses-paid trips to China in order to persuade them to change their views by seeing actual conditions in China. Finally, President Clinton, like President George H. W. Bush, often was not in a position to risk other legislative goals by punishing members critical of his China policy. In short, from a congressional perspective and a broader perspective in American politics, sharp congressional criticism of China in the 1990s became a "free ride" with many benefits for those doing the criticizing and few perceived drawbacks.

As President Clinton and his staff took more control over China policy after the face-off with Chinese forces in the Taiwan Strait in 1996, they emphasized—like George H. W. Bush—a moderate policy of engagement, seeking change in offensive Chinese government practices through a gradual process involving closer Chinese integration with the world economic and political order. The U.S.-China relationship improved but also encountered significant setbacks and resistance. The president's more activist and positive policy of engagement with China brought such high points as the China-U.S. summits in 1997 and 1998, the Sino-American agreement on China's entry into the WTO in 1999, and passage of U.S. legislation in 2000 granting China permanent normal trade relations status. Low points in the relationship during this time included strong congressional opposition to the president's stance against Taiwan independence in 1998; the May 1999 bombing of the Chinese embassy in Belgrade and Chinese demonstrators trashing U.S. diplomatic properties in China; strident congressional criticism in the so-called Cox Committee report of May 1999 charging administration officials with gross malfeasance in guarding U.S. secrets and weaponry from Chinese spies; and partisan congressional investigations of Clinton administration political fund-raising that highlighted some illegal contributions from sources connected to the Chinese regime and the alleged impact they had on the administration's more moderate approach to the PRC.[39]

Chinese leaders had long sought the summit meetings with the United States. Coming in the wake of Chinese meetings with other world leaders in the aftermath of the international isolation of China caused by the Tiananmen crackdown, the summit meetings with the American president were a clear signal that the Communist administration of China had growing international status and that its position as the legitimate government of China now was recognized by all major world powers.[40]

The benefits for the United States in the summit meetings were more in question, though the Clinton administration justified these steps as part of its efforts to use engagement in seeking change in offensive Chinese government practices through a gradual process involving closer Chinese integration with the world economic and political order. American and other critics failed to accept this rationale and honed their criticism of what they viewed as unjustified U.S. concessions to Chinese leaders. Heading the list were perceived concessions in the U.S. president articulating limits on American support for Taiwan in the so-called three nos. Speaking in Shanghai in June 1998 during his visit to China, President Clinton affirmed that the United States did not support Taiwan independence, two Chinas, or one Taiwan and one China, and that the United States did not believe Taiwan should be a member of an organization where statehood is required. The Clinton administration claimed the three nos were a reaffirmation of long-standing U.S. policy, but the president's action was roundly criticized in Congress and the U.S. media as a new gesture made to accommodate Beijing and undermine Taipei.[41]

Progress in U.S. negotiations leading to eventual agreement on China's entry into the WTO was not without serious difficulties and negative consequences. The United States took the lead among the organization's contracting parties in protracted negotiations (1986–1999) to reach agreements with China on a variety of trade-related issues before Chinese accession could move forward. Chinese Premier Zhu Rongji visited Washington in April 1999 hoping to reach agreement with the United States on China's entry into the World Trade Organization. An agreement was reached and disclosed by the Americans, only to be turned down by President Clinton. The setback embarrassed Zhu and raised serious questions in the Chinese leadership about the intentions of President Clinton and his administration. Recovering from the setback, Zhu was able to complete the U.S.-China negotiations in November 1999, paving the way for China's entry into the WTO in 2001. After the United States agreed in late 1999 to China joining the World Trade Organization, U.S. legislation passed granting China permanent normal trade relations (PNTR) in 2000. This ended the need for annual presidential requests and congressional reviews regarding China keeping normal trade relations (NTR) tariff status, previously known as most favored nation tariff status.[42]

Making such progress in Sino-American relations was difficult because of incidents and developments affecting U.S.-China relations and vitriolic American debate over the Clinton administration's China policy. In particular, the accidental U.S. bombing of the Chinese embassy in Belgrade was the most important incident in U.S.-China relations after the Tiananmen crackdown. The reaction in China included mobs stoning the U.S. embassy in Beijing and burning U.S. diplomatic property in Chengdu. Both governments restored calm and dealt with some of the consequences of the bombing, but China and the United States never came to an agreement on what happened and whether the United States explained its actions appropriately.[43]

Taiwan President Lee Teng-hui added to Taiwan Strait tension that worried American policy makers when he asserted in July 1999 that Taiwan was a state separate from China and that China and Taiwan had "special state-to-state relations." Chinese leaders saw this as a step toward Taiwan independence and reacted with strong rhetoric, some military actions, and by cutting off cross-strait communication links.[44]

Complementing difficulties abroad were the many challenges at home to the Clinton administration's moderate policy of engagement toward China. The U.S. media ran repeated stories in the second term of the Clinton administration linking the president, Vice President Gore, and other administration leaders with illegal political fund-raising involving Asian donors, some of whom were said to be connected with the Chinese government. Congressional Republican Committee Chairmen, Senator Fred Thompson and Representative Dan Burton, held hearings, conducted investigations, and produced information and reports regarding various unsubstantiated allegations of illegal contributions from Chinese backers in return for the Clinton administration turning a blind eye to Chinese illegal trading practices and Chinese espionage activities in the United States.[45]

More damaging to the administration and its engagement policy toward China was the report of the so-called Cox Committee. Formally known as the Select Committee on U.S. National Security and Military/Commercial Concerns with the People's Republic of China, and named for its chairman, Republican congressman Christopher Cox, the committee released in May 1999 an eight-hundred-page unclassified version of a larger classified report. It depicted long-standing and widespread Chinese espionage efforts against U.S. nuclear weapons facilities, allowing China to build advanced nuclear warheads for use on missiles that were made more accurate and reliable with the assistance of American companies. It portrayed the Clinton administration as grossly negligent in protecting such vital U.S. national security secrets. The report added substantially to concerns that the United States faced a rising security threat posed by China's rapidly expanding economic and military power. [46]

DEVELOPMENTS DURING THE
GEORGE W. BUSH ADMINISTRATION

George W. Bush became president in 2001 with a policy toward China tougher than the policy of his predecessor. Seeking to sustain economic relations with China, the new president was wary of China's strategic intentions and took steps to deter China from using military force against Taiwan. Most notably, he departed sharply from past U.S. practice since the U.S. normalization of relations with China by announcing in April 2001 that the United States would do "whatever it takes" to help defend Taiwan in the face of military attack from China. Relations deteriorated when on April 1, 2001, a Chinese jet fighter collided with a U.S. reconnaissance plane, the EP-3, in international waters off the coast of China. The jet was destroyed and the pilot killed. The EP-3 was seriously damaged but managed to make an emergency landing on China's Hainan Island. The U.S. crew was held for eleven days and the U.S. plane much longer by Chinese authorities. Weeks of negotiations produced compromises that allowed the crew and plane to return to the United States, but neither side accepted responsibility for the incident. [47]

Many specialists predicted continued deterioration of relations, but both governments worked to resolve issues and establish a businesslike relationship that emphasized positive aspects of the relationship and played down differences. The terrorist attack on America on September 11, 2001, diverted U.S. attention away from China as a potential strategic threat. Chinese officials privately indicated that they sought a constructive relationship with the new U.S. government, and in the process they publicly showed remarkable deference in the face of the Bush government's uniquely assertive stance on Taiwan as well as its strong positions on regional and national ballistic missile defense, expansion of U.S.-Japanese defense cooperation, NATO expansion, and other sensitive security issues that had been focal points of Chinese criticism of the United States in the recent past. The Chinese leaders seemed preoccupied at home, notably focusing on a very important and somewhat irregular leadership transition and related issues of power sharing and development policy. Against this background, Chinese leaders worked hard to moderate previous harsh rhetoric and pressure tactics in order to consolidate relations with the United States.

Specialists offered different explanations for what they viewed as a surprising improvement in American-Chinese relations during the administration of President George W. Bush. Some focused on greater Chinese leadership confidence and maturity as the cause for the turnabout in relations, arguing that such confidence and maturity prompted the Chinese government to deal more moderately and with restraint regarding some of the challenges posed by the new U.S. administration and its assertive policies.[48]

Another group of specialists was less convinced that U.S.-China relations were destined to converge substantially over Asian and world affairs. These specialists emphasized the importance of what they saw as the Bush administration moving fairly rapidly from an initial toughness toward China to a stance of accommodation and compromise. In their judgment, the shift toward a moderate U.S. stance prompted Chinese leaders to pursue greater moderation in turn in their overall approach to Asian and world affairs.[49]

A third view involved specialists who gave more weight to the Bush administration's initially firm and effective policies toward China, which were seen to have curbed assertive and potentially disruptive Chinese tendencies and served to make it in China's interests to avoid confrontation, seek better U.S. ties, and avoid challenge to U.S. interests in Asian and world affairs. This view held that it was more China than the United States that took the lead in seeking better ties in 2001, and that greater U.S.-China cooperation in Asian affairs depended not so much on Chinese confidence and maturity as on effective U.S. use of power and influence to keep Chinese tendencies in check and to prevail upon China to limit emphasis on differences with the United States.[50]

All three schools of thought judged that the improvement in U.S.-China relations reinforced generally moderate Chinese tendencies in Asian and world affairs, but their differences over the causes of the American-Chinese thaw had implications for assessing future Chinese policy and behavior. In the first instance, the key variable seemed to be Chinese confidence and maturity, which presumably would continue to grow along with Chinese development and moderation, suggesting a continued moderate Chinese approach for the next several years if not longer. The latter two views depended heavily on the United States, with the first view arguing that continued U.S. moderation and accommodation of Chinese interest was required, as a more firm American stance presumably could lead to a more assertive and aggressive Chinese stance in the region. The second of the latter two views indicated that much depended on continued U.S. resolve, power, and effectiveness in dealing with China. Weakness or extremism in the American stance could reverse the prevailing trend of Chinese moderation in the region and lead to a more assertive and disruptive approach.

In any event, the course of U.S.-China relations was smoother than at any time since the normalization of U.S.-China relations. American preoccupation with the wars in Afghanistan and Iraq and the broader war on global terrorism meant that U.S. strategic attention to China as a threat remained a secondary consideration for American policy makers. Chinese leaders for their part continued to deal with an incomplete leadership transition and the broad problem of trying to sustain a one-party authoritarian political regime amid a vibrant economy and rapid social change. In this context, the two powers, despite continuing differences ranging from Taiwan and Tibet to trade issues and human rights, managed to see their interests best served by generally emphasizing the positive. In particular, they found new common ground in dealing with the crisis caused by North Korea's nuclear weapons program beginning in 2002, and the Chinese appreciated Bush's warning in December 2003 to Taiwan's leader Chen Shui-bian to avoid steps toward independence for Taiwan that could lead to conflict in the Taiwan Strait.

It is easy to exaggerate the speed and consistency of growing Sino-American convergence during the Bush administration. The antiterrorism campaign after September 11, 2001, saw an upswing in U.S.-China cooperation, though China was somewhat tentative and reserved in supporting the U.S. war against Afghanistan. President Bush's visits to Shanghai in October 2001 and Beijing in February 2002 underlined differences as well as common ground. The U.S. president repeatedly affirmed his strong support for

Taiwan and his firm position regarding human rights issues in China. His aides made clear China's lower priority in the administration's view of U.S. interests as the Bush administration continued to focus on relations with Japan and other allies in Asia and the Pacific. In its first year, the Bush administration imposed sanctions on China over issues involving China's reported proliferation of weapons of mass destruction more times than during the eight years of the Clinton administration. The Defense Department's Quadrennial Defense Review unmistakably saw China as a potential threat in Asia. American ballistic missile defense programs, opposed by China, went forward, and rising U.S. influence and prolonged military deployments were at odds with Chinese interest to secure China's western flank.[51] The Defense Department's annual reports on the Chinese military pulled few punches in focusing on China's military threat to Taiwan and to U.S. forces that might come to Taiwan's aid in the event of a conflict with the PRC. The Bush administration's September 2002 National Security Strategy Report called for better relations with China but clearly warned against any power seeking to challenge U.S. interests with military force.[52]

It was notable that China's increased restraint and moderation toward the United States came even in the face of these new departures in U.S. policy and behavior under the Bush administration, particularly presidential pledges along with military and political support for Taiwan, strong missile defense programs, and strong support for alliance strengthening with Japan and expanded military cooperation with India. In the recent past, such U.S. actions would have prompted strong Chinese public attacks and possibly military countermeasures.

American leaders showed an increased willingness to meet Chinese leaders' symbolic needs for summitry, and the U.S. president pleased his Chinese counterpart by repeatedly endorsing a "constructive, cooperative, and candid" relationship with China. Amid continued Chinese moderation and concessions in 2002 and reflecting greater U.S. interest in consolidating relations and avoiding tensions with China at a time of growing U.S. preoccupation with the war on terrorism, Iraq, and North Korea, the Bush administration broadened cooperation with China and gave U.S. relations with China a higher priority as the year wore on. An October 2002 meeting between President Bush and President Jiang Zemin at the U.S. president's ranch in Crawford, Texas, highlighted this trend. Concessions and gestures, mainly from the Chinese side, dealing with proliferation, Iraq, the release of dissidents, U.S. agricultural imports, Tibet, and Taiwan, facilitated the positive Crawford summit.[53] Meanwhile, senior U.S. leaders began to refer to China and Jiang Zemin as a "friend."[54] They adhered to public positions on Taiwan that were acceptable to Beijing, and they sanctioned an anti-PRC terrorist group active in China's Xinjiang region. The Defense Department was slow to resume high-level contacts with China, reflecting continued wariness in the face of China's ongoing military buildup focused on dealing with Taiwan and U.S. forces that might seek to protect Taiwan, but formal relations at various senior levels were resumed by late 2002.[55]

Looking back, it appears that patterns of Bush administration policy and behavior toward China began to change significantly in 2003. American officials sometimes continued to speak in terms of "shaping" Chinese policies and behavior through tough deterrence along with moderate engagement. However, the thrust of U.S. policy and behavior increasingly focused on positive engagement. China also received increasingly high priority in U.S. foreign policy.

The determinants of the U.S. approach appeared to center on the Bush administration's growing preoccupations with the war in Iraq, its mixed record in other areas of the war on terror and broader complications in the Middle East, and growing international and domestic disapproval of Bush administration policies. The North Korean nuclear program emerged as a major problem in 2003, and the U.S. government came to rely heavily on China to help manage the issue in ways that avoided major negative fallout for the interests of the U.S. government. Although Asian policy did not figure prominently in the 2004 presidential campaign, Senator John Kerry, the Democratic candidate, used a televised presidential debate to challenge President Bush's handling of North Korea's nuclear weapons development. President Bush countered by emphasizing his reliance on China in order to manage the issue in accord with U.S. interests.[56]

With the Bush administration's determination to avoid trouble with China at a time of major foreign policy troubles elsewhere, the president strongly pressured Taiwan's government to stop initiating policies seen as provocative by China and possible causes of confrontation in U.S.-China relations.[57] The strong rhetorical emphasis on democracy promotion in the Bush administration's second term notably avoided serious pressures against China's authoritarian system.

The U.S. government's emphasis on positive engagement with China did not hide the many continuing differences or U.S. efforts to plan for contingencies in case a rising China turned aggressive or otherwise disrupted U.S.

interests. The United States endeavored to use growing interdependence, engagement, and dialogues with China to foster webs of relationships that would tie down or constrain possible Chinese policies and actions deemed negative to U.S. interests.[58]

On the whole, the administration of President Hu Jintao welcomed and supported the new directions in U.S.-China policy. The Chinese leaders endeavored to build on the positives and play down the negatives in relations with the United States. This approach fit well with the Chinese leadership's broader priorities of strengthening national development and Communist Party legitimacy that were said to require China to use carefully the "strategic opportunity" of prevailing international circumstances seen as generally advantageous to Chinese interests. As in the case of U.S. policy toward China, Chinese engagement with the United States did not hide Chinese contingency plans against suspected U.S. encirclement, pressure, and containment and the Chinese use of engagement and interdependence as a type of Gulliver strategy to constrain and tie down possible U.S. policies and actions deemed negative to Chinese interests.[59]

As China expanded military power along with economic and diplomatic relations in Asian and world affairs at a time of U.S. preoccupation with the war in Iraq and other foreign policy problems, debate emerged inside and outside the U.S. government about the implications of China's rise for U.S. interests. Within the Bush administration, there emerged three viewpoints or schools of thought, though U.S. officials frequently were eclectic, holding views of the implications of China's rise from various perspectives.[60]

On one side were U.S. officials who judged that China's rise in Asia was designed to dominate Asia and in the process to undermine U.S. leadership in the region.[61] A more moderate view of China's rise in Asia came from U.S. officials who believed China's focus in the region was to improve China's position in Asia mainly in order to sustain regional stability, promote China's development, reassure neighbors and prevent balancing against China, and isolate Taiwan. Officials of this school of thought judged that China's intentions were not focused on isolating and weakening the United States in Asia. Nevertheless, the Chinese policies and behavior, even though not targeted against the United States, contrasted with perceived inattentive and maladroit U.S. policies and practices. The result was that China's rise was having an indirect but substantial negative impact on U.S. leadership in Asia.

A third school of thought was identified with U.S. Deputy Secretary of State Robert Zoellick, who by 2005 publicly articulated a strong argument for greater U.S. cooperation with China on Asian and other issues as China rose in regional and international prominence.[62] This viewpoint held that the United States had much to gain from working directly and cooperatively with China in order to encourage the PRC to use its rising influence in "responsible" ways in accord with broad U.S. interests in Asian and world affairs. This viewpoint seemed to take account of the fact that the Bush administration was already working closely with China in the six-party talks to deal with North Korea's nuclear weapons development and that U.S. and Chinese collaboration or consultations continued on such sensitive topics as the war on terror, Afghanistan, Pakistan, Iran, Sudan, Burma, and even Taiwan as well as bilateral economic, security, and other issues. Thus, this school of thought gave less emphasis than the other two on competition with China and more emphasis on cooperation with China in order to preserve and enhance U.S. leadership and interests in Asia as China rises.

Bush administration policy came to embrace the third point of view. Senior U.S. leaders reviewed in greater depth the implications of China's rise and the strengths and weaknesses of the United States in Asia. The review showed that U.S. standing as Asia's leading power was basically sound. American military deployments and cooperation throughout the Asia-Pacific region were robust. The U.S. economic importance in the region was growing, not declining. Overall, it was clear that no other power or coalition of powers was even remotely able or willing to undertake the costs, risks, and commitments of the United States in sustaining regional stability and development essential for the core interests of the vast majority of regional governments.[63] Thus, China's rise—while increasingly important—posed a less substantial and significant challenge for U.S. interests than many of the published commentaries and specialists' assessments might have led one to believe.

On this basis, the U.S. administration increasingly emphasized positive engagement and dialogues with China, encouraging China to act responsibly and building ever-growing webs of relationships and interdependence. This pattern fit well with Chinese priorities regarding national development in a period of advantageous international conditions while building interdependencies and relationships that constrain possible negative U.S. policies or behaviors.

DEVELOPMENTS DURING THE
BARACK OBAMA ADMINISTRATION

Presidential candidate Barack Obama was unusual in recent U.S. presidential politics in not making an issue of his predecessor's China policy. Like President Bush, the new president showed a course with China involving pursuing constructive contacts, preserving and protecting American interests, and dealing effectively with challenges posed by rising Chinese influence and power.[64]

A strong theme in President Obama's initial foreign policy was to seek the cooperation of other world powers, including China, to deal with salient international concerns such as the global economic crisis and recession, climate change, nuclear weapons proliferation, and terrorism. He and his team made strong efforts to build common ground with China on these and related issues. China's leaders offered limited cooperation; they focused much more on their own interests than on the need for global responsibility urged by President Obama. Chinese officials suspected that added global responsibilities would hold back China's economic development and modernization.[65]

More worrisome, some Chinese actions and assertions in 2009 and 2010 directly challenged the policies and practices of the United States. Chinese government patrol boats confronted U.S. surveillance ships in the South China Sea; China challenged U.S. and South Korean military exercises against North Korea in the Yellow Sea; Chinese treatment of U.S. arms sales to Taiwan and President Obama's meeting with the Dalai Lama was harsher than in the recent past; Chinese officials threatened to stop investing in U.S. government securities and to move away from using the U.S. dollar in international transactions; and the Chinese government for a time reacted very harshly to American urging for collective efforts to manage tensions in the South China Sea and affirming that the U.S.-Japan alliance provides for American support for Japan over such disputed territories as islands in the East China Sea controlled by Japan but claimed by China.[66]

The Obama government reacted calmly and firmly to what Secretary of State Hillary Clinton called these "tests" or manifestations of new assertiveness by China. It gave no ground on any of the Chinese demands. It also found that prominent Chinese assertiveness and truculence with the United States and neighboring Asian countries over maritime, security, and other issues seriously damaged China's efforts to portray a benign image in Asia. Asian governments became more active in working more closely with the

United States and in encouraging an active U.S. presence in the Asia-Pacific. Their interest in closer ties with the United States meshed well with the Obama government's broad effort to reengage with the countries of the Asia-Pacific, ranging from India to the Pacific Islands. The overall effect was a decline in China's position in the Asia-Pacific and a rise in the position of the United States.[67]

Meanwhile, the Obama government made clear to the Chinese government and the world that the United States was prepared to undertake military measures needed to deal with the buildup of Chinese forces targeting Americans and American interests in the Asia-Pacific. U.S. officials also helped to move China to curb North Korea's repeated provocations by warning privately as well as publicly that the United States viewed North Korea's nuclear weapons development as not just a regional issue and concern for global nonproliferation but a direct threat to the United States.[68]

During the period leading up to the January 18–20, 2011, visit of President Hu Jintao to Washington, China tried to ease recent tensions and set a smoother course for U.S.-China relations. The harsh rhetoric criticizing American policies and practices subsided, the Chinese put aside their objections to high-level military exchanges, and Secretary of Defense Robert Gates reestablished businesslike ties at the top levels of the Chinese military during a visit to Beijing in early January 2011. China also used its influence to get North Korea to stop its provocations against South Korea and to seek negotiations over nuclear weapons issues. Regarding Iran, China avoided undercutting international sanctions pressuring Iran to give up its nuclear weapons program. On the economic front, China allowed the value of its currency to appreciate. Finally, Chinese officials were more cooperative over climate change issues at an international meeting in Cancun than they had been a year earlier.[69]

The successful U.S.-China summit helped to sustain positive momentum in U.S.-China relations, even though the many differences between the two countries continued. President Obama made clear that he wanted to pursue closer engagement with China as part of his administration's overall reengagement with the Asia-Pacific. His administration also made clear that it would not give in to Chinese assertiveness or pressure, and, if needed, it would respond to such Chinese actions with appropriate military, diplomatic, or other means.[70] On the domestic front, the president was sometimes sharply critical of China in response to anti-China charges by his opponent in the 2012 election campaign. After winning reelection, President Obama resumed a moderate public posture toward China. He took steps during his November 2012 visit to Asia to underline that American reengagement in Asia was not focused on balancing China's rise.

Given more recent signs of renewed Chinese assertiveness amid evidence of a broader debate on the future course of Chinese foreign policy, it was less certain that President Hu Jintao shared President Obama's interest in reengagement. China's recent assertiveness against the United States and other countries over differences on territorial and other issues seemed to be more costly than beneficial for China's broader interests. On balance, it weakened China's position and strengthened the position of the United States in the Asia-Pacific.[71] Against this background, leading officials responsible for Chinese foreign policy and authoritative commentators in late 2010 and early 2011 reaffirmed that Chinese interests were best served by a moderate approach that avoided "reckless" actions and assertions that undermined China's international position and regional stability.

Unfortunately for those seeking coherence, predictability, and moderation in Chinese actions, these commentaries were overshadowed in 2012 by unprecedented demonstrations of Chinese power short of using military force in defense of Chinese claims to disputed territories in the South China Sea and the East China Sea. As noted in chapter 1, such actions went well beyond established international norms and resulted in extralegal measures and in some cases in widespread violence and property destruction. They placed China's neighbors and concerned powers, notably the United States, on guard. They compelled the neighbors and the United States not only to consider methods of dealing effectively with Chinese pressures, but also to consider more carefully the wide range of differences they have with China that might set off highly disruptive and assertive actions by the now second-ranking and rapidly growing power in world politics. The implications for regional order clearly took a negative turn in 2012.[72]

The recent negatives in U.S.-China relations seem balanced by numerous positive developments that serve to underline a pragmatic interest on both sides in sustaining positive engagement and managing differences to avoid confrontation and conflict. Among instruments serving to moderate the Sino-American frictions, the wide range of official Chinese-American exchanges through an array of over seventy bilateral dialogues continue to make significant progress in several areas, notably a strengthening in bilateral military exchanges. The so-called Taiwan issue—historically the leading cause of friction between the United States and China—remains on a recent trajectory of easing tensions. Sino-American handling of the complicated case of a prominent Chinese dissident, Chen Guangcheng, who sought refuge in the U.S. embassy in April 2012, was resolved by mutual agreement. Chinese authorities almost certainly were relieved that the U.S. government remained silent on what it was told when in February 2012 Wang Lijun, head of police in Chongqing municipality and a key actor in what would turn out to be the most important Chinese leadership purge in many years, drove to Chengdu and entered the American consulate there in February 2012, reportedly fearing for his life and seeking refuge.

By the end of 2012, some specialists saw a decline in U.S.-China relations, but a number of specialists on both the American and Chinese sides seemed to agree that effectively managing differences through a process of constructive engagement remains in the interests of both countries. American specialists noted important reasons for this judgment:

- Both administrations benefit from positive engagement in various areas. Such engagement supports their mutual interests in stability in the Asia-Pacific, a peaceful Korean peninsula, and a peaceful settlement of the Taiwan issue; the U.S. and Chinese leaders recognize the need to cooperate to foster global peace and prosperity, to advance world environmental conditions, and to deal with climate change and nonproliferation.
- Both administrations see that the two powers have become so interdependent that emphasizing the negatives in their relationship will hurt the other side but also will hurt their own. Such interdependence is particularly strong in Sino-American economic relations.
- Both leaderships are preoccupied with a long list of urgent domestic and foreign priorities; in this situation, one of the last things they would seek is a serious confrontation in relations with one another.

Prominent Chinese specialists visiting Washington at the end of 2012 underscored the futility of conflict and the need for cooperation in a somewhat different way. They averred that the U.S.-China relationship has become increasingly important to both sides and that three "realities" compel the two governments to seek ways to manage their differences while trying to broaden common ground. Those realities are:

- Each country is too big to be dominated by the other.
- Each country has too unique a political and social structure to allow for transformation by the other.

- Each country has become too interdependent with the other to allow conflicts to disrupt their relationship.[73]

NOTES

1. Chen Jian, *Mao's China and the Cold War* (Chapel Hill: University of North Carolina Press, 2001); Thomas Christensen, *Useful Adversaries: Grand Strategy, Domestic Mobilization, and Sino-American Conflicts, 1949–1958* (Princeton, NJ: Princeton University Press, 1996).

2. Bruce Cummings, *The Origins of the Korean War* (Princeton, NJ: Princeton University Press, 1990); William Stueck, *The Korean War: An International History* (Princeton, NJ: Princeton University Press, 1997).

3. Warren Cohen, *America's Response to China* (New York: Columbia University Press, 2000), pp. 169–72.

4. Robert Sutter, *Historical Dictionary of United States-China Relations* (Lanham, MD: Scarecrow, 2006), pp. 65–66.

5. Michael Schaller, *The United States and China: Into the Twenty-First Century* (New York: Oxford University Press, 2002), pp. 144–46.

6. Ralph Clough, *Island China* (Cambridge, MA: Harvard University Press, 1978), pp. 10–14.

7. Steven Goldstein, "Dialogue of the Deaf? Sino-American Ambassadorial-Level Talks, 1955–1970," in *Re-examining the Cold War: U.S.-China Diplomacy, 1954–1973*, ed. Robert Ross and Jiang Changbin (Cambridge, MA: Harvard University Press, 2001), pp. 200–237; Zhang Baijia and Jia Qingguo, "Steering Wheel, Shock Absorber, and Diplomatic Probe in Confrontation: Sino-American Ambassadorial Talks Seen from the Chinese Perspective," in Ross and Jiang, eds., *Re-examining the Cold War*, pp. 173–99.

8. Nancy Bernkopf Tucker, *Strait Talk: United States-Taiwan Relations and the Crisis with China* (Cambridge, MA: Harvard University Press, 2009), pp. 14–17.

9. Alice Lyman Miller and Richard Wich, *Becoming Asia* (Stanford, CA: Stanford University Press, 2011), pp. 122–137.

10. Tucker, *Strait Talk*, pp. 17–21.

11. Cohen, *America's Response to China*, pp. 190–94; Goldstein, "Dialogue of the Deaf?" pp. 229–37.

12. Sutter, *Historical Dictionary of United States-China Relations*, p. lvii.

13. Robert Sutter, *China-Watch* (Baltimore: Johns Hopkins University Press, 1978), pp. 1–62.

14. These American events are recounted in Robert Sutter, *U.S.-Chinese Relations: Perilous Past, Pragmatic Present* (Lanham, MD: Rowman & Littlefield, 2010), pp. 67–69.

15. Thomas Gottlieb, *Chinese Foreign Policy Factionalism and the Origins of the Strategic Triangle* (Santa Monica, CA: Rand, 1977).

16. Thomas Robinson, "The Sino-Soviet Border Dispute: Background, Development and the March 1969 Clashes," *American Political Science Review* 66, no. 4 (December 1972): pp. 1175–78.

17. Sutter, *China-Watch*, pp. 78–102.

18. Robert Ross, *Negotiating Cooperation: The United States and China, 1969–1989* (Stanford, CA: Stanford University Press, 1995), pp. 28, 34–35.

19. Schaller, *The United States and China*, pp. 178–84; Tucker, *Strait Talk*, pp. 29–68; Ross, *Negotiating Cooperation*, pp. 17–54.

20. Warren Cohen, *America's Response to China: A History of Sino-American Relations* (New York: Columbia University Press, 2000), pp. 198–200.

21. John Garver, *Foreign Relations of the People's Republic of China* (Englewood Cliffs, NJ: Prentice Hall, 1993), pp. 166–77, 310–11.

22. Cohen, *America's Response to China*, p. 201.

23. James Mann, *About Face: A History of America's Curious Relationship with China, from Nixon to Clinton* (New York: Knopf, 1999), pp. 82–92.

24. Ross, *Negotiating Cooperation*, pp. 125–26; Mann, *About Face*, pp. 98–100.

25. House Committee on Foreign Affairs, *Executive-Legislative Consultations over China Policy, 1978–1979* (Washington, DC: U.S. Government Printing Office, 1980).

26. Harry Harding, *A Fragile Relationship: The United States and China since 1972* (Washington, DC: Brookings Institution, 1992), pp. 86–87.

27. Tucker, *Strait Talk*, pp. 129–52.

28. Tony Saich, *Governance and Politics of China* (New York: Palgrave Macmillan, 2004), pp. 70–74.

29. David M. Lampton, *Same Bed, Different Dreams: Managing U.S.-China Relations, 1989–2000* (Berkeley: University of California Press, 2001), pp. 17–55.

30. Barry Naughton, *The Chinese Economy* (Cambridge, MA: MIT Press, 2007), pp. 98–100.

31. Michael Swaine, *Reverse Course? The Fragile Turnabout in U.S.-China Relations*, Policy Brief 22 (Washington, DC: Carnegie Endowment, February 2003).

32. Schaller, *The United States and China*, pp. 204–5.

33. Robert Sutter, *U.S. Policy toward China: An Introduction to the Role of Interest Groups* (Lanham, MD: Rowman & Littlefield, 1998), pp. 26–44.

34. Mann, *About Face*, pp. 274–78.

35. Cohen, *America's Response to China*, pp. 229–31.

36. Schaller, *The United States and China*, pp. 214–19.

37. Cohen, *America's Response to China*, pp. 234–39.

38. For this and the next two paragraphs, see Robert Sutter, *Historical Dictionary of United States-China Relations* (Lanham, MD: Scarecrow Press, 2006), pp. lxix–lxx.

39. Schaller, *The United States and China*, pp. 219–27.

40. Cohen, *America's Response to China*, pp. 235–36.

41. Tucker, *Strait Talk*, pp. 217–18, 231–43.

42. Sutter, *Historical Dictionary of United States-China Relations*, p. lxxi.

43. Robert Suettinger, *Beyond Tiananmen* (Washington, DC: Brookings Institution, 2003), pp. 369–77.

44. Tucker, *Strait Talk*, pp. 239–44.

45. Lampton, *Same Bed, Different Dreams*, pp. 95–97.

46. Jean Garrison, *Making China Policy: From Nixon to G.W. Bush* (Boulder, CO: Lynne Rienner, 2005), pp. 148–152.

47. For background, see Sutter, *U.S.-Chinese Relations*, pp. 147–68.

48. Kenneth Lieberthal, "Behind the Crawford Summit," *Pac Net 44* (October 24, 2002), www.csis.org/pacfor.

49. Michael Swaine, *Reverse Course: The Fragile Turnabout in US-China Relations*, Policy Brief 22 (Washington, DC: Carnegie Endowment for International Peace, February 2003).

50. Hugo Restall, "Tough Love for China," *Wall Street Journal*, October 21, 2002, p. A14.

51. "Concern over US Plans for War on Terror Dominate Jiang Tour," Reuters, April 7, 2002, www.taiwansecurity.org (accessed April 9, 2002); Willy Wo-Lap Lam, "US, Taiwan Catch Jiang Off-Guard," *CNN.com*, March 19, 2002.

52. Bonnie Glaser, "Playing Up the Positive on the Eve of the Crawford Summit," *Comparative Connections*, October 2002, www.csis.org/pacfor.

53. "U.S. Says China Regulations Should Free Up Soybean Exports," statement of the Office of the U.S. Trade Representative, October 18, 2002, www.ustr.gov; "Mainland Offers Taiwan Goodwill Gesture," *China Daily*, October 18, 2002, www.taiwansecurity.org (accessed October 20, 2002); "China Tightens Rules on Military Exports," Reuters, October 21, 2002, www.taiwansecurity.org (accessed October 23, 2002); "Ashcroft to Open China FBI Office," Reuters, October 22, 2002, www.taiwansecurity.org (accessed October 24, 2002); "US and China Seal Billion Dollar Deals," BBC, October 22, 2002, www.taiwansecurity.org (accessed October 24, 2002); "U.S. and China Set New Rights Talks," *Washington Post*, October 24, 2002, www.taiwansecurity.org (accessed October 26, 2002).

54. Lu Zhenya, "Jiang Zemin, Bush Agree to Maintain High-Level Strategic Dialogue," *Zhongguo Xinwen She* (Beijing), October 26, 2002 (online version).

55. Shirley Kan, *U.S.-China Military Contacts: Issues for Congress*, Report RL32496 (Washington, DC: Library of Congress, Congressional Research Service, June 19, 2012), pp. 2–4.

56. "Bush, Kerry Square Off in 1st Debate," *Japan Today*, October 1, 2004, www.japantoday.com (accessed March 21, 2008).

57. Robert Sutter, "The Taiwan Problem in the Second George W. Bush Administration—US Officials' Views and Their Implications for US Policy," *Journal of Contemporary China* 15, no. 48 (August 2006): pp. 417–42.

58. Secretary of State Condoleezza Rice, remarks at Sophia University, Tokyo, Japan, March 19, 2005, 2001-2009.state.gov/secretary/rm/2005/43655.htm; Evan Medeiros, "Strategic Hedging and the Future of Asia-Pacific Stability," *Washington Quarterly* 29, no. 1 (2005–2006): pp. 15–28.

59. Rosemary Foot, "Chinese Strategies in a US-Hegemonic Global Order: Accommodating and Hedging," *International Affairs* 82, no. 1 (2006): pp. 77–94; Wang Jisi, "China's Search for Stability with America," *Foreign Affairs* 84, no. 5 (September–October 2005): pp. 39–48; Yong Deng and Thomas Moore, "China Views Globalization: Toward a New Great-Power Politics," *Washington Quarterly* 27, no. 3 (Summer 2004): pp. 117–36.

60. Off-the-record interviews with U.S. officials reviewed in Robert Sutter, "Dealing with a Rising China: US Strategy and Policy," in *Making New Partnership: A Rising China and Its Neighbors*, ed. Zhang Yunlin (Beijing: Social Sciences Academic Press, 2008), 370–74.

61. Among published sources, see US-China Economic and Security Review Commission, *2005 Report to Congress* (Washington, DC: U.S. Government Printing Office, 2005), pp. 143–90.

62. Remarks of Deputy Secretary of State Robert Zoellick, "Wither China? From Membership to Responsibility," National Committee for U.S.-China Relations, September 21, 2005, www.ncuscr.org/files/2005Gala_RobertZoellick_Whither_China1.pdf.

63. Victor Cha, "Winning Asia: Washington's Untold Success Story," *Foreign Affairs* 86, no. 6 (November–December 2007): pp. 98–133; Daniel Twining, "America's Grand Design in Asia," *Washington Quarterly* 30, no. 3 (2007): pp. 79–94; Robert Sutter, *The United States in Asia* (Lanham, MD: Rowman & Littlefield, 2008), pp. 270–76, 281–83.

64. For an overview of the Obama administration's approach to China, see notably Jeffrey Bader, *Obama and China's Rise* (Washington, DC: Brookings Institution, 2012).

65. Robert Sutter, *U.S.-Chinese Relations: Perilous Past, Pragmatic Present* (Lanham, MD: Rowman & Littlefield, 2010), pp. 161–67.

66. Minxin Pei, "China's Bumpy Ride Ahead," *The Diplomat*, February 16, 2011, thediplomat.com; Robert Sutter, *Positive Equilibrium in U.S.-China Relations: Durable or Not?* (Baltimore: University of Maryland School of Law, 2010).

67. Thomas Christensen, "The World Needs an Assertive China," *New York Times*, February 21, 2011, www.nytimes.com; Greg Sheridan, Interview of Hillary Clinton, *Australian*, November 8, 2010, www.state.gov.

68. Elisabeth Bumiller, "U.S. Will Counter Chinese Arms Buildup," *New York Times*, January 8, 2011, www.nytimes.com; David Sanger, "Superpower and Upstart: Sometimes It Ends Well," *New York Times*, January 22, 2011, www.nytimes.com.

69. Sanger, "Superpower and Upstart"; "Beyond the U.S.-China Summit," *Foreign Policy Research Institute*, February 4, 2011, www.fpri.org.

70. Mark Landler and Martin Fackler, "U.S. Warning to China Sends Ripples to the Koreas," *New York Times*, January 20, 2011, www.nytimes.com.

71. Pei, "China's Bumpy Ride"; Christensen, "The World Needs."

72. Wang Jisi, "China's Search for a Grand Strategy," *Foreign Affairs* 90, no. 2 (March/April 2011): pp. 68–79; Dai Bingguo, "Stick to the Path of Peaceful Development," *China Daily*, December 13, 2010, pp. 9–10; Robert Sutter, "U.S. and China: Competition Challenges Engagement," paper for the Annual Meeting of the Association for Asian Studies, March 21–24, 2013.

73. Sutter, "U.S. and China: Competition Challenges Engagement."

Chapter Eight

Relations with Neighboring Asian Countries

The history of the foreign relations of the People's Republic of China shows strong and generally consistent attention of China's leaders to international trends influenced heavily by the United States, and for a long period the Soviet Union, that could impact Chinese interests. Though China often has aspired to and in the recent decades has attained considerable global prominence and influence, the main arena where Chinese foreign relations have focused remains the periphery of the PRC. Even in the recent period of China's wide international economic footprint as the world's largest exporter, second-largest economy, and largest creditor, it is estimated by some experienced Chinese officials that 70 percent of Chinese leaders' attention in foreign affairs remains focused on nearby Asia.[1]

The reasons for this priority seem obvious. Nearby Asia holds the areas of disputed territories that patriotic Chinese officials and people are committed to return to Chinese rule. The many security threats China has faced throughout most of its recent history came from large powers building strategic forces and influence along China's periphery. With the opening to the United States under President Nixon and Chairman Mao and the demise of the Soviet Union at the end of the Cold War, the danger of superpower threat to and attack on China declined. Nevertheless, Chinese officials showed continued strong concern over perceived U.S.-led efforts in the post–Cold War period to use strategic deployments as well as economic and political pressures, especially along China's periphery, in order to "encircle" and "contain" China's rising influence in Asian and world affairs. China's negative assessment of the implications for China of recent initiatives of the Obama administration regarding American reengagement in the Asia-Pacific underlines such long-standing Chinese concerns with superpower influence along China's rim.[2]

Meanwhile, the stability of nearby Asia has a direct impact on the beneficial international environment China has been seeking in order to foster economic growth—the key determinant of Chinese Communist Party legitimacy in the post-Mao period. And nearby Asia is much more important to Chinese economic interests than world areas farther away from China. Thus, China receives wide publicity as it has risen to become the largest trader in Africa in recent years, but its trade with South Korea each year is more than its trade with the entire African continent.[3]

The findings of this and earlier chapters show that the wide array of key Chinese territorial, security, economic, and other concerns in nearby Asia have prompted Chinese leaders repeatedly to take decisive actions to protect their interests, even in the face of strong and adverse international circumstances. This pattern has not been followed in other world regions, where Chinese interests are less important and willingness to stand against strong international opposition is weaker. Mao Zedong's repeated confrontations with nuclear-armed American and Soviet intervention and pressure focused on nearby Asia. Deng Xiaoping showed consistent support for the internationally abhorrent Khmer Rouge in Cambodia in the face of Soviet Union–backed Vietnamese opposition; Deng decided to invade Vietnam despite the danger of Soviet attack on China in order to counter the Vietnamese invasion of Cambodia. More recent Chinese leaders have been much less prone than Mao and Deng to undertake risky initiatives that would seriously complicate Chinese international relationships. But they have shown continued resolve in pledging to put aside the benefits of the recent period and attack Taiwan if it declares independence. They have undermined China's image as a responsible and moderate rising power with repeated resort to coercion, intimidation, extralegal measures, and violence beyond the pale of international norms in support of territorial claims and ambitions around China's rim. And they have stood in the way of international pressure on North Korea, and to a lesser degree Myanmar, that would jeopardize Chinese interests in sustaining a stable situation in these areas along China's periphery.

The wide range of international variables influencing Chinese interests in nearby Asia over the years have mixed with changing and often conflicting

Chinese policy priorities. The result has been patterns of advancing relations compromised by negative legacies and inconsistent directions. An assessment in chapter 10 sees China's rising influence in Asia encumbered by these changing circumstances, negative legacies, and inconsistent imperatives.

RELATIONS WITH JAPAN

China's historic antipathy toward Japan on account of Japan's record as the most brutal imperialist power in China during the nineteenth and twentieth centuries and China's deep suspicion of Japan's close alignment with the United States in recent periods of tension between Beijing and Washington have been at the forefront in Chinese foreign relations in Asia. As in the case of Chinese disputes with Japan over the Senkaku/Diaoyu Islands during 2012, Chinese animosity toward Japan sometimes receives enormous publicity and is depicted as the unquestioned determinant in Sino-Japanese relations. Nevertheless, the salience of these negative historical Chinese legacies and ongoing strategic concerns in fact has waxed and waned over the decades. The negatives flowing from theses legacies and concerns often have been balanced with strong Chinese economic and strategic interests in cooperating closely with Asia's leading developed country. In particular, the Chinese leadership more often than not has sought to keep open channels of beneficial foreign trade, investment, assistance, and other interchange with Japan, even when political and security relations have been tense and confrontational.

Japan became the major base used by the United States in the policy of containment of China during the Cold War. China opposed the United States-Japan Security Treaty and the large presence of U.S. military forces in Japan. At the same time, Chinese officials in the 1950s and 1960s engaged in active interchange with opposition politicians and opinion leaders in Japan. Public opinion in Japan tended to favor improved relations with China. Business interests there chafed at U.S.-led efforts to restrict Japanese and other allied economic interchange with China.[4]

China toughened its public posture toward Japan as part of its broadly more radical approach to domestic and foreign policy issues during the period of the Great Leap Forward in the late 1950s. The collapse of the Sino-Soviet alliance coincided with more pragmatic economic policies in China during the early 1960s. Against this background, Chinese leaders came to welcome Japan's interest in developing trade and other economic relations.

An agreement in 1962 governed five years of trade anticipated at a value of $100 million annually. In fact, the new arrangement and other channels of exchange saw Sino-Japanese trade grow from $137 million in 1963 to over $600 million in 1966 before declining during the violent period of China's Cultural Revolution and then recovering again to about $600 million in 1969. Japan became an increasingly important source for material needed for China's economic modernization; the pragmatic Sino-Japanese relationship continued even during disruptions of the Cultural Revolution. Japan was the major developed country involved in the support of China's economy.[5]

While continuing to trade with Japan even during the most disruptive and violent years of the Cultural Revolution in the late 1960s, Beijing also strove to use its nascent opening to the Nixon administration and growing pro-PRC sentiment in Japan in order to isolate Japanese prime minister Eisaku Sato and his conservative Liberal Democratic Party (LDP) government over their refusal to break ties with Taiwan and establish ties with Beijing. Richard Nixon's surprise opening to China forced a change in government in Japan. Sato, with a tough policy toward China, was replaced and the new Japanese administration quickly adjusted policy, setting the stage for improved political as well as economic relations for much of the rest of the Cold War. A highlight of progress was the establishment of official diplomatic relations in 1972 using an arrangement to deal with continued unofficial Japanese relations with Taiwan that became known as the Japanese formula, which was followed by the United States in its normalization of relations with China. Another highlight was the signing of the China-Japan Peace and Friendship Treaty in 1978, in which China pressed to include a clause opposing "hegemony," a reference to joint opposition to Soviet international expansion. As in the case of Chinese interaction with the United States and U.S. allies, China at this time urged strong Japanese defense and other measures as part of an international united front to deal with the menace seen in expanding Soviet international power and influence. Chinese long-standing concerns with the historical legacies of Japan's aggression against China leading to World War II and the perceived potential revival of what China called Japanese militarism were played down in the interest of seeing stronger Japanese national security efforts against the Soviet danger.[6]

As post-Mao China developed an "open door" foreign economic policy in the late 1970s, Japan loomed large in China's development calculus. Japan was China's largest trading partner. Aid relations grew rapidly, and by 1982 China was the largest recipient of official Japanese development assistance.

Nonetheless, Chinese discontent grew in the 1980s over what China's officials and opinion leaders perceived as asymmetrical aspects of the economic relationship. For example, China sold Japan coal, oil, and raw materials; Japan sold China higher-value-added machinery, autos, and other equipment. Uncertain about the overall business climate in China, Japanese business and government representatives eschewed large-scale direct investment in China; Japan also shared less technology with China than with some other developing countries. Combined with Chinese irritation over the refusal of Japanese officials to take what Beijing saw as an appropriately contrite posture regarding Japan's negative war record in China, the seeming imbalance in economic benefits led to sharp criticisms and demonstrations against Japan by students, opinion leaders, and some officials. Both governments moved to minimize the disputes, with Japan notably stepping up its aid efforts in China and curbing official references to the war record that were likely to elicit a sharp Chinese response.[7]

There also was some ambivalence in China's attitude to growing U.S.-Japan security relations, which became especially close during the rule of President Ronald Reagan and Prime Minister Yasuhiro Nakasone. As explained in chapter 3, China shifted in the early 1980s to a more evenhanded posture in dealing with the superpowers and was less supportive of strengthening U.S. security measures around China's periphery in Asia; the phase didn't last long, and China eventually came to support American and Japanese approaches in the face of a continued Soviet hard line in Asia up to the mid-1980s.

A period of several years after the Tiananmen incident of 1989 was widely acknowledged as the most positive and cooperative period in Sino-Japanese relations since World War II. Japan's initial response to the incident was muted. Initially Tokyo went along with the United States and other leading developed countries in the so-called Group of Seven (G-7) as it imposed sanctions against China. In July 1990, however, Tokyo diverged from the rest of the G-7 to announce a resumption of lending to China. The Chinese government strongly supported the Japanese move, which ushered in a three-year period of cooperation and cordiality.[8]

A visit to China by Prime Minister Toshiki Kaifu in 1991 confirmed that Tiananmen was no longer an obstacle to a cordial relationship. The change in Japanese policy coincided with a surge in Japanese investment in China; many Japanese business leaders judged that Chinese authorities had shown themselves to be capable of maintaining stability, and this and later rapid

Chinese economic growth encouraged Japanese investment. In a notable departure from past Japanese practice emphasizing the primacy of relations with the United States and the U.S.-Japan alliance, Japanese prime minister Morihiro Hosokawa declared in late 1991 that Japan's relationship with China was as important as its relationship with the United States. A successful visit to China by the Japanese emperor in 1992 indicated just how far the two sides were willing to go in order to put the past behind them, at least for the time being. More forthright expressions of regret by Japanese leaders, including Hosokawa's in 1993 for past Japanese aggression against China, also were appreciated by the Chinese. Economic relations developed rapidly, with China becoming Japan's second-largest destination for direct foreign investment after the United States. Official dialogues and intergovernmental cooperation expanded, including cooperation in military and security matters. [9]

The broad trends in relations since the mid-1990s have featured serious differences over historical, territorial, diplomatic, and security issues, even though economic ties and interdependence continue to advance. Japanese elite and public opinion has turned against China, and Chinese opinion of Japan remains suspicious and largely negative. Both sides demonstrate a tendency to react in nationalistic ways in response to perceived affronts by the other. Chinese official interaction with Japan has been the least forthcoming in the general Chinese efforts in the post–Cold War period to reassure its neighbors that China's rise will not threaten their interests. Although some Japanese leaders have tried to give greater priority to improving relations with China, more common is a defensive concern about rising Chinese power asserting leadership in Asia at odds with fundamental Japanese political, economic, and security interests. As a result, Japanese leaders have sought closer security ties with the United States and have broadened relationships with Australia, India, and other powers seen useful in securing an Asian environment that would support and protect the interests of Japan as its power diminishes in the face of China's rise.

Against this background, a range of specialists foresee Sino-Japanese rivalry and confrontation characterizing the order in Asia for many years to come. [10] They highlight changes in attitudes of Japanese and Chinese decision makers, opinion leaders, and popular opinion about the status and outlook of their mutual relations. They tend to see initiatives reflecting strong Sino-Japanese friction and rivalry. Signs of Sino-Japanese competition and rivalry include the following:

- Separate and seemingly competing proposals by China and Japan to establish free-trade arrangements with the ten Southeast Asian nations in the Association of Southeast Asian Nations (ASEAN) and other signs of competition for leadership in Asian regional organizations, notably the Sino-Japanese struggle for influence in the lead-up to the East Asian Summit (EAS) of December 2005
- Intensifying competition for control of energy and other resources and disputed territory in the East China Sea
- Active Chinese international lobbying against high-priority Japanese efforts in 2005–2006 to gain a permanent seat in the UN Security Council
- Strong Japanese competition with China to gain improved access to Russian oil in the Far East
- Greater Japanese support for Taiwan at a time of stronger U.S. backing of Taiwan during the Bush administration
- The first significant cutbacks in Japanese aid to China since the normalization of relations in the 1970s
- Increased Japanese willingness to deploy military forces in Asia in support of U.S. and UN initiatives
- Stepped up Japanese efforts to improve security, aid, and/or other relations with Australia, India, and other nations on China's southern and western flanks, including strong Japanese aid efforts for Pakistan, Afghanistan, and central Asian countries
- Increased Japanese efforts to solidify relations with South Korea and the United States to form a closer Japan-South Korea-U.S. alignment in reaction to China's refusal to condemn repeated North Korean aggression against South Korea in 2010 and related Chinese truculence over its territorial claims in the Yellow Sea.

Other specialists give greater weight to the common interests and forces that continue to bind Sino-Japanese relations and to limit the chances of serious confrontation or conflict. Mutual interests center on strong, growing economic and strategic interdependence between Japan and China, and the influence of the United States and other third parties, including other national powers in Asia—all of whom favor and could be expected to work to preserve Sino-Japanese stability. Specific elements of the argument against the development of serious Sino-Japanese confrontation involve the following:

- Both the Japanese and Chinese governments remain domestically focused, and continue to give top priority to the economic development of their countries, which they believe require a prolonged, peaceful, and cooperative relationship with their Asian neighbors, notably one another.
- China values Japan for some economic assistance, for technology and investment, and as a market for Chinese goods; Japan is increasingly dependent on China as a market, source of imports, and offshore manufacturing base.
- Personnel exchanges between Japan and China have grown markedly. Tens of thousands of Japanese students have visited or studied in China each year. Government-sponsored exchange programs abound, and even if they do not always promote positive feelings, they probably promote more realistic mutual perceptions.
- No other government in Asian affairs—with the possible exception of North Korea—would benefit from or seek to promote greater Sino-Japanese friction. This includes the United States, which remains careful to balance its strong alliance with Japan with emphasis on closer mutually beneficial relations with China. [11]

RELATIONS WITH TAIWAN

As discussed in chapter 2, Mao Zedong repeatedly probed U.S. and Nationalist Chinese defenses in the Taiwan Strait during the 1950s. There were major episodes of military conflict during the so-called Taiwan Strait crises of 1954–1955 and again in 1958. Mao's actions were in line with broader efforts to confront and counter American-backed security measures in the ring of containment established following the start of the Korean War. The actions concerned and sometimes alarmed Nikita Khrushchev and the other Soviet leaders who were linked with China and wary of getting dragged into a war with the United States over Taiwan or other issues. Aligned with Chiang Kai-shek's Nationalist forces on Taiwan, the U.S. leadership also was wary of getting involved in direct combat with China, though it showed resolve and repeatedly used threats of nuclear war and thereby engaged in what was pejoratively called "nuclear blackmail" in order to get the Communists to stop their aggression.

Communist military probes subsided with the massive economic collapse of the failed Great Leap Forward and the public break between China and its superpower ally in Moscow. The United States worked to insure a stasis in the Taiwan Strait by curbing Chiang Kai-shek's ambitions to exploit the Chinese difficulties and launch an attack on the mainland. The Communists on the mainland arguably enjoyed more support than the Nationalists in Taiwan among the newly emerging former colonies obtaining independence in the 1950s and 1960s. Nevertheless, Taiwan competed actively through foreign assistance efforts and other measures to win support in the developing world. Beijing's attraction also was overshadowed by the frequent xenophobic outbursts evident during the radical stage of "Red Guard diplomacy" during the early years of China's Cultural Revolution. [12]

The opening of China to relations with the United States and its allies and associates fundamentally changed the cross-strait dynamic. China enjoyed broad international support as it took the China seat on the United Nations Security Council and related bodies and Taiwan lost official representation. Chinese leaders used negotiations on diplomatic relations with the United States, Japan, and dozens of other countries establishing official relations with Beijing at this time to require breaking official ties with Taiwan. Within a few years, Taiwan was isolated with only two dozen states sustaining official relations. The loss of U.S. official recognition and the ending of the U.S.-Taiwan defense treaty and all other official connections placed the Nationalist Party government, now led by Chiang Kai-shek's son, Chiang Ching-kuo, under enormous pressure. Not only was Taiwan less secure vis-à-vis China and acutely isolated internationally, it was under attack domestically from large and growing numbers of Taiwan's citizens who were unsympathetic with the authoritarian regime and favored a greater voice for their ambitions for Taiwan to be an independent government separate from China. [13]

Building on its international advantages, China appealed to Taiwan to pursue a "peaceful" path to reunification and as part of the first steps to open links for direct trade, transportation, and other communication across the strait. Taiwan rebuffed the Chinese initiatives. It sustained close unofficial ties with the United States, including active arms sales, despite U.S.-Chinese agreements ostensibly limiting such sales. Taiwan's economy was strong and deeply integrated with Japan, the United States, and other major trading powers. Politically, the Chiang Ching-kuo government moved toward liberalization and democracy, which eased the split between the "mainlanders," those who came from mainland China with Chiang Kai-shek and their descendents, and the "Taiwanese," those whose roots in Taiwan went back to before the Chiang Kai-shek government, which was imposed on them after World War II.[14]

As martial law and other features of the authoritarian regime in Taiwan ended in the late 1980s, Chiang Ching-kuo's successor, Lee Teng-hui, took power as president and chairman of the Nationalist Party. Lee encouraged an emerging two-party political system as his Nationalist Party government sought its legitimacy at the ballot box from the voters of Taiwan. Unlike Chiang Kai-shek and his son, who stayed in Taiwan during their presidencies, Lee sought international travel as a means to highlight his importance to Taiwan's voters and to enhance Taiwan's international stature. As explained in chapter 4, international circumstances were favorable as China was isolated on account of the harsh crackdown after the Tiananmen incident, and Taiwan's emerging democracy and vibrant economy appeared very positive by comparison. Even the Clinton administration was persuaded to change policy and allow Lee to visit the United States in 1995.

Lee's American visit prompted an extraordinary Chinese response, with a string of live-fire military exercises including ballistic missile tests in sensitive areas of the Taiwan Strait for the next nine months. The exercises were designed to deter Lee and others in Taiwan whom China suspected of working toward Taiwan independence. They also seemed designed to influence and perhaps intimidate the Taiwan voters in the lead-up to the first direct election of the Taiwan president in March 1996. And they demonstrated to the United States the risks and costs it would bear in the event that it supported Lee in further moves toward Taiwan independence.[15]

The Clinton administration delayed reaction to the Chinese military exercise for seven months. As the exercises continued and reached a crescendo prior to the Taiwan presidential election, the U.S. government sent two aircraft carrier battle groups to the Taiwan area, marking the most serious U.S.-China military faceoff over Taiwan since the 1950s.[16]

Subsequently, cross-strait dynamics changed markedly.[17] An important area of continuity was that China continued to encourage cross-strait economic and social exchanges, and these were attractive to many business people and others in Taiwan who pressed their government to allow for closer economic and other advantageous relations with China.

Significant change came as China increased diplomatic pressure to isolate and punish Taiwan for its efforts to seek greater international representation through presidential visits and other means. In the wake of China's show of resolve in the Taiwan Strait following the Lee Teng-hui visit to the United

States, few nations—including the United States—were ready to bear the responsibility and costs associated with hosting the Taiwan president. Many nations that had been open to informal contacts with Taiwan's leaders pulled back in the face of intense pressure from China.

Perhaps the most important change came in military preparations. The U.S. deployment of aircraft carriers showed China that its military preparations would need to be sufficient to offset U.S. military intervention to support Taiwan. The double-digit increases in the Chinese defense budgets for the next two decades focused importantly on building capabilities not only to intimidate Taiwan but to deter American intervention.

A new political order in Taiwan under President Chen Shui-bian began in May 2000, ending fifty years of rule by the Nationalist Party. Many in Taiwan, the PRC, and the United States linked Chen with the past strongly pro-independence stance of his party, the Democratic Progressive Party (DPP). There were widespread predictions of an imminent crisis in cross-strait relations when Chen was elected. In fact, Chen initially appeared more moderate than was widely anticipated.[18]

A turn for the worse in cross-strait relations came with Chen Shui-bian's shift to a much more assertive and pro-independence stance in 2003–2004, which Chinese officials watched with dismay. Chen's government rejected the principle of one China, condemned China's pressure tactics, and pushed hard for broad-ranging legal and institutional reforms in civil service practices, education, cultural support, public information, diplomacy, and other areas. The reforms, which included major constitutional changes, sought to end past government practices that identified Taiwan with China and reinforced Taiwan's identity as a country permanently separate from China.[19]

Chinese and U.S. officials viewed the reforms as steps toward independence and as making it increasingly unlikely that Taiwan ever would voluntarily agree to be part of China.[20] Chinese officials focused on possible changes in provisions in the Republic of China constitution that identified Taiwan with China. They warned that removing those provisions and establishing a formal and legally binding status for Taiwan as a country permanently separate from China would result in China's use of force. Officials from the United States were anxious to avoid this outcome. Overall, the situation in the Taiwan Strait became tenser. China's leaders found that their mix of economic incentives, proposals for talks, military threats, and coercive diplomacy had obviously failed to stop Taiwan's moves toward greater separation.[21]

Seeing the rise of instability and an increased danger of conflict in the Taiwan area, U.S. president George W. Bush publicly rebuked Taiwan's president on December 9, 2003. Chinese officials urged U.S. and international pressure to rein in Chen. They judged that a strident public Chinese stance probably would increase support for him in the prevailing atmosphere in Taiwan and thus be counterproductive for China's purposes.[22]

Chen's narrow reelection victory in March 2004 showed Chinese and other observers how far the Taiwan electorate had moved from the 1990s, when pro-independence was a clear liability among the Taiwanese voters. Chinese officials were pleased that U.S. pressure sought to curb Chen's more ambitious reform efforts that flirted with de jure independence, but they pushed for more overt U.S. pressure, including curbs on U.S. arms sales.[23] Officials from the United States continued to press Chen to avoid provocative actions but remained firm in maintaining military support for Taiwan as a means to deter China from using force against Taiwan. They intervened repeatedly in the lead-up to the 2004 legislative elections to highlight differences between U.S. policy and the assertive positions of President Chen and his supporters.[24]

In the end, the turmoil in Taiwan's relations with China and with the United States caused by Chen's maneuvers and their negative consequences for cross-strait and U.S.-Taiwan relations, along with Chen's apparent deep personal involvement in corruption scandals, seemed to undermine the attractiveness of DPP candidates in Taiwan's legislative elections in January 2008 and the presidential election in March 2008. The result was a landslide victory for the Nationalist Party (Kuomintang, KMT) candidates. The party gained overwhelming control of the legislature; the new president, Ma Ying-jeou, had a strong political mandate to pursue policies of reassurance and moderation in cross-strait relations.[25]

President Ma came to power with an agenda emphasizing that his government would not move Taiwan toward independence and stressing closer economic, social, and other contacts across the strait. Ma and his colleagues in Taiwan and their counterparts in China have emphasized that progress will be easier in building closer and mutually advantageous economic and social ties; however, issues of security and sovereignty posed by the growing Chinese military buildup opposite Taiwan and reaching agreement on Taiwan's desired greater international participation will be harder to deal with.[26]

On the whole, the improvements in cross-strait relations have been rapid and impressive. The security situation in the Taiwan Strait has entered a period of relaxing tensions. Both Beijing and Taipei have emphasized enhancing people-to-people contacts and expanding economic ties. A major development was an agreement in 2010 establishing free trade between China and Taiwan known as the Economic Cooperation Framework Agreement (ECFA), which provided privileged access to Chinese markets and other economic benefits for various important constituencies in Taiwan.[27] On balance, Taiwan's voters saw the benefits as sufficient and supported President Ma's reelection in 2012. Also, the opposition DPP gradually moved its cross-strait policies away from past challenges to China and toward a more cooperative approach favored by the Taiwan electorate.[28]

There was no significant action on the part of the Chinese government to reduce its military presence directly opposite Taiwan. President Ma also was reluctant to engage in talks with China on a possible peace agreement, and he argued that discussion on possible reunification between Taiwan and China would have to await developments after his term in office.

The numerous cross-strait agreements brought burgeoning face-to-face interaction between Taiwan's and China's governments after decades of no direct dealings. The agreements were between ostensibly unofficial organizations—Taiwan's Straits Exchange Foundation (SEF) and China's Association for Relations across the Taiwan Strait (ARATS)—but they required officials of the two governments to deal with each other on a host of transportation, food safety, financial regulation, and law enforcement issues. In effect, three channels of communication were now active between Taiwan and China: the SEF-ARATS exchanges; exchanges between the leaders of the Chinese Communist Party (CCP) and Taiwan's KMT; and widening government-to-government coordination and cooperation on a variety of cross-strait issues. Many of the agreements, interactions, and understandings focused on managing the large-scale trade and investment between Taiwan and China.[29]

Meanwhile, the Ma Ying-jeou government achieved a breakthrough in getting China to allow Taiwan to participate in the annual World Health Assembly (WHA) meeting as an observer using the name "Chinese Taipei." Other evidence of progress in China-Taiwan relations over issues regarding Taiwan's participation in international affairs was the diminishment of what had been intense Taiwan-China competition for international recognition.[30]

U.S. reaction to recent developments in China-Taiwan relations has been positive. The Bush administration welcomed the efforts of the Ma government and China's positive response as stabilizing and beneficial for all parties concerned. It turned aside an initiative by President-elect Ma to visit the United States for talks with U.S. officials prior to his inauguration. Ma made no other such requests to the U.S. government; he worked hard to keep his transit stops in the United States discreet in ways that would not complicate U.S. relations with China. High-level contacts occurred between the United States and Taiwan in quiet and private ways that avoided upsetting China, and ongoing U.S. military consultations with and advice to Taiwan's armed forces continued.[31]

The Bush administration delayed until close to the last minute approval of a large arms sales package for Taiwan. The approved package worth $6.5 billion was the largest during the tenure of the Bush government. Initial generous offers from the United States during Bush's first year in office were repeatedly delayed and whittled down on account of partisan bickering and funding delays for many years in Taiwan; this was followed by U.S. reluctance to provide arms that would appear to support President Chen Shui-bian's provocative stance toward China. In the end, the package in 2008 represented about half of what Taiwan said it wanted, and it did not include sixty-six F-16 fighters that Taiwan had been trying for years to get the U.S. government to consider selling to Taiwan. China reacted to the sale with strong criticism and suspension of military contacts with the United States. Those contacts were resumed in mid-2009.[32]

The Barack Obama government welcomed the new stability in cross-strait ties. Like the outgoing Bush government, the Obama administration appeared to be relying on President Ma and his team to continue to manage cross-strait ties in positive ways that would not cause the Taiwan "hot spot" to reemerge on the already crowded list of policy priorities needing urgent attention by the new U.S. leader.[33] The Obama government followed through with a $6 billion arms package for Taiwan in 2010 and a similarly large package in 2011. The packages did not include F-16 fighters; they prompted sometimes strident public complaints from China, along with limited substantive retaliation.[34]

RELATIONS WITH THE KOREAN PENINSULA

In the wake of the Korean War, discussed in chapter 2, China had strong advantage over the Soviet Union in relations with Kim Il Sung and his Communist administration in North Korea. At enormous cost in manpower and resources, China's military rescued the North Korean regime from annihilation at the hands of the United States and provided secure "rear area" support against strengthening South Korea and the United States building the sinews of containment on the peninsula. Solicitous of Chinese assistance and maintaining close North Korean-Chinese relations, Kim Il Sung nonetheless established a position as the sole major Communist leader in Asia able to sustain a balanced position without taking sides in what emerged as intense Sino-Soviet competition for international support. As the Soviet leadership of Leonid Brezhnev expanded involvement in Asia in competition with China for influence in the region, Kim maneuvered between Moscow and Beijing.[35]

China's Cultural Revolution featured Red Guard attacks against Kim Il Sung as a "fat revisionist," and normal Sino–North Korean interchange was disrupted with the collapse of regular lines of communication and command. There was possible danger to China caused by the so-called *Pueblo* incident, involving North Korean capture in January 1968 of a U.S. ship and crew engaged in gathering electronic intelligence off the coast of North Korea. However, the impact of the incident was overshadowed in the United States by the Communist Tet offensive in Vietnam. China meanwhile was in the throes of violent internal turmoil during this phase of the Cultural Revolution.[36]

Chinese leaders endeavored to reach out to international leaders including Kim Il Sung as they sought to build leverage and avoid isolation in the face of burgeoning pressure and threat from the Soviet Union in 1969. Kim disapproved of China's opening to the United States, though he came to engage in talks and reach agreements with South Korea, temporarily easing tensions on the peninsula. Chinese leader Deng Xiaoping reportedly counseled Kim Il Sung at the time of the U.S. retreat from Vietnam in 1975 that North Korea should not use the occasion to attack South Korea.[37]

After Deng was again purged in early 1976 and then returned to power beginning in 1977, the Chinese reformer pursued closer relations with the United States and Japan in opposition to what China called Soviet "hegemonism." Deng worked hard, notably during a five-day visit to North Korea in 1978, to prevent Kim Il Sung's strong disagreement with China's pro-U.S. and pro-Japan positions from driving North Korea to the Soviet side in the intense Sino-Soviet rivalry.[38] As discussed in chapter 3, China in 1981 came to play down ties with the United States and Japan while opening to more exchanges with the Soviet Union in a brief period of "independent" foreign policy. The Chinese change opened greater common ground between China

and North Korea. Improvement in North Korean–Chinese relations continued during the visit to China of Kim Il Sung's son and heir apparent, Kim
Jong Il, in mid-1983. China's relations with North Korea then declined after
North Korea's assassination of South Korean leaders in a bombing in Ran-
goon, Burma, in October 1983. Continuing to play both sides of the street in
a continuing strong Sino-Soviet competition for influence, Kim Il Sung in
1984 made his first visit to the Soviet Union in over twenty years.[39]

Mikhail Gorbachev's Soviet Union steadily withdrew the expensive support the USSR had been providing to North Korea and began reciprocating
strong South Korean interest in improving relations with Moscow as well as
Beijing. The Soviet Union and South Korea established diplomatic relations
in 1990. Post-Mao China also was interested in closer relations with South
Korea and its vibrant economy. Trade grew rapidly in the 1980s despite the
absence of official relations between the two governments. China endeavored to sustain good relations with North Korea while moving forward incre-
mentally with South Korea, eventually establishing official diplomatic relations in 1992.[40]

Chinese policy and practice toward North and South Korea following the
end of the Cold War showed China endeavoring to sustain a leading position
in relations with both North and South Korea as it reacted to changing
circumstances on the Korean peninsula. Growing Chinese frustration with
the twists and turns of North Korean behavior, especially Pyongyang's nuclear weapons development, has not resulted in a major change in China's
reluctance to pressure North Korea to conform more to international norms
and eschew provocations and confrontation. China's focus has been to preserve stability in an uncertain environment caused by internal pressures and
international provocations of North Korea and erratic policies by the United
States and South Korea. China continues to follow practices that give priority
to positive incentives rather than pressure in order to elicit North Korean
willingness to avoid further provocations and to return to negotiations on
eventual denuclearization.

Developments in the two decades since the end of the Cold War can be
divided into three periods:[41]

• 1989–2000 featured Chinese angst over North Korean leadership transi-
  tion and instability and economic collapse as well as a crisis with the
  United States prompted by North Korea's nuclear weapons development.
  China supported U.S. efforts to negotiate the Agreed Framework of 1994,

which eased tensions over North Korea's suspected nuclear weapons program; it provided measured material support for North Korea in a period of economic collapse; and it markedly improved economic and political ties with South Korea.

- 2000–2001 featured a period of unprecedented détente, where China facilitated North Korean outreach and endeavored to keep pace with expanding North Korean contacts with South Korea, the United States, Russia, and others.
- 2002–2009 featured periodic and intense North Korean provocations and wide swings in U.S. policy ranging from thinly disguised efforts to force regime change in North Korea to close collaboration with Pyongyang negotiators. South Korean policy also shifted markedly from a soft to a harder line in dealing with North Korea.

A careful review of the gains China has made in improving relations with Asian neighbors and elsewhere in recent years shows South Korea to have been an area of considerable achievement, until very recent years. The Chinese advances with South Korea also coincided with the most serious friction in U.S.–South Korean relations since the Korean War during the first term (2001–2005) of the George W. Bush administration. Thus, China's influence relative to the United States grew on the Korean peninsula.

Meanwhile, U.S. policy evolved in dealing with North Korea. By 2003 the George W. Bush administration was working much more closely with China in order to facilitate international talks on North Korea's nuclear weapons program. North Korea at that time seemed to prefer to deal directly with the United States on this issue. While such bilateral interchange with North Korea presumably would have boosted U.S. influence relative to that of China in peninsula affairs, the U.S. government tended to see such U.S.-North Korean contacts as counterproductive for U.S. interests in securing a verifiable end of North Korea's nuclear weapons program. Thus, China's influence grew as it joined with the United States in the multilateral efforts to deal with the North Korean nuclear weapons issue on the one hand, while Beijing sustained its position as the foreign power having the closest relationship with the reclusive North Korean regime on the other. [42]

Against this background, China's relations with South Korea improved markedly. [43] China became South Korea's leading trading partner, the recipient in some years of the largest amount of South Korean foreign investment, and the most important foreign destination for South Korean tourists and students. For many years, it was a close and often like-minded partner in dealing with issues posed by North Korea's nuclear weapons program and related provocations on the one hand, and dealing with the Bush administration's hard-line policy toward North Korea on the other.

South Korea's trade with China grew rapidly in recent years. Despite the global economic crisis of 2008–2009, the two countries met a goal of $200 billion in trade in 2010, according to Chinese figures. Chinese trade figures showed that about 30 percent of South Korean exports went to China and that China ran a $70 billion trade deficit with South Korea in 2010. South Korea has become the third largest source of foreign investment in China, and China is the largest destination of foreign investment from South Korea. Meanwhile, in the face of the Bush administration's tough stance toward North Korea, 2001–2006, South Korea and China were close partners in dealing more moderately than the United States with issues posed by North Korea's nuclear weapons program and related provocations.[44]

As relations developed, however, China's economic importance for South Korea was seen by South Koreans more in both negative and positive ways. Periodic trade disputes came with growing concerns by South Korean manufacturers, political leaders, and public opinion about competition from fast-advancing Chinese enterprises. China's economic attractiveness to South Korean consumers declined markedly as a result of repeated episodes of Chinese exports of harmfully tainted consumer products to South Korean and other markets. South Korean leaders strove to break out of close dependence on economic ties with China through free-trade agreements and other arrangements with the United States, Japan, and the European Union that would insure inputs of foreign investment and technology needed for South Korea to stay ahead of Chinese competitors.

Other differences between the two countries focused on competing Chinese and Korean claims regarding the scope and importance of the historical Goguryeo kingdom, China's longer-term ambitions in North Korea, and Chinese treatment of North Korean refugees in China and of South Koreans endeavoring to assist them there. The disputes had a strong impact on nationalistic South Korean political leaders and public opinion. Public opinion polls showed a significant decline in South Korean views of China and its policies and practices since earlier in the past decade.[45]

Regarding Chinese relations with North Korea, China's frustration followed the North Korean nuclear weapons tests in 2006 and 2009 and other provocations.[46] The evidence of growing Chinese frustration with North Korea was strong; contrary to past practice, the Chinese government allowed a public debate where relations with North Korea often were depicted as a liability for China, requiring serious readjustment in Chinese policy. On balance, the overall record of Chinese policy and practice has shown continuing caution; China endeavors to preserve important Chinese interests in stability on the Korean peninsula through judicious moves that strike an appropriate balance among varied Chinese relations with concerned parties at home and abroad. China remains wary that North Korea, the United States, and others could shift course, forcing further Chinese adjustments in response.

Chinese leaders recognize that their cautious policies have failed to halt North Korea's nuclear weapons development; they probably judge that they will be living with a nuclear North Korea for some time to come, even as they emphasize continued diplomatic efforts to reverse North Korea's nuclear weapons development and create a nuclear-free peninsula. They appear resigned to joining with U.S. and other leaders in what is characterized as "failure management" as far as North Korean nuclear weapons development is concerned.[47] They will endeavor to preserve stability and Chinese equities with concerned powers. As in the recent past, they probably will avoid pressure or other risky initiatives on their own, waiting for the actions of others or changed circumstances that would increase the prospects of curbing North Korea's nuclear challenge and allow for stronger Chinese measures to deal with nuclear North Korea.

Recent Developments—Setbacks for China

China continued to make gains since the start of 2010 in solidifying its position as the most important and avid supporter of the North Korean leadership as North Korea undergoes the most significant leadership transition in a generation amid poor domestic conditions and generally unfriendly international circumstances.[48] China also deepened economic relations with both North and South Korea. Though discussions between China and North Korean remain secret, it appears that bilateral relations have registered significant improvement despite differences over North Korea's proliferation and military provocations.

The same cannot be said about China's relations with South Korea. In 2010, those ties reached the lowest point since the establishment of diplomatic relations. Recent contacts designed to improve relations, notably a visit of one of China's rising "fifth generation" leaders, Vice Prime Minister Li

Keqiang, to Seoul in 2011 and a visit of President Lee Myung-Bak to Beijing in 2012, have barely hidden deep differences. China's refusal to criticize North Korean military attacks against South Korea left a lasting and widespread impression of where China's priorities lie when choosing between North and South Korea. In particular, China refused to join strong international condemnation of North Korea's sinking in March 2010 of the South Korean warship *Cheonan*, which killed forty-three South Korean military personnel, and the North Korean artillery barrage in November 2010 attacking South Korean soldiers and civilians on a coastal island, killing four and injuring others. China also blocked or weakened efforts in the United Nations against the North Korean aggression. Against this background and contrary to China's longer-term objective to diminish U.S. and Japanese influence on the Korean peninsula, China has faced strengthened U.S.–South Korean and U.S.-Japanese alliance relationships, and off-again on-again efforts to forge closer strategic coordination between South Korea and Japan over North Korean issues. Adding to South Korean and U.S. differences with China was Beijing's unexpectedly strong public opposition in 2010 to U.S.-ROK military exercises in the Yellow Sea that were targeted at showing allied resolve and deepening deterrence against further North Korean military provocations.[49]

RELATIONS WITH SOUTHEAST ASIA AND THE ASIA-PACIFIC

It has not been easy for the People's Republic of China to sustain an approach or approaches to Southeast Asia that allow for steady progress for China in this important neighboring region. The 1950s featured strong Chinese political, military, and economic support for the Vietnamese and other Communist-led forces in Indochina battling U.S.-backed French forces up to 1954 and then American-backed indigenous leaders. China was generally critical of regional governments that sided with the United States and established formal security relationship with the United States.[50]

The mid-1950s featured an interlude of "peaceful coexistence" consistent with the efforts of the Soviet Union to ease international tensions and advance relations with independent-minded governments emerging in the developing world. As discussed in chapter 2, China became more radical in foreign affairs as its domestic policies swung to extremes in the Great Leap Forward and disagreements with the Soviet Union led to an open Sino-Soviet rift by 1960. In Southeast Asia, China continued overt support for Communists in Vietnam and Laos. Thinly disguised Chinese propaganda, financial, and military support grew for Communist-led insurgencies targeting several pro-Western governments (Thailand, Malaysia, and the Philippines). Better hidden—even from the pro-China leader of Cambodia at the time, Prince Norodom Sihanouk—was Chinese support for Pol Pot and other Cambodian Communists who would form the Khmer Rouge. In 1960, China settled its disputed border with Burma—which in recent years had seen Chinese military forces cross into Burma repeatedly to deal with remnants of Chiang Kai-shek Nationalist forces operating there as well as other concerns for China.[51]

As noted in chapter 2, China for several years in the 1960s placed great emphasis on its ever-closer relationship with Indonesia and its leader, Sukarno, who increasingly favored left-leaning policies. China supported President Sukarno in his radical nationalist policies of confrontation with Malaysia, which was backed by Great Britain, over whether Malaysia or Indonesia should control the disputed regions of Sarawak and Sabah. China also cooperated closely with the Indonesian Communist Party (PKI), the world's largest nonruling Communist party, which was growing rapidly in influence under Sukarno's policies.

In September 1965, radical officers attempted a coup against the top-level, anti-Communist leadership of the army. Several army leaders were assassinated. General Suharto took control of the army and put down the abortive coup. The army blamed the coup attempt on the PKI and instigated an Indonesia-wide anti-Communist propaganda campaign. An anti-Communist reign of terror developed. Hundreds of thousands of Communists, ethnic Chinese, and others were killed; the PKI was crushed. General Suharto sidelined Sukarno and took power as president in 1968, consolidating his influence over the military and government. Indonesian relations with China were suspended and would not be resumed for over twenty years.[52]

Faced with the deepening American military involvement in Vietnam and among Western-leaning Southeast Asian governments in the 1960s, China expanded its support and involvement in backing North Vietnam and Communist-led fighters against the Americans. China also upped the ante in supporting the Communist-led insurgences targeting Southeast Asian states with pro-U.S. leanings. Meanwhile, Red Guard diplomacy beginning in 1966 alienated several Southeast Asian governments that had been favorable to China, notably Cambodia and Burma.

In Burma, relations deteriorated seriously in 1967 when clashes inspired by Cultural Revolution zealots led to full-scale anti-Chinese riots leaving over one hundred Chinese dead. China subsequently organized, armed, and trained a large (twenty thousand fighters) insurgency against the Burmese administration under the rubric of the Burmese Communist Party, which posed the major security threat to the Burmese government for the next twenty years.[53]

Cambodia's Prince Sihanouk overcame difficulties with China during the early years of the Cultural Revolution. When he was toppled from power in 1970 by generals backed by the United States, Sihanouk was supported by Chinese leaders who encouraged him to align with the Chinese-backed Khmer Rouge guerrillas in Cambodia. China continued support for Sihanouk and the Khmer Rouge regime that followed the defeat of the U.S.-backed government in 1975 with such egregious misrule and terror that over one million Cambodians died.[54]

As discussed in chapter 3, China's strong equities with the Vietnamese Communists and their associates in Laos were undermined as a result of China's alignment with the United States in the early 1970s against the USSR and the latter's strengthening relationship with Communist Vietnam. Le Duan, the Communist leader of Vietnam at the time, directed deliberations that decided to rely more closely on the Soviet Union and seek a military solution of Vietnamese reunification at odds with the Paris Peace Agreement of 1973. The decision strongly alienated China. After the Communist takeover of South Vietnam in 1975, Le Duan became leader of a unified Vietnamese state. He aligned Vietnam formally with the Soviet Union and then approved a Vietnamese invasion of Cambodia late in 1978 to overthrow the Chinese-backed Khmer Rouge government of that country. The movement toward this invasion caused a major disruption in relations between Vietnam and China; Vietnam expelled ethnic Chinese residents of the country as it cultivated a closer alliance with the Soviet Union. China launched a retaliatory invasion of Vietnam in February 1979 and maintained strong military pressure along the Sino-Vietnamese border throughout the 1980s; China also supported Khmer Rouge and other armed guerrillas resisting Vietnamese forces in Cambodia until the Vietnamese forces withdrew and peace was restored in Cambodia as a result of the Paris Peace Agreement of 1991.[55]

Against the background of the demise of the USSR in 1991 at the end of the Cold War, Chinese foreign relations with Southeast Asian neighbors went through distinct phases in the following decades. In the shifts from one phase to the next Chinese leaders reversed or revised policy actions and goals seen as having failed or otherwise become counterproductive for Chinese interests, and added policy actions and goals better suited to advancing Chinese interests.[56]

1989–1996: The first phase witnessed strong Chinese efforts to break out of the post Tiananmen isolation and pressure imposed by the United States and Western-aligned countries by means of more active Chinese diplomacy. Chinese diplomacy focused on neighboring countries and other developing states that were more inclined to deal with China pragmatically and without pressure regarding China's political system or other internal affairs. The Chinese government emphasized sovereignty and nationalism and passed a territorial law in 1992 strongly asserting claims to disputed territories, especially along China's eastern and southern maritime borders. The Chinese military backed efforts by Chinese oil companies, fishing enterprises, and others to advance Chinese claims in the Spratly Islands of the South China Sea against the expansion of such activities by Vietnam, the Philippines, Malaysia, and other claimants. A major incident in 1995 brought the leading states of ASEAN together to stand against Chinese territorial expansion, and the United States also publicly weighed-in in support of peaceful resolution of regional disputes. During the nine months of off-and-on large-scale Chinese military exercises against Taiwan in 1995–1996, few of China's neighbors explicitly sided either with China or the United States. But many were seriously concerned with the implications of China's assertiveness and ambitions.

1996–2001: Chinese leaders in this period played down military actions and assertive commentary as they demonstrated more concern to reassure neighbors in Southeast Asia and other countries that China was not a threat. They propounded principles related to a "new security concept" that built on the moderate approach China had adopted sometimes in the past regarding the so-called Five Principles of Peaceful Coexistence in international affairs. Chinese diplomacy was very active in bilateral relations, establishing various types of special partnerships and fostering good-neighbor policies. China also increased interaction with the Association for Southeast Asian Nations (ASEAN), the ASEAN Regional Forum, and other Asian regional organizations. Chinese trade relations with neighboring countries generally grew at twice the rate of China's rapidly growing economy, which remained stable amid the Asian economic crisis of 1997–1998. China did not devalue its currency, it sustained economic growth, and it supported some international efforts to assist failing regional economies—developments that boosted China's stature in the region.

The Chinese government continued strong public opposition to perceived U.S. efforts to pressure and weaken China and strong public opposition to U.S. domination and "hegemonism" in various world areas, notably including Southeast Asia. Beijing told neighboring states that its "new security concept" was in opposition to the archaic "Cold War thinking" seen in U.S. efforts to sustain and strengthen alliance relations, including U.S. alliances in Asia, notably with Japan, South Korea, Australia, and some Southeast Asian nations. Beijing indicated that these states would be wise to follow China's approach and to eschew closer alliance and military ties with the United States.

2001–present: The coming to power of the George W. Bush administration coincided with a further demonstrated shift in China's policy in Asia and elsewhere. As discussed in chapter 7, the initially tough Bush administration approach on supporting Taiwan, and opposing China's military buildup and Chinese proliferation practices, as well as other Bush administration initiatives on issues sensitive for China, such as strengthening U.S.-Japanese alliance relations and developing ballistic missile defenses in Asia and the United States, did not elicit strident criticism by Chinese officials and in official Chinese media. In the recent past, even less serious U.S. steps against Chinese interests had been routinely denounced as perceived manifestations of U.S. hegemonism and Cold War thinking.

Over time, it became clear that China was endeavoring to broaden the scope of its ongoing efforts to reassure its neighbors that China was not a threat. The broadened efforts now included and focused on the United States. The previous Chinese efforts attacking U.S. policies and alliance structures in order to get Asian governments to choose between closer relations with China and closer relations with the United States had failed and were put aside. In their place emerged a new and evolving Chinese emphasis focused on Washington as well as on Asian and other powers that China's "rise" would be a peaceful one that represented many opportunities and no threat to concerned powers. China's initial emphasis on "peaceful rise" eventually evolved into the even more moderate rubrics focused on "peaceful development" and seeking "harmony" in relations with all powers. The shift in China's approach reinforced the positive momentum in China's relations with Asian neighbors, notably in Southeast Asia and South Korea.

As in the case of Chinese relations with South Korea, the gains in Chinese relations with Southeast Asia proved difficult to sustain. China in 2009–2010 adopted what many outside of China and some in China assessed as "assertive" practices particularly regarding territorial claims with its Southeast Asian and other neighbors and the United States. The Chinese actions helped to forge growing common ground between U.S. efforts to reengage with Southeast Asia and Southeast Asian efforts to seek American support in the face of China's perceived truculence backed by an ever-increasing Chinese military buildup.[57]

Rising frictions between China and Southeast Asian neighbors, especially over the South China Sea, came along with rising frictions in China's relations with the United States over a range of issues including American military presence in the South China Sea and other waters near China. The United States and Vietnam, the Philippines, and other Southeast Asian countries appeared to deepen military, political, and other cooperation in part in order to support their interests in their respective disputes with China. The cooperation came as the United States and many other countries in the Asia-Pacific region reacted negatively to what was widely seen as new and assertive Chinese approaches—in some cases backed by military or other government-supported maritime shows of force—to disputed territories and other issues around its periphery.[58] By solidifying cooperation with the United States in a period of enhanced disputes with China, many Southeast Asian governments appeared to join the United States and other regional governments in signaling to China that its assertive actions were fostering regional trends adverse to China's interests.

Against this background, American and regional leaders tended to see as a positive development a shift beginning in late 2010 toward greater moderation in Chinese policy in regard to disputes over regional waters near China, including the South China Sea. Chinese commentary muted differences with the United States over Southeast Asian and other issues in the lead-up to President Hu Jintao's summit in Washington, D.C., in January 2011.[59] The moderate Chinese public profile toward Southeast Asian neighbors, the United States, and others was broadly welcomed by regional governments and the United States.

Unfortunately, Chinese truculence and assertiveness reemerged strongly in 2012. Chinese authorities took extraordinary measures and used impressive demonstrations of Chinese security, economic, administrative, and diplomatic power to have their way in the South China Sea:[60]

- China employed its large and growing force of maritime and fishing security ships, targeted economic sanctions, and repeated diplomatic warnings to intimidate and coerce Philippine officials, security forces, and fishermen to respect China's claims to disputed Scarborough Shoal.
- China showed stronger resolve to exploit more fully the contested fishing resources in the South China Sea with the announced deployment of one of the world's largest (thirty-two-thousand-ton) fish-processing ships to the area and the widely publicized dispatch of a fleet of thirty fishing boats supported by a supply ship to fish in disputed South China Sea areas.
- China created a new, multifaceted administrative structure backed by a new military garrison that covered wide swaths of disputed areas in the South China Sea. The coverage was reported to be in line with China's broad historical claims depicted in Chinese maps with a nine-dashed line encompassing most of the South China Sea. The large claims laid out in Chinese maps also were seen by foreign experts to provide the justification for a state-controlled Chinese oil company to offer nine new blocks of foreign oil companies' development in the South China Sea that were far from China but very close to Vietnam, with some of the areas already being developed by Vietnam. Against this background, little was heard in recent Chinese commentary of the more moderate explanation of Chinese South China Sea territorial claims made by the Chinese Foreign Ministry spokesperson on February 29, 2012, who said that China did not claim the "entire South China Sea" but only its islands and adjacent waters.
- China advanced cooperative relations with the 2012 ASEAN chair, Cambodia, thereby insuring that with Cambodia's cooperation South China Sea disputes did not receive prominent treatment in ASEAN documents in the 2012 ASEAN Ministerial Meeting. A result was strong division in ASEAN on how to deal with China that resulted in a remarkable display of ASEAN disunity in the first failure of the annual ASEAN Ministerial Meeting to conclude with an agreed-upon communiqué in the forty-five-year history of the group.

Chinese officials and official Chinese media commentaries endeavored to bound and compartmentalize the South China Sea disputes. Their public emphasis remained heavily on China's continued pursuit of peaceful development and cooperation during meetings with Southeast Asian representatives and those of other concerned powers including the United States. Thus, what emerged was a Chinese approach having at least two general paths:

- One path showed South China Sea claimants in the Philippines, Vietnam, and others in Southeast Asia, as well as their supporters in the United States and elsewhere how powerful China had become in disputed South China Sea areas, how China's security, economic, administrative, and diplomatic power was likely to grow in the near future, and how Chinese authorities could use those powerful means in intimidating and coercive ways short of overt use of military force in order to counter foreign "intrusions" or public disagreements regarding Chinese claims.
- Another path forecast ever-closer "win-win" cooperation between China and Southeast Asian countries, ASEAN, and others including the United States. It focused on burgeoning Chinese–Southeast Asian trade and economic interchange and was premised on treatment of the South China Sea dispute and others in ways that avoided public controversy and eschewed actions challenging or otherwise complicating the extensive Chinese claims to the area. In this regard, China emphasized the importance of all concerned countries to adhere to efforts to implement the 2002 Declaration of the Conduct of the Parties in the South China Sea (DOC). It duly acknowledged recent efforts supported by ASEAN to reach the "eventual" formulation of a code of conduct (COC) in the South China Sea, implying that the process of achieving the latter may take some time.

In sum, China set forth an implicit choice for the Philippines, Vietnam, other Southeast Asian disputants of China's South China Sea claims, ASEAN, and other governments and organizations with an interest in the South China Sea, notably the United States. On the one hand, based on recent practice, pursuit of policies and actions at odds with Chinese claims in the South China Sea would meet with more demonstrations of Chinese power along the lines of the first path above. On the other hand, recent Chinese leaders' statements and official commentary indicated that others' moderation and/or acquiescence regarding Chinese claims would result in the mutually beneficial development seen in the second path. At the end of 2012, the Philippines, Vietnam, and other disputants of Chinese claims did not seem to be in an advantageous position in the face of Chinese power and intimidation. ASEAN remained divided on how to deal with China. And options of the United States and other concerned powers to deal effectively with the new situation of greater muscle short of use of military force remained to be determined.

Relations with Australia, New Zealand, and the Pacific Islands

The growing disputes over the South China Sea and nearby sea-lanes, the stronger involvement of Australia and New Zealand in Asian regional bodies influencing China's position along its periphery, and the expanded U.S. role in the area under President Obama's reengagement with the Asia-Pacific have reinforced growing Chinese interests and concerns in relations with Australia, New Zealand, and the Pacific Island countries. China's economic and political prominence has grown, notably in the Pacific Islands, an area where the United States, its ally Australia, and closely associated states like New Zealand monitor and intervene in regional security and stability and where Japan and Taiwan also remain active along with China and others in seeking political influence. China's relations with Australia have improved markedly over the years, based notably on an upswing in Australian raw material exports to China and a marked increase in Chinese exports to Australia. Official Chinese attention to Australia, New Zealand, and the Pacific Islands has been extraordinary, with numerous high-level and other official visits. Nonetheless, apart from business interests in Australia backed by sometimes positive Australian media coverage, pro-China "fever" seen in some other states around China's periphery has been limited. Officials and elites in regional governments often register wariness as they carefully calculate the pros and cons of closer China ties.[61]

Australia was among the group of leading Western nations establishing diplomatic relations with China in the early 1970s as China reached out for greater international contact and support in the face of growing power and pressure of the Soviet Union directed at China at that time. It became a major trading partner of China. China's rapid economic development required increasing imports of energy, iron ore, foods, and other resources, which Australia willingly provided; Chinese exports of manufactured goods to Australia also grew. A close ally of the United States, Australia generally adhered to a moderate policy and developed positive approaches in engagement with China, seeking to avoid the acrimonious disputes and controversies that sometimes marked the erratic course of U.S.-Chinese relations in the recent period. However, Australia publicly sided with Washington during the Taiwan Strait crisis of 1996. In the face of China's steady military buildup and assertive policies along its rim in recent years, Australia adopted a planned military buildup in 2009 and coordinated closely with the United States in countering perceived Chinese coercive practices in nearby seas and in support of the American strategic reengagement with the Asia-Pacific, including deployments of U.S. forces to Australia.[62]

China and New Zealand established diplomatic relations in 1972. In following years, relations developed along the lines of Chinese relations with Australia and other Western-oriented governments. New Zealand welcomed and sought economic opportunities in China as a result of post-Mao economic reforms and supported China's entry into the World Trade Organization. In 2004 it was the first developed country to recognize China's market economy status, which provided China more assurances regarding possible trade protection and restrictions by New Zealand. And in 2008 New Zealand was the first developed country to sign a free-trade agreement with China. China became an important partner in foreign trade; it was New Zealand's second-greatest export destination in 2010. The two countries also maintained active political and defense interchanges. Among recent differences or controversial developments, New Zealand joined with Australia and India in participating in the East Asian Leadership Summit meetings beginning in 2005. China had not favored broadening the scope of these meetings to include these three countries. New Zealand also joined with Australia to sharply criticize the competition between the governments of the People's Republic of China (PRC) and the Republic of China (ROC) for diplomatic recognition among states in the Pacific Islands, arguing that the competition led to poor governance and instability in a region of high importance for New Zealand. Like Australia, New Zealand warmly welcomed the Obama government's reengagement in the Asia-Pacific, which was viewed negatively by China but included U.S. initiatives to improve relations with New Zealand and the Pacific Island countries that were long favored by the New Zealand government.[63]

RELATIONS WITH SOUTHERN ASIA

The People's Republic of China's interaction with southern Asia involves China's long-standing concern to control Tibet. In October 1950, China began to consolidate its control of Tibet as tens of thousands of Chinese military forces entered eastern regions of Tibet and defeated Tibetan defenders. In May 1951, China and Tibet reached a seventeen-point agreement deepening China's control of Tibet.[64]

Neighboring India was under the leadership of Jawaharlal Nehru. As the first prime minister of newly independent India until his death in 1964,

Nehru presided over, and in many cases directed, the tortuous turns of Sino-Indian relations during this formative period of relations. Nehru chartered a course for India independent of the United States and the Soviet Union. He pioneered a policy on nonalignment and became a leader of the international Non-Aligned Movement. He quickly established diplomatic relations with China, argued in favor of China's entry into the United Nations, and refused to condemn China as the aggressor in the Korean War.[65]

In the mid-1950s, Nehru built a relationship with Chinese premier Zhou Enlai, then emphasizing Chinese moderation consistent with the Five Principles of Peaceful Coexistence. He seemed surprised by revelations in 1958 of Chinese road building across Indian-claimed territory known as the Aksai Chin. Amid a Tibetan uprising and Chinese crackdown in 1959, the Dalai Lama and many thousands of Tibetans fled to India. Backing the Dalai Lama's cause, the United States government clandestinely supported armed resistance to Chinese rule in Tibet during the 1960s. Some reports also highlighted the role of Taiwan and Indian authorities in these clandestine operations. Nehru allowed the Dalai Lama and the many thousands of his followers escaping a Chinese crackdown to reside in India. Chinese-Indian border tensions worsened, though Nehru again seemed surprised by the Chinese military action overrunning Indian defenses along the eastern boundary in 1962, the nadir of Sino-Indian relations in the modern period.[66]

The rising border tension with India added incentives for China to settle boundaries and build constructive relations with Burma in 1960, noted in the previous section on Southeast Asia, and other neighboring states. Nepal, a Himalayan mountain state bordering China, at first deepened economic and security ties with India in the aftermath of China's military occupation of Tibet in 1950. Nepal improved relations with China in the mid-1950s in tandem with improvement in India's relations with China. Nepal and China established diplomatic relations in 1955. Subsequently, relations continued to improve while Indian-Chinese relations declined. Nepal recognized Tibet as part of China and exchanged resident ambassadors by 1960. That year, Nepal and China signed a boundary settlement agreement and a treaty of peace and friendship. Nepal also began supporting China's entry into the United Nations. In 1961, Nepal and China agreed to build an all-weather road connecting the Nepalese capital, Kathmandu, with Tibet. During the Sino-Indian War of 1962, Nepal maintained neutrality.[67]

As China's relations with India worsened leading to the border war of 1962, Beijing moved to establish close ties with Pakistan, India's South

Asian rival and main security concern. Since then, China and Pakistan have established an unbroken record of continued close relations, often bordering on an alliance, which has been unique in the history of twists and turns in the foreign relations of the People's Republic of China. A tentative border agreement was reached in 1962, contingent on the settlement of India and Pakistan's differences over Kashmir. China for years supported Pakistan's claims to this disputed territory along the India-Pakistan border, the catalyst of repeated military clashes and confrontations between the two South Asian powers. China in the mid-1960s appeared to prepare to take military actions against India in order to assist Pakistan in its conflict with India over Kashmir and other issues. [68]

Chinese relations with India were poor during the lengthy tenure of Indian prime minister, Indira Gandhi, 1966–1977, 1980–1984. During this time, India aligned more closely with China's main international adversary, the Soviet Union. India became directly involved in the breakup of China's main South Asian partner, Pakistan, supporting East Pakistan's independence as Bangladesh. In response to the perceived threat from nuclear-armed China, India developed a nuclear weapons program and carried out an underground nuclear test in 1974. Tensions over the Sino-Indian border dispute remained high during the period. China did little against India when India backed the breakaway of East Pakistan in 1971, leading to the creation of Bangladesh. But strong Chinese military, political, and economic support for Pakistan continued, including the reported provision of nuclear weapons technology and missile delivery systems. China worked closely with Pakistan and the United States in supporting armed resistance to the Soviet Union's military presence in Afghanistan in the 1980s. [69]

Indira Gandhi's son Rajiv Gandhi served as prime minister of India from the death of his mother in 1984 until 1989. China was critical of his continued close relationship with the Soviet Union and also India's intervention in the domestic politics of South Asian states, notably sending Indian troops into the civil war in Sri Lanka. Nevertheless, Chinese-Indian relations began to improve with Gandhi's December 1988 visit to China, the first by an Indian prime minister in thirty-four years. Both sides appeared interested in avoiding conflict, expanding exchanges, and managing differences in less acrimonious ways than in the recent past. [70]

Post–Cold War Chinese policy toward southern Asia generally was in line with broader efforts by China to reduce tensions around its periphery. This was part of its larger goal of stabilizing the "peaceful international environment" needed for China's ambitious agenda of economic and other domestic changes and reforms. Using "dialogues," high-level visits, and other diplomatic measures, Beijing publicly emphasized the positive and endeavored to minimize the negative with all its southern Asian neighbors, including India. In this process, Chinese authorities avoided compromising important Chinese territorial, economic, political, and other interests while they sought to benefit through methodical and generally constructive interaction with the southern Asian countries.[71]

Several problems complicated the new Chinese approach. Amid territorial disputes and conflicting interests between China and India, China faced a difficult task in influencing India. India remained at odds with China over territorial issues and over China's long-standing support for Pakistan. India and China also tended to be seen at home and abroad as rivals for influence and leadership in Asian and world affairs. In recent years, the two countries' industries competed actively for international energy to fuel their respective burgeoning economies. Energy security added to factors influencing each power to view warily the other's military improvements and alignments, especially those affecting transportation routes from the oil-rich Middle East.[72]

The incremental efforts to ease tensions and improve relations moved forward in the 1980s and appeared to receive an added boost from the collapse of the Soviet Union. For many years, the latter had fostered a close strategic relationship with India based in part on Soviet-Indian mutual suspicion of China. Following Prime Minister Rajiv Gandhi's visit to China in 1988, Premier Li Peng visited India in 1990, and President Jiang Zemin traveled there in 1996.[73] The regular visits by top-level Chinese and Indian leaders in following years were accompanied by many agreements, along with positive rhetoric asserting mutual determination to settle the border issue and other differences and to build on rapidly expanding economic cooperation and trade.[74]

As India and China improved relations, China continued to modify its long-standing support for Pakistan.[75] It was already evident in the 1970s that China was unwilling to take significant military action against India in the event of an Indo-Pakistani war. During the 1965 Indo-Pakistani war, Chinese forces did take assertive actions along the Indian border in order to divert Indian forces and weaken their assault against Pakistan. But when India defeated Pakistan in the late 1971 war, which brought about the dismemberment of Pakistan and the creation of an independent Bangladesh, China took no significant military action.

In the 1980s and 1990s, China further modified its public stance in support of Pakistani claims against India over territorial and other issues. Beijing notably adhered to an increasingly evenhanded approach over the sensitive Indo-Pakistani dispute over Kashmir. By 2008 it was reported that Chinese president Hu Jintao offered to mediate between India and Pakistan in order to help resolve the issues regarding Kashmir. Terrorist attacks in Mumbai's financial district in November 2008 were linked to a Pakistani-based organization reportedly involved in resisting Indian control in Kashmir. China changed its past unwillingness to have the UN Security Council condemn the group and sided with a UN Security Council vote declaring the group to be a terrorist organization. [76]

China continued its close military and economic support for Pakistan. Numerous reports showed that China played a major role for many years in assisting Pakistan's development of nuclear weapons and related ballistic missile delivery systems, though Chinese officials denied this. In an interview published on June 3, 1998, President Jiang Zemin was asked, "Has China helped Pakistan to make its nuclear bomb?" He replied, "No, China has not helped Pakistan."[77] Continuing to benefit from Chinese military, economic, and political support, Pakistan chose to emphasize the positive in Sino-Pakistani relations and deemed counterproductive any significant show of irritation with Beijing's shift toward a more evenhanded public posture in the subcontinent.

Recent high points of Chinese interaction with Pakistan included repeated visits by the Pakistan prime minister to China, reports of transfers of jet fighters and other advanced Chinese military equipment to Pakistan, and advances in China's nuclear power cooperation with Pakistan, reportedly in response to India's success in achieving a major nuclear cooperation agreement with the United States. Chinese Premier Wen Jiabao spent three days in Pakistan following a visit to India in December 2010. He announced an increase in what had been seen as a small (initially $10 million) Chinese donation for relief from a flood disaster in Pakistan in the summer and various commercial deals and assistance. [78]

As Sino-Indian relations improved, both sides saw their interests best served by giving less attention than in the past to continued significant areas of disagreement, noted below. [79] On the other hand, the issues continued to be raised periodically and often strongly by officials on both sides, demonstrating slow overall progress in improving relations.

- *Border issues:* Large expanses of territory along India's northwestern and northeastern frontier remain in dispute. In many rounds of border talks since 1981, the two sides made slow progress in their putative effort to delineate the so-called line of actual control (LOAC) and other lingering problems. During Jiang Zemin's 1996 visit to India, the two sides codified many of the ad hoc confidence-building measures that had evolved over the years along the mostly quiet frontiers. Determination to settle the border issue was a focal point in senior-level dialogue between Chinese and Indian diplomats begun in 2003, though concrete results were slow to be announced, and occasional public assertions by Chinese and Indian government officials of claims to disputed border territories continued.

- *Chinese ties with Pakistan, Myanmar, and other southern Asian states:* Long-standing close Chinese military ties with Pakistan and more recently with Myanmar were viewed by some Indian officials as a Chinese "pincer movement" to contain India. Long-standing Chinese ties with Bangladesh, Sri Lanka, and Nepal added to the Indian suspicion that China sought to use such ties to hobble India's ambitions by causing New Delhi strategic concerns in southern Asia. China's military and political support assisted the Sri Lankan government in its final victory in the long-running war with the separatist Tamil Tigers in 2009, opening the way to closer strategic as well as economic and political cooperation. At times in the past, some in India also saw the United States playing a supporting role through its engagement policy toward China. Over the past decade, however, India transformed this concern by nurturing a closer relationship, notably closer military relations, with the United States. Officials in the United States said that they were interested in developing these ties with India, along with nuclear, economic, and other ties, for a variety of important reasons, including as a strategic hedge in case of Chinese moves contrary to American interests.

- *Tibet:* Beijing gave high priority in the post–Cold War period to countering the efforts by the Dalai Lama and his supporters to seek a greater international profile for Tibet. Despite some greater Indian recognition of China's control of Tibet, China remained at odds with New Delhi over India's continued hosting of the spiritual leader and his government in exile.

- *Trade, energy, and energy security:* Continued Indian efforts to open the economy and increase exports led to greater cooperation between the economies of China and India but also Indian economic competition with China for investment and markets and more direct competition for international energy resources. Concern over securing sea-lanes from the oil-rich Persian Gulf prompted India to increase its already powerful naval force in the Indian Ocean and China to develop closer ties with Pakistan, Myanmar, Sri Lanka, and others in developing port and communications assets that would help secure Chinese access to Persian Gulf oil. Chinese naval forces could also be involved in the region at some point in the future.
- *Asian and world leadership:* India wanted a permanent seat on the UN Security Council. China on the one hand said that it supported India's bid and on the other hand made sure that UN reform was so slow that China would remain Asia's only permanent member on the council. India reportedly resented Chinese efforts to gain admission to the Indian-dominated South Asian Association for Regional Cooperation, while New Delhi was pleased that Japan and some Southeast Asian powers resisted Chinese efforts to exclude India and other interested outside powers from the new East Asian Summit of December 2005; New Delhi played a prominent role in the new organization. China appeared unenthusiastic in the face of India's efforts with support of Russia to gain observer status in the Shanghai Cooperation Organization (SCO). China, India, and others competed for influence in Southeast Asia through their respective free-trade initiatives and involvement with efforts to secure sea-lanes through the region. China also maneuvered unsuccessfully within the Nuclear Suppliers Group to thwart approval in 2008 of India's landmark nuclear cooperation agreement with the United States.

As suggested above, further complicating smooth Sino-Indian relations has been the prominent role of the United States. India has benefited substantially from strong U.S. support under the Clinton, Bush, and Obama administrations. The record of arms sales, military exchanges and exercises, trade, investment, and nuclear cooperation between Washington and New Delhi has underscored the repeated U.S. declaration that it seeks to support India's rise as a major power. U.S. relations with China involve many areas of competition and controversy as well as cooperation. U.S. policy is not nearly as enthusiastic about China's rising power as it is about India's ascendance.

RELATIONS WITH RUSSIA AND CENTRAL ASIA

Relations with Russia

The role of the Soviet Union in China's relations with Asia is discussed at some length in chapters 2 and 3. China and Russia have had a long and often troubled history. Czarist Russia's expansion into the Far East came largely at the expense of the declining Chinese empire. Nineteenth-century treaties made vast stretches of territory formerly under China's rule part of the Russian empire. China's internal weakness and political dislocation during the first half of the twentieth century provided opportunities for Soviet leaders Vladimir Lenin and Joseph Stalin to seek allies and foster revolutionary movements favorable to the Soviet Union. Soviet involvement was often ham-handed and, on occasion, worked against the immediate interests of the Communist guerrilla movement in China led by Mao Zedong. [80]

Seeking economic support and strategic backing in the face of an indifferent or hostile West, Mao Zedong's newly formed People's Republic of China (PRC) sought an alliance with Stalin's Soviet Union in 1949. After many weeks of hard bargaining, the alliance was signed on February 14, 1950. The alliance relationship was essential to China's security and its military, economic, and social development in the 1950s. Soviet aid, advisers, and guidelines were key features fostering the changes under way in China. But steadily escalating differences arose over strategy toward the United States and international affairs, the proper ideological path to development, and the appropriate leadership roles of Mao Zedong and Soviet leader Nikita Khrushchev in the world communist movement. Soviet aid was cut off in 1960. Polemics over strategy and ideology led to more substantive disputes over competing claims to border territories. Armed border clashes reached a point in 1969 at which the Soviet Union threatened to attack Chinese nuclear installations, and Chinese leaders countered with a nationwide war preparations campaign against the "war maniacs" in the Kremlin. Party relations were broken, trade fell to minimal levels, and each side depicted the other in official media as a dangerous international predator. [81]

The start of Sino-Soviet talks on border issues in October 1969 eased the war crisis, but each side continued preparations for the long-term struggle against its neighboring adversary. As the weaker party in the dispute, China attempted to break out of its international isolation and gain diplomatic leverage against perceived Soviet efforts at intimidation and threat. Beijing's opening to the Nixon administration was an important element in this policy.

The Soviet Union continued its previous efforts to build up military forces along the Sino-Soviet and Sino-Mongolian borders in order to offset any perceived threat from China. It also pursued this course to provide a counter-weight against any Chinese effort to exert pressure on countries around China's periphery that were interested in developing closer relations with the Soviet Union (for example, India and Vietnam). [82]

The death of Mao Zedong in 1976 and the gradual emergence of a more pragmatic leadership in China reduced the importance of ideological and leadership issues in the Sino-Soviet dispute, but the competition in Asia again reached a crisis in 1979. China countered Soviet-backed Vietnam's invasion of Cambodia by launching a limited military incursion into Vietnam. The Soviet Union responded with warnings and large-scale military exercises along China's northern border. China also denounced the Soviet invasion of Afghanistan in 1979 and sided with the U.S.-backed anticommunist guerrillas in Afghanistan. [83]

Chinese leaders spent much of the two decades from the late 1960s building military defenses and conducting diplomatic and other international maneuvers to deal with the perceived dangers of the prime strategic threat to China posed by the Soviet Union. Particularly important were the buildup of Soviet military forces along the Sino-Soviet and Sino-Mongolian borders and Soviet military and political presence and influence in key areas along China's periphery, notably Vietnam, Laos, Cambodia, India, Afghanistan, North Korea, and the western Pacific and Indian oceans. [84]

Over time, both countries attempted to moderate the tensions. Soviet leader Leonid Brezhnev made several public gestures calling for improved economic, government, and party relations with China before he died in 1982. This prompted the start of a series of political, economic, technical, and cultural contacts and exchanges.

By 1982, the Soviet leadership concluded that its post-1969 strategy toward China (including the massing of forces along the eastern sector of the border and media campaigns against China's domestic and international policies) had backfired. The post-1972 normalization of China's relations with the United States and Japan and the signing of the 1978 China-Japan friendship treaty showed a strategic convergence among the United States, China, and Japan, which added to the Soviet defense burden and worsened the security environment on its long, remote, and thinly populated eastern flank. To undo this problem, Brezhnev and later leaders held out an olive branch to the Chinese leadership. Political contacts and trade increased and polemics subsided, but real progress came only after Mikhail Gorbachev consolidated his power in the mid-1980s and made rapprochement with China a priority.[85]

Gorbachev was prepared to make major changes in what China referred to as the "three obstacles" to improved Sino-Soviet relations: Soviet troops in Afghanistan, the buildup of Soviet forces along the border (including the deployment in Mongolia), and the Soviet-backed Vietnamese military occupation of Cambodia.[86] Motivated by a desire to repair relations with China, to ease the defense burden on the Soviet economy, and to reciprocate China's reduction of its 4 million troops to 2.95 million from 1982 to 1986, the Soviet government announced in 1987 that a phased reduction of its troops (roughly 65,000 in total number) from Mongolia would be initiated with the aim of eliminating the deployment by 1992.[87] The Soviet formations in Mongolia had been kept at a higher level of readiness than others along the border, and the Chinese had long viewed them as a first-echelon strike force aimed at Beijing. In December 1988, Gorbachev announced at the United Nations that Soviet conventional forces would unilaterally be reduced by 500,000. Soviet spokesmen later clarified that, of the total, 120,000 would come from the troops arrayed against China and that remaining Far East units would progressively be configured in a defensive mode. In late 1989, following Gorbachev's visit to Beijing in May, Chinese and Soviet officials began negotiations on reducing forces along the border, and during Prime Minister Li Peng's visit to Moscow in April 1990, an agreement was reached on governing principles regarding force reductions. By the time the Soviet Union collapsed in 1991, five rounds of talks on force reductions had been conducted.

The reduction of the conventional threat to China was complemented by the 1987 U.S.-Soviet intermediate nuclear forces (INF) treaty, under which Moscow dismantled all its medium- and intermediate-range nuclear missiles, including 180 advanced mobile SS-20 missiles that were based in the Asian regions of the Soviet Union with missions including targeting China. Meanwhile, the Soviet Union agreed under the April 1988 Geneva Accords to withdraw its combat forces from Afghanistan by May 1989 and Moscow encouraged Vietnam to evacuate its troops from Cambodia by the end of 1989.

High-level political contacts helped to alter the adversarial character of Sino-Soviet relations, the most important being the visits of Foreign Minister Eduard Shevardnadze and Gorbachev to Beijing in 1989 and of Li Peng and Chinese Communist Party General Secretary Jiang Zemin to Moscow in 1990 and 1991, respectively. Talks on resolving the border dispute, which had been derailed by the Soviet invasion of Afghanistan, resumed in 1987. A treaty delimiting the eastern sector of the border was signed in May 1991. These military and political transformations in Sino-Soviet relations were supplemented by a significant growth in trade—especially along the border—and agreements providing for thousands of Chinese workers to be employed in construction projects in Siberia and the Soviet Far East.[88]

With the demise of the Soviet Union following the end of the Cold War, Beijing's relationship with Moscow further improved amid massive changes in the relative power between the two former adversaries. China advanced dramatically in economic modernization and international prominence, becoming the world's fastest-rising power. Russia seemed to flounder for a decade, losing the military, economic, and other elements that had made the Soviet Union a major power in Asian as well as European and global affairs. The sparsely populated eastern Russia saw a steep decline in population, living standards, and military readiness as neighboring China boomed and its military modernized rapidly, partly with the help of Russian weapons and technical specialists.[89]

In recent years, international energy scarcities and the more disciplined administration of Vladimir Putin raised Russia's economic importance as an exporter of oil, gas, and other commodities to Asian as well as other consumers. Russia was positioned as a key player in international disputes such as the controversies over the U.S.-led invasion of Iraq and Iran's nuclear development program. Russia also remained critically important for Chinese interests in central Asia and for supplies of modern weaponry. However, Chinese efforts in the 1990s to forge a united front with Russia against U.S. "hegemonism" failed in part because Putin in early 2001 steered Russian policy in a direction that gave primacy to businesslike relations with the United States. China soon followed suit.

Chinese and Russian leaders subsequently issued occasional joint statements and engaged in some military and diplomatic activities in opposition to U.S. interests and international leadership. Under Putin's leadership, Russia shifted for a time to a tougher stance against the United States and the West on a variety of issues, including perceived intrusions on Russia's power and influence along its periphery, notably NATO expansion and planned deployment of U.S.-backed antiballistic missile systems (ABM) in the Czech Republic and Poland. China gave some political support to the Russian position, but when Russian military forces in August 2008 attacked Western-backed Georgia over territorial issues, Chinese leaders avoided taking sides.

The weakness of any Russian-Chinese commitment against the United States and the West showed again when Russia shifted in 2010 to a more cooperative stance with the United States and NATO on arms control, security, and economic issues that stood in contrast with Chinese truculence toward the United States at this time over Taiwan arms sales, Tibet, U.S. military surveillance near China, and economic issues. Putin's resumption as Russian president in 2012 was accompanied by some hardening in Russian positions at odds with the United States and signs of strengthening Russian ties with China, but analysts had a hard time discerning a major departure from the often expedient twists and turns in the recent Sino-Russian relationship vis-à-vis the United States and the West.[90]

In sum, the post–Cold War Russia-China relationship proved to be mixed and somewhat volatile regarding political cooperation despite the signing of a friendship treaty in 2001 and numerous bilateral agreements:

- Arms sales and technology transfers kept growing for many years, primarily because Russian economic difficulties and Putin's emphasis on defense industries complemented China's need for advanced military equipment and technology to prepare for regional contingencies. They reached a point of diminishing returns for China and declined in very recent years.
- Economic relations moved forward. For a time, Putin tried to link arms sales to an expansion of commercial trade, but this did not succeed, especially given Moscow's need for the arms sales and Beijing's limited interest in other Russian exports. As China showed greater interest in Russian oil and other resources, Putin tried, again with little success, to link provision of these Russian supplies with demands that China purchase more Russian industrial goods. Negotiations, declarations, and agreements on large-scale energy and infrastructure projects—some dating back to the 1990s—continued. The flow of Russian oil to China increased via rail shipment. More efficient and expensive pipelines were slow to develop though one was eventually completed.
- Russia and China continued to pursue good-neighborly relations and bilateral confidence-building measures (CBMs). Although both moderated their respective public criticism of U.S. leadership in Asian and world affairs, in principle they remained opposed to the regional and global domination of a single power and occasionally jointly criticized evidence of U.S. "unilateralism" or "interventionism."

There was an upsurge in public Russian-Chinese assertiveness against the United States in 2005. The Russian and Chinese leaders met in July and issued a formal statement widely seen as an attack on U.S. international leadership. Both governments joined with the SCO that month in calling for U.S. and allied forces to set a deadline for withdrawal from central Asia. They subsequently backed the authoritarian government of Uzbekistan, which disputed U.S. support for political opposition in the country, and called for U.S. forces to withdraw from Uzbekistan. In August, about ten thousand Chinese and Russian forces held sophisticated military exercises, ostensibly under the auspices of the SCO that were focused in waters east of China and appeared directed at warning Taiwan and its supporters in Japan and the United States.[91] Both Russia and China resisted U.S.-backed efforts in 2005–2006 to pressure Iran to end suspected nuclear weapons development. These developments added to differences in Russian relations with the United States over Putin's authoritarian internal policies and other issues. Taken together, they complicated U.S. efforts to manage relations with Russia and China but did not appear to change the overall orientation of Russian and Chinese policies, which continued to give primacy to relations with the United States over relations with one another.[92]

Russian–Chinese political cooperation against the United States remained limited as both Moscow and Beijing seemed to maintain a grudging respect for U.S. power and influence and a calculation that constructive bilateral relations with the United States and its allies were essential to their respective development and reform programs. Russian-Chinese political cooperation also was limited by historical mutual suspicions, their respective concerns about each other's long-term threat potential, their occasional maneuvers at the other's expense for international advantages, and the preoccupation of both leaderships with domestic priorities.[93] As noted above, China straddled the fence in regard to Russia's assertive stance against the United States and military intervention into Georgia in 2008; Russia's moderation with the Obama administration in 2010 was at odds with China's harder line toward the United States at that time.[94]

Economic cooperation focused on trade in energy. Bilateral trade dropped from $56.8 billion in 2008 to $38.8 billion in 2009 and returned to the 2008 level in 2010.[95] Trade relations also reflected repeated signs of China-Russia differences. Moscow's maneuvering between Japan and China over a Russian oil pipeline in Asia reached a new stage in 2009 when China agreed to a large, $25 billion loan to Russia in return for oil shipments and the Russian

decision to construct and open earlier than expected an oil pipeline spur to
China on the proposed Russian oil pipeline to the Russian Pacific coast.[96]
Friction also was reported between Russia and China over the Russian leadership's efforts to control the export of oil and gas from central Asian republics on the one hand and Chinese efforts to build pipelines outside of Russian
control and encourage exports of these commodities from central Asian
countries to China on the other.[97]

The resiliency of the strong mutual interests behind Chinese-Russian
cooperation in arms sales and military technological cooperation was tested
as the two sides endeavored to overcome differences resulting in a marked
decline in the arms sales beginning around the middle of the past decade. The
decline contrasted with the record of the previous ten years when $25 billion
worth of Russian air, naval, and ground military equipment was delivered to
China. A major part of the problem was Russian complaints about Chinese
reverse-engineering Russian arms; also involved was Russian inability to
fulfill some contracts.[98] There were conflicting reports in 2010 and later
about when and if strong Russian arms sales to China would be resumed.[99]

Despite China's recent mixed experience in cooperation with Russia as it
changed positions regarding the United States and the West and Russia's
overall decline in international power and influence, especially in Asia, since
the end of the Cold War, Chinese relations with Russia remained among the
top priorities in Chinese foreign policy. Russia's geographic location, energy
resources, nuclear arsenal, great power position, and relatively modern weaponry warranted continued close attention by Chinese leaders.

Relations with Central Asia

After the end of the Cold War and the fall of the Soviet Union, China
expanded its ties across central Asia in order to stabilize its western frontier,
gain access to the region's energy resources, and balance Western influence
in an area Beijing traditionally viewed as Russia's reserve.[100] Beijing calculated that improved ties with central Asian states, which were also concerned
about problems arising from the linkage of religion and politics, could shield
Xinjiang Province and its ethnically Turkic Uighur population from outside
Muslim and pan-Turkic influence. China worried that its neighbors might
lack sufficient resolve to control and suppress the threat. In this context, U.S.,
Russian, and Chinese efforts to support antiterrorist initiatives in central Asia
beginning in 2001 seemed to reflect some important common ground among
the three powers.[101]

China's central Asian energy projects reflected PRC efforts to obtain secure supply lines and avoid overdependence on a few sources of energy. Beijing concluded agreements to develop Kazakhstan oil and gas fields and construct a pipeline to Xinjiang, and China developed gas pipeline links with Uzbekistan, Turkmenistan, and other countries. As in the case of pipeline and related energy deals involving Russia, the projects were expensive, logistically difficult, and complicated by inadequate energy-processing and transport systems. There were many signed agreements but slower progress toward completing the pipelines and filling them to capacity.[102]

On September 24, 1997, China and Kazakhstan signed agreements worth $9.5 billion that involved development of two major oil and gas fields and the construction of pipelines in Kazakhstan. One pipeline covered 3,000 kilometers from Kazakhstan into western China and began operation in 2006. China signed an agreement with Turkmenistan in 2006 to export natural gas through a new pipeline reaching China through Uzbekistan and Kazakhstan. This pipeline was completed expeditiously, and was supported by a separate natural gas pipeline linking Uzbekistan and Kazakhstan with China. The new efforts undercut what had been a situation of control of the exporting of central Asian natural gas by Russian pipeline administrators.[103]

Beijing adopted an evenhanded public stance on the most contentious political issue in central Asian politics since the 1990s: the continuing civil war in Afghanistan. China urged all warring parties to stop fighting and to discuss their problems among themselves without any outside interference. China typically supported a major role for the United Nations, where China had a permanent seat on the Security Council. With the increase of U.S.-led combat operations against a resurgent Taliban threat during the administration of U.S. President Barack Obama, China was careful to straddle the fence and avoid commitments not seen in its longer-term interests. China endorsed the May 2, 2011, killing of Osama Bin Laden by American special forces in Pakistan as "a positive development in the international struggle against terrorism."[104]

China continued to monitor carefully the growing Western commercial presence in central Asia and tended to view expanding NATO activities as indicative of U.S. efforts to extend its influence to the region, squeeze out Russia, and contain China. China's expanding influence in central Asia generally prompted little overt opposition from Moscow. China usually pursued its interests in central Asia cautiously, presumably in part to avoid provoking its Russian strategic partner into discontinuing the supply of arms to China and possibly risking a strong nationalist backlash from Russia's leadership.[105]

China's interest in using multilateral organizations to pursue Chinese interests around its periphery in the post–Cold War period showed first in central Asia. Building on a growing "strategic partnership" with Russia, China hosted in Shanghai in April 1996 the first meeting of representative leaders of what became known as the Shanghai Five. The Shanghai Five consisted of China, Russia, and the three other former Soviet republics that border on China: Kazakhstan, Kyrgyzstan, and Tajikistan. The group focused at first on finalizing border settlements between China and the four former Soviet republics, demilitarizing their frontiers, and establishing confidence-building measures. Uzbekistan joined the group in July 2001, establishing the SCO, with six members: Russia, China, Kazakhstan, Kyrgyzstan, Tajikistan, and Uzbekistan. The declaration on the creation of the SCO showed strong attention to regional security issues involving terrorism, drug trade, and other transnational crimes affecting the countries. Work in subsequent annual summit meetings of the group included efforts to establish a charter and small budget for the organization, to start a small antiterrorism center in Kyrgyzstan, and to set up an SCO secretariat headquartered in Beijing and paid for by China to foster cooperation on terrorism and other transnational issues. Chinese leaders showed strong interest in broadening the scope of the SCO to include strong economic development efforts, notably in building transportation infrastructure that would benefit western China.[106] At the SCO prime ministers' meeting in Tajikistan in September 2006, Prime Minister Wen Jiabao announced that China had set a goal of doubling the current level ($40 billion) of Chinese trade with SCO members in the next few years.[107]

Looking out, China's approach to the central Asian region seemed coherent, reasonably successful, and likely to continue along existing lines. While Chinese leaders have had several important interests and goals in pursing relations with central Asia, they have managed them without significant conflict, reinforcing the likelihood of continuity and durability in China's approach to the region. Notably in contrast to Chinese approaches in eastern and southern Asia, there has been less tension between China's national development emphasis on promoting peace and development abroad and Chinese national security, territorial, and national unification objectives that emphasize China's use of force against foreign threats in ways that have alienated and alarmed some of China's neighbors and other concerned powers.

Chinese interests and goals in central Asia continued to focus on the following:

- Borders and security, curbing outside support to separatists in Xinjiang province, and seeking common ground with regional governments in working against terrorist and criminal elements
- Access to central Asian oil and gas supplies and development of strong trade relations
- Fostering a stable and productive environment along this segment of China's periphery while enhancing China's regional and international prominence through effective bilateral and multilateral diplomacy

One of the reasons that China's government has been able to develop and sustain a coherent approach in post–Cold War central Asia despite potentially conflicting goals is that external forces that the Chinese administration does not control and that strongly influence Chinese foreign policy in other areas do not play much of a role in its relations with central Asia. For example, Taiwan is insignificant in central Asia. Chinese threats to use force against Taiwan separatism have much less disruptive impact on China's central Asian neighbors than they do elsewhere around China's periphery. Japan's role in central Asia also is relatively small. China's sometimes strident reactions to disputes with Japan have a less disruptive impact on China's relations with central Asian neighbors than on Chinese relations with neighbors in other parts of China's periphery.

The upswing in U.S. military presence and influence in central Asia after the terrorist attack on the United States in 2001 was an important change impacting China's strategic calculus in central Asia. However, its overall importance has been offset by the fact that the foundation of U.S. power in central Asia is much weaker than in other parts of China's periphery. In addition, the record of relatively low levels of follow-on U.S. aid and official involvement in the region and Russia's continued leading importance among the central Asian republics also have diminished Chinese concerns about the U.S. military presence and influence in central Asia.[108]

Meanwhile, changes in Chinese foreign policy and behavior influenced by Chinese leaders' lack of confidence and uncertainty in their legitimacy at home and abroad are less in the case of central Asia than in other parts of China's periphery.[109] Notably, the need for Chinese leaders to adopt tough policies on territorial or other nationalistic issues with central Asian neighbors is less than in the case of Chinese relations with some neighbors to China's east and south. Part of the reason is that the Chinese government has been successful in keeping Chinese media and other public attention focused away from territorial and nationalistic issues with central Asian neighbors. In addition, Chinese territorial and nationalistic issues with central Asian neighbors seem less salient to important Chinese interests in development and national power than such Chinese issues with some other neighbors. And the generally authoritarian central Asian governments have endeavored to deal constructively, pragmatically, and generally quietly with China over territorial and other disputes, a contrast with the nationalistic posturing of some of China's eastern and southern neighbors.

Although the course of China's strategy toward central Asia seems more stable than in other areas of Chinese foreign relations, there remain significant uncertainties clouding the longer-term outlook. For one thing, specialists are divided on China's long-term goals in the region and how these goals could lead to a major change in China's approach to the region. Some emphasize strongly that the prevailing Chinese interest in regional stability and energy trade will remain the important determinants of Chinese policy and will reinforce continuity in the Chinese policy and behavior we see today.[110] However, others argue that recent accommodating and moderate Chinese policies and behavior presage the creation of an emerging central Asian order dominated by China that will be reminiscent of the Sino–central Asian relationship during the strong dynasties in Chinese history.[111]

Meanwhile, China's influence in central Asia and developments in the region depend heavily on the power and policies of Russia. Russian weakness in the 1990s provided the opportunity for expanding Chinese influence in central Asia and the foundation of Russian inclination to cooperate closely with rising China on trade, including arms trade, and a variety of international issues. Under the leadership of Vladimir Putin, Russia has endeavored to rebuild elements of national strength and to use them to reassert Russian interests against those perceived as encroaching on Russian interests. Thus far, the Russian relationship with China generally has remained cordial and cooperative, though Russia-China competition for influence in central Asia and over other issues continues.[112] If China were to be seen to seek regional dominance in central Asia, Russia might adopt more competitive and perhaps confrontational policies that would have a major impact on China's existing approach to the region. At the same time, if Russia successfully pursues a more assertive leadership role in the region, China's leaders presumably would be forced to choose between accommodating rising Russian power and possibly losing Chinese equities and influence or resisting the Russian advances.

NOTES

1. Findings from an off-the-record seminar with U.S. government and nongovernment China specialists, Washington, D.C., area, November 10, 2011.

2. Martin Indyk, Kenneth Lieberthal, and Michael O'Hanlon, *Bending History: Barack Obama's Foreign Policy* (Washington, DC: Brookings Institution, 2012), pp. 61–62.

3. Trade figures used in this section are from the UN COMTRADE database at comtrade.un.org/db.

4. Chae-Jin Lee, *Japan Faces China* (Baltimore: Johns Hopkins University Press, 1978).

5. A. Doak Barnett, *China and the Major Powers in East Asia* (Washington, DC: Brookings Institution, 1977), pp. 105–8.

6. Barnett, *China and the Major Powers in East Asia*, pp. 108–22. Ezra Vogel, *Deng Xiaoping and the Transformation of China* (Cambridge, MA: Harvard University Press, 2011), pp. 294–310.

7. Allen Whiting, *China Faces Japan* (Berkeley: University of California Press, 1989); Robert Sutter, *China's Rise in Asia* (Lanham, MD: Rowman & Littlefield, 2005), pp. 131–32.

8. Donald Klein, "Japan and Europe in Chinese Foreign Relations," in *China and the World*, ed. Samuel Kim (Boulder CO: Westview,1998), pp. 137–46.

9. Robert Sutter, *Chinese Policy Priorities and Their Implications for the United States* (Lanham MD: Rowman & Littlefield, 2000), p. 82.

10. Minxin Pei and Michael Swaine, *Simmering Fire in Asia: Averting Sino-Japanese Strategic Conflict*, Policy Brief 44 (Washington, DC: Carnegie Endowment for International Peace, December 1, 2005); Susan Shirk, *China: Fragile Superpower* (New York: Oxford University Press, 2007), pp. 140–80; Richard Bush, *The Perils of Proximity: China-Japan Security Relations* (Washington, DC: Brookings Institution, 2010).

11. Robert Sutter, "China-Japan: Trouble Ahead?" *The Washington Quarterly* 25, no. 4 (2002): pp. 37–49; Mike Mochizuki, "Terms of Engagement: The U.S.-Japan Alliance and the Rise of China," in *Beyond Bilateralism: U.S.-Japan Relations in the New Asia-Pacific*, ed. Ellis Krauss and T. J. Pempel (Stanford, CA: Stanford University Press, 2004), pp. 96–100; Michael Yahuda, *The International Politics of the Asia-Pacific* (London: Routledge, 2011), pp. 324–28.

12. Ralph Clough, *Island China* (Cambridge, MA: Harvard University Press, 1978), pp. 148–72.

13. John Copper, *Taiwan: Nation State or Province?* (Boulder, CO: Westview, 2009), pp. 50–53.

14. Denny Roy, *Taiwan: A Political History* (Ithaca, NY: Cornell University Press, 2003), pp. 152–82.

15. Charles Freeman, "Preventing War in the Taiwan Strait," *Foreign Affairs* 77, no. 4 (July–August 1998): pp. 6–11; Steven Goldstein, *Taiwan Faces the Twenty-First Century* (New York: Foreign Policy Association, 1997).

16. John Garver, *Face-Off* (Seattle: University of Washington Press, 1997).

17. Richard Bush, *Untying the Knot* (Washington, DC: Brookings Institution, 2005), pp. 27–141.

18. Steven Goldstein and Julian Chang, eds., *Presidential Politics in Taiwan: The Administration of Chen Shui-bian* (Norwalk, CT: Eastbridge, 2008).

19. Nancy Bernkopf Tucker, *Strait Talk: United States-Taiwan Relations and the Crisis with China* (Cambridge, MA: Harvard University Press, 2009); Philip Yang, "Cross Strait Relations under the First Chen Administration," in Goldstein and Chang, eds., *Presidential Politics in Taiwan*, pp. 211–22.

20. Robert Sutter, *Chinese Foreign Relations* (Lanham, MD: Rowman & Littlefield, 2012), p. 158.

21. David G. Brown, "China-Taiwan Relations: Campaign Fallout," *Comparative Connections*, January 2005, www.csis.org/pacfor.

22. Brown, "China-Taiwan Relations"; interviews with Chinese government officials and specialists, Washington, DC, January–March 2004.

23. Sutter, *Chinese Foreign Relations*, p. 159.

24. At this time, Taiwan media reported that George Bush had used an epithet to refer to Chen Shui-bian (Brown, "China-Taiwan Relations").

25. David Brown, "Taiwan Voters Set a New Course," *Comparative Connections* 10, no. 1 (April 2008): p. 75.

26. Dennis Hickey, "Beijing's Evolving Policy toward Taipei: Engagement or Entrapment," *Issues and Studies* 45, no. 1 (March 2009): pp. 31–70; Alan Romberg, "Cross Strait Relations: 'Ascend the Heights and Take a Long-Term Perspective,'" *China Leadership Monitor* 27, Winter 2009, www.chinaleadershipmonitor.org; author's interviews and consultations with international affairs officials, including repeated meetings with senior officers up to minister level, Taipei, May, July, August, and December 2008, April 2009.

27. David Brown, "Economic Cooperation Framework Agreement Signed," *Comparative Connections* 12, no. 2 (July 2010): pp. 77–79.

28. David Brown, "Post-Election Continuity," *Comparative Connections* 14, no. 1 (May 2012): pp. 81–86.

29. David Brown, "Looking Ahead to 2012," *Comparative Connections* 12, no. 4 (January 2011), www.csis.org/pacfor.

30. Donald Zagoria, *Trip to Seoul, Taipei, Beijing, Shanghai, and Tokyo—May 8–25, 2010* (New York: National Committee on American Foreign Policy, 2010), pp. 2–6.

31. Author's interviews and consultations with international affairs officials, including repeated meetings with senior officers up to minister level, Taipei, May, July, August, and December 2008, April 2009.

32. Shirley Kan, *Taiwan: Major US Arms Sales since 1990*, Report RL 30957 (Washington, DC: Library of Congress, Congressional Research Service, October 8, 2008); Kathrin Hille and Demetri Sevastopulo, "US and China Set to Resume Military Talks," *Financial Times*, June 21, 2009, www.ft.com.

33. David Shear, "Cross-Strait Relations in a New Era of Negotiation," remarks at the Carnegie Endowment for International Peace, Washington, DC, July 7, 2010, www.state.gov/.

34. Bonnie Glaser, "The Honeymoon Ends," *Comparative Connections* 12, no. 1 (April 2010): pp. 23–27; Bonnie Glaser, "US Pivot to Asia Leaves China Off Balance," *Comparative Connections* 13, no. 3 (January 2012): pp. 37–38.

35. Samuel Kim, *The Two Koreas and the Great Powers* (New York: Cambridge University Press, 2006).

36. Robert Sutter, *China-Watch* (Baltimore: Johns Hopkins University Press, 1978), p. 65.

37. Sutter, *China-Watch*, pp. 85, 95–96; Ria Chae, "East German Documents on Kim Il Sung's April 1975 Visit to China," *North Korea International Documentation Project* (Washington, DC: Woodrow Wilson Center for Scholars, 2012), www.wilsoncenter.org/publication/

east-german-documents-kim-il-sung%E2%80%99s-april-1975-trip-to-beijing (accessed July 7, 2012).

38. Ezra Vogel, *Deng Xiaoping and the Transformation of China* (Cambridge, MA: Harvard University Press, 2011), pp. 278–80.

39. Robert Sutter, *Chinese Foreign Policy: Developments after Mao* (New York: Praeger, 1986), pp. 185, 189–91.

40. Kim, *The Two Koreas and the Great Powers*, pp. 52–63, 118–21.

41. Robert Sutter, "China and North Korea after the Cold War: Wariness, Caution and Balance," *International Journal of Korean Studies* 14, no. 1 (2010): pp. 19–34.

42. Samuel Kim, "The Changing Role of China on the Korean Peninsula," *International Journal of Korean Studies* 8, no. 1 (2004): pp. 79–112.

43. Chung, Jae Ho, "China's 'Soft' Clash with South Korea," *Asian Survey* 49, no. 3 (2009): pp. 468–83.

44. Snyder, Scott, "Post Olympic Hangover: New Backdrop for Relations," *Comparative Connections* 10, no. 3 (October 2008): pp. 101–7.

45. Scott Snyder, "Lee Myung-bak and the Future of Sino-South Korean Relations," Jamestown Foundation, *China Brief* 8, no. 4 (February 14, 2008): pp. 5–8.

46. Bonnie Glaser, "China's Policy in the Wake of the Second DPRK Nuclear Test," *China Security* 5, no. 2 (2009): pp. 1–11.

47. Christopher Twomey, "Chinese Foreign Policy toward North Korea," *Journal of Contemporary China* 17, no. 56 (2008): p. 422.

48. Scott Snyder, "DPRK Provocations Test China's Regional Role," *Comparative Connections* 12, no.4 (January 2011), www.csis.org/pacfor.

49. Scott Snyder, "Consolidating Ties with New DPRK Leadership," *Comparative Connections* 12, no. 3 (October 2010), www.csis.org/pacfor.

50. Harold Hinton, *Communist China in World Politics* (Boston: Houghton Mifflin Company, 1966), pp. 394–441.

51. Nayan Chanda, *Brother Enemy* (New York: Harcourt, 1986): Hinton, *Communist China in World Politics*, 408–22.

52. Robert Sutter, *Historical Dictionary of Chinese Foreign Policy* (Lanham, MD: Scarecrow, 2011), p. 125.

53. Sutter, *Historical Dictionary of Chinese Foreign Policy*, p. 55.

54. Chanda, *Brother Enemy*; Sophie Richardson, *China, Cambodia, and the Five Principles of Peaceful Coexistence* (New York: Columbia University Press, 2010).

55. Richardson, *China, Cambodia, and the Five Principles of Peaceful Coexistence*, pp. 110–98.

56. Robert Sutter, *China's Rise: Implications for US Leadership in Asia*, Policy Studies 21 (Washington, DC: East-West Center, 2006), pp. 9–16.

57. "US Profile Rises, China Image Falls, North Korea Changes?" *Comparative Connections* 12, no. 3 (October 2010): pp. 1–11.

58. "China Reassures Neighbors, Wary of US Intentions," *Comparative Connections* 12, no. 4 (January 2011), www.csis.org/pacfor.

59. "China-Southeast Asia Relations," *Comparative Connections* 13, no. 1 (May 2011): p. 65.

60. "China–Southeast Asia Relations," *Comparative Connections* 14, no. 2 (September 2010): pp. 61–62.

61. *The Rise of China in the Pacific*, Policy Briefing Note, no. 2 (Canberra: Australian National University, 2007); *China and Taiwan in the South Pacific: Diplomatic Chess versus Pacific Political Rugby* (Sydney: Lowy Institute, 2007); Tamara Shie, "Rising Chinese Influ-

ence in the South Pacific," *Asian Survey* 47, no. 2 (March–April 2007): pp. 307–26; Linda Jacobson, "Australia-China Ties: In Search of Political Trust," *Policy Brief*, Lowy Institute, June 2012.

62. Sutter, *Historical Dictionary of Chinese Foreign Policy*, p. 49; Jacobson, "Australia-China Ties."

63. Sutter, *Historical Dictionary of Chinese Foreign Policy*, pp. 179–80; Mark Manyin, coord., *Pivot to the Pacific? The Obama Administration's "Rebalancing" Toward Asia*, Report R42448 (Washington, DC: Library of Congress, Congressional Research Service, March 28, 2012), pp. 2–6.

64. Sutter, *Historical Dictionary of Chinese Foreign Policy*, pp. 241–42.

65. Sutter, *Historical Dictionary of Chinese Foreign Policy*, p. 178.

66. John Garver, *Protracted Contest* (Seattle: University of Washington Press, 2001), pp. 3–109; Alice Lyman Miller and Richard Wich, *Becoming Asia* (Stanford, CA: Stanford University Press, 2011), pp. 90–93.

67. Garver, *Protracted Contest*, pp. 138–66; Sutter, *Historical Dictionary of Chinese Foreign Policy*, pp. 178–79.

68. Garver, *Protracted Contest*, pp. 187–215; Miller and Wich, *Becoming Asia*, pp. 179–82.

69. Miller and Wich, *Becoming Asia*, pp. 182–93.

70. Sutter, *Historical Dictionary of Chinese Foreign Policy*, p. 105.

71. Abu Taher Salahuddin Ahmed, "India-China Relations in the 1990s," *Journal of Contemporary Asia* 26, no. 1 (1996): pp. 100–115; Robert Sutter, *China's Rise in Asia: Promises and Perils* (Lanham, MD: Rowman & Littlefield, 2005), pp. 231–48.

72. Gurpreet Khurana, "Securing the Maritime Silk Route: Is There a Sino-Indian Confluence?" *China and Eurasia Forum Quarterly* 4, no. 3 (August 2006): pp. 89–103.

73. Denny Roy, *China's Foreign Relations* (Lanham, MD: Rowman & Littlefield, 1998), pp. 170–74.

74. "Indian Prime Minister Ends China Visit," *China Daily*, January 15, 2008, p. 1; Fu Xiaoqiang, "Wen's Visit Benefits South Asia," *China Daily*, December 23, 2010, p. 8.

75. Garver, *Protracted Contest*, pp. 216–42.

76. Tarique Niazi, "Sino-Pakistani Relations Reach New Level after Zadari's Visit," *China Brief* 8, no. 24 (December 19, 2008): pp. 7–9; Christopher Griffin, "Hu Loves Whom? China Juggles Its Priorities on the Subcontinent," *China Brief* 6, no. 25 (December 19, 2006): pp. 1–3.

77. *Hong Kong AFP in English*, June 3, 1998, www.afp.com (accessed June 4, 1998) cited in Robert Sutter, *Chinese Policy Priorities and Their Implications for the United States* (Lanham, MD: Rowman & Littlefield, 2000), p. 135.

78. Stephanie Ho, "China to Sell Outdated Nuclear Reactors to Pakistan," *VOANews.com*, March 24, 2011, www.voanews.com; Li Xiaokun and Ai Yang, "Wen Delivers on Flood Aid as Visit to Pakistan Begins," *China Daily*, December 18–19, 2010, p. 1; L. C. Russell Hsiao, "China and Pakistan Enhance Strategic Partnership," *China Brief* 8, no. 19 (October 7, 2008).

79. Mohan Malik, "Chinese-Indian Relations in the Post-Soviet Era," *China Quarterly* 142 (June 1995): pp. 317–55; Garver, *Protracted Contest*; Sutter, *China's Rise in Asia*, 233; Jonathan Holslag, *China and India: Prospects for Peace* (New York: Columbia University Press, 2010); C. Raja Mohan, "Sino-Indian Relations: Growing Yet Fragile," *RSIS Commentaries* 174, December 20, 2010; "India and China Eye Each Other Warily," *IISS Strategic Comments* 9, no. 27 (December 2010).

80. John Garver, *Foreign Relations of the People's Republic of China* (Englewood Cliffs, NJ: Prentice Hall, 1993), pp. 31–39, 304–13; Lowell Dittmer, *Sino-Soviet Normalization and Its International Implications, 1945–1990* (Seattle: University of Washington Press, 1992).

81. Miller and Wich, *Becoming Asia*, pp. 116–36.

82. Miller and Wich, *Becoming Asia*, pp. 161–93.

83. Sutter, *Chinese Foreign Relations*, p. 270.

84. Robert Ross, ed., *China, the United States and the Soviet Union: Tripolarity and Policy Making in the Cold War* (Armonk, NY: M. E. Sharpe, 1993).

85. Miller and Wich, *Becoming Asia*, pp. 196–201.

86. Rajan Menon, "The Strategic Convergence between Russia and China," *Survival* 39, no. 2 (Summer 1997): pp. 101–25.

87. James Clay Moltz, "Regional Tension in the Russo-Chinese Rapprochement," *Asian Survey* 35, no. 6 (June 1995): pp. 511–27.

88. Stephen Uhalley, "Sino-Soviet Relations: Continued Improvement amidst Tumultuous Change," *Journal of East Asian Affairs* 6, no. 1 (Winter–Spring 1992): pp. 171–92.

89. Sutter, *Chinese Foreign Relations*, pp. 272–78.

90. Bobo Lo, *Axis of Convenience: Moscow, Beijing, and the New Geopolitics* (Washington, DC: Brookings Institution, 2008); Bobo Lo "A Partnership of Convenience," *New York Times*, June 7, 2012, www.nytimes.com/.

91. Yu Bin, "The New World Order According to Moscow and Beijing," *Comparative Connections*, October 2005, www.csis.org/pacfor.

92. Yu Bin, "Pragmatism Dominates Russia-China Relations," *PACNET* 11 (March 20, 2006), www.csis.org/pacfor.

93. Yu Bin, "China-Russia: Embracing a Storm and Each Other?" *Comparative Connections* 10, no. 4 (January 2009): pp. 131–40.

94. Yu Bin, "China-Russia Relations: Reset under Medvedev: Zapad-Politik and Vostok 2010," *Comparative Connections* 12, no. 2 (July 2010), pp. 135–38; Yu Bin, "China-Russia Relations: Guns and Games of August: Tales of Two Strategic Partners," *Comparative Connections* 10, no. 3 (October 2008): pp. 131–38.

95. "China-Russia Economic, Trade Co-Op New Starts: Minister," *China Daily*, November 25, 2010, www.chinadaily.com.cn/.

96. "China, Russia Sign $25-Billion Loan-for-Oil Deal," *Financial Times*, February 18, 2009, www.ft.com (accessed February 19, 2009).

97. Michael Richardson, "China and Russia Spread Their Influence over Central Asia," *Canberra Times*, August 2, 2007, www.canberratimes.com.au (accessed February 16, 2009).

98. Stephen Blank, "Recent Trends in Russo-Chinese Military Relations," *China Brief* 9, no. 2 (January 22, 2009): pp. 6–8.

99. Jeremy Page, "China Clones, Sells Russian Fighter Jets," *Wall Street Journal*, December 6, 2010, www.wsj.com; Minnie Chan, "Russia Will Sell Beijing Hi-Tech Jets," *South China Morning Post*, December 2, 2010, www.scmp.com.

100. Bates Gill and Matthew Oresman, *China's New Journey to the West* (Washington, DC: Center for Strategic and International Studies, August 2003).

101. Gill and Oresman, *China's New Journey to the West*, pp. viii–ix.

102. Zhou Yan, "A Lifeline from Central Asia," *China Daily*, February 17, 2011; Sebastien Peyrouse, "Sino-Kazakh Relations: A Nascent Strategic Partnership," *China Brief* 8, no. 21 (November 7, 2008): pp. 11–15.

103. Peyrouse, "Sino-Kazakh Relations," p. 12; Kevin Sheives, "China and Central Asia's New Energy Relationship: Keeping Things in Perspective," *China-Eurasia Forum Quarterly*, April 2005, p. 18; Stephen Blank, "The Strategic Implications of the Turkmenistan-China Pipeline Project," *China Brief* 10, no. 3 (February 4, 2010): pp.10–12.

104. "China Says Bin Laden's Death a Milestone for Anti-Terrorism," *China Daily*, May 3, 2011, www.chinadaily.com.cn; Andrew Small, "China's Caution on Afghanistan-Pakistan," *Washington Quarterly* 33, no. 3 (July 2010): pp. 81–97.

105. Sutter, *Chinese Policy Priorities and Their Implications for the United States*, p. 143.

106. Wang Jianwei, "China's Multilateral Diplomacy in the New Millennium," in *China Rising: Power and Motivation in Chinese Foreign Policy*, ed. Yong Deng and Fei-Ling Wang (Lanham, MD: Rowman & Littlefield, 2005), pp. 177–87.

107. Qin Jize, "Wen: SCO Trade Is Set to Double," *China Daily*, September 16–17, 2006, p. 1.

108. Michael Mihalka, "Not Much of a Game: Security Dynamics in Central Asia," *China and Eurasia Quarterly* 5, no. 2 (2007): pp. 21–39; Dan Burghart, "The New Nomads? The American Military Presence in Central Asia," *China and Eurasia Quarterly* 5, no. 2 (2007): pp. 5–19.

109. Compare Susan Shirk, *China: Fragile Superpower* (New York: Oxford University Press, 2007), pp. 140–254, with Matthew Oresman, "Repaving the Silk Road: China's Emergence in Central Asia," in *China and the Developing World*, ed. Joshua Eisenman, Eric Heginbotham, and Derek Mitchell (Armonk, NY: M. E. Sharpe, 2007), pp. 60–83.

110. Kevin Sheives, "China Turns West: Beijing's Contemporary Strategy toward Central Asia," *Pacific Affairs* 79, no. 2 (summer 2006): pp. 205–24.

111. Niklas Swanstrom, "China and Central Asia: A New Great Game or Traditional Vassal?" *Journal of Contemporary China* 14, no. 45 (November 2005): pp. 569–84.

112. Celeste Wallander, "Russia: The Domestic Sources of a Less-Than-Grand Strategy," in *Strategic Asia 2007–2008*, ed. Ashley Tellis and Michael Wills (Seattle, WA: National Bureau of Asian Research, 2007), pp. 138–75.

Chapter Nine

Relations beyond Nearby Asia

In the post–Cold War period, China has established a wide economic footprint as the world's largest exporter and second-largest economy throughout regions of the world distant from China where past Chinese influence had been episodic and comparatively small. With a highly resource-intensive economic growth trajectory and legions of highly competitive producers of manufactured products and builders of modern infrastructure projects backed in many cases by well-funded Chinese financial institutions, contemporary China needs massive inputs of raw materials from abroad to keep its fast growing economy moving forward smoothly. (A Chinese government specialist wrote in an editorial in 2010 that China "consumed 0.82 ton of standard oil for every \$1,000 increase in GDP value" while "in the U.S. and Japan, the figure was 0.20 ton and 0.10 ton respectively.")[1] And the Chinese government has been effective in working closely with competitive Chinese enterprises in selling Chinese products and services abroad in ways that have sustained a favorable Chinese trade balance despite China's position as the world's largest importer of commodities.

The negative legacies, policy inconsistencies, and other contemporary complications and encumbrances facing China's rise in nearby Asia are not present or are much less important in China's rise as an economic power with growing political influence in regions farther from China. Part of the reason is that China has much less at stake in those regions than in nearby Asia. Not present are issues of disputed territorial claims and the security and stability of the Chinese homeland in the face of wary regional powers and the United States. China's use of its growing military, other national security, economic,

267

and political power for purposes of coercion and fostering Chinese interests remains focused on nearby Asia. The volatile and occasionally violent patriotic Chinese public and various segments in the Chinese administration that emphasize defense of Chinese nationalistic claims and interests generally devote less attention to issues beyond China's periphery.

At bottom, China's main interests in these areas are heavily commercial. Though China welcomes the international status and political influence that attends its growing economic role, it uses its influence in these areas to advance fairly narrow and concrete Chinese interests in a win-set emphasized in the ubiquitous "win-win" formula governing contemporary Chinese foreign relations. In the post–Cold War period, this pervasive element in Chinese foreign policy and behavior is part of a broad-ranging effort to reassure other countries, international groups, or other world actors that Chinese behavior and interaction with them will benefit them as well as China.

The Chinese government has pursued reassurance by developing common ground and putting aside differences. Under the win-win concept, China makes clear to foreign governments, organizations, and others that it will work with them in areas of mutual interest and that China does not expect them to do things that they would not ordinarily do. There are a few exceptions to this general rule. China usually demands adherence to "one China" that does not allow contacts with Taiwan, and it expects the foreign party to avoid contacts with the Dalai Lama, the Falun Gong, and prominent dissidents from Xinjiang and other parts of China. In general, this Chinese approach has been widely welcomed by those seeking closer interaction with China.[2]

What the win-win concept means for China is that China is prepared to work with foreign parties in areas of mutual interest but is not going to take actions or adopt changes in policy and behavior that are not within the limited scope of carefully defined Chinese national interests. Against this background, in regions of the world beyond the scope of Chinese nationalistic, security, and related interests in nearby Asia, China has followed practices that avoid involvement in contentious disputes and foster as stable an environment as possible that is beneficial for Chinese commercial and related interests.

RELATIONS WITH THE MIDDLE EAST

During the Cold War, Chinese officials viewed the Middle East as an arena of the so-called East-West (i.e., U.S-Soviet) competition for world domination and of resistance by developing countries and liberation movements against outside powers and their local allies. Beijing lined up on the side of what it conceived of as progressive forces resisting the United States. It later encouraged opposition as well to the Soviet Union in the 1960s. China supported Gamal Abdel Nasser leading Egypt against Western powers in the 1950s. It supported Arab countries backing Palestinian resistance to Israel and the United States. China provided some military training, assistance, and other support to some resistance movements, notably the Palestine Liberation Organization under the leadership of Yasir Arafat. In general, however, Chinese leaders saw the Middle East as distant from primary Chinese foreign policy concerns. It avoided major commitments and was in a good position to change policies and practices in the region as Chinese foreign policy priorities shifted, sometimes dramatically.[3]

That China's policies in the Middle East for many years involved more rhetoric than substance was evident in relations with Egypt under Nasser. As noted in chapter 2, China showed strong interest in ties with Egypt following Nasser's coming to power in the 1950s. The Egyptian leader gave an anti-Western cast to the prevailing ideas in the Afro-Asian and Non-Aligned movements. He also was a proponent of pan-Arabism and sought to reduce Western influence in Egypt, notably by nationalizing the Suez Canal.

Egypt's confrontation with Great Britain and France led it to reach out to China and establish diplomatic relations in 1956, and China responded positively. Egypt became the first country in Africa or the Middle East to establish diplomatic relations with the People's Republic of China. Egypt's militant anticolonialist stance and its role as the largest and most influential Arab state reinforced Chinese interest in close relations. However, the two governments came to differ, notably over China's increasingly strident opposition to the Soviet Union, which caused a major split in the Afro-Asian People's Solidarity Organization and other Afro-Asian groups. China made the case that participants should receive assistance from only Afro-Asian countries, thereby excluding not only the West but also the Soviet Union, a major economic partner of and aid provider to Egypt. It opposed efforts by Cairo to include Soviet delegates in the proceedings of Afro-Asian groups in the 1960s. China's advice to Nasser and the Egyptians after the defeat at the hands of U.S.-backed Israeli forces in the 1967 war was to engage in protracted guerrilla war with Israel; this advice was deemed unhelpful and naïve among the Arab leaders.[4]

In the 1960s and 1970s, China actively supported the armed struggle of the PLO as a Palestinian political and paramilitary organization against the policies and practices of Israel. It recognized and had diplomatic relations with the PLO, supported its observer status in the United Nations, and maintained close relations with its longtime leader, Yasir Arafat.[5]

As China in the 1970s changed foreign policy priorities to emphasize an international front targeting Soviet expansion and to improve relations with the United States and Western-aligned countries, policy shifts in the Middle East resulted. In 1967 China began supporting Dhofar Province's struggle for independence from the central authority of the Sultanate of Oman. Chinese assistance diminished and ended in the middle 1970s in favor of Chinese diplomatic ties with the Shah of Iran, who was aligned with the United States and wary of the Soviet Union. Iran supported the Sultanate of Oman as a force for regional stability.[6]

China's strong interest in developing closer relations with the pro-Western Iranian leader brought expanding Chinese diplomatic, foreign trade, and other commercial ties with Iran. Chinese leader Hua Guofeng was one of the last major international leaders to visit the Shah prior to his overthrow in the Iranian revolution of 1979. China adjusted quickly and pragmatically to the change and was able to build ties with the new, more radical Iranian regime, which strenuously opposed the United States.[7]

China approved when Anwar Sadat of Egypt in 1972 expelled Soviet military personnel and abrogated the Egyptian Friendship Treaty with the Soviet Union. It offered immediate Chinese economic and military aid in response. By the end of the decade, China was reported to be selling to Egypt advanced weapons like submarines, jet fighters, and surface-to-air missiles worth hundreds of millions of dollars.[8]

China eschewed joining the harsh Arab criticism of Anwar Sadat for signing the Camp David Accords of 1978 and seeking peace with Israel. It came to view the accords negotiated by Sadat and the Israeli prime minister with mediation provided by U.S. President Jimmy Carter as a positive step toward regional stability.

Other changes in Chinese policy at this time included a large cutback in Chinese military supplies, training, and other support for radical groups engaged in terrorist acts against Israel. By 1980, China clearly indicated opposition to terrorist acts and supported Israel's right to exist. During these years, Israel and China maintained a variety of intelligence operations and arms trade relationships, which helped to provide a foundation for China's decision to establish diplomatic relations with Israel in 1992. [9]

The twists and turns in Chinese Middle East policy at this time were also reflected in policy toward Iraq. China established relations with Iraq in 1958 after it withdrew from the U.S.-backed Central Treaty Organization. China for years duly supported Iraq and other Arab governments opposed to Israel's policies and practices. As noted above, China's concern with the expansion of Soviet power and influence in the Middle East prompted its strong relations with Iraq's regional rival Iran in the 1970s. And China also diverged from Iraq in avoiding sharp criticism of Egypt in seeking peace with Israel in the Camp David Accords. [10]

China's maneuvering following the Iranian revolution of 1979 and subsequent war between Iran and Iraq (1980–1988) was a remarkable display of pragmatism and fence straddling that benefited China's economic growth and military modernization. China was broadly successful in efforts to stay on good terms with both powers. While Chinese diplomats routinely denied reports of large Chinese arms sales to the combatants in the protracted conflict that killed a half million people, China's actual supplying each with large amounts of weapons for the first time put China among the leading arms exporters in the international arms trade. China also developed close economic ties involving large purchases of oil and numerous Chinese construction and other projects in these two countries. The United States was critical of Chinese sales of missiles and other military equipment that Iran could use to threaten U.S. forces and oil shipping in the Persian Gulf. [11]

Beijing was less successful in positioning China in reaction to Iraq's invasion of Kuwait in 1990. China opposed the invasion, but it also had reservations about efforts led by the United States to organize efforts to drive out the Iraqi forces. China had developed important economic interests in Iraq, a supplier of oil to China. China's resistance slowed United Nations Security Council decisions condemning Iraq, and it abstained from endorsing the use of force against Iraq. When the U.S.-led allied forces were successful in driving out Iraqi invaders and restoring stability in Kuwait with minimal allied casualties, China appeared temporarily isolated. China later criticized and resisted U.S.-led efforts in the 1990s to continue military restrictions and other punishments against Iraq and to pressure Iraq to comply with international norms regulating the development of weapons of mass destruction. [12]

In the twenty-first century, Chinese policy and behavior toward the Middle East followed a pattern seen in Chinese policy and behavior toward the other regions of developing countries far from China—Africa and Latin America. On the one hand, there was an upswing of Chinese attention to the region, notably because of growing Chinese need for oil and other energy sources and resources that are required to support China's remarkable economic growth. On the other hand, there were complications in China's expanding engagement. In the Middle East, China's close relations with Iran complicated China's efforts to stay on good terms with the United States and developed countries important in Chinese foreign policy.[13] In much of the past two decades, Iran was seen as a major deviant from world norms regarding nuclear weapons proliferation, terrorism, human rights, and other sensitive issues that were supported by the United States, the EU, and other powers of importance to China.

The Chinese government was more reluctant than in the 1990s to take strong public positions against the United States and its allies in dealing with Iran, as well as Iraq and other issues of controversy, as it gave high priority to persuading Washington and others of China's avowed intention to develop peacefully and in a way seen as responsible and attentive to international norms.[14] In the 1990s, China's often tough public line made clear its opposition to U.S. strategic dominance in the Persian Gulf and elsewhere in the region. However, the Chinese administration generally did not allow its pervasive anti-U.S. rhetoric to spoil its more important effort to stabilize U.S.-China relations. For example, when the Chinese government came under pressure from the United States in the late 1990s to end nuclear cooperation with Iran, Chinese leaders did so. They suffered a serious downturn in relations with Tehran for the sake of ensuring smooth summit meetings with U.S. leaders seriously concerned with Iran's nuclear weapons ambitions. Meanwhile, Chinese policy aimed at keeping on good terms with all sides, including notably Israel, in the often contentious politics of the region. In this way, China could serve its economic interests of ensuring diverse supplies of oil and access to regional markets for economic benefit and arms transfers.[15]

Chinese maneuvering over Iran underlines that Chinese policy and behavior in the Middle East in the twenty-first century features salient decision points involving often contradictory imperatives. These imperatives pose sometimes serious dilemmas for Chinese leaders and seem to require pragmatic and careful cost-benefit assessments by Chinese officials. One-sided decisions run the risk of serious negative consequences for Chinese interests.

In general, the Chinese leaders have tried to adopt positions that are well balanced, have the broadest international appeal, and do the least damage to China's often conflicting interests in the Middle East. [16]

Heading the list of complications and conflicting imperatives in Chinese policy toward the Middle East is Chinese leaders' need to strengthen their relations with oil and gas exporters, including targets of U.S.-backed international pressure (like Iran) and countries that periodically wish to show greater independence from the United States (like oil-rich Saudi Arabia). Building better Chinese relations with these two energy giants is further complicated by their deep mutual suspicion and conflicting interests. At the same time, Chinese leaders are seeking to tone down their anti-U.S. posturing seen in the 1990s in order to strengthen Chinese moderation toward the United States; this more moderate approach is in the interest of avoiding conflict and convincing the United States and its partners of China's determination to conform to international norms as it seeks greater economic development, international influence, and power. China also does not wish to appear to challenge the long-standing U.S. relationship with Saudi Arabia for fear of seriously antagonizing the United States. Chinese strategists see their access to the energy resources of the Persian Gulf heavily influenced by the strong U.S. military presence in the gulf and the broader Middle East. Taken together, the previously mentioned imperatives and trends are often at odds. They appear contradictory, and they complicate China's approach toward the region.

Deepening the trend of the previous decade, Chinese policy aims as much as possible at keeping on good terms with all sides in the often contentious politics of the region. [17] The logic behind the Chinese approach to the Middle East seems clear, even though the Chinese goals seem in conflict and the resulting Chinese actions appear to be somewhat ambivalent and muddled. Chinese domestic economic growth and political stability depend on stable energy supplies. The main sources of Chinese energy demand involve industrial activities, infrastructure development, and transportation growth. The large increase in the number of cars in China strengthens the need for imported oil. Despite China's efforts to diversify the sources of oil imports, the Middle East accounts for over half of China's overall imports, with Saudi Arabia and Iran being the biggest suppliers in the region. [18]

Graphic examples of China's stronger drive for international energy resources include a variety of high-level Chinese visits and energy-related agreements with Iran as well as even more interactions and agreements with the major energy power in the region, Saudi Arabia. Saudi Arabia was the largest supplier of oil to China for most recent years, accounting for about 15 percent of Chinese imports. In 1999, President Jiang Zemin visited Saudi Arabia and signed accords, including a Strategic Oil Cooperation Agreement. In 2006, the head of state of Saudi Arabia visited China in his inaugural trip abroad. President Hu Jintao reciprocated a few months later. The Chinese president followed up with a widely publicized visit in 2009. While more oil sales and closer bilateral relations seemed in the offing, it was unclear how far the two governments would go in solidifying their bilateral relationship and what meaning this would have for the United States, which historically is the major power backing the Saudi ruler. Although Saudi Arabia reportedly has an interest in showing greater independence from the United States, Chinese interest in posturing against the United States in such a sensitive area as relations with Saudi Arabia seems low. China notably continues to rely on the U.S. military to ensure secure transit for its growing energy imports from Saudi Arabia and other Middle Eastern suppliers. Further, Chinese leaders continue to emphasize to U.S. counterparts China's interest is seeking partnership with the United States as China seeks to develop "peacefully" and without the disruptive opposition that could come from an aroused U.S. superpower.[19]

By the time of Chinese President Hu Jintao's visit to Saudi Arabia in February 2009, Sino–Saudi Arabian trade amounted to over $42 billion a year. This was almost half of China's overall trade with the Middle East. Bilateral trade declined along with international energy demand during the global economic downturn in 2009, but it rebounded to a value of $43 billion in 2010. China became the largest importer of Saudi oil. Trade was projected to reach $60 billion by 2015.[20]

Meanwhile, even though China was well aware that Saudi Arabia and Iran had a number of serious differences and were often on opposite sides regarding Middle Eastern problems, China pursued its long-standing ties with Tehran with new vigor given its ever-growing energy needs. Chinese firms also were deeply involved in developing the Tehran subway, electricity, dams, and other industries and infrastructure. These steps reinforced Chinese reluctance to see sanctions or other pressure imposed on Tehran by the United States and Western powers concerned with Iran's nuclear development program, though China continued to show reluctance to stand alone against such international opposition.[21] Top-level Chinese leaders visited Iran less frequently than Saudi Arabia, but they met cordially with the controversial Iranian president in China and at international meetings elsewhere. Iranian officials said in 2011 that direct Chinese trade with Iran was valued at $29 billion, and indirect trade through countries neighboring Iran brought the total to $38 billion in 2010. They added that Iran is currently China's third largest supplier of crude, providing China with roughly 12 percent of its total annual oil consumption. Trade was slated to reach a value of $50 billion in 2015.[22] Active collaboration between Iranian and Chinese energy firms indicated that China would continue to rely heavily on imports from the country, though the need to adhere to tightening U.S.-backed international sanctions against Iran over its nuclear development programs were obstacles to oil trade between Iran and China.[23]

At the same time, strong examples of China's moderation toward the United States and its interests in the Middle East included China's reluctance to stand against the U.S.-led military assault against Saddam Hussein in 2003. Chinese officials repeatedly assured U.S. officials that China would not block the U.S.-led attack. As one Chinese diplomat said in the interview in 2007, "China will not challenge the presence of the United States in the Middle East." Instead, China will focus on strengthening relations with Middle Eastern countries beneficial for the supply of oil and other energy to China.[24]

Regarding the controversy over Iran's nuclear program, the Chinese government has acted as though it did not want to choose between its important energy and other ties with Iran and its concern to nurture the continued cooperation of the United States, the EU, and others who have strongly pressed Iran over a variety of issues, notably its suspected efforts to develop nuclear weapons. Chinese officials at times endeavored to slow and delay actions in the United Nations that would result in condemnation of or sanctions against Iran, and at times they worked closely with Russia in fending off pressure from the United States and the EU powers for more decisive UN action. However, China was reluctant to stand alone against the Western pressure, and it bent to such pressure in allowing the issue to be brought before the UN Security Council despite earlier pledges to resist such a step. In June 2010 China voted for a UN Security Council resolution approving new sanctions against Iran on account of its suspected nuclear weapons development.[25]

Chinese relations with Israel have posed another set of contradictions and complications for Chinese foreign policy in the Middle East. China benefited greatly from economic and military transfers from Israel; the latter were especially valuable to China because of the continued Western arms embargo against China. China resented U.S. pressure to curb Israeli military transfers to China.[26] Beijing accepted Israel's right to exist and eschewed past support for radical elements aiming at Israel's destruction—steps that significantly improved China's relations with the United States and other concerned Western powers. At the same time, China supported the Palestinian Authority (PA) in its opposition to various Israeli pressures and maneuvers seen as designed to weaken the PA and what were deemed legitimate Palestinian territorial claims. China was sharply critical of Israel's December 2008 invasion of Gaza and the resulting humanitarian crisis. The victory of the radical Hamas movement in PA legislative elections in the middle of the past decade and growing control of the radical movement over the PA posed a serious complication. China was low keyed in accepting Hamas in the face of strong U.S. and Israeli opposition to international support for what they viewed as a terrorist organization. The Chinese Foreign Ministry spokesperson welcomed the April 2011 agreement between Hamas and its Fatah rival as paving the way to the formation of an interim government to prepare for elections determining the future administration of the PA.[27]

A more serious set of complications was raised by the war in July–August 2006 between Israeli and Hezbollah forces based in southern Lebanon. Chinese commentary moved from a more or less evenhanded position to one that sided against Israel and to a degree the United States. China did not want to seriously alienate any major party or make major commitments or take risks in the volatile situation; this finding was illustrated by the bland and noncommittal remarks of the Chinese media and the foreign ministry "special envoy" sent to tour the region. The United States, European powers, Israel, Iran, and Syria loomed much more important in the conflict and the efforts to resolve the conflict. As one veteran scholar of China–Middle East relations concluded, China's behavior during the crisis showed that Beijing continued to talk much and do little regarding serious regional issues.[28] China did respond to UN and European requests for peacekeeping forces and agreed to provide one thousand personnel for the UN peacekeeping operation in Lebanon. The Chinese personnel were used in support functions, according to Chinese diplomats.[29]

An additional set of contradictions is posed by China's ongoing efforts to suppress dissent and so-called "splitist" activities by Muslim adherents in Xinjiang. It is deemed essential that these elements be suppressed in order to preserve order and stability in China. At the same time, the tough Chinese measures negatively affect China's image among the Islamic governments in the Middle East. Finally, Chinese antiterrorist efforts at home and abroad, notably in the Shanghai Cooperation Organization (SCO), are seen as vital to Chinese national security and regional stability and an important foundation for greater Chinese cooperation with the United States and other Western powers. At the same time, China's interests with Iran required Chinese leaders to allow the president of Iran to participate in the elaborate fifth anniversary summit of the SCO in Shanghai and later meetings of the group despite strong accusations from Israel, the United States, and Western powers that Tehran supports terrorist activities against Israel, in Iraq, and elsewhere. [30]

More recent Chinese fence straddling showed in avoiding a veto of UNSC Resolution 1973 in March 2011 against the Gadhafi regime while complaining at the highest levels about the violence in Libya resulting from NATO forces employing military coercion in the country under the auspices of the UNSC resolution. China joined with Russia in vetoing a UNSC resolution in February 2012 applying pressure over Syria amid mass killings of oppositionists by the Syrian armed forces. The hardening Chinese stance against pressure on existing regimes came as China lost billions of dollars of investment because of the fighting in Libya. More generally, China strongly opposed the so-called Arab Spring popular uprisings against authoritarian rulers and the graphically negative implications it had for continued Communist Party rule in China. [31]

RELATIONS WITH AFRICA

China's early involvement with Africa reflected efforts to throw off outside influence and foster rapid development and social progress. Chinese officials to this day continue a long-standing practice of comparing Africa's suffering under the European colonialists with China's so-called hundred years of humiliation. As in the Middle East and other areas of the developing world, Beijing aligned with what it saw as progressive forces resisting the United States and its Western allies and associates. It later encouraged opposition as well to the Soviet Union as China broke with the USSR in the 1960s. [32]

China was a disruptive force in African regional groups and liberation movements as it competed for influence against both the Western countries and the USSR and its allies. China's commitment to the efforts of liberation groups and states supporting armed struggles against colonial powers, white-ruled states, and African regimes closely aligned with the West or the USSR at times was substantial. China warned newly emerging African officials and leaders of militant liberation movements against Western and Soviet intentions, including foreign assistance from these governments, and it was for many years prepared to provide substantial assistance to favored governments and liberation movements despite its own pervasive poverty at home. Beijing was an important supplier of basic military equipment and training to a number of liberation groups and newly emerged governments. Premier Zhou Enlai in a wide-ranging visit to Africa in 1964 proclaimed that Africa was ripe for revolution, and China subsequently provided a variety of assistance to favored governments and resistance movements. The assistance ranged from providing help to dissident factions opposed to the UN-backed regime in Congo-Leopoldville to providing backing for the regime of President Mobutu in Zaire to help check Soviet-backed incursions from Angola in the 1970s. The Chinese were key backers of liberation fighters against the Portuguese in Angola and Mozambique, they supported Robert Mugabe in his struggle against white-ruled Rhodesia, and they backed other radical groups in South Africa and elsewhere.[33]

Among African leaders who stayed close to China were Julius Nyerere of Tanzania and Kenneth Kaunda of neighboring Zambia. China nurtured ties with these long-serving presidents who enjoyed prominence among African leaders. In the 1960s and 1970s, China was a strong supporter of several of the armed resistance groups active in Nyerere's Tanzania and Kaunda's Zambia that were focused on opposition to white-ruled and colonial regimes in Africa. The groups included FRELIMO, Frente de Libertação de Moçambique, also known as the Liberation Front for Mozambique. This guerilla movement founded in 1962 was focused on gaining freedom from Portugal's colonial rule; over the years it received important training and material support from China. Mozambique became an independent country under FRELIMO's rule in 1975 and soon established and sustained friendly ties with China. Also active in these countries was Robert Mugabe, who struggled for decades against the white-ruled government of Rhodesia. He led the Zimbabwe African National Movement (ZANU), which received support from China, in contrast to a competing resistance movement, the Zimbabwe African People's Union (ZAPU), which received support from the Soviet Union. China sustained support for Mugabe as he succeeded in his struggles against the white-ruled government and opposing forces, becoming head of government in Zimbabwe in the 1980s.[34]

As China developed close relations with Nyerere's Tanzania and Kaunda's Zambia, it provided favorable publicity to their international and domestic policies. A favorite subject highlighted for many years by Chinese media was Nyerere's socialist and rural-based development policies and practices that many foreign specialists and commentators now see as having been ineffective or counterproductive.

Tanzania under Nyerere's leadership and Zambia under Kaunda's leadership were among the few nations to remain on good terms with China during the radical policies and practices of the Cultural Revolution. Chinese assistance to Africa during this period and later involved building prominent demonstration projects. Most involved sports stadiums, government buildings, or roads, but a few were truly monumental. At the urging of Nyerere and Kaunda, Mao Zedong was willing to make the enormous Chinese sacrifices necessary to build the TanZam Railway that Zambia and Tanzania sought in order to allow Zambian copper to transit from landlocked Zambia through routes not controlled by white minority or colonial regimes. The TanZam Railway, designed to link Zambia's copper fields and the Tanzanian coast, was undertaken by Chinese engineers even though it was previously judged ill-advised by Western and other international experts. Despite great obstacles, Chinese government workers completed the project after many years of effort, the loss of many lives, and great expense. The railway was poorly maintained at various times during ensuing years, making it less than reliable or efficient as a transportation route.[35]

As noted in chapter 3, China relied heavily on backing from African countries in its efforts to rally so-called third world support in order to gain entry for China and to remove Taiwan from the United Nations in 1971. Competition between China and Taiwan for diplomatic recognition in Africa and elsewhere continued.

The dramatic Chinese opening to improved relations with the United States and Western countries during an intensifying struggle against the expansion of the Soviet Union in the 1970s resulted in shifts in Chinese foreign relations in Africa. Chinese officials showed pragmatism as they developed relations with previously alienated African leaders who had strong ties with the United States. And unlike in the Maoist period, Chinese leaders became unwilling to make major economic or security commitments to these regimes. Focused on Chinese domestic needs and development, Deng Xiaoping and his colleagues proved much less generous in providing aid and other assistance.

Emblematic of the pragmatic and arguably expedient turns in Chinese policy at this time is the Chinese relationship with Sese Mobutu. China and this long-serving (1965–1997) president of Zaire (also known at various times as the Democratic Republic of the Congo) were at first on opposite sides of the struggles afflicting the country. Mobutu seemed as suspicious of Chinese actions and motives as he was of the actions and motives of the Soviet Union. Mobutu opposed seating China at the United Nations.

However, by 1972, he began to see the Chinese in a different light, as a counterbalance to both the Soviet Union and his close ties with the United States, Israel, and South Africa. In November 1972, Mobutu extended diplomatic recognition to China, and the two governments established diplomatic relations. In 1973, he visited Beijing, where he met personally with Mao Zedong and received promises of $100 million in technical foreign assistance.

In 1974, Mobutu made a surprise visit to both China and North Korea. At the time, China and Zaire shared a common goal in central Africa, namely opposing the expansion of Soviet power through Soviet-backed African resistance forces in Angola. Accordingly, both Zaire and China covertly funneled aid to Angolan resistance groups opposed to the Soviet-supported forces that seemed ascendant in Angola. The Soviet-backed forces also received the support of tens of thousands of combat troops from Cuba. China provided training, weapons, and money to the Angolan forces also backed by Zaire. Zaire itself launched an ill-fated, preemptive invasion of Angola in a bid to install a pro-Zaire government, but the invasion was repulsed by Cuban troops. China sent military aid to Zaire during counterstrikes led by Cuban troops against Zaire.[36]

China subsequently pulled away from overt resistance to Soviet-backed movements in Angola and other parts of Africa. The shift involved ending support for the National Union for the Total Independence of Angola (União Nacional para a Independência Total de Angola—UNITA). This guerilla movement founded in 1966 was one of the important African resistance movements that long received Chinese support. Largely peasant based, UNITA focused its armed struggle against the colonial rule by Portugal in Angola. Its leader was Jonas Savimbi, who had received paramilitary training in China and who adopted Maoist guerrilla tactics in his resistance against the Portuguese and competing resistance groups. After the end of Portuguese rule in Angola in 1975, a civil war among UNITA and competing resistance groups emerged that endured for more than two decades.[37]

China withdrew support from UNITA and generally eschewed involvement in the civil war. It remained on good terms with Mobutu, who visited China three times after his 1973 and 1974 visits. Chinese assistance projects were followed by a variety of commercial deals and China continued to provide some military assistance to Zaire. When Mobutu was overthrown in 1997, China continued normal relations with the now renamed Democratic Republic of the Congo without serious interruption.[38]

Post-Mao Chinese leaders were much less interested in spending money overseas, especially when their political standing at home rested heavily on their ability to improve economic conditions for the Chinese people. By the late 1970s, the overriding focus of domestic modernization led to a reduction in Chinese enthusiasm for funding expensive African assistance programs. Chinese officials also recognized that past efforts to roll back superpower influence in the region had not worked well. Aid levels dropped markedly in the late 1970s and remained around $100 million annually for the whole world. Chinese assistance increasingly took the form of training, export credits for Chinese goods, or joint financing plans. As the Chinese export-oriented economy grew, so did Chinese trade, from about $300 million with Africa in 1976 to $2.2 billion in 1988. Of course, this still was only a small fraction of overall Chinese trade.[39]

As post-Mao China was willing and anxious to receive foreign aid from the World Bank, the International Monetary Fund (IMF), and other international bodies and donor countries, this put China in direct competition with African states seeking aid from the same sources. The newly open Chinese economy also was seen by some to be taking foreign investment that might have gone to African ventures. African grumbling over these trends grew. Even some longtime African friends felt increasing ambiguity in their ties with China. With mixed results, Chinese officials used diplomacy, propaganda, and exchanges to preserve Beijing's self-described position as an intimate supporter of struggling African states. While acknowledging Chinese political support, African governments often recognized that they had to follow China's example in cultivating ties with developed economies, including the United States, Europe, and Japan, if they expected markedly to boost their modernization efforts. Meanwhile, long-standing Chinese efforts to offer university and other training for African students were clouded by several publicized incidents showing apparent Chinese social bias against Africans in the late 1980s.[40]

Chinese incentives to improve relations with African countries increased after the Tiananmen incident of 1989.[41] Officials anxiously sought African and other third world support to offset Beijing's isolation and to reduce international pressure against China. The period also saw Taiwan launch its pragmatic or flexible diplomacy policy. Taipei used offers of aid or other means to woo aid-dependent African countries and to have them establish official diplomatic relations with Taiwan even though they had diplomatic relations with Beijing. Whenever this occurred, Beijing broke ties with the African state concerned, providing a net diplomatic gain for Taipei. As discussed in chapter 8, China strongly intensified competition with Taiwan in Africa when Beijing gave higher priority to checking Taiwan's flexible diplomacy, especially following the visit by Taiwan's president, Lee Teng-hui, to the United States in 1995. Its efforts proved successful, diminishing Taiwan's official recognition in Africa to a few small states.

The deepening and broadening Chinese interaction with African countries in the twenty-first century has featured an upsurge in Chinese trade, investment financing, and high-level official interaction with African countries that stands in contrast with the stagnant and contentious relations African countries often have had with developed countries and international financial institutions. A marked increase in Chinese purchases of oil and other raw materials from Africa and a concurrent effort to foster Chinese exports to African markets and an increase in Chinese construction projects throughout Africa are new and important drivers of Chinese interest in the continent. Other patterns of the post–Cold War period have continued without major change. China continues to devote strong political attention to African countries in order to compete with Taiwan, enhance solidarity with members of the third world bloc in the United Nations and other world organizations, facilitate growing trade, and portray China internationally as a power of growing stature and importance. The Chinese government has had an active aid program in several African countries, but the cost of the program to China (that is, the amount of funds leaving China to aid African countries and not guaranteed to be paid back in commodities or other forms) remains small. With a few exceptions, Chinese arms transfers to Africa are small, and China has avoided taking positions that might be seen as interfering in the internal affairs of African countries or antagonistic to disputants in the continent's many conflicts. Consistent with its recent emphasis on avoiding difficulties with the United States and other powers as it endeavors to pursue a path of "peaceful development," the Chinese government has tended to avoid being seen as criticizing U.S. and other powers' policies that are incompatible with Chinese goals on the continent.[42]

In general, the advance of Chinese relations in Africa has faced fewer contradictions or complications than concurrent Chinese advances among developing countries in the Middle East or Latin America. In the latter two areas, the security, political, and economic roles of the United States, European countries, and other foreign powers generally have been significantly more important than China's newly rising prominence. Taken together, the roles of these other foreign powers have added to factors constraining the influence of China in those regions. In the case of Africa and especially sub-Saharan Africa, however, China's involvement has reached high prominence in a setting where other powers have appeared less vigorously involved. China, while not achieving the status of Africa's leading foreign power, clearly has played a leading role in regional affairs along with the United States and European countries and the international organizations they support. The latter powers sometimes have criticized aspects of Chinese involvement in Africa, but they also have moved to consult with and work more closely with China in dealing with regional issues. Meanwhile, though the Chinese government usually has sustained good relations with African government leaders, it has found that China's increasing impact on Africa has resulted in mixed reactions below the national government level, with some strong negative responses on the part of constituencies adversely affected by Chinese interaction with their countries.[43]

A landmark in China's efforts to formulate a comprehensive outreach to Africa came in October 2000 when China's leaders and the leaders of forty-five African countries met in Beijing to form the China-Africa Cooperation Forum (CACF). They agreed that CACF would meet every three years to further mutual economic development and cooperation. The Chinese government endeavored to enhance cooperation by using the first CACF meeting to pledge forgiveness of $1.2 billion in African debt covering thirty-two nations and to expand Chinese foreign aid to Africa. At the second ministerial CACF conference held in Addis Ababa, Ethiopia, in December 2003, China promised to cooperate with Africa in priority sectors identified in the African governments' New Partnership for African Development. These African priorities included infrastructure development, prevention and treatment of diseases such as HIV/AIDS, human resources development, and agricultural development. China also agreed to begin negotiations on reducing tariffs to zero for some exports to China of the least-developed African countries.[44]

Continued high-level attention to Africa included the release in January 2006 of the Chinese government's first official white paper on African policy, prior to Foreign Minister Li Zhaoxing's visit to several African countries. The document was broad ranging and basically restated official Chinese positions on Africa, which were also highlighted in President Hu Jintao's visit to Morocco, Kenya, and Nigeria in April 2006. This was followed by Prime Minister Wen Jiabao's visit to seven African countries in mid-2006. At the time, Chinese media reported that Chinese trade with Africa reached $40 billion in 2005, up rapidly from $10 billion in 2000.[45]

China hosted the CACF summit in November 2006. Representatives of forty-eight African countries and Chinese leaders capped the meeting with a joint declaration that provided an action plan for the next three years. The emphasis in the declaration was on expanding exchanges, trade, investment, and mutually beneficial ties as well as calling on the United Nations and the international community to strengthen support for African interests. At the summit, China pledged $5 billion in preferential loans and credits and to double aid to Africa by 2009. It announced support for health and education efforts in Africa and said that trade would expand from the 2005 level of $40 billion to reach $100 billion by 2010. Meanwhile, Chinese companies signed fourteen commercial contracts and agreements valued at $1.9 billion.[46]

Chinese government figures on Chinese investment in Africa tended to be significantly lower than figures used in Western and African media and other international reports. Thus, even with a widely reported and dramatic rise in Chinese involvement in gaining access to African oil and other natural resources needed for China's heavily resource-intensive economic growth trajectory, a Chinese government official put a recent rise in Chinese investment in Africa in some perspective during an interview with official Chinese media in April 2011. The official said that Chinese investment in Africa, then "about $1 billion" a year, was "dwarfed by the West" in contributions to overall annual foreign investment in Africa amounting to $80–90 billion.[47]

Chinese foreign assistance to African states also received prominent treatment in Chinese and international media and among concerned international relations specialists, even though the actual amounts of Chinese assistance to Africa (as opposed to large amounts of financing provided by China to be paid for with African commodities or other means) seemed modest and less than that provided by developed countries and international financial institutions.[48] For a variety of reasons, the actual amounts of Chinese foreign assistance have not been released in a comprehensive way by the Chinese government. China did issue an official document on Chinese foreign assistance in April 2011; but the information was very broad ranging and foreign analysts have continued to rely on piecing together information supplied by Chinese media and other official sources and on data from foreign sources in order to discern contributions and costs regarding specific countries and programs. Deborah Brautigam, a specialist on foreign aid and Chinese involvement in Africa, estimated that Chinese aid in Africa in 2001–2009 amounted to $2.1 billion.[49]

Salient indicators[50] underlining the importance of Africa in Chinese foreign relations at the start of the current decade include the following:

- *Leadership attention and contacts:* President Hu Jintao visited four African countries in February 2009, marking his fourth visit to Africa since becoming president in 2003. Premier Wen Jiabao led China's delegation to the fourth China-Africa Cooperation Forum (CACF) held in Egypt in November 2009. He pledged to double the $5 billion low-cost loan for African development promised at the 2006 CACF, and he detailed a wide range of debt relief, environmental, education, training, and other Chinese offers and opportunities for African countries. China had diplomatic relations and embassies in all but a small handful of African states (four still recognized Taiwan), maintained extensive party ties with African political parties, and developed growing relations with regional and subregional organizations like the African Development Bank.
- *Economic relations:* China's trade with Africa grew by 30 percent a year in the past decade reaching $106.8 billion in 2008. The trade was spread among various countries with Angola (one of China's top oil suppliers) and South Africa being the most important trading partners. Chinese success in selling manufactured and other goods to Africa generally balanced China's large-scale imports of African commodities. Trade dipped in value in 2009 but revived to a level of $114.8 billion in 2010 and reportedly exceeded $160 billion in 2011.[51] In 2009 China became Africa's largest trading partner, surpassing the United States and the European Union. The Chinese government also set up a series of commercial and investment centers called special economic zones (SEZs) that provided special privileges and incentives to Chinese firms in Africa. Cumulative Chinese investment at the end of 2010 was said to be worth $9.3 billion by official Chinese media. Chinese aid included forgiveness of debts to China by poorer African countries valued at almost $3 billion, several billions of

dollars of financing provided by a special Sino–African development fund, and financing, including loans from official Chinese banks backed by commodities and other collateral in support of large-scale infrastructure projects in Angola, Sudan, Congo, and other resource-rich countries. China's provision of such financing engendered serious controversy among Western countries and some African constituencies that were concerned with China's provisions to support corrupt or otherwise unsavory regimes.

- *Social, cultural, and other interchange:* The over one million Chinese working in Africa included professionals in Chinese commercial and government institutions, Chinese laborers working on projects throughout the continent, and Chinese traders and small-business people focused on selling Chinese commodities to African consumers. The Chinese government followed past practice in pursuing active cultural exchange programs with African countries and sending Chinese medical personnel to Africa. Chinese-funded Confucius Institutes, whose mission is to spread Chinese language and culture abroad, were established in a dozen locations in Africa.

- *Military relations:* China sustained an active program of military exchanges throughout Africa. Chinese arms sales generally remained at a modest level, though Chinese arms sales to controversial governments like Sudan and Zimbabwe received critical attention in international media. Chinese military and other security forces were active participants in UN-backed peacekeeping efforts in several African countries. Since 2009, China maintained warships along the Horn of Africa to work with international security efforts to counter pirate attacks against international shipping off the coast of Somalia.

RELATIONS WITH LATIN AMERICA AND THE CARIBBEAN

China historically has paid less attention to Latin America and the Caribbean than to any other region in the developing world. Geographic distance and China's preoccupation with issues closer to home put Latin American issues low on China's list of priorities. In the East-West and Sino-Soviet competition for global influence during the Cold War, Beijing at first tried to make headway among radical Latin American groups. In general, however, there was little to show for this effort. The power and influence of the United States remained very strong among most established governments in Latin

America, while leftists in Cuba, Chile, Nicaragua, and elsewhere tended to look to the Soviet bloc for tangible assistance rather than to seek the political advice and rhetorical support offered by Maoist China. [52]

Chinese leaders maneuvered to gain Fidel Castro's support in Cuba during the acrimonious Sino-Soviet split beginning in the 1960s. Pro-Chinese and pro-Cuban groups for several years pursued revolutionary tactics in ideological association. The break came in the mid-1960s, when the Cubans, presumably under Soviet pressure, became more cautious in exporting revolution. China went on giving financial aid and political encouragement to revolutionary groups in Latin America in the 1960s, but most of them adopted strongly pro-Soviet, pro-Cuban orientations. [53]

As China in the late 1960s and early 1970s opened to relations with the United States and a wide range of governments useful in China's search for greater recognition and international leverage against the growing coercion of the Soviet Union, China's past advocacy of violent revolution was replaced by championing the interests of third world governments. Forecasting themes seen in Deng Xiaoping's famous speech to the United Nations in 1974 announcing China's "Three Worlds" theory was the Chinese address at the UN Conference on Trade and Development meeting in Chile in 1972. China assumed the role as spokesperson for the developing world and chief opponent of both the Soviet Union and the United States in Latin America and elsewhere. Such rhetoric did not go very far in advancing Chinese regional influence, as China had few interests that coincided with those of the countries in Latin America and it had few resources to expend there. [54]

Later in the 1970s, Beijing for several years attempted to fit its Latin American policy into its dominant anti-Soviet orientation, but the results led to sometimes egregious excesses, notably China's support for the right-wing policies of General Augusto Pinochet in Chile. China's relations with Cuba worsened as Beijing strongly condemned Cuba's provision of thousands of combat forces in support of Soviet-backed regimes in Africa during the 1970s. [55]

China's more evenhanded criticism of the Soviet Union and the United States was evident at the turn of the decade and the emergence of China's "independent foreign policy" in the early 1980s. At an international summit in Cancun Mexico in October 1981, Chinese Premier Zhao Ziyang stressed strong support for developing countries' demands for establishment of a new economic order, opposed by the United States and other developed countries. China sided with Argentina against U.S.-backed Great Britain in the war over the disputed Falkland Islands in 1982. Regarding the conflicts in Nicaragua and El Salvador, China opposed the U.S. use of force while supporting American and other efforts to use multilateral aid programs backed by political initiatives as the best means to achieve regional stability and keep out the USSR.[56]

Throughout much of the post–Cold War period, China followed a low-key and pragmatic effort to build better relations with Latin American countries. Beijing was well aware of China's limited standing in the region. The region has long been dominated by U.S. power and influence and has also been developing improved economic and political relations with European powers, Japan, South Korea, and others. Radical movements in the region in the past looked to Moscow rather than Beijing for support and guidance. Throughout the 1990s and into the next decade, China maintained an active diplomatic presence; engaged in a wide variety of government-sponsored political, economic, and military contacts; and grew economic relations with the region to a point where China–Latin America trade, while only a small fraction of Chinese overall trade, surpassed Chinese trade with Africa.[57]

A rapid increase in Chinese purchases of Latin American commodities along with widely publicized Chinese leaders' visits to the region in 2004, 2005, and 2008 appeared to mark a significant change in China's approach to Latin America. President Hu Jintao's regional tour and participation at the November 2004 Asian-Pacific Economic Cooperation (APEC) summit in Chile saw an outpouring of media and specialist commentary that provided sometimes grossly exaggerated assessments of China's rising investments and other economic interests in Latin America. The commentary also exaggerated Chinese support for some regional leaders, such as Venezuela's president Hugo Chavez, who were determined to stand against U.S. interests and influence in the region. Subsequent assessments provided a more sober view of China's increased interest in the region. China's interest appeared to focus heavily on obtaining access to resources needed for Chinese economic development; it showed little sign of a Chinese desire to undertake the costs and commitments involved in challenging the United States or adopting a significant leadership role in Latin America. The increased Chinese interest in acquiring Latin American resources generally was welcomed by regional leaders but also was accompanied by strong opposition and complaints over the impact of Chinese economic relations on regional economies.[58]

Throughout the post–Cold War period, Chinese motives in Latin America were similar to Chinese motives in the Middle East, Africa, and other developing countries without major strategic significance for China. Beijing sought to nurture common bonds with Latin American countries and strove to win their support for China's positions in the United Nations and other international organizations. Latin America, especially Central America and the Caribbean, represented the main battleground in Beijing's international competition with Taiwan. Chinese officials went to extraordinary lengths, even using China's veto power in the UN Security Council, in order to curb the still strong support for Taiwan on the part of many regional states.[59] Chinese commentaries until 2001 also routinely criticized U.S. policy in Latin America and highlighted European and Japanese resistance to the U.S. efforts to have its way in the region. The rhetoric fit into the broader Chinese tendency at that time to see and encourage signs of emerging multipolarity in the world when the U.S. superpower met resistance from other powers determined to protect their interests in an economically and politically competitive world environment. As a result of the improvement in U.S.-Chinese relations in 1997–1998, Chinese officials and commentary devoted less attention to these themes, suggesting that China was inclined, at least for the time being, to pursue its interests by not standing against the United States on a variety of world issues. This trend became more pronounced as in mid-2001 China muted most routine rhetoric against U.S. hegemonism and later adopted an emphasis on peaceful development that sought closer partnership and cooperation with the United States.[60]

By all accounts, economic relations between China and Latin American countries have taken off over the past decade. Growth in trade and investment has been large. Two-way trade flows increased over 500 percent, from $8 billion in 1999 to $40 billion in 2004, and kept growing. Much of the activity centered on Chinese efforts to secure access to natural resources. As a result, the large increases in trade have focused on a few Latin American countries that provide the raw materials that China has been looking for, notably copper, nickel, iron ore, petroleum, grains, wood, frozen fish, fish meal, sugar, leather, and chemical substances. Increased trade also has seen a large upsurge in Chinese manufactured goods exported throughout Latin American markets.[61]

Measuring the increasing importance of China as a trading partner for Latin America, total China–Latin America trade flows were valued at $178.6 billion in 2010. The trade was balanced, with Chinese exports to Latin America valued at $88.3 billion and imports valued at $90.3 billion. Brazil was the standout in the growing economic ties with China. Bilateral trade in 2010 was valued at $56.2 billion. Commodities such as iron ore made up the vast bulk (90 percent) of Brazilian exports, and manufactured goods were the main products imported from China. In 2011, the value of China's trade with Latin America was $200 billion. This value was one-fourth of the trade that occurred between Latin American countries and the United States. Canada and the European Union also remained major Latin American trading partners. The relative importance of Latin America to China likewise was significant but not overwhelming, especially given that the expansion of Chinese trade on a global level was remarkable in recent years.[62]

Until recently, Chinese outflows of foreign direct investment (FDI) in Latin America were very small. In 2004, 0.71 percent of Latin America's cumulative stock of FDI was from China; Chinese FDI represented 2.46 percent of inflows to Latin American countries that year (compared to 29 percent from the United States). Reflecting China's need for resources and its large foreign exchange holdings, the turn of the decade registered a big increase in Chinese investment. Official Chinese media reported in April 2011 that cumulative Chinese investment in Latin America had reached $41.2 billion at the end of 2009. The upswing continued in later years. China's investments were directed toward projects that facilitate the procurement of natural resources (for example, roads, and port facilities), and they concentrated in a few countries where the resources base was significant (Brazil, Argentina, Chile, Peru, and Venezuela). Brazil was a major target of investment. Various Chinese investment deals in Brazil in 2010 were valued at $17 billion. If China does ultimately reach a reported goal of $100 billion in investment in Latin America by 2015, China's portion of Latin America's cumulative stock likely would still be a distinct minority share. In 2010, over 90 percent of foreign direct investment flowing into Mexico and Brazil, the region's two biggest economies, came from developed countries.[63]

As in the case of Chinese financing of infrastructure efforts in African and other developing countries, China has engaged in similar financing efforts to build roads, railroads, refineries, ports, and other facilities in Latin America. Little of this financing would be considered foreign assistance by Western standards, and Chinese foreign assistance to Latin America is thought to be very low. In 2009 and 2010, the China Development Bank extended multibillion-dollar lines of credits to energy companies and government entities notably in Brazil, Ecuador, and Venezuela. The loans were secured by revenue earned from the sale of oil at market prices to Chinese national oil companies. The loans were distinguished by their large size and long terms. They were attractive at that time because many companies were postponing major investments in oil development on account of cash flow problems, and other financial institutions were unwilling to lend such large amounts of capital for such long terms. [64]

The positive effects of growing economic ties on Chinese relations with Latin America were reduced to some degree by a variety of complications and negative features of the economic ties:

- Countries in Latin America that were not major exporters of resources tended to focus on the fact that they could not compete with incoming Chinese manufactured goods and that those goods also took their important markets in the United States and elsewhere. Countries that export products similar to those of China (notably Mexico but also many Central American and Caribbean countries) experienced intense competition with China.
- Chinese "tied loans," which carried low interest rates and led to the project being carried out by Chinese state-owned enterprises, tended not to increase local employment or related poverty reduction. [65]
- Important constituents in the resource-exporting countries have reacted negatively to incoming Chinese manufactured imports and overall Chinese competition for world markets. Despite the rapid increase in Brazil-China trade and Chinese investment in Brazil, incoming Brazilian president Dilma Rousseff in 2011 steered policy in directions to defend Brazilian manufacturers suffering in the face of imported Chinese goods benefiting from the low value of China's currency; she also pressed China to open its market more to Brazilian aircraft and other manufactured goods. [66]
- Latin American countries had long been suppliers of raw materials to extra-regional powers, and they often resented this role as well as the unfavorable terms of trade and environmental degradation that inevitably followed. As the pattern of Chinese trade and investment became more important and clear, past practice indicated that Latin American countries would see that the kind of relationship China was attempting to forge with the region was not all that different from the past imperialist and neo-imperialist models that Latin American had come to resent. Some Chinese commentators expert in regional issues showed an awareness of negative features in China's developing relationship with Latin America; they urged steps to foster a more balanced and complementary relationship in the broad interests of both sides. [67]

The Taiwan factor continued to drive China's political relations in Latin America. Almost half of the governments that officially recognized Taiwan were in Latin America. Other than Paraguay, all were in Central America and the Caribbean. Given the "dollar diplomacy" of Beijing and Taipei as they competed with each other for international recognition, small countries often switched recognition when given a good offer from one side or the other. As noted in chapter 8, the coming to power in 2008 of the moderate Ma Ying-jeou administration in Taiwan changed the competition between China and Taiwan for international recognition. Seeking to reassure China and ease cross-strait relations, Ma reached an informal understanding with China whereby neither would pursue new advances in diplomatic relations at the expense of the other. Paraguay and perhaps other countries in Latin America were prepared to switch recognition from Taipei to Beijing, but such moves did not take place, presumably because of the informal Taiwan-China under-standing.[68]

Latin America, including Central America and the Caribbean, also re-mained significant to China because of the number of votes the region repre-sents in international bodies, especially the United Nations. China also was quietly seeking admittance to a number of regional organizations. It obtained observer status in the Organization of American States (OAS), the Associa-tion for Latin American Integration, and the Caribbean Development Bank; it sought to join and eventually did join the Inter-American Development Bank.

China's relations with Latin American countries also had a South-South dimension that supported Chinese efforts to work over the long-term against U.S. dominance and to create a multipolar world. China's support for Bra-zil's bid to become a permanent member of the UN Security Council, its cooperation agreements with regional governments in the areas of science and technology, and Chinese solidarity with developing countries in pushing for a favorable international trade regime were part of Beijing's South-South agenda that has long existed in Chinese foreign policy. Chinese leaders also participated actively and often cooperatively with Brazilian leaders in vari-ous international groups dealing with global development and governance. Notably, China collaborated closely with Brazil, India, and Russia in a new international grouping known as the BRIC, an acronym containing each member country's first letter. Another new grouping included South Africa along with China, India, and Brazil and it was known as BASIC. As noted earlier, South Africa was asked and agreed to join the BRIC countries in 2011, with that organization becoming BRICS.[69]

China's political relationship with Latin America's leftist leaders was more complicated. Available evidence suggested that China was being cautious in its relations with Venezuela, a country of strong interest in the PRC's increasingly active quest for oil and other energy resources.[70] Moreover, China's broad interest in Latin America and elsewhere was to convey an image as a reliable and stable trade partner. Close Chinese association with Venezuela's support of indigenous populism and antiglobalization causes could have led to instability among China's trading partners and undermined Chinese access to the resources of the region.[71]

Following the end of the Cold War and the termination of Soviet aid to Cuba, Sino-Cuban relations increased. China's top leaders have visited the island, highlighting modest levels of Chinese assistance. There also were repeated reports of deepening Chinese-Cuban military and intelligence cooperation. They centered on reported Chinese arms sales and Chinese acquisition of former Soviet-operated signals intelligence outposts in Cuba.[72] Whatever was taking place was not seen as posing a threat to the United States, according to U.S. officials.[73]

Another cluster of allegations against China focused on supposed Chinese maneuvers to control the Panama Canal. The concern stemmed from the fact that Hong Kong–based Hutchinson Whampoa Limited, a company that had links to China, owned the port facilities in Cristobel and Balboa, at each end of the canal, and had received an offer to develop a former U.S. facility at Rodman's Point. Some judged that the company was a cover for the Chinese government and that it engaged in surveillance and might resort to sabotage in the event of a Sino-U.S. war over Taiwan.[74] On reflection, most U.S. policy makers presumably found this scenario far-fetched, as no action was taken.

RELATIONS WITH EUROPE

During the Cold War, Europe was viewed by China as an arena of competition between the United States and the Soviet Union that featured generally secondary concerns for China. East Germany and other countries aligned with the Soviet Union provided significant material and technical assistance to China during the 1950s. China took important positions in the discussions among Communist countries regarding the controversies involving the Soviet Union's relations with Poland and Hungary in 1956. China also was able to establish diplomatic and foreign trade relations with some non-Communist western European countries despite U.S. pressure to impose a diplomatic and economic embargo against China. Amid the thaw in Chinese foreign relations after the Korean War and while China was joining the Soviet Union in highlighting the Five Principles of Peaceful Coexistence, Beijing reciprocated Great Britain's earlier appointment of a chargé d'affaires to its embassy, sent a trade delegation to London, signed a trade agreement with Finland, and began negotiations with the recently arrived Norwegian envoy on establishing formal diplomatic relations.[75]

Despite its alignment with the United States during the Cold War, Britain quickly recognized the People's Republic of China and worked to preserve its colonial administration in Hong Kong. As noted in chapter 2, a low point in relations came in 1967 at the height of China's Red Guard diplomacy during a particularly violent stage of the Cultural Revolution when a mob in Beijing protesting police arrests of pro-China demonstrators in Hong Kong burned the British mission, and assaulted its officers.

French forces in Vietnam and Indochina were the target of the Viet Minh insurgents strongly backed by China in the early 1950s. Under the leadership of President Charles de Gaulle, France broke with its Western partners and in 1964 it established relations with the People's Republic of China (PRC) and ended ties with the Republic of China (ROC) based on Taiwan.[76]

The international communist movement was an important arena of early Sino-Soviet polemics over issues regarding Soviet leadership of world Communist parties and states, debates over how to assess Stalin's leadership, appropriate economic development strategies in Communist countries, and relations with the United States and other Western countries. Enver Hoxa was the leader of Albania's government, Communist Party, and military from the end of World War II until his death in the 1980s. As serious ideological and foreign policy issues emerged between the People's Republic of China (PRC) and the Soviet Union at the end of the 1950s, Albania under Hoxa's leadership sided with China and was publicly rebuked by Moscow beginning in the early 1960s. China provided strong material and political support for the hard-line leadership of the small European state for over a decade until relations declined as a result of disagreements over China's rapprochement with the United States and with Albania's more powerful regional neighbor, Yugoslavia.[77]

Regarding the latter, for many years, Chinese officials joined Albanians and a few others with similar views in attacking the "revisionist" policies of Josip Tito, the independent-minded Communist leader of Yugoslavia. China also encouraged Romania's Nicolai Ceauşescu to assert independence from policies in the Warsaw Pact favored by the Soviet Union. Signs of close relations included Chinese leaders using Ceauşescu to convey sensitive messages to and from leaders of the United States and the Soviet Union. The main Communist parties of Western Europe tended to side with Moscow against Beijing's challenges in the international communist movement. For many years, they were viewed critically by Chinese officials. [78]

The Chinese opening to the United States in the late 1960s and early 1970 was accompanied by many non-Communist governments in Europe establishing and upgrading official relations with China. China encouraged the trend and used the opportunity to urge European leaders to increase vigilance against the international expansion of the Soviet Union. China established official relations with West Germany in 1973, and it endeavored to balance these new relations with long-standing Chinese ties with East Germany. Beijing was wary of the implications of the moderate West German policy toward the Soviet Union and the Warsaw Pact under the leadership of Chancellor Willy Brant (1969–1974). At that time, China was under great pressure from the Soviet Union and was concerned that détente in Europe, the fulcrum of East-West confrontation, would allow Moscow to muster more forces to coerce China. [79]

Facing this strategic threat and pressure from the Soviet Union, Chinese officials moved pragmatically to improve relations with Yugoslavia, welcoming Tito on a landmark visit to China in 1977. They revived formal Communist Party relations, and sent Party Chairman Hua Guofeng to Tito's funeral in 1980. The improvement of relations with Yugoslavia along with China's opening to the United States lay behind long-standing ally Albania's open break with China.

Beijing endeavored to keep on good terms with Ceauşescu's Romania, but while Chinese leaders were abandoning Maoist excesses and opening to the outside world in the late 1970s, Ceauşescu was moving toward erratic policies, a strong cult of personality, nationalism, and deterioration in relations with the West and the USSR. His eventual overthrow and execution by firing squad in 1989 as Communist regimes were collapsing throughout the world stood as a graphic reminder to leaders in China as to what can happen to authoritarian rulers who lose control of the levers of power.

China had mixed views of the implications of the labor strikes that under-mined pro-Soviet rule in Poland in the early 1980s. On the one hand, China saw the workers' strikes and organization of Solidarity, a powerful indepen-dent labor organization, as weakening Moscow's international position in ways beneficial to China. On the other hand, the Polish example showed Communist rulers in China the kinds of challenges they would also face from an independent labor organization. [80]

China's pragmatic search for greater international influence, especially leverage to use against the USSR, brought changes in its approach to the main Communist parties in Western Europe. By 1976, official Chinese com-mentary no longer portrayed the Italian Communist Party, the largest in Western Europe, as subservient to the interests of the Soviet Union, but it continued to treat it as a revisionist party. Over time, China's commentary came to treat the party in an uncritical fashion, signaling an imminent recon-ciliation, which came during a summit meeting between the Chinese Com-munist Party and the Italian Communist Party leaders in 1980. [81]

Significant developments in Chinese relations with Europe in the 1980s included the Sino-British agreement on the future of Hong Kong, an impor-tant British colony. Interests in Hong Kong influenced Great Britain's deci-sions on policy toward China, notably its decision to recognize the People's Republic of China (PRC) in 1950. China generally was pragmatic in seeking economic and other advantage from interchange with Hong Kong, despite its colonial status. Hong Kong also served as a base for U.S. and other foreign commercial and government activities dealing with China. Though Western trade with China was restricted during the first two decades of the Cold War, foreign trade and foreign investment in Hong Kong grew. As the Chinese government opened to foreign economic exchange in the 1970s, many foreign businesses used Hong Kong as a base of operations to take advantage of China's opening. [82]

Under the leadership of Prime Minister Margaret Thatcher, Britain was compelled to put aside colonial rights and negotiate the return of Hong Kong to Chinese sovereignty. Sino-British negotiations in 1982–1984 to define Hong Kong's future status led to the Joint Declaration, an agreement in 1984 calling for the British colony to return to Chinese sovereignty in 1997. The Tiananmen crackdown and large-scale demonstrations in Hong Kong in 1989 prompted greater British interest in securing guarantees for democracy and stability in the territory. The United States shared this concern. U.S. legisla-tion conditioning the annual U.S. renewal of most favored nation (MFN) tariff status for China routinely had provisions dealing with China's policy toward Hong Kong. The last British governor of Hong Kong, Christopher Patten, and prominent Hong Kong Democratic Party leader Martin Lee made annual visits to the United States seeking support while urging continued open U.S. trade with China, an essential element in Hong Kong's economy. At congressional initiative, the United States passed the Hong Kong Policy Act in 1992 laying out U.S. concerns about Hong Kong's future and calling for regular U.S. reports monitoring China's treatment of the territory.[83]

In 1997, the territory of Hong Kong reverted to Chinese sovereignty as the Hong Kong Special Administrative Region (HKSAR) of the People's Republic of China (PRC). China followed through on commitments reached in the Joint Declaration while opposing efforts to advance democracy by advocates in Hong Kong and abroad. The Hong Kong administration integrated the region ever more closely to China's economy and sought to avoid controversy with Beijing over issues sensitive to the Chinese government. Hong Kong's status as a foreign gateway to China declined with the opening and development of the modern commercial hubs in Shanghai and other major Chinese cities. Foreign media and government attention to perceived Chinese efforts to curb those in Hong Kong seeking greater democracy for the people of Hong Kong also declined.

Although China strongly supported liberation movements engaged in armed struggle against Portuguese colonial rule in Angola, Mozambique, and other colonial possessions in Africa in the 1960s and the 1970s, China adopted a very different approach to the Portuguese colonial territory of Macao, which was near Hong Kong and was also claimed as part of China. The Portuguese government appeared willing to end colonial rule after changes in governments and colonial policies in the mid-1970s. Nevertheless, China waited until after reaching the Sino-British Joint Declaration, governing Hong Kong's transfer to China, before reaching agreement with Portugal on Macao's transfer to China. Macao was returned to Chinese rule in 1999, further advancing Portugal's relations with China under the rubric of a "strategic partnership."[84]

With its strong emphasis on economic modernization in recent decades, Beijing has remained anxious to gain economically from improved relations with Europe. The European powers joined the United States and Japan in imposing economic and other sanctions on China following the Tiananmen crackdown in 1989. Japan was the first in the group to break with the sanctions and resume trade, investment, and aid. It was followed by Great Britain and other European states.

Beijing also has shown interest from time to time in fostering greater European political and strategic independence from the United States. This is part of broader PRC efforts to develop a multipolar world more advantageous to China than the prevailing international order with the United States in the leading position. Throughout the 1990s and until 2001, Beijing publicly chafed under an international order where the Chinese saw the United States as the dominant power; this international order often pressed the PRC hard on a variety of sensitive international and domestic questions. Thus, for China, relations with Europe were viewed with an eye to other Chinese interests; Europe was said to represent a "card" China could play in the more important contest of U.S.-Chinese relations. This line of thinking underscored the limits of Chinese interests in Europe and reflected the fact that in the order of PRC foreign policy priorities, primacy was given to the United States, followed by Japan and important countries in the Asian area. Europe and other areas more distant from China came in behind them. [85]

China notably opposed U.S.-led NATO expansion and tried from time to time to play up intra-alliance rivalries and differences, especially between the U.S. and French governments. But this effort was largely in vain given the strong and broad European alliance support for NATO and its expansion. Chinese opposition looked weak in the face of the U.S.-led NATO war against Serbia in 1999. Chinese officials also had a long history of thinking of the EU and its members as oriented to protectionist tendencies that would try to impede the flow of Chinese exports to European markets. [86]

Because of organizational and institutional weaknesses, the European Union (EU) and its members had a hard time developing a comprehensive and coherent policy toward China. As Europe's interest in China was mainly economic, the EU and its members were seen as most effective when dealing with a country like China on the basis of economic issues, with other channels of interaction remaining weak.

As a diplomatic actor or as a force on security issues, the EU and its members were said to be less well suited to take action in relation to China, especially as EU members were reluctant to allow the EU very much leeway to deal with important defense and security issues. The EU was very slow to come out in support of the American show of force off the Taiwan Strait in the face of provocative PRC military exercises in 1996, though some member governments were prompt in supporting the move. [87]

Though some observers saw Sino-European relations in the early twenty-first century as "a comprehensive and multidimensional relationship," a "strategic partnership," and "a new axis in world affairs,"[88] later development supported a less positive view. On balance, the recent record along with past practice suggest that the growing China-Europe ties will remain hampered by substantial and sometimes growing problems and competing interests.

Trade and economic ties are the foundation of the relationship. In January 2005, official Chinese media reported that according to Chinese trade data, the EU in 2004 surpassed Japan and the United States to become China's largest trade partner, and China became the second-largest trade partner of the EU, following the United States. The account acknowledged that the expansion of the EU to twenty-five members in 2004 obviously increased the size of the Chinese trade figures with the EU, though the main EU countries involved in China trade were those that were long-standing EU members—Germany, Holland, the United Kingdom, France, and Italy, which were said to account for 72 percent of EU trade with China at that time.[89] Trade grew impressively until the economic crisis of 2009. It rebounded and reached a value close to $500 billion in 2010 and $567.2 billion in 2011.[90]

Chinese sources reported in late 2010 that the EU countries were the third-largest source of foreign investment in China. The total stock of European foreign direct investment in China amounted to more than $70 billion. According to Chinese and European sources, the European countries also were the largest exporter of technologies to China, which allowed for upgrades to Chinese manufacturing and related capabilities. China and the EU also participated in a number of joint technology projects, including the European Galileo satellite navigation program, an alternative to the U.S. Global Positioning System, and the world's largest cooperative science and technology research project, the EU-China Framework Agreement. Meanwhile, Chinese investment in Europe became significant. By 2009, it amounted to $6.28 billion involving 1,400 Chinese-funded enterprises. Of this total, Chinese investment in Europe in 2009 amounted to $2.97 billion.[91]

That not all was positive in Chinese-European economic relations was seen in a growing trade deficit Europe ran with China. It tripled in size in five years, amounting to around $127 billion in 2005. The trend was exacerbated by the fact that China remained the main beneficiary of the EU's Generalized System of Preferences (GSP) program, which granted trade preferences to China. In 2010, the trade deficit was $142.8 billion.[92]

The large trade deficit and Chinese commercial competitiveness fed senti-ment in Europe against Chinese imports. Significant curbs were introduced beginning in 2005 against incoming Chinese products. European complaints against Chinese trade practices, intellectual property rights protection, and currency valuation policies grew. Chinese efforts to gain market economy status from WTO partners had some success in some quarters (Association of Southeast Asian Nations, Australia, New Zealand, and some Latin American countries), but the EU and many of its members, along with the United States, stood firm against strong Chinese pressure. China's status as a non-market economy meant among other things that the EU did not have to rely on cost figures given by Chinese exporters when determining if goods were being sold below cost in the EU. The EU instead could consider cost and price data from other countries when it decided whether to apply duties to Chinese exports in defense of European producers or to launch antidumping procedures.[93]

Scandals in 2007–2008 over the safety of consumer products from China added to the negative European views of China. Economic data from the European Commission in early 2009[94] showed a mixed picture for European interests in trade with China. The European stake in the foreign-invested enterprises in China amounted to 8 percent of such foreign investment in the country. China was the fastest-growing export market for Europe, growing 75 percent between 2003 and 2007 to a level valued at well over $100 billion a year. Nonetheless, the EU still exported more to Switzerland than it did to China. European imports from China also increased an average of over 20 percent per year for the previous six years. They were more than three times the value of European exports to China, resulting in a large trade deficit. The small surplus Europe ran on trade in services with China (worth $5 billion to $6 billion in 2007) had only a small effect on the overall trade imbalance.

Barriers to trade in China were estimated to cost EU businesses close to $30 billion in lost trade opportunities annually, and major losses came from counterfeiting and intellectual property rights violations in China. China was the largest target of trade defense investigations by the EU. In early 2009, the EU had forty-nine antidumping measures in force against Chinese imports. European service companies repeatedly complained about Chinese restric-tions on granting telecom licenses and on investment in banking, construc-tion, and other sectors.

In the political realm, Chinese and European leaders held regular meet-ings. President Hu Jintao and Premier Wen Jiabao visited Europe on official business annually. An annual China-EU summit has rotated between Brussels and Beijing. Both the EU and China learned how to deal with one another in the sometimes difficult negotiations, notably concerning China's entrance into the WTO.[95]

China canceled the China-EU summit in 2008 over the French president's planned meeting with the Dalai Lama. Smooth relations took over a year to revive.[96]

Chinese leaders were particularly active in visiting European capitals and hosting European leaders in 2010. Chinese and foreign media portrayed China as able and willing to make investments and promote mutually beneficial economic relations even with European countries with questionable credit ratings following the 2009 economic crisis.[97] In fact, China seemed careful to avoid commitments to European countries that might not be repaid.

Regarding foreign assistance, in 2003, the EU Commission calculated that programs it was running in China amounted to annual expenditures of over $300 million. These programs did not take into account the sometimes large (e.g., in the case of Germany) assistance programs in China offered by individual European countries.[98]

Regarding continuing Chinese efforts to overturn the EU arms embargo against China, in 2004 China secured the support of the French government on this issue, and the French promised to persuade other EU members to lift the ban that had been in place since 1989. France managed to get the German government to change its view and to erode British opposition. However, U.S. opposition was strong and firm, leading to a major crisis with the EU over whether to end the embargo. The United States was backed by many within Europe, including the new government in Germany in 2005, and had the strong support of Japan, which agreed with the United States that lifting the embargo would enhance the ability of Chinese forces to confront America and its allies in the event of a conflict over Taiwan. China's passage of a tough Anti-Secession Law directed at Taiwan in March 2005 halted the European movement to lift the embargo, at least for the time being. At this time, European leaders also showed greater interest to coordinate policies with the United States on sensitive issues involving China, including the buildup of Chinese military forces and its implications for Taiwan and broader Asian security and stability.[99]

This string of setbacks for Chinese interests combined with rising trade frictions in EU-Chinese relations; a Chinese reassessment of European policy followed, according to specialists. While clearly determined to develop advantageous economic and other ties with European counterparts, Chinese officials were more realistic about developing any sort of a meaningful strategic partnership with Europe for the foreseeable future.

China viewed the EU and its members as collectively too weak, divided, and dependent on the United States to become an independent great power in international relations. Thus, the EU was not a particularly promising partner for China in its rise to power and influence in world affairs. Further, the EU was much more prone to side with the United States than with China on issues sensitive to China involving democracy and the rule of law in China, stability in eastern Asia, climate change, the implications of China's growing trade surpluses with both the United States and the EU members, antiterrorist efforts, and curbs on nuclear weapons proliferation in Iran. [100]

Recent developments underscore strong problems complicating Chinese-European relations. When French president Nicolas Sarkozy, then also serving as head of the European Union, indicated that he would meet the Dalai Lama and did so in late 2008, Beijing abruptly postponed the planned EU-China annual summit scheduled to be held in France. Premier Wen Jiabao traveled to Europe in early 2009 in an effort to shore up relations, but he also continued Chinese efforts to isolate the French president until the French administration worked to fix the damage caused by the meeting with the Dalai Lama. China's efforts to improve ties with European countries were complicated by widespread disapproval in Europe over what was seen as China's role as a major impediment to progress at the international conference on climate change in Copenhagen in December 2009. Also, China alienated many in Europe with its strident reaction and pressure on Norway and other European governments participating at the Nobel awards ceremonies in honor of a Chinese dissident receiving the 2010 Nobel peace prize. [101]

A gradual Chinese-French reconciliation culminated in Hu Jintao's visit to Paris in November 2010—part of a trip to European capitals seeking advantageous economic ties with China during a period of protracted economic recession in the West. President Sarkozy traveled to China in 2011 to further cement ties, but that visit was overshadowed by differences in Chinese-European relations, in this case Hu Jintao's and other Chinese complaints about NATO—urged on by France—employing military force against the regime of Libya's Muammar Gadhafi. [102]

CANADA, THE ARCTIC, ANTARCTICA

A NATO member with strong ties to Europe and the United States, Canada was among the first of leading Western nations in establishing diplomatic relations with China, in 1970, as China reached out for greater international contact and support in the face of the growing power and pressure of the Soviet Union at that time. It became a major trading partner of China. China's rapid economic development required more imports of energy, foods, and other resources, which Canada willingly provided, while Chinese exports of manufactured goods to Canada grew enormously, leading to a large trade deficit for Canada.

Generally following a moderate course in dealing with China, Canada usually sought to avoid the acrimonious disputes and controversies that sometimes marked the erratic course of U.S.-China relations in the recent period. An exception was the leadership of Prime Minister Stephen Harper whose government for several years in the first decade of the twenty-first century highlighted political disputes with China, notably over human rights and Tibet, before calming disputes in a more pragmatic pursuit of closer economic contacts. [103]

As post-Mao Chinese foreign relations developed, China began to play a more active role in Antarctica. Chinese scientists joined an Australian research expedition to the continent in 1979. In the 1980s, China set up its own scientific expedition bases and launched independent expeditions. China in the past decade has stepped up funding for upgrading existing Antarctic bases, establishing a new base, and increasing research involving Antarctica. China's overall involvement on the continent remained modest, comparable to that of India and much smaller than that of the United States. [104]

China since 2008 has sought to become a permanent observer on the Arctic Council, an exclusive regional forum of eight member states (Canada, Denmark, Finland, Iceland, Norway, Russia, Sweden, and the United States) that was created in 1996 to promote collaboration and cooperation on Arctic issues. There are currently six non-Arctic observer states—France, Germany, the Netherlands, Poland, Spain, and the United Kingdom.

The five coastal states bordering the Arctic Ocean, Canada, Denmark, Norway, Russia, and the United States, signed a declaration in 2008 signaling that by virtue of their sovereignty, sovereignty rights, and jurisdiction in large areas of the Arctic Ocean, they are uniquely positioned to address the evolving contemporary issues of the Arctic. The declaration represented an explicit statement that there was no need for a comprehensive Arctic Treaty on the lines of what exists in Antarctica. Chinese commentary has taken the position that the Arctic region possesses a "shared heritage of humankind," suggesting China could oppose some of the Arctic states' sovereignty claims and assert claims of its own as the melting ice creates easier access to resources in the area and eases barriers to more efficient sea transportation between China and European and North American ports.[105]

NOTES

1. Feng Zhaokui, "China Still a Developing Nation," *China Daily*, May 6, 2010, p. 12.

2. Michael Chambers, "China and Southeast Asia: Creating a 'Win-Win' Neighborhood," in *China's "Good Neighbor" Diplomacy* (Washington, DC: Woodrow Wilson Center for Scholars Asia Program Special Report 126, January, 2005); "Wen Rolls Out 'Win-Win' Strategy in Africa," IPS News, June 21, 2006, ipsnews.net/news.asp?idnews=33702 (accessed July 16, 2010).

3. Harold Hinton, *Communist China in World Politics* (Boston: Houghton Mifflin, 1966), pp. 178–87; Lillian Harris, *China Considers the Middle East* (London: Tauris, 1993); Guang Pan, "China's Success in the Middle East," *Middle East Quarterly*, December 1997, pp. 35–40; Lillian Harris, "Myth and Reality in China's Relations with the Middle East," in *Chinese Foreign Policy: Theory and Practice*, ed. Thomas W. Robinson and David Shambaugh (New York: Oxford University Press, 1994), pp. 322–47.

4. Robert Sutter, *Historical Dictionary of Chinese Foreign Policy* (Lanham, MD: Scarecrow, 2011), pp. 41, 88–89.

5. Harris, "Myth and Reality in China's Relations with the Middle East," p. 336.

6. Sutter, *Historical Dictionary of Chinese Foreign Policy*, p. 85.

7. John Garver, *China and Iran* (Seattle: University of Washington Press, 2006), pp. 27–56.

8. Sutter, *Historical Dictionary of Chinese Foreign Policy*, p. 215.

9. Mao Yufeng, "China's Interests and Strategy in the Middle East," in *China and the Developing World: Beijing's Strategy for the Twenty-First Century*, ed. Joshua Eisenman, Eric Heginbotham, and Derek Mitchell (Armonk, NY: M. E. Sharpe, 2007), pp. 113–32; Yitzhak Shichor, "China's Middle East Strategy" in *China and the Developing World*, ed. Lowell Dittmer and George Yu (Boulder, CO: Lynne Rienner, 2010), pp. 157–76; Sutter, *Historical Dictionary of Chinese Foreign Policy*, p. 130.

10. Harris, "Myth and Reality in China's Relations with the Middle East," p. 332.

11. Garver, *China and Iran*, pp. 57–94.

12. Alexander Lennon, "Trading Guns, Not Butter," *China Business Review*, March–April 1994, pp. 47–49; Pan, "China's Success in the Middle East."

13. Garver, *China and Iran*, pp. 95–128.

14. Jon B. Alterman and John Garver, *The Vital Triangle: China, the United States, and the Middle East* (Washington, DC: Center for Strategic and International Studies, 2008); John W. Garver, "Is China Playing a Dual Game in Iran?" *Washington Quarterly* 34, no. 1 (Winter 2011), pp. 75–88.

15. Harris, *China Considers the Middle East*; Pan, "China's Success in the Middle East."

16. Alterman and Garver, *The Vital Triangle*; Garver, "Is China Playing"; Mao Yufeng, "China's Interests and Strategy in the Middle East," in *China and the Developing World: Beijing's Strategy for the Twenty-First Century*, ed. Joshua Eisenman, Eric Heginbotham, and Derek Mitchell (Armonk, NY: M. E. Sharpe, 2007), pp. 113–32; Yitzhak Shichor, "China's Middle East Strategy" in *China and the Developing World*, ed. Lowell Dittmer and George Yu (Boulder, CO: Lynne Rienner, 2010), pp. 157–76; Daniel Blumenthal, "Providing Arms," *Middle East Quarterly*, Spring 2005: pp. 11–19; Jing-dong Yuan, "China and the Iranian Nuclear Crisis," *China Brief* 6, no. 3 (February 1, 2006): pp. 6–8; Yitzhak Shichor, "China's Kurdish Policy," *China Brief* 6, no. 1 (January 3, 2006): pp. 3–6.

17. SUSRIS interview with Jon Alterman October 13, 2008, www.saudi-us-relations.org/articles/2008/interviews/081013-alterman-interview.html (accessed October 14, 2008).

18. Flynt Leverett and Jeffrey Bader, "Managing China-U.S. Energy Competition in the Middle East," *Washington Quarterly* 29, no. 1 (Winter 2005/2006): pp. 187–201.

19. "Saudi Arabia Ties Get a Boost," *China Daily*, February 12, 2009, p. 1; John Calabrese, "Saudi Arabia and China Extend Ties beyond Oil" *China Brief* 5, no. 12 (May 24, 2005): pp. 1–4; Australian Parliamentary Library Research Service, *Directions in China's Foreign Relations: Implications for East Asia and Australia*, Parliamentary Library Research Brief 9:2005–2006 (Canberra: Australian Parliamentary Library Research Service, December 5, 2005), pp. 16–20.

20. "China-Saudi Trade Reached Record High in 2010," Chinese embassy in Saudi Arabia, February 9, 2011, sa2.mofcom.gov.cn.

21. Borzou Daragahi, "Iran Signs $3.2 Billion Natural Gas Deal with China," *Los Angeles Times*, March 14, 2009, www.latimes.com (accessed March 18, 2009); Garver, "Is China Playing."

22. "Iran-China Trade Volume Reaches $38 billion," *PressTV*, February 13, 2011, www.presstv.ir/detail/165011.html (accessed May 18, 2011).

23. Mark Landler, "China Is Excluded from Waivers for Oil Trade with Iran," *New York Times*, June 11, 2012, www.nytimes.com/.

24. Interview with Chinese Ambassador Hua Liming, cited in Shuang Wen, "From Brothers to Partners: The Evolution of China's Foreign Policy to the Middle East," master's thesis, The American University of Cairo, 2008, p. 75.

25. Bonnie Glaser, "Pomp, Blunders and Substance: Hu's Visit to the U.S.," *Comparative Connections* 8, no. 2 (July 2006): pp. 35–36, 40; and Bonnie Glaser, "Cooperation Faces Challenges," *Comparative Connections* 12, no. 2 (July 2010): pp. 38–39.

26. Blumenthal, "Providing Arms," p. 6.

27. Chris Zambelis, "China's Palestine Policy," *China Brief* 9, no. 5 (March 4, 2009): pp. 9–12; "China Welcomes Hamas-Fatah Unity Deal," *China Daily*, April 29, 2011, www.chinadaily.com.cn/.

28. Yitzhak Shichor, "Silent Partner: China and the Lebanon Crisis," *China Brief* 6, no. 17 (August 16, 2006): pp. 2–4.

29. Consultations with Chinese diplomats, Washington, DC, December 18, 2006.

30. Yu Bin, "SCO Five Years On: Progress and Growing Pains," *Comparative Connections* 8, no. 2 (July 2006): p. 140.

31. "Hu Slams Use of Force, Seeks Libyan Ceasefire," *China Daily*, March 31, 2011, www.chinadaily.com.cn; Indira A. R. Lakshmanan, "Leaders in Beijing Feared Arab Spring Could Infect China," *Bloomberg*, May 1, 2012.

32. Hinton, *Communist China in World Politics*, pp. 188–96; Gerald Segal, "China and Africa," *Annals of the American Academy of Political and Social Science* 519 (January 1992):

pp. 115–26; Philip Snow, "China and Africa: Consensus and Camouflage," in Robinson and Shambaugh, eds., *Chinese Foreign Policy*, pp. 283–321.

33. Philip Snow, *The Star Raft: China's Encounter with Africa* (Ithaca, NY: Cornell University Press, 1988); Alaba Ogunsanwo, *China's Policy in Africa, 1958–1971* (New York: Cambridge University Press, 1979); Peter Van Ness, *Revolution and Chinese Foreign Policy* (Berkeley: University of California Press, 1970).

34. Sutter, *Historical Dictionary of Chinese Foreign Policy*, pp. 140, 171–72, 185.

35. Deborah Brautigam, *The Dragon's Gift: The Real Story of China in Africa* (New York: Oxford University Press, 2010), pp. 40–41, 83–85.

36. Sutter, *Historical Dictionary of Chinese Foreign Policy*, p. 169.

37. Philip Snow, *The Star Raft*; Sutter, *Historical Dictionary of Chinese Foreign Policy*, p. 248.

38. Sutter, *Historical Dictionary of Chinese Foreign Policy*, p. 76

39. Robert Sutter, *Chinese Policy Priorities and Their Implications for the United States* (Lanham, MD: Rowman & Littlefield, 2000), pp. 163–64.

40. Brautigam, *The Dragon's Gift*, pp. 22–70; Sutter, *Chinese Policy Priorities and Their Implications for the United States*, p. 164.

41. Snow, "China and Africa," pp. 318–21.

42. Brautigam, *The Dragon's Gift*; George Yu, "China's Africa Policy," in *China and the Developing World*, ed. Lowell Dittmer and George Yu (Boulder, CO: Lynne Rienner, 2010), pp. 129–56; Christopher Alden, Daniel Large, and Ricardo de Oliveria, *China Returns to Africa: A Superpower and a Continent Embrace* (New York: Columbia University Press, 2008); Ian Taylor, *China's New Role in Africa* (Boulder, CO: Lynne Rienner, 2008); Robert I. Rotberg, ed., *China into Africa: Trade, Aid, and Influence* (Washington, DC: Brookings Institution, 2008); David Shinn and Joshua Eisenman, *Responding to China in Africa* (Washington, DC: American Foreign Policy Council, July 2008); Council on Foreign Relations, *More Than Humanitarianism: A Strategic U.S. Approach toward Africa*, Independent Task Force Report 56 (New York: Council on Foreign Relations, January 2006); *China and Sub-Saharan Africa*, Congressional Research Service Report RL 33055 (Washington, DC: Library of Congress, August 29, 2005).

43. *Africa and China: Issues and Insights—Conference Report* (Washington, DC: Georgetown University, School of Foreign Service, Asian Studies Department, November 7, 2008).

44. Chin-Hao Huang, *China's Rising Stakes in Africa*, Asian Studies Research Paper (Washington, DC: Georgetown University, April 2006), p. 7 (also reviewed in *China and Sub-Saharan Africa*).

45. *China's African Policy* (Beijing: State Council Information Office, January 2006), english.people.com.cn/200601/12/print20060112_234894.html; Yan Yang, "China-Africa Trade Prospects Look Promising: President Hu Jintao Promotes Nation on Tour of the Continent," *China Daily*, April 26, 2006, p. 9; "Support for Africa 'Not a Temporary Measure,'" *China Daily*, July 3, 2006, p. 3; Wenran Jiang, "China's Booming Energy Relations with Africa," *China Brief* 6, no. 13 (June 21, 2006): pp. 3–5.

46. Sun Shangwu, "Bright, Prosperous Relations," *China Daily*, November 6, 2006, p. 1.

47. Ding Qingfen, "Countries 'Seek More Investment for Development,'" *China Daily*, April 27, 2011, p 1.

48. Phillip C. Saunders, *China's Global Activism: Strategy, Drivers, and Tools*, Occasional Paper 4 (Washington, DC: National Defense University Institute for National Strategic Studies, June 2006), p. 2; Thomas Lum, coord., *Comparing Global Influence: China's and U.S. Diplomacy, Foreign Aid, Trade, and Investment in the Developing World*, Report RL 34620 (Wash-

ington, DC: Library of Congress, Congressional Research Service, August 15, 2008), pp. 62, 65.

49. Brautigam, *The Dragon's Gift*, p. 168.

50. Zeng Qiang, "FOCAC: A Powerful Engine for the Continued Development of Friendship between China and Africa," *Contemporary International Relations* (Beijing) 20, no. 6 (November/December 2010): pp. 45–59; "White Paper on China-Africa Economic Cooperation and Trade Cooperation" *China Daily*, December 23, 2010, www.chinadaily.com.cn/; David Smith, "China Poised to Pour $10bn into Zimbabwe's Ailing Economy," *Guardian*, February 1, 2011, www.guardian.co.uk; He Wenping, "Equal Platform, Mutual Benefit," *China Daily*, July 17, 2010, p. 5; "China-Africa Trade Hits Record High," *China Daily*, December 24, 2010, p. 3.

51. "Sino-Africa Agri Trade Spike," *China Daily*, May 21, 2012, www.chinadaily.com.cn/bizchina/2012-05/21/content_15348005.htm (accessed July 18, 2012).

52. Hinton, *Communist China in World Politics*, pp. 197–204; Cecil Johnson, *Communist China and Latin America* (New York: Columbia University Press, 1970); Robert Worden, "China's Balancing Act: Cancun, the Third World, Latin America," *Asian Survey* 23, no. 5 (May 1983), 619–36.

53. Sutter, *Historical Dictionary of Chinese Foreign Policy*, p. 61.

54. Robert Sutter, *Chinese Foreign Policy: Developments after Mao* (New York: Praeger, 1986), p. 200.

55. Sutter, *Historical Dictionary of Chinese Foreign Policy*, pp. 65, 78.

56. Worden, "China's Balancing Act"; Sutter, *Chinese Foreign Policy*, pp. 200–202.

57. Samuel Kim, *The Third World in Chinese World Policy* (Princeton, NJ: Princeton University Press, 1989); Frank O. Mora, "Sino–Latin American Relations: Sources and Consequences," *Journal of Interamerican Studies and World Affairs* 41, no. 2 (Summer 1999): pp. 91–116; Chein-hsun Wang, "Peking's Latin American Policy in the 1980s," *Issues and Studies* 27, no. 5 (May 1991): pp. 103–18.

58. Jorge Dominguez, *China's Relations with Latin America: Shared Gains, Asymmetrical Hopes*, Working Paper (Washington, DC: Inter-American Dialogue, June 2006); R. Evan Ellis, *U.S. National Security Implications of Chinese Involvement in Latin America* (Carlisle, PA: U.S. Army War College Strategic Studies Institute, June 2005); R. Evan Ellis, *China in Latin America* (Boulder, CO: Lynne Rienner 2009); Kerry Dumbaugh and Mark Sullivan, *China's Growing Interest in Latin America*, Report RS22119 (Washington, DC: Library of Congress, Congressional Research Service, April 20, 2005); Riordan Roett and Guadalupe Paz, eds., *China's Expansion into the Western Hemisphere* (Washington, DC: Brookings Institution, 2007); Robert Delvin et al., *The Emergence of China: Challenges and Opportunities for Latin America and the Caribbean* (Cambridge, MA: Harvard University Press, 2006); David Shambaugh, "China's New Foray into Latin America," *YaleGlobal* Online, November 17, 2008, www.yaleglobal.com (accessed November 18, 2008); Cynthia Watson, "Adios Taipei, Hola Beijing: Taiwan's Relations with Latin America," *China Brief* 4, no. 11 (May 27, 2004): pp. 8–10, and "A Warming Friendship," *China Brief* 4, no. 12 (June 10, 2004): pp. 2–3.

59. Robert Sutter, *Chinese Foreign Relations: Power and Policy since the Cold War* (Lanham, MD: Rowman & Littlefield, 2012), pp. 326, 327, 333.

60. Sutter, *Chinese Foreign Relations*, pp. 327–28.

61. *Asia and Latin America and the Caribbean: Economic Links, Cooperation and Development Strategies*, Discussion Paper for Annual Meeting of Governors (Washington, DC: Inter-American Development Bank, March 21, 2005); John Paul Rathbone, "China Is Now Region's Biggest Partner," *Financial Times*, April 26, 2011, www.ft.com/.

62. Rathbone, "China Is Now Region's Biggest Partner"; Qin Jize and Wang Chenyan, "Argentina Visit to Boost Ties," *China Daily*, June 25, 2012, www.chinadaily.com.cn/.

63. Wang Xiaotian and Chen Ma, "RMB Fund Planned to Aid Latin America," *China Daily*, April 29, 2011, p. 13; Brian Winter and Brian Ellsworth, "Brazil and China: A Young Marriage on the Rocks," Reuters, February 3, 2011, www.reuters.com; "Brazil Leads Surge in Latam Foreign Investment," *UV10*, May 18, 2011, www.uv10.com/brazil-leads-surge-in-latam-foreign-investment_800548463/.

64. Thomas Lum, *China's Foreign Aid Activities in Africa, Latin America, and Southeast Asia*, Report R40361 (Washington, DC: Library of Congress, Congressional Research Service, February 25, 2009), p. 15; Erica Downs, *Inside China, Inc: China Development Bank's Cross-Border Energy Deals*, John Thornton China Center Monograph Series 3 (Washington, DC: Brookings Institution, March 2011), p. 1.

65. "Magic or Realism: China and Latin America," *Economist*, December 29, 2004, www.economist.com (accessed January 10, 2005); Stuart Grudgings, "Analysis: Surge in Chinese Investment Reshapes Brazil Ties," Reuters, August 10, 2010, www.reuters.com.

66. Larry Rohter, "China Widens Economic Role in Latin America," *New York Times*, November 20, 2004, www.nytimes.com (accessed November 20, 2004); Winter and Ellsworth, "Brazil and China: A Young Marriage on the Rocks."

67. Sun Hongbo, "Tapping the Potential," *China Daily*, April 16, 2010, p. 9.

68. "Ma Reaffirms 'Modus Vivendi' Diplomatic Approach," *China Post*, March 15, 2011, www.chinapost.com.tw.

69. Sutter, *Chinese Foreign Relations*, p. 334.

70. "Testimony of Cynthia Watson, Professor of Strategy, National Defense University, Washington, DC, before the House Committee on International Relations, Subcommittee on Western Hemisphere Affairs," April 6, 2005, www.house.gov (accessed May 7, 2005).

71. William Ratliff, "Pragmatism over Ideology: China's Relations with Venezuela," *China Brief* 6, no. 6 (March 15, 2006): pp. 3–5; "Venezuela's Crude Oil Exports to U.S. Average 1 Million Bpd," *El Universal*, April 4, 2011, www.eluniversal.com (accessed May 18, 2011).

72. Guillermo Delamer et al., "Chinese Interest in Latin America," in *Latin American Security Challenges* (Newport, RI: Naval War College, 2004), p. 94; Shambaugh, "China's New Foray into Latin America."

73. "Testimony of Rogelio Pardo-Maurer, Assistant Secretary of Defense for Latin America, before the House Committee on International Affairs, Subcommittee on Western Hemisphere Affairs," April 6, 2005, www.house.gov (accessed May 7, 2005).

74. Stephen Johnson, *Balancing China's Growing Influence in Latin America* (Washington, DC: Heritage Foundation, October 24, 2005), p. 5.

75. Robert Sutter, *China-Watch* (Baltimore: Johns Hopkins University Press, 1978), p. 36.

76. Hinton, *Communist China in World Politics*, pp. 149–51.

77. Sutter, *Historical Dictionary of Chinese Foreign Policy*, p. 42.

78. Hinton, *Communist China in World Politics*, pp. 171–75; Sutter, *Historical Dictionary of Chinese Foreign Policy*, p. 94.

79. Sutter, *Historical Dictionary of Chinese Foreign Policy*, 107.

80. Sutter, *Chinese Foreign Policy*, pp. 57, 131, 145; Sutter, *Historical Dictionary of Chinese Foreign Policy*, pp. 61, 201, 242.

81. Sutter, *Historical Dictionary of Chinese Foreign Policy*, p. 131.

82. John Garver, *Foreign Relations of the People's Republic of China* (Englewood Cliffs, NJ: Prentice Hall, 1993), pp. 231–37.

83. Ezra F. Vogel, *Deng Xiaoping and the Transformation of China* (Cambridge, MA: Harvard University Press, 2011), pp. 495–511.

84. Sutter, *Historical Dictionary of Chinese Foreign Policy*, pp. 157, 202.

85. Michael Yahuda, "China and Europe: The Significance of a Secondary Relationship," in *Chinese Foreign Policy: Theory and Practice*, ed. Thomas Robinson and David Shambaugh (New York: Oxford University Press, 1994), pp. 266–82.

86. Sutter, *Chinese Policy Priorities and Their Implications for the United States*, pp. 149–56.

87. Sutter, *Chinese Policy Priorities and Their Implications for the United States*, p. 152; Wayne Morrison, *Chinese Economic Conditions*, Report RL 33534 (Washington, DC: Library of Congress, Congressional Research Service, June 26, 2012, p. 30.

88. David Shambaugh, "China and Europe: The Emerging Axis," *Current History* 103, no. 674 (September 2004): pp. 243–48.

89. "EU Becomes China's Largest Trade Partner," *Xinhua*, January 10, 2005, www.taiwansecurity.org (accessed January 19, 2005).

90. Stanley Crossick, Fraser Cameron, and Alex Berkofy, *EU-China Relations—Toward a Strategic Partnership*, Working Paper (Brussels: European Policy Centre, July 2005), p. 26; "Senior Chinese Official Calls for Enhanced Trade, Economic Cooperation with EU," *Xinhua*, December 29, 2010, www.xinhua.com.

91. "Senior Chinese Official Calls"; Crossick et al., *EU-China Relations*, 26–27; "Li's Visit Pushes China-EU Ties toward New Stage," *China Daily*, January 6, 2011, p. 8.

92. Jean-Pierre Cabestan, "European Union–China Relations and the United States" (paper prepared for the 58th annual meeting of the Association for Asian Studies, April 6–9, 2006, San Francisco); "Senior Chinese Official Calls"; Crossick et al., *EU-China Relations*, 26–27.

93. Jean-Pierre Cabestan, "European Union–China Relations and the United States," *Asian Perspective* 30, no. 4 (Winter 2006): pp. 19–20.

94. *EU-China Trade in Facts and Figures*, EUROPA MEMO/09/40, January 30, 2009, europa.eu (accessed February 16, 2009).

95. "Full Text of Joint Statement Issued at 8th China-EU Summit," *Xinhua*, September 5, 2005, www.xinhuanet.com/english (accessed September 9, 2005).

96. Sutter, *Historical Dictionary of Chinese Foreign Policy*, p. 215.

97. Huang Shuo, "New Year, Old EU Woes for China," *China Daily*, January 7, 2011, www.chinadaily.com.cn.

98. Gillian Wong, "China Rises and Rises, Yet Still Gets Foreign Aid," Associated Press, September 27, 2010, www.ap.com.

99. Cabestan, "European Union–China Relations and the United States," pp. 6–8.

100. Neil King and Marc Champion, "EU, US Policy on China Converges on Key Issues: Trade, Defense Spats Foster Alignment, Worrying Beijing," *Wall Street Journal*, May 4, 2006, www.wsj.com (accessed May 4, 2006); Cabestan, "European Union–China Relations and the United States," p. 7.

101. Tania Branihan and Jonathan Watts, "Chinese PM Rebuts Criticism over Copenhagen Role," *Guardian*, March 14, 2010, www.guardian.uk.com; Goeff Dyer and Andrew Ward, "Europe Defies China's Nobel Threat," *Financial Times*, November 5, 2010, www.tf.com.

102. "China's Attitude on Libya: Give Peace a Chance," *Peoples Daily*, english.people.com.cn.

103. Sutter, *Historical Dictionary of Chinese Foreign Policy*, p. 60.

104. Anne-Marie Brady, "China's Rise in Antarctica," *Asian Survey* 50, no. 4 (2010): pp. 759–85.

105. Francois Perreault, "Can China Become a Major Arctic Player?" *RSIS Commentaries* 073/2012 (April 24, 2012), www.rsis.edu.sg/publications/Perspective/RSIS0732012.pdf (accessed July 8, 2012).

Chapter Ten

Implications and Outlook

The analyses and discussion in this volume explain significant developments in the evolution and status of China's international relationships since 1949. They do so in part to better judge China's actual influence in contemporary world affairs and its likely role in the future. By drawing implications from the findings of this study, this chapter endeavors to present such judgments.

As noted in chapter 1, there is a large literature assessing China's rising role in world affairs. Common in the literature is a tendency to employ a selected set of indicators focused on the growing size of China's economy; China's leading role as an international manufacturer and trader, consumer of raw materials, and holder of foreign exchange reserves; and China's widespread international impact backed by active diplomacy and steadily increasing military capabilities. These indicators support assessments of China's rapidly growing role in world affairs. They contrast with indicators of slow growth or stagnation on the part of other world powers, notably Japan, Europe, and the United States. As a result, many specialists have come to the conclusion that China has risen to the point where a power transition is under way in China's surroundings in Asia, with Beijing emerging as the region's new leading power and with the United States, heretofore the leading power around Asia's rim, moving to a secondary position. Some specialists go further in judging that the power transition from U.S. leadership to that of China is more global in scope.[1]

Of course, there are specialists who employ other indicators and evidence to conclude that rising China has a long way to go to be in a position to challenge America's leading role in Asian and world affairs. The indicators include China's internal preoccupations with sustaining leadership legitima-cy amid prevalent social turmoil, widespread corruption, widening income gaps, highly resource-intensive economic development, environmental dam-age, and slowing economic reform of an economic model seen as unsustain-able. They also involve the enormous obligations and demonstrated strengths shown by the United States in supporting regional and international mecha-nisms and order that China generally avoids as it "cheap rides" and exploits the existing international system in pursuit of narrowly defined Chinese interests.[2]

The debate over China's rise and its implications remains inconclusive. Some of the indicators used in assessments on one side or the other are subject to dispute. Thus, for example, measuring the impact of China's obvi-ous internal preoccupations on the conduct of Chinese foreign policy remains difficult. The calculations of Chinese leaders as they deal with domestic political, economic, and social problems remain obscured by prevailing se-crecy surrounding Chinese decision making on these matters. How serious these matters are in their judgment cannot be known with assurance.[3]

This study employs analysis based on Chinese international behavior that can be measured and is supported with evidence from both Chinese and international sources. It endeavors to examine how well China is doing in exerting actual influence in Asian and world affairs. China's relationships with Asian and other countries can be measured fairly accurately to deter-mine the extent of Chinese influence. The strengths and limitations of China as a leader in Asian and world affairs can be compared with that of the United States. One also can discern and measure indications of the prefer-ences of Asian and other states for a leading role played by China or a leading role played by the United States. This study identifies such indicators and related evidence, which can be used by readers to make their own judg-ments as to whether or not a power transition is under way in Asia and what China's rising influence actually means for the Asian and world order.

IMPLICATIONS

Relations beyond Nearby Asia

As reviewed in chapter 9, Chinese behavior in world areas distant from China shows growing Chinese activism in pursuit of fairly narrowly defined interests focused on commercial relations involving acquisition of raw materials and foreign investment and broadening markets for Chinese sales abroad. Negative legacies, policy inconsistencies, and other contemporary complications and encumbrances facing China's rise in nearby Asia and in relations with the United States are much less important in China's rise as a new economic power with growing political influence in regions further from China.

China has much less at stake in the regions further from China than those in nearby Asia. There are no disputed territorial claims and few concerns involving Chinese national security. China does not employ military coercion in these areas. Patriotic Chinese public opinion and various segments in the Chinese administration that emphasize defense of Chinese nationalistic claims and interests generally devote less attention to issues beyond China's periphery.

As China has pursued its commercial interests, it has employed with considerable success the "win-win" formula emphasizing converging interests between China and concerned countries distant from China. Under the win-win concept, China makes clear to foreign governments, organizations, and others that it will work with them in areas of mutual interest and that China does not expect them to do things that they would not ordinarily do. What the win-win concept means for China is that China is prepared to work with the other foreign parties in areas of mutual interest, but China is not going to take actions or adopt changes in policy and behavior that it would not ordinarily do if they are not within a restricted scope of Chinese national interests. Against this background, in regions of the world beyond the scope of Chinese nationalistic, security, and related interests in nearby Asia, China has followed practices that avoid involvement in contentious disputes and has endeavored to foster as stable an environment as possible that is beneficial for Chinese commercial and related interests.[4]

As discussed in chapter 9, China does face some serious obstacles even as it pursues its fairly restricted set of interests in world regions beyond nearby Asia. China takes great care to avoid taking positions on the many sensitive disputes in Middle East affairs and it tries to stay on good terms with the United States in part to insure secure access to the region's energy resources through sea-lanes controlled by the United States. China similarly avoids strong opposition to the United States in Latin America, recognizing that China's increasing importance as a regional trading partner and investor still pales in comparison with the region's dependence on the United States. China at times has endeavored to use growing economic interaction with

Europe to maneuver for change in Europe's adherence to a U.S.-backed arms embargo against China. It also has attempted to foster greater European independence from the United States on issues ranging from Iraq to NATO expansion. The results have been poor. On balance, sub-Saharan Africa has provided the world area of smoothest advance of Chinese commercial interests and related political influences under the "win-win" formula.[5]

The overall importance of China's rising role in world areas distant from China does not go much beyond China's strong and growing commercial importance. China does not try hard to get these states to do things that they wouldn't ordinarily do. The focus of Chinese attention rests on exploiting economic interests of mutual benefit. One can assume that China sustains an interest in changing the world international order along the lines advocated more vocally by Chinese officials and media in the immediate post–Cold War period and earlier. But that policy priority has been overshadowed by the prevailing need to work with the United States and other world powers in constructive ways that avoid creating obstacles in China's pursuit of its restricted interests in these international areas.

Relations with Nearby Asia

As discussed in chapter 8, China demonstrates many strengths as it rises in power and influence in the Asia-Pacific region. The region has long been the international area where China has exerted the greatest influence and has long been the focal point of Chinese foreign policy concerns. It contains sovereignty, security, and development issues of top priority in Chinese foreign relations. The region also is the arena where China interacts most directly with the United States, the prevailing international superpower seeking to sustain and expand its influence in the region in ways opposed by China.[6]

Among the most important Chinese strengths in the Asia-Pacific region are

- China's position as the leading trading partner with most neighboring countries and the heavy investment many of those countries make in China;
- China's active leadership attention and active diplomacy in interaction with neighboring countries both bilaterally and multilaterally; and
- China's expanding military capabilities.

Chapter 8 and earlier discussion make clear that these strengths are offset by some general Chinese practices in world affairs and by some Chinese practices specific to the Asia-Pacific region. Meanwhile, added in this chapter is a brief examination of the strengths and weaknesses of the United States in the Asia-Pacific region in order to provide additional indicators of how far China has to go before it can assume the mantle of regional leadership.

Practices Limiting Chinese Influence in Asian and World Affairs

As demonstrated in the discussion of the U.S. role in the Asia-Pacific region, leadership in the region involves strong efforts to support common interests involving regional security and development. The examination of Chinese international behavior in this volume shows that China has a well-developed tendency to avoid risks, costs, or commitments to the common good unless there is adequate benefit for tangible Chinese interests. Like many other world governments with a strong sense of nationalism, the Chinese leadership continues to emphasize a restricted scope of national interests and ensures that its policies and practices serve those interests.

Examples abound of China pursuing narrow interests, often to the detriment of others in the Asia-Pacific region and elsewhere. Although it has over $3 trillion in foreign exchange reserves, China continues to run a substantial trade surplus and to accumulate large foreign exchange reserves supported by currency policies widely seen to disadvantage trading competitors in the Asia-Pacific and elsewhere. Despite its economic progress and role as an international creditor comparable to international financial institutions, China annually receives over $6 billion a year of foreign assistance loans and lesser grants from international organizations like the World Bank and the Asian Development Bank, the United Nations Development Program, and over twenty other UN agencies, and foreign government and nongovernment donors that presumably would otherwise be available for other deserving clients in the Asia-Pacific and the world. It carefully adheres to UN budget formulas that keep Chinese dues and other payments remarkably low for a country with Chinese international prominence and development. It tends to assure that its contributions to the broader good of the international order (e.g., use of Chinese personnel in UN peacekeeping operations) are paid for by others. Despite its status as a leader in production and export of wind power, solar power, and other alternative energy products, China remains one of the top two users of provisions in the Kyoto Protocol giving cost-free access to the advanced environmental technologies of developed countries. At bottom, the "win-win" principle that undergirds recent Chinese foreign policy means that Chinese officials make sure that Chinese policies and practices provide a "win" for generally narrowly defined national interests of China. They eschew the kinds of risky and costly commitments for the broader regional and global common good that Asian leaders have come to look to U.S. leadership to provide.[7]

A major reason for China's continued reluctance to undertake costs and commitments for the sake of the common interests of the Asia-Pacific and broader international affairs is the long array of domestic challenges and preoccupations faced by Chinese leaders. As noted earlier, the impact of these domestic issues on the calculations of Chinese leaders is hard to measure with any precision, but their overall impact appears substantial. Those domestic issues include securing smooth leadership succession and Communist Party unity; battling pervasive corruption in order to foster good governance for Chinese constituents; sustaining strong economic growth in order to insure employment and material benefits for the vast majority of Chinese people; boosting administrative support for those left behind by China's economic modernization so that the gap between the rich and poor in China will stop widening and narrow somewhat; ending grossly wasteful use of China's limited resources and those imported from abroad; and finding efficient and economical means to gradually reduce the widespread environmental damage caused by Chinese economic development.

Given these preoccupations as well as China's heavy interdependence with the United States and other leading powers, it has appeared that the Chinese leadership, unless provoked, would seek to avoid substantial confrontation with the United States and other powers over issues in Asian and world affairs. Though some opinion leaders in China from time to time have argued for challenging the United States in Asian and world affairs in defense of Chinese interests, the senior Chinese leaders generally have adhered to a more reassuring approach. They usually have sought to avoid serious complications as China exploits what it views as the current period of generally peaceful and advantageous strategic opportunity for China's development and the advancement of Communist rule in China.[8]

China's Encumbered Rise in Asia

China appears to have far to go in reassuring Asia-Pacific neighbors of its intentions. Over the past four years, episodes of Chinese assertiveness toward several neighbors and the United States have reminded China's neighbors that the sixty-year history of the PRC has much more often than not featured China acting in disruptive and domineering ways in the region.

Those seeking verification of China's encumbered rise can take account of the fact that China has been rising in the Asia-Pacific region free from superpower threat since the end of the Cold War over twenty years ago. The record of Chinese advance in the region since then can be measured using Chinese and international evidence. What is shown is a mixed record of accomplishment with China far from a position of leadership.

As discussed in chapter 8 and chapter 1, China faces major impediments as it endeavors to reassure Asian neighbors and advance Chinese regional influence. China's long-standing practice of building an image of consistent and righteous behavior in foreign affairs blocks realistic appraisal of the wary view of China held by most neighbors and the United States. The latter countries fear another in the long series of historical shifts in Chinese policies away from current emphasis on reassurance and toward past practices of intimidation and aggression. Absorbed in Chinese publicity regarding China's exceptional position of consistent, moral, and benign foreign behavior, the Chinese have a poor appreciation of regional and American concerns. Both elite and public opinion compel Chinese policy makers to adhere to a firm line when dealing with disputes and differences with neighbors and the United States, especially when those disputes are publicized by Chinese media, as they usually are, in ways that foster an attitude of exceptional self-righteousness in popular opinion in China on these topics.

At the same time, the Chinese media tend to emphasize China's historic victimization at the hands of outside powers like the United States, Japan, and others. They have long registered deep opposition to foreign powers like the United States establishing and deepening a strategic presence along China's periphery. Such attitudes have reinforced depiction of the United States and the Soviet Union as always trying to encircle and contain China.

China's relationship with Japan, arguably Asia's richest country and the key ally of the United States, exemplifies the significant limitations and shortcomings of China's recent relations in Asia, despite the many positive economic and other connections linking the two countries. During the tenure of Japanese prime minister Junichiro Koizumi (2001–2006), China engaged in an effort to isolate Japan and diminish its prominence in Asian and world affairs. In general, the effort did not work well and was quickly put aside once Koizumi left office. Recent relations have worsened because of disputes

involving violence, extra-legal trade sanctions, and intimidation over territorial and resource claims in the East China Sea, as well as intrusions of
Chinese naval vessels into Japanese-claimed areas and competition for influence in Southeast Asia and in the United Nations.[9]

Asia's other large powers, India and Russia, have showed ambivalence
about relations with China. The border issue between China and India has
run hot and cold, as has their competition for influence among the countries
surrounding India and in Southeast Asia and central Asia. The limited
progress in Sino-Indian relations became overshadowed by a remarkable
upswing in India's strategic cooperation with the United States during the
past decade.[10] Meanwhile, Russian and Chinese interest in close alignment
has waxed and waned and has appeared to remain secondary to their respective relationships with the West. Key differences were on display when President Vladimir Putin in 2001 abruptly reversed policy strongly supported by
China against the U.S. development of a ballistic missile defense system, and
again in 2008 when Russia sought in vain Chinese support for the Russian
military attacks on Georgia.[11]

Until recently, China had a very negative record in relations with Taiwan.
The election of a new Taiwanese government in 2008 bent on reassuring
Beijing changed relations for the better. China's economic, diplomatic, and
military influence over Taiwan grew. The government was reelected in 2012,
but the political opposition in Taiwan remained opposed to recent trends and
improved its standing with Taiwan voters.

Strong Chinese nationalism and territorial claims have complicated China's efforts to improve relations with its other Asian neighbors, including
South Korea. South Korean opinion of China declined sharply from a high
point in 2004, initially because of nationalist disputes over whether a historic
kingdom controlling much of Korea and northeastern China was Chinese or
Korean. South Koreans also became increasingly suspicious over growing
Chinese trade with and investment in North Korea and enhanced political
support for the Pyongyang regime. China's efforts seemed designed to sustain a viable state in North Korea friendly to China—an objective at odds
with South Korea's goal to reunify North and South Korea. China's refusal in
2010 to condemn North Korea's killing of forty-six South Korean sailors in
the sinking of a South Korean warship and the killing of South Korean
soldiers and civilians in an artillery attack strongly reinforced anti-China
sentiment.

Chinese diplomacy at times endeavored to play down territorial disputes with Southeast Asian countries, but clear differences have remained unresolved and have become more prominent in recent years, especially over disputed claims in the South China Sea. In disputes with the Philippines and Vietnam in 2012, China used a range of diplomatic threats, occupation of disputed territories by powerful surveillance ships, offshore oil lease offers reflecting egregious expansion of Chinese claims in line with sometimes very large territorial claims, administrative fiats, and extra-legal economic coercion to put both Manila and Hanoi on the defensive. These steps implicitly warned other claimants and the United States not to challenge China regarding the disputed sea regions. To support its objectives, China used its influence with Cambodia, the chair of ASEAN for the year, to split the group over the South China Sea disputes and thereby reduce the group's ability to counter or complicate Chinese coercion and intimidation. On balance, the continued disputes served as a substantial drag on Chinese efforts to improve relations in the region.

China's remarkable military modernization and its sometimes secretive and authoritarian political system have raised suspicions and wariness on the part of a number of China's neighbors, including such middle powers as Australia.[12] They sought more transparency regarding Chinese military intentions as they endeavored to build their own military power and work cooperatively with one another and the United States in the face of China's military advances.

During the forty-year rule of Mao Zedong and Deng Xiaoping, the People's Republic of China had a record of aggression and assertiveness toward many Asian countries that remains hard to live down. This experience has left China with few positive connections on which to build friendly ties with its neighbors. Chinese interchange with Asian neighbors has depended heavily on the direction and leadership of the Chinese government. Nongovernment channels of communication and influence have been limited.

An exception may be seen in the so-called Overseas Chinese communities in Southeast Asian countries. These people have provided important investment and technical assistance to China's development and have represented political forces supportive of their country's good relations with China. At the same time, however, the dominant ethnic, cultural, and religious groups in Southeast Asia often have a long history of wariness of China and sometimes have promoted violent actions and other discrimination against ethnic Chinese.

Limitations and complications also show in the areas of China's greatest strength in Asia—economic relations and diplomacy.[13] Double counting associated with processing trade exaggerated Chinese trade figures. As foreign-invested enterprises in China conduct over half of Chinese trade, the resulting processing trade means that China often adds only a small amount to the product, and the finished product often depends on sales to the United States or the European Union. Taken together, these facts seem to offset China's stature in Asia as a powerful trading country.

The large amount of Asian and international investment that has gone to China means that other Asian countries' economic development is hurt. For many years until very recently, China invested little in Asia apart from Hong Kong, a reputed tax haven and source of "round-trip" monies leaving China and then returning to China as foreign investment.

China's government does not clearly present its aid figures. What is known, however, shows that China's aid to Asia is very small, especially in comparison to other donors, with the exception of aid to North Korea and, at least until recently, Myanmar. China's large foreign exchange reserves have served many purposes for the Chinese government's effort to maintain stability amid many domestic preoccupations. They have not translated into big Chinese grants of assistance abroad. China's attractiveness to Asian producers of raw materials is not shared by workers in Asian manufacturing. Asian entrepreneurs tended to relocate to China and appeared to do well, but they left their workers jobless back home.

In keeping with China's "win-win" diplomacy, the sometimes dizzying array of meetings, agreements, and pronouncements in Chinese diplomacy in Asia does not hide the fact that China remains reluctant to undertake significant costs, risks, or commitments in dealing with difficult regional issues.

North Korea remains a special case in Asian and world affairs. It reflects an unusual mix of Chinese strengths and weaknesses in Asia. China provides considerable food aid, oil, and other material support as North Korea's largest trading partner and foreign investor. In addition, China often shields Pyongyang from U.S.-led efforts at the United Nations to sanction or otherwise punish North Korea over its nuclear weapons development, ballistic missile development, proliferation activities, and military aggression against South Korea. The United States and other participants in the six-party talks rely on China to use its standing as the foreign power with the most influence in North Korea to get Pyongyang to engage in negotiations over its weapons development and proliferation activities. On the other hand, North Korea repeatedly rejects Chinese advice and warnings, and North Korean officials make no secret of their disdain for China. Nonetheless, Chinese leaders are loath to cut off their aid or otherwise increase pressure on North Korea to conform to international norms for fear of a backlash from the Pyongyang regime that would undermine Chinese interest in preserving stability on the Korean peninsula and in northeastern Asia. The net effect of these contradictions is that while China's influence in North Korea is greater than other major powers, it is encumbered and limited.[14]

Standards of Leadership: The United States in the Asia-Pacific

Readers interested in assessing China's rise in the Asia-Pacific and its possible leadership in a purported power transition in the region can usefully compare the indicators of the often encumbered Chinese advances in the region noted above with the strengths and weaknesses of American leadership in the region explained in this section. What the comparison shows is that China has far to go in undertaking even a fraction of the leadership responsibilities that continue to be carried out by the United States in the Asia-Pacific region.[15]

Of course, readers need to give careful attention to U.S. weaknesses as well as strengths in the Asia-Pacific region. As China and other Asian powers have risen to new prominence in the post–Cold War period, much commentary has focused on U.S. weaknesses and decline in the Asia-Pacific and elsewhere. The policies of the George W. Bush administration were very unpopular in the region. The United States was seen as inattentive to regional concerns, preoccupied with wars in Southwest Asia and the broader war on terrorism, and prone to crude and unilateral use of military coercion in dealing with sensitive international issues. The Barack Obama administration has refocused U.S. attention on the Asia-Pacific region, and regional concerns have shifted to worries that U.S. budget difficulties and political gridlock undermine the ability of the United States to sustain its regional responsibilities.

To assist readers in determining the degree of purported U.S. decline and how this impacts China's rising role in Asia, the discussion below provides indicators for readers to watch as future events in the region unfold. Recent practice shows that U.S. priorities, behavior, and power mesh well with the interests of the majority of Asia-Pacific governments that seek legitimacy through development and nation building in an uncertain security environment and an interdependent world economic order. The drivers of America

undertaking leadership responsibilities in the Asia-Pacific region remain
strong:

- The region is an area of ever-greater strategic and economic importance
  for the United States.
- The United States remains strongly committed to long-standing goals of
  supporting stability and balance of power, sustaining smooth economic
  access, and promoting U.S. values in this increasingly important world
  area.
- U.S. leadership in the Asia-Pacific arose in World War II. It has faced
  repeated major challenges—often much more serious than challenges
  faced today.

The basic determinants of U.S. strength and influence in the Asia-Pacific
region involve the following factors.[16]

Security: In most of Asia, governments are strong and viable, making the
decisions that determine direction in foreign affairs. Popular, elite, media,
and other opinion sources may influence government officials in policies
toward the United States and other countries, but in the end the officials
make decisions on the basis of their own calculus. In general, the officials see
their governments' legitimacy and success resting on nation building and
economic development, which require a stable and secure international environment. Unfortunately, Asia is not particularly stable, and most regional
governments privately are wary of and tend not to trust each other. As a
result, they look to the United States to provide the security they need to
pursue goals of development and nation building in an appropriate environment. They recognize that the U.S. security role is very expensive and involves great risk, including large-scale casualties if necessary, for the sake of
preserving Asian security. They also recognize that neither rising China nor
any other Asian power or coalition of powers is able or willing to undertake
even a fraction of these risks, costs, and responsibilities. Several U.S. allies
and associates in the Asia-Pacific support the U.S. security role through
provision of monetary support, access to bases and supplies, and defense
buildups providing greater synergy with American forces in the region.

A key set of indicators readers should monitor involves the ability of the
U.S government to sustain such support for security in the region. If the
United States declines, withdraws military forces, or becomes "isolationist,"
such developments are certain to lead to recalibrations by Asia-Pacific

governments on how best to secure their interests in a newly uncertain security environment.

Economic: The nation-building priority of most Asian governments depends importantly on export-oriented growth. Chinese officials recognize this; officials in other Asia-Pacific countries recognize the rising importance of China in their trade; but they all also recognize that half of China's trade is done by foreign-invested enterprises in China, and a large portion of the trade is processing trade—both features that make Chinese and Asian trade heavily dependent on exports to developed countries, notably the United States. The United States has run a massive trade deficit with China and a total trade deficit with Asia valued at over $350 billion at a time of a much larger overall U.S. trade deficit. Asian government officials recognize that China, which runs an overall trade surplus, and other trading partners of Asia are unwilling and unable to bear even a fraction of the cost of such large trade deficits, that nonetheless are very important for Asian governments.

Obviously, the global economic crisis and downturn beginning in 2008 are having an enormous impact on trade and investment. Some Asian officials are talking about relying more on domestic consumption, but tangible progress seems slow. They appear determined to preserve market share and export-oriented growth involving the U.S. and other world markets. How cooperative China has been and will be in working with the United States to deal with the various implications of the economic crisis also remains an open question, though the evidence on balance appears to show great care on the part of the Chinese government to avoid pushing controversial policies that would further undermine international confidence in the existing economic system and thwart meaningful efforts at economic recovery. The Chinese leadership appears to give priority to stability in its continued adherence to international economic patterns that feature the leading role of the U.S. dollar, strong direct and indirect U.S. influence on foreign investors in China, and the United States as a market of priority for Chinese products.

A key set of indicators readers should monitor involves the ability of the U.S. government to sustain such support for economic interests in the region. If the United States declines or resorts to economic policies designed to protect American companies at the expense of Asian exporters, such developments are certain to lead to recalibrations by Asia-Pacific governments on how best to secure their interests in a newly uncertain economic environment.

Government engagement: The Obama administration inherited a U.S. position in the Asia-Pacific buttressed by generally effective interaction with Asia's powers. It is very rare for the United States to enjoy good relations with Japan and China at the same time, but the Bush administration carefully managed relations with both powers effectively. It is unprecedented for the United States to be the leading foreign power in South Asia and to sustain close relations with both India and Pakistan, but that was the case since relatively early in the Bush administration. And it is unprecedented for the United States to have good relations with Beijing and Taipei at the same time, but that situation emerged during the Bush years and strengthened with the election of Taiwan President Ma Ying-jeou in March 2008.

The Obama government has moved to build on these strengths; a series of initiatives removed obstacles to closer U.S. cooperation with ASEAN and Asian regional organizations. The Obama government's wide-ranging "reengagement" with regional governments and multilateral organizations has a scope going from India to the Pacific Island states. The Obama administration's emphasis on consultation and inclusion of international stakeholders before coming to policy decisions on issues of importance to Asia and the Pacific also has been broadly welcomed and stands in contrast with the perceived former unilateralism of the U.S. government.

Meanwhile, in recent years, the U.S. Pacific Command and other U.S. military commands and security and intelligence organizations have been at the edge of wide-ranging and growing U.S. efforts to build and strengthen webs of military and related intelligence and security relationships throughout the region. In an overall environment where the United States remains on good terms with major powers and most other Asian governments, building military and other security ties through education programs, on-site training, exercises, intelligence cooperation, and other means enhances American influence in generally quiet but effective ways.

A key set of indicators readers should monitor involves the ability of the U.S government to sustain a well-balanced policy toward all of Asia's powers, including China, which tends to worry about the Obama government's regional reengagement. The success of the Obama administration in continuing to engage positively with China as it enhances engagement with the Asia-Pacific region remains to be determined. Meanwhile, the webs of U.S. security relationships in the region depend on continued budget support, which is not guaranteed given the continuing budget debates in Washington.

Nongovernment engagement and immigration: For much of its history, the United States exerted influence in Asia and the Pacific much more through business, religious, educational, and other interchange than through channels dependent on government leadership and support. Active American nongovernmental interaction with the countries of the region continues today, putting the United States in a unique position where the American nongovernment sector has such a strong and usually positive impact on the influence the United States exerts in the region. Meanwhile, almost fifty years of generally color-blind U.S. immigration policy since the ending of discriminatory U.S. restrictions on Asian immigration in 1965 has resulted in the influx of millions of Asia-Pacific migrants who call America home and who interact with their countries of origin in ways that undergird and reflect well on the American position in the region. No other country, with the exception of Canada, has such an active and powerfully positive channel of influence in the Asia-Pacific.

Indicators for readers to monitor regarding this set of factors involve American attitudes toward immigration. Should the United States restrict immigration, or revert to the discriminatory practices against Asians seen in the past, the result would weaken American influence in the Asia-Pacific region.

Asia-Pacific contingency planning: Part of the reason for the success of U.S. efforts to build webs of security and related cooperation with Asia-Pacific countries has to do with active contingency planning by many Asia-Pacific governments. As power relations change in the region, notably on account of China's rise, regional governments generally seek to work positively and pragmatically with China, but they also seek the reassurance of close security, intelligence, and other ties with the United States in case rising China shifts from its current avowed benign approach to one of greater assertiveness or dominance.

Chinese assertiveness over territorial claims along its maritime frontier rose in 2009–2010, prompting many Asia-Pacific governments to reinforce their security relationships with the United States, which worked methodically to preserve stability by dissuading China from pursuing aggressive tendencies. The Asia-Pacific governments' interest in closer ties with the United States meshed well with the Obama administration's engagement with regional governments and multilateral organizations. The U.S. concern to keep stability in the broad region while fostering economic growth overlapped constructively with the priorities of the vast majority of regional governments as they pursued their respective nation-building agendas. North Korea has remained opposed to the United States, and Myanmar has been suspicious, at least until recently. China's suspicions seem outweighed, at least for the time being, by the benefits derived from pragmatic cooperation with the United States.

Readers are advised to monitor this set of indicators for evidence of greater regional acceptance of China's rise as a benign and positive force in regional affairs. Such a change would presumably reduce regional interest in sustaining close ties with the United States as a potential counter to possible Chinese intimidation and coercion. Also, readers should monitor this set of indicators for signs that regional governments may come to judge the United States as unable or unwilling to strike a proper balance to allow them to remain secure without causing U.S.-Chinese friction that destabilizes the regional environment.

CONCLUSION AND OUTLOOK

The effort in this volume to provide reliable and realistic ways to assess China's rise and the purported power shift in Asia shows the following conclusions:

1. China's recent relationships in Asia can be measured accurately.
2. Salient strengths and limitations of China's rising influence in Asia can be measured accurately.
3. Significant strengths and limitations of the United States in the Asia-Pacific region can be measured accurately.
4. The contingency planning of Asia-Pacific governments can be measured accurately.

Taken together, these conclusions show a continued Chinese advance in importance and influence. But the United States remains the region's leading power, and other governments are wary of implications of China's rise as they seek mutual benefit in greater economic and other interaction with China. China has always exerted its greatest influence and devoted the lion's share of its foreign policy attention in Asia, but that does not mean that China will come to dominate the region. Prevailing conditions, which take into account the broad-gauge data used in assessments predicting a power shift in the Asia-Pacific, nonetheless make it hard to foresee how China could emerge in a dominant position in Asia.

As a result, the reported danger of confrontation and/or conflict predicted to emerge in Sino-American relations amid projections of China rising to challenge the leading position of the United States appears to be reduced. Moreover, if China is not in a position to challenge the United States in nearby Asia, it will be less able to do so in other areas farther from China's scope of influence and concern. Indeed, it appears more likely that Chinese policy makers and strategists will continue incremental efforts and adjustments in order to overcome obstacles as they seek to improve Chinese influence, interests, and status. This difficult and protracted task adds to China's array of domestic challenges and other preoccupations. It argues for continued reserve in broader foreign policies and practices as Chinese leaders take account of the sustained but substantial limits of Chinese international power and influence.

Variables that could upset the above forecast include how well China's leaders manage such a moderate approach to world affairs. A major challenge comes from Chinese elites and public opinion that discount any negative legacies China has as a result of past behavior. The acute sense of righteousness of these Chinese groups is accompanied by prickly patriotic inclinations that are quick to find fault with the United States and some of China's neighbors. Such frustrations can grow and spill over to impact Chinese leaders and the policies they follow in regard to China's neighbors and the United States.

Other variables that could change the forecast include U.S. policy. Should the United States reverse policy and withdraw from security commitments to the Asia-Pacific or close American markets to regional exporters, the prevailing order in the Asia-Pacific would change significantly, with the future order very much in doubt. The United States also could craft its reengagement in Asia as balancing against and excluding China, thereby forcing Asian governments to choose between Beijing and Washington. Meanwhile, abrupt and provocative actions by the always unpredictable North Korean government or by claimants in territorial disputes along China's rim could easily escalate tensions and possibly lead to military conflict involving China and the United States.

NOTES

1. Arvind Subramanian, "The Inevitable Superpower: Why China's Rise Is a Sure Thing," *Foreign Affairs* 90, no. 5 (September–October 2011): pp. 66–78; Stefan Halper, *The Beijing Consensus: How China's Authoritarian Model Will Dominate the 21st Century* (New York: Basic Books, 2010); Martin Jacques, *When China Rules the World: The Rise of the Middle Kingdom and the End of the Western World* (New York: Penguin, 2009).

2. Joseph Nye, *The Future of Power* (New York: Perseus, 2011), chap. 6; Evan Medeiros, "Is Beijing Ready for Global Leadership?" *Current History* 108, no. 719 (September 2009): pp. 250–56.

3. Michael Beckley, "China's Century? Why America's Edge Will Endure," *International Security* 36, no. 3 (Winter 2011/2012): pp. 41–78.

4. Michael Chambers, "China and Southeast Asia: Creating a 'Win-Win' Neighborhood," *China's "Good Neighbor" Diplomacy*, Special Report 126 (Washington, DC: Woodrow Wilson Center for Scholars Asia Program, January 2005); "Wen Rolls Out 'Win-Win' Strategy in Africa," IPS News, June 21, 2006, ipsnews.net/news.asp?idnews=33702 (accessed July 16, 2010).

5. Deborah Brautigam, *The Dragon's Gift* (New York: Oxford University Press, 2010).

6. Mark Manyin, coord., *Pivot to the Pacific? The Obama Administration's "Rebalancing" Toward Asia*, Report 42448 (Washington, DC: Library of Congress, Congressional Research Service, March 28, 2012).

7. Xin Zhiming, "Government Clears $5.4b World Bank Loan," *China Daily*, July 25, 2008, p. 13; Asian Development Bank, *Asian Development Bank and the People's Republic of China: 2008: A Fact Sheet*, www.adb.org; Fu Jing and Hu Haiyan, "China, UN Jointly Unveil Five-Year Aid Framework," *China Daily*, April 2, 2010; Gillian Wong, "China Rises and Rises, Yet Still Gets Foreign Aid," Associated Press, September 27, 2010, www.ap.com; Antoine Dechezlepretre, et al., "Technology Transfer by CDM Projects," *Energy Policy* 37, no. 2 (2009): p. 1; Keith Bradsher, "China Leading Global Race to Make Clean Energy," *New York Times*, January 31, 2010, www.nytimes.com (accessed February 2, 2010); The World Bank, "Global Environmental Facility (GEF) Projects in China," July 2009; The World Bank, "World Bank, GEF-Backed Energy Efficiency Program Expands in China," January 2008; Asian Development Bank, *Asian Development Bank and People's Republic of China: Fact Sheet*, December 2008, p. 3.

8. Douglas Paal, "The United States and Asia in 2011," *Asian Survey* 52, no. 1, p.7.

9. Peter Ford, "Japan Abandons Bid to Make China a Key Pillar of Its Foreign Policy," *Christian Science Monitor*, November 17, 2010, www.CSMonitor.com.

10. Lawrence Saez and Crystal Chang, "China and South Asia: Strategic Implications and Economic Imperatives," in *China, The Developing World, and the New Global Dynamic*, ed. Lowell Dittmer and George Yu (Boulder, CO: Lynne Rienner, 2010), pp. 83–108; John Garver and Fei-ling Wang, "China's Anti-Encirclement Struggle," *Asian Security* 6, no. 3 (2010): pp. 238–63.

11. Yu Bin, "China-Russia Relations: Guns and Games of August: Tales of Two Strategic Partners," *Comparative Connections* 10, no. 3 (October 2008): pp. 131–38.

12. Linda Jacobson, "Australia-China Ties: In Search of Political Trust," *Policy Brief*, Lowy Institute, June 2012.

13. Thomas Lum, coord., *Comparing Global Influence: China's and U.S. Diplomacy, Foreign Aid, Trade, and Investment in the Developing World*, Report RL34620 (Washington, DC: Library of Congress, Congressional Research Service, August 15, 2008); Yu Yongding,

"A Different Road Forward," *China Daily*, December 23, 2010, p. 9; "China's Reforms: The Second Long March," *Economist*, December 11, 2008, www.economist.com.

14. Scott Snyder, "China's Post–Kim Jong Il Debate," *Comparative Connections* 14, no. 1 (2012): pp. 107–14.

15. Robert Sutter, "Assessing China's Rise and U.S. Influence in Asia—Growing Maturity and Balance," *Journal of Contemporary China* 19, no. 65 (June 2010): pp. 591–604.

16. Robert Sutter, "China's Rise: Evolution and Implications," in *The Far East and Australasia 2011*, ed. Lynn Daniel (London: Routledge, 2010), pp. 3–9; see also this author's findings based on interviews with over two hundred officials from ten Asia-Pacific countries discussed in Robert Sutter, *China's Rise in Asia* (Lanham, MD: Rowman & Littlefield, 2005) and Robert Sutter, *The United States in Asia* (Lanham, MD: Rowman & Littlefield, 2009).

Selected Bibliography

Alden, Christopher, Daniel Large, and Ricardo de Oliveria. *China Returns to Africa: A Super-power and a Continent Embrace*. New York: Columbia University Press, 2008.

Alterman, Jon, and John Garver. *The Vital Triangle: China, the United States, and the Middle East*. Washington, DC: Center for Strategic and International Studies, 2008.

Austin, Greg, and Stuart Harris. *Japan and Greater China*. Honolulu: University of Hawaii Press, 2001.

Ba Zhongtan et al. *Zhongguo Guojia Anquan Zhanlue Wenti Yanjiu*. Beijing: Zhongguo Junshi Kexue Chubanshe, 2003.

Bachrack, Stanley D. *The Committee of One Million: "China Lobby" Politics, 1953–1971*. New York: Columbia University Press, 1976.

Bader, Jeffrey. *Obama and China's Rise*. Washington, DC: Brookings Institution, 2012.

Barnett, A. Doak. *China and the Major Powers in East Asia*. Washington, DC: Brookings Institution, 1977.

———. *Communist China and Asia: Challenge to American Policy*. New York: Harper and Brothers, 1960.

Barnouin, Barbara, and Yu Changgen. *Chinese Foreign Policy during the Cultural Revolution*. New York: Columbia University Press, 1997.

Bergsten, C. Fred, et al. *China's Rise: Challenges and Opportunities*. Washington, DC: Peterson Institute for International Economics and Center for Strategic and International Studies, 2008.

Bhattasali, Deepak, Shantong Li, and Will Martin. *China and the WTO*. Washington, DC: World Bank, 2004.

Blasko, Dennis. *The Chinese Army Today*. London: Routledge, 2012.

Brautigam, Deborah. *The Dragon's Gift*. New York: Oxford University Press, 2009.

Bush, Richard. *The Perils of Proximity: China-Japan Security Relations*. Washington, DC: Brookings Institution, 2010.

———. *Unchartered Strait: the Future of China-Taiwan Relations*. Washington, DC: Brookings Institution, 2012.

———. *Untying the Knot: Making Peace in the Taiwan Strait*. Washington, DC: Brookings Institution, 2005.

Bush, Richard, and Michael O'Hanlon. *A War Like No Other: The Truth about China's Challenge to America*. Hoboken, NJ: John Wiley & Sons, 2007.

Cabestan, Jean-Pierre. "European Union-China Relations and the United States." *Asian Perspective* 30, no. 4 (Winter 2006): 11–38.

Carlson, Allen. "More Than Just Saying No: China's Evolving Approach to Sovereignty and Intervention." In *New Directions in the Study of China's Foreign Policy*, edited by Alastair Iain Johnston and Robert S. Ross, 217–41. Stanford, CA: Stanford University Press, 2006.

Chanda, Nayan. "China and Cambodia." *Asia-Pacific Review* 9, no. 2 (2002): 1–11.

Chang, Gordon. *Friends and Enemies: The United States, China, and the Soviet Union, 1948–1972*. Stanford, CA: Stanford University Press, 1990.

Chen Jian. *China's Road to the Korean War*. New York: Columbia University Press, 1994.

———. *Mao's China and the Cold War*. Chapel Hill: University of North Carolina Press, 2001.

Cheng Ruisheng, "China-India Diplomatic Relations: Six Decades' Experience and Inspiration," *Foreign Affairs Journal* (Beijing) 96 (Summer 2010): 59–70.

Cheung, Joseph Y. S. "Sino-ASEAN Relations in the Early 21st Century." *Contemporary Southeast Asia* 23, no. 3 (December 2001): 420–52.

Chi, Su. *Taiwan's Relations with Mainland China: A Tail Wagging Two Dogs*. New York: Routledge, 2008.

Christensen, Thomas. "Fostering Stability or Creating a Monster? The Rise of China and US Policy toward East Asia." *International Security* 31, no. 1 (Summer 2006): 81–126.

———. *Useful Adversaries: Grand Strategy, Domestic Mobilization, and Sino-American Conflicts, 1949–1958*. Princeton, NJ: Princeton University Press, 1996.

———. "Windows and War: Trends Analysis and Beijing's Use of Force." In *New Directions in the Study of China's Foreign Policy*, edited by Alastair Iain Johnston and Robert S. Ross, 50–85. Stanford, CA: Stanford University Press, 2006.

Chu Shulong. "Quanmian jianshe xiaokang shehui shiqi de zhongguo waijiao zhan-lue." *Shijie Jingji yu Zhengzhi* 8 (August 2003).

Chung, Jae Ho. "From a Special Relationship to a Normal Partnership?" *Pacific Affairs* 76, no. 3 (2003): 549–68.

Clough, Ralph. *Cooperation or Conflict in the Taiwan Strait?* Lanham, MD: Rowman & Littlefield, 1999.

———. *Island China*. Cambridge, MA: Harvard University Press, 1978.

Cohen, Jerome, and Hungdah Chiu. *People's China and International Law*. Princeton, NJ: Princeton University Press, 1974.

Cohen, Warren I. *America's Response to China: A History of Sino-American Relations*. New York: Columbia University Press, 2010.

———. "China's Rise in Historical Perspective." *Journal of Strategic Studies* 30, nos. 4–5 (August–October 2007): 683–704.

Cole, Bernard. *Great Wall at Sea*. Annapolis, MD: Naval Institute, 2010.

Council on Foreign Relations. *More Than Humanitarianism: A Strategic U.S. Approach toward Africa*. Independent Task Force Report 56. New York: Council on Foreign Relations, January 2006.

———. *U.S.-China Relations: An Affirmative Agenda, a Responsible Course*. New York: Council on Foreign Relations, 2007.

Cui Liru. "A Multipolar World in the Globalization Era." *Contemporary International Relations* (Beijing) 20, Special Issue (September 2010): 1–11.

Cumings, Bruce. *The Origins of the Korean War*. Princeton, NJ: Princeton University Press, 1990.

Dahlman, Carl. *The World under Pressure: How China and India Are Influencing the Global Economy and Environment.* Stanford, CA: Stanford University Press, 2011.

Dai Bingguo. "Stick to the Path of Peaceful Development." *Beijing Review* 51 (December 23, 2010). www.beijinreview.com.cn.

Deng Hao. "China's Relations with Central Asian Countries: Retrospect and Prospect." *Guoji Wenti Yanjiu* (Beijing), May 13, 2002, 8–12.

Deng Xiaoping. *Selected Works of Deng Xiaoping, 1982–1992.* Beijing: Foreign Languages Press, 1994.

Deng, Yong. *China's Struggle for Status: The Realignment of International Relations.* New York: Cambridge University Press, 2008.

———. "The Chinese Conception of National Interests in International Relations." *China Quarterly* 154 (June 1998): 308–29.

———. "Hegemon on the Offensive: Chinese Perspectives on U.S. Global Strategy." *Political Science Quarterly* 116, no. 3 (Fall 2001): 343–65.

Deng, Yong, and Thomas Moore. "China Views Globalization: Toward a New Great-Power Politics." *Washington Quarterly* 27, no. 3 (Summer 2004): 117–36.

Deng, Yong, and Fei-Ling Wang, eds. *China Rising: Power and Motivation in Chinese Foreign Policy.* Lanham, MD: Rowman & Littlefield, 2005.

Dittmer, Lowell. *Sino-Soviet Normalization and Its International Implications, 1945–1990.* Seattle: University of Washington Press, 1992.

Dittmer, Lowell, and George T. Yu, eds. *China, the Developing World and the New Global Dynamic.* Boulder, CO: Lynne Rienner, 2010.

Downs, Erica. *Brookings Foreign Policy Studies Energy Security Series: China.* Washington, DC: Brookings Institution, 2006.

———. *Inside China, Inc: China Development Bank's Cross-Border Energy Deals.* John Thornton China Center Monograph Series 3. Washington, DC: Brookings Institution, March 2011.

Dulles, Foster Rhea. *American Policy toward Communist China, 1949–1969.* New York: Thomas Y. Crowell, 1972.

Dumbaugh, Kerry. *China-U.S. Relations: Current Issues and Implications for U.S. Policy.* Report RL32804. Washington, DC: Library of Congress, Congressional Research Service, June 8, 2006.

———. *Taiwan-US Relations: Recent Developments and Their Policy Implications.* Report RL 34683. Washington, DC: Library of Congress, Congressional Research Service, October 27, 2008.

Economy, Elizabeth. "China's Environmental Challenge." *Current History,* September 2005, 278–82.

Eisenman, Joshua, Eric Heginbotham, and Derek Mitchell, eds. *China and the Developing World.* Armonk, NY: M. E. Sharpe, 2007.

Ellis, R. Evan. *China in Latin America.* Boulder, CO: Lynne Rienner, 2009.

Fairbank, John. *The United States and China.* Cambridge, MA: Harvard University Press, 1983.

Fairbank, John, and Merle Goldman. *China: A History.* Cambridge, MA: Harvard University Press, 1999.

Fang Ning, Wang Xiaodong, and Qiao Liang. *Quanqihua Yinying xia de Zhongguo Zhilu.* Beijing: Chinese Academy of Social Sciences, 1999.

Feng Zhongping. "China-EU Relationship." *Xiandai guoji guanxi* (Beijing) 17 (January 2007): 47–55.

———. "EU's China Policy Analyzed." *Contemporary International Relations* (Beijing) 8, no. 4 (April 1998): 1–6.

Fewsmith, Joseph. *China since Tiananmen*. New York: Cambridge University Press, 2008.

Fewsmith, Joseph, and Stanley Rosen. "The Domestic Context of Chinese Foreign Policy: Does 'Public Opinion' Matter?" In *The Making of Chinese Foreign and Security Policy in the Era of Reform*, edited by David M. Lampton, 179–86. Stanford, CA: Stanford University Press, 2001.

Finkelstein, David. *China Reconsiders Its National Security: The Great Peace and Development Debate of 1999*. Alexandria, VA: CNA, December 2000.

Foot, Rosemary. "China and the ASEAN Regional Forum." *Asian Survey* 38, no. 5 (1998): 425–40.

———. "Chinese Strategies in a U.S.-Hegemonic Global Order: Accommodating and Hedging." *International Affairs* 82, no. 1 (2006): 77–94.

———. *The Practice of Power: U.S. Relations with China since 1949*. New York: Oxford University Press, 1997.

Foot, Rosemary, and Andrew Walter. *China, the United States and the Global Order*. New York: Cambridge University Press, 2011.

Fravel, M. Taylor. "China's Search for Military Power" *Washington Quarterly* 33, no. 3 (Summer 2008): 125–41.

———. *Strong Borders, Secure Nation: Cooperation and Conflict in China's Territorial Disputes*. Princeton, NJ: Princeton University Press, 2008.

Fravel, M. Taylor, and Evan Medeiros. "China's Search for Assured Retaliation," *International Security* 35, no. 2 (Fall 2010): 48–87.

Friedberg, Aaron. *A Contest for Supremacy: China, America, and the Struggle for Mastery in Asia*. New York: W. W. Norton, 2011.

———. "The Future of U.S.-China Relations: Is Conflict Inevitable?" *International Security* 30, no. 2 (2005): 7–45.

———. "'Going Out': China's Pursuit of Natural Resources and Implications for the PRC's Grand Strategy." *NBR Analysis* 17, no. 3 (September 2006): 1–40.

Fu Mengzi. "China and Peace Building on the Korean Peninsula." *Xiandai guoji guanxi* (Beijing) 17 (July 2007): 27–40.

———. "Sino-US Relations." *Xiandai guoji guanxi* (Beijing) 17 (January 2007): 32–46.

Gao Lianfu. "East Asia Regional Cooperation Entered the Stage of Institutionalization." *Taipingyang Xuebao* 2 (2001).

Gao Zugui. "An Analysis of Sino-U.S. Strategic Relations on the 'Western Front.'" *Xiandai Guoji Guanxi* 12 (December 20, 2004).

Garnett, Sherman, ed. *Rapprochement or Rivalry? Russia-China Relations in a Changing Asia*. Washington, DC: Carnegie Endowment for International Peace, 2000.

Garver, John. *China and Iran: Ancient Partners in a Post-Imperial World*. Seattle: University of Washington Press, 2006.

———. "Development of China's Overland Transportation Links with Central, Southwest, and South Asia." *China Quarterly* 185 (March 2006): 1–22.

———. *Face-Off*. Seattle: University of Washington Press, 1997.

———. *Foreign Relations of the People's Republic of China*. Englewood Cliffs, NJ: Prentice Hall, 1993.

———. "Is China Playing a Dual Game in Iran?" *Washington Quarterly* 34, no. 1 (Winter 2011): 75–88.

———. *Protracted Contest: Sino-Indian Rivalry in the 20th Century*. Seattle: University of Washington Press, 2001.

Gill, Bates. "China's Evolving Regional Security Strategy." In *Power Shift: China and Asia's New Dynamics*, edited by David Shambaugh, 247–65. Berkeley: University of California Press, 2005.

———. *Rising Star: China's New Security Diplomacy*. Washington, DC: Brookings Institution, 2007.

———. "Two Steps Forward, One Step Back: The Dynamics of Chinese Nonproliferation and Arms Control Policy-Making in an Era of Reform." In *The Making of Chinese Foreign and Security Policy in the Era of Reform*, edited by David M. Lampton, 257–88. Stanford, CA: Stanford University Press, 2001.

Gill, Bates, and Melissa Murphy. "China's Evolving Approach to Counterterrorism." *Harvard Asia Quarterly,* Winter/Spring 2005, 21–32.

Gill, Bates, and Matthew Oresman. *China's New Journey to the West*. Washington, DC: Center for Strategic and International Studies, August 2003.

Glaser, Bonnie, and Evan Medeiros. "The Changing Ecology of Foreign Policy Making in China: The Ascension and Demise of the Theory of 'Peaceful Rise.'" *China Quarterly* 190 (2007): 291–310.

Glosny, Michael. "Heading toward a Win-Win Future? Recent Developments in China's Policy toward Southeast Asia." *Asian Security* 2, no. 1 (2006): 24–57.

Godwin, Paul. "China as a Major Asian Power: The Implications of Its Military Modernization (a View from the United States)." In *China, the United States, and Southeast Asia: Contending Perspectives on Politics, Security, and Economics*, edited by Evelyn Goh and Sheldon Simon, 145–66. New York: Routledge, 2008.

Goh, Evelyn. *Constructing the US Rapprochement with China, 1961–1974: From "Red Menace" to "Tacit Ally."* Cambridge: Cambridge University Press, 2005.

———. *Meeting the China Challenge: The United States in Southeast Asian Regional Security Strategies*. Policy Studies 21. Washington, DC: East-West Center, 2006.

———. "Southeast Asia: Strategic Diversification in the 'Asian Century.'" In *Strategic Asia 2008–2009*, edited by Ashley Tellis, Mercy Kuo, and Andrew Marble, 261–96. Seattle, WA: National Bureau of Asian Research, 2008.

Goldstein, Avery. *Rising to the Challenge: China's Grand Strategy and International Security*. Stanford, CA: Stanford University Press, 2005.

Goldstein, Lyle, and Vitaly Kozyrev. "China, Japan, and the Scramble for Siberia." *Survival* 48, no. 1 (Spring 2006): 163–78.

Goldstein, Steven. *Taiwan Faces the Twenty-First Century*. New York: Foreign Policy Association, 1997.

Goldstein, Steven, and Julian Chang, eds. *Presidential Politics in Taiwan: The Administration of Chen Shui-bian*. Norwalk, CT: Eastbridge, 2008.

Gong Li. "Deng Xiaoping Dui Mei Zhengce Sixing yu Zhong-Mei Guanxi." *Guoji Wenti Yanjiu* 6 (2004): 13–17.

———. *Kuayue: 1969–1979 nian Zhong Mei guanxi de yanbian* [Across the chasm: The evolution of China-US relations, 1969–1979]. Henan: Henan People's Press, 1992.

———. "The Official Perspective: What Chinese Government Officials Think of America." In *Chinese Images of the United States*, edited by Carola McGiffert, 25–32. Washington, DC: CSIS, 2006.

Green, Michael. *Japan's Reluctant Realism*. New York: Palgrave, 2003.

Green, Michael, and Benjamin Self. "Japan's Changing China Policy: From Commercial Liberalism to Reluctant Realism." *Survival* 38, no. 2 (Summer 1996): 34–58.

Gries, Peter. *China's New Nationalism*. Berkeley: University of California Press, 2004.

Guoji Zhanlue yu Anquan Xingshi Pinggu 2001–2002. Beijing: Shishi Chubanshe, 2002.

Guoji Zhanlue yu Anquan Xingshi Pinggu 2003–2004. Beijing: Shishi Chubanshe, 2004.

Guoji Zhanlue yu Anquan Xingshi Pinggu 2004–2005. Beijing: Shishi Chubanshe, 2005.

Hagerty, Devin. "China and Pakistan: Strains in the Relationship." *Current History*, September 2002, 284–89.

Halper, Stephan. *The Beijing Consensus.* New York: Basic Books, 2010.

Harding, Harry. *China's Foreign Relations in the 1980s.* New Haven, CT: Yale University Press, 1984.

———. *China's Second Revolution.* Washington, DC: Brookings Institution, 1987.

———. *A Fragile Relationship: The U.S. and China Since 1972.* Washington, DC: Brookings Institution, 1992.

Harris, Lillian Craig, and Robert Worden, eds. *China and the Third World.* Dover, MA: Auburn House, 1986.

Henderson, John, and Benjamin Reilly. "Dragon in Paradise." *National Interest*, Summer 2003, 93–102.

Herberg, Mikkal, and Kenneth Lieberthal. "China's Search for Energy Security: Implications for U.S. Policy." *NBR Analysis* 17, no. 1 (April 2006): 1–54.

Hinton, Harold. *China's Turbulent Quest.* New York: Macmillan, 1972.

———. *Communist China in World Politics.* Boston: Houghton Mifflin, 1966.

Holslag, Jonathan. *China and India: Prospects for Peace.* New York: Columbia University Press, 2010.

Hou Yousheng. "Oumeny yu Meiguo dai Hua zhanlue bijiao." *Xiandai guoji guanxi* (Beijing) 8 (August 2006): 1–6.

Hou Zhengdo. "Guanyu Zhong Ou zhanlue guanxi jige xiangfa." *Guoji Wenti Yanjiu* (Beijing) 2 (April 2005).

Hu Angang. *Daguo Zhanlue Liyi yu Shiming.* Liaoning: Liaoning Renmin Chubanshe, 2000.

Hu Angang and Meng Honghua. "Zhongmeiriieying youxing zhanlue ziyuan bijiao." *Zhanlue yu Guanli* 2 (2002): 26–41.

———, eds. *Jiedu Meiguo Dazhanlue.* Hangzhou: Zhejiang Renmin Chubanshe, 2003.

Hu Guocheng. "Chinese Images of the United States: A Historical Review." In *Chinese Images of the United States*, edited by Carola McGiffert, 3–8. Washington, DC: CSIS, 2006.

Hu, Sheng. *Imperialism and Chinese Politics.* Beijing: Foreign Language Press, 1985.

Huang Renwei. *Zhongguo Jueji de Shijian he Kongjian.* Shanghai: Shanghai Academy of Social Sciences, 2002.

Huchet, Jean-Francois. "Emergence of a Pragmatic India-China Relationship: Between Geo-strategic Rivalry and Economic Competition." *China Perspectives* 3 (2008): 50–67.

Hunt, Michael H. *The Genesis of Chinese Communist Foreign Policy.* New York: Columbia University Press, 1996.

Institute for International and Strategic Studies. *China's Grand Strategy: A Kinder, Gentler Turn.* London: Institute for International and Strategic Studies, November 2004.

Institute of Strategic Studies, CCP Central Party School. *Zhongguo Heping Jueji Xindaolu.* Beijing: Zhonggong Zhongyang Dangxiao Chubanshe, 2004.

International Crisis Group. *China and North Korea: Comrades Forever?* Asia Report 112. Brussels: International Crisis Group, February 1, 2006.

———. *China's Growing Role in UN Peacekeeping.* Asia Report 166. Brussels: International Crisis Group, April 17, 2009.

———. *China's Myanmar Strategy.* Asia Briefing No.112. Brussels: International Crisis Group, September 21, 2010.

———. *China's Thirst for Oil.* Asia Report No. 153-9. Brussels: International Crisis Group, June 2008.

————. *China-Taiwan: Uneasy Détente.* Asia Briefing 42. Brussels: International Crisis Group, September 21, 2005.

————. *North Korea's Nuclear Test: The Fallout.* Asia Briefing 56. Brussels: International Crisis Group, November 13, 2006.

Jacobson, Linda, and Dean Knox. *New Foreign Policy Actors in China.* SIPRI Policy Paper 26. Stockholm: Stockholm International Peace Research Institute, September 2010.

Ji Zhiye. "Strategic Prospects for Russia," *Contemporary International Relations* (Beijing) 20, no. 5 (September/October 2010): 1–16.

Jia Qingguo. "Peaceful Development: China's Policy of Reassurance." *Australian Journal of International Affairs* 59, no. 4 (December 2005): 493–507.

Jiang Changbin and Robert S. Ross, eds. *1955–1971 Nian de Zhong Mei Guanxi—Huanhe Zhigian: Lengzhan Chongtu yu Keshi de Cai Tantao* [U.S.-China relations 1955–1971— before détente: An examination of Cold War conflict and restraint]. Beijing: Shijie Zhishi Chubanshe, 1998.

————. *Cong Duizhi zouxiang Huanhe: Lengzhan Shiqi Zhong Mei Guanxi zai Tantao* [From confrontation toward détente: A Reexamination of U.S.-China relations during the Cold War]. Beijing: Shijie Zhishi Chubanshe, 2000.

Johnston, Alastair Iain. *Social States: China in International Institutions, 1980–2000.* Princeton, NJ: Princeton University Press, 2008.

Johnston, Alastair Iain, and Paul Evans. "China's Engagement." In *Engaging China: The Management of an Emerging Power*, edited by Alastair Iain Johnston and Robert Ross, 235–72. New York: Routledge, 1999.

Johnston, Alastair Iain, and Robert S. Ross, eds. *New Directions in the Study of China's Foreign Policy.* Stanford, CA: Stanford University Press, 2006.

Kan, Shirley. *China and Proliferation of Weapons of Mass Destruction and Missiles: Policy Issues.* Report RL31555. Washington, DC: Library of Congress, Congressional Research Service, January 31, 2006.

Kan, Shirley, Christopher Bolkcom, and Ronald O'Rourke. *China's Foreign Conventional Arms Acquisitions.* Report RL30700. Washington, DC: Library of Congress, Congressional Research Service, November 6, 2001.

Kang, David. *China Rising: Peace, Power, and Order in East Asia.* New York: Columbia University Press, 2007.

————. "Getting Asia Wrong: The Need for New Analytical Frameworks." *International Security* 27, no. 4 (2003): 57–85.

Keefe, John. *Anatomy of the EP-3 Incident.* Alexandria, VA: Center for Naval Analysis, January 2002.

Keller, William, and Thomas Rawski, eds. *China's Rise and the Balance of Influence in Asia.* Pittsburgh, PA: University of Pittsburgh Press, 2007.

Kim, Samuel. *China, the United Nations and World Order.* Princeton, NJ: Princeton University Press. 1979.

————. "Chinese Foreign Policy Faces Globalization Challenges." In *New Directions in the Study of China's Foreign Policy*, edited by Alastair Iain Johnston and Robert S. Ross, 276–308. Stanford, CA: Stanford University Press, 2006.

————. *The Third World in Chinese World Policy.* Princeton, NJ: Center of International Studies, Woodrow Wilson School of Public and International Affairs, Princeton University, 1989.

————. *The Two Koreas and the Great Powers.* New York: Cambridge University Press, 2006.

————, ed. *China and the World: New Directions in Chinese Foreign Relations.* Boulder, CO: Westview, 1989.

Kim, Taeho. "Sino-ROK Relations at a Crossroads: Looming Tensions amid Growing Interdependence." *Korean Journal of Defense Analysis* 17, no. 1 (2005): 129–49.

Kissinger, Henry. *On China.* New York: Penguin, 2011.

————. *White House Years.* Boston: Little, Brown, 1979.

————. *Years of Upheaval.* Boston: Little, Brown, 1983.

Kleine-Ahlbrandt, Stephanie, and Andrew Small. "China's New Dictatorship Diplomacy." *Foreign Affairs* 87, no. 1 (January–February 2008): 38–56.

Koen, Ross Y. *The China Lobby in American Politics.* New York: Harper and Row, 1974.

Kurlantzick, Joshua. *Charm Offensive: How China's Soft Power Is Transforming the World.* New Haven, CT: Yale University Press, 2007.

Lall, Arthur. *How Communist China Negotiates.* New York: Columbia University Press, 1968.

Lampton, David M., ed. *The Making of Chinese Foreign and Security Policy in the Era of Reform, 1978–2000.* Stanford, CA: Stanford University Press, 2001.

————. *Power Constrained: Sources of Mutual Strategic Suspicion in US-China Relations NBR Analysis* (June 2010): 5–25.

————. *Same Bed, Different Dreams.* Berkeley: University of California Press, 2001.

————. *The Three Faces of Chinese Power: Might, Money, and Minds.* Berkeley: University of California Press, 2008.

Lancaster, Carol. *The Chinese Aid System.* Washington, DC: Center for Global Development, June 2007.

Lardy, Nicholas. *Integrating China in the Global Economy.* Washington, DC: Brookings Institution, 2002.

Larkin, Bruce. *China and Africa, 1949–1970.* Berkeley: University of California Press, 1971.

Lee, David Tawei. *The Making of the Taiwan Relations Act.* New York: Oxford University Press, 2000.

Lee Teng-hui. *Creating the Future: Towards a New Era for the Chinese People* (a compilation of speeches and remarks by President Lee Teng-hui). Taipei: Government Information Office, 1992.

Leverett, Flynt, and Jeffrey Bader. "Managing China-U.S. Energy Competition in the Middle East." *Washington Quarterly* 29, no. 1 (Winter 2005/2006): 187–201.

Lewis, Joanna. "China's Strategic Priorities in International Climate Change Negotiations." *Washington Quarterly* 31, no. 1 (Winter 2007–2008): 155–74.

————. "The State of US-China Relations on Climate Change." *China Environmental Series* 11 (2010/2011): 7–39.

Li, Cheng, ed. *China's Changing Political Landscape: Prospects for Democracy.* Washington, DC: Brookings Institution, 2008.

————. *China's Leaders: The New Generation.* Lanham, MD: Rowman & Littlefield, 2001.

Li Li. "India's Engagement with East Asia and the China Factor." *Contemporary International Relations* (Beijing) 20, no. 5 (September/October 2010): 97–109.

Li Shaoxian. "China-Russia Bond." *Xiandai guoji guanxi* (Beijing) 17 (January 2007): 5–21.

Li Shaoxian and Tang Zhichao. "China and the Middle East." *Xiandai guoji guanxi* (Beijing) 17 (January 2007): 22–31.

Li Shaoxian and Wei Liang. "New Complexities in the Middle East since 9.11." *Contemporary International Relations* (Beijing) 20, Special Issue (September 2010): 22–32.

Li Shengming and Wang Yizhou, eds. *Nian quanqiu Zhengzhi yu Anquan Baogao.* Beijing: Shehui Kexue Wenxian, 2003.

Lieberthal, Kenneth. "Preventing a War over Taiwan." *Foreign Affairs* 84, no. 2 (March–April 2005): 53–63.

Lieberthal, Kenneth, and Mikkal Herberg. "China's Search for Energy Security: Implications for U.S. Policy." *NBR Analysis* 17, no. 1 (April 2006): 1–54.

Lieberthal, Kenneth, and David Sandalow. *Overcoming Obstacles to US-China Cooperation on Climate Change.* John L. Thornton China Center Monograph Series, no. 1. Washington, DC: Brookings Institution, January 2009.

Lieberthal, Kenneth, and Wang Jisi. *Addressing U.S.-China Strategic Distrust.* Brookings Institution, March 2012.

Liu Baolai. "Broad Prospects for China-Arab Relations." *Foreign Affairs Journal* (Beijing) 79 (March 2006): 38–44.

Liu Jianfei. *Meiguo yu Fangong Zhuyi: Lun Meiguo Dui Shehui Zhuyi Guojia de Yishixingtai Wijiao.* Beijing: Chinese Social Science Press, 2001.

Liu Ming. "China and the North Korean Crisis." *Pacific Affairs* 76, no. 3 (Fall 2003): 347–73.

Liu Tainchun. *Riben Dui Hua Zhengce yu Zhongri Guanxi.* Beijing: Renmin Chubanshe, 2004.

Lo, Bobo. *Axis of Convenience: Moscow, Beijing, and the New Geopolitics.* Washington, DC: Brookings Institution, 2008.

Lou Yaoliang. *Diyuan Zhengzhi yu Zhongguo Guofang Zhanlue.* Tianjin: Tianjin Press, 2002.

Lu Fanghua. "An Analysis of U.S. Involvement in the South China Sea." *Contemporary International Relations* (Beijing) 20, no 6 (November/December 2010): 132–41.

Lu Gang and Guo Xuetang. *Zhongguo Weixie Shui: Jiedu "Zhong Weixie Lun."* Shanghai: Xueling Chubanshe, 2004.

Lu Ning. *The Dynamics of Foreign Policy Decision Making in China.* Boulder, CO: Westview, 1997.

Lum, Thomas, coord. *Comparing Global Influence: China's and U.S. Diplomacy, Foreign Aid, Trade, and Investment in the Developing World.* Report RL34620. Washington, DC: Library of Congress, Congressional Research Service, August 15, 2008.

Luthi, Lorenz M. *The Sino-Soviet Spilt: Cold War in the Communist World.* Princeton, NJ: Princeton University Press, 2008.

Ma Jiali. "Emerging Sino-Indian Relations." *Xiandai guoji guanxi* (Beijing) 17 (May 2007): 71–80.

Ma Licheng. "Duiri Guanxi Xinsiwei." *Zhanlue yu Guanli* 6 (2002): 41–47.

MacFarquhar, Roderick, and John K. Fairbank, eds. *The Cambridge History of China,* Vol. 14: *The People's Republic, Part 1: The Emergence of Revolutionary China, 1949–1965.* Cambridge: Cambridge University Press, 1987.

———. *The Cambridge History of China,* Vol. 15: *The People's Republic, Part 2: Revolutions within the Chinese Revolution, 1966–1982.* Cambridge: Cambridge University Press, 1991.

MacFarquhar, Roderick, and Michael Schoenhals. *Mao's Last Revolution.* Cambridge, MA: Harvard University Press, 2006.

Malik, J. Mohan. "The China Factor in the India-Pakistan Conflict." *Parameters,* Spring 2003, 35–50.

———. "Chinese-Indian Relations in the Post-Soviet Era." *China Quarterly* 142 (June 1995): 317–55.

Mann, Jim. *About Face: A History of America's Curious Relationship with China, from Nixon to Clinton.* New York: Knopf, 1999.

McGiffert, Carola, ed. *Chinese Images of the United States.* Washington, DC: CSIS, 2006.

Medeiros, Evan. "Is Beijing Ready for Global Leadership?" *Current History* 108, no. 719 (September 2009): 250–56.

———, ed. *Pacific Currents: The Responses of U.S. Allies and Security Partners in East Asia to China's Rise*. Santa Monica, CA: RAND Corporation, 2008.

———. *Reluctant Restraint: The Evolution of China's Nonproliferation Policies and Practices, 1980–2004*. Stanford, CA: Stanford University Press, 2007.

———. "Strategic Hedging and the Future of Asia-Pacific Stability." *Washington Quarterly* 29, no. 1 (2005–2006): 145–67.

Medeiros, Evan, and R. Taylor Fravel. "China's New Diplomacy." *Foreign Affairs* 82, no. 6 (November–December 2003): 22–35.

Mei Zhaorong. "Sino-European Relations in Retrospect and Prospect." *Foreign Affairs Journal* (Beijing) 79 (March 2006): 17–27.

Men Honghua. *China's Grand Strategy: A Framework Analysis*. Beijing: Beijing Daxue Chubanshe, 2005.

Menon, Rajan. "The Strategic Convergence between Russia and China." *Survival* 39, no. 2 (Summer 1997): 101–25.

Miller, Alice Lyman, and Richard Wich. *Becoming Asia*. Stanford, CA: Stanford University Press, 2011.

Miller, H. Lyman, and Liu Xiaohong. "The Foreign Policy Outlook of China's 'Third Generation' Elite." In *The Making of Chinese Foreign and Security Policy in the Era of Reform*, edited by David M. Lampton, 123–50. Stanford, CA: Stanford University Press, 2001.

Mitter, Rana. *A Bitter Revolution: China's Struggle with the Modern World*. New York: Oxford University Press, 2004.

Mochizuki, Mike. "Terms of Engagement: The U.S.-Japan Alliance and the Rise of China." In *The U.S.-Japan Relationship in the New Asia-Pacific*, edited by Ellis Krauss and T. J. Pempel, 87–115. Stanford, CA: Stanford University Press, 2004.

Moltz, James Clay. "Regional Tension in the Russo-Chinese Rapprochement." *Asian Survey* 35, no. 6 (June 1995): 511–27.

Moore, Thomas. "Chinese Foreign Policy in an Age of Globalization." In *China Rising: Power and Motivation in Chinese Foreign Policy*, edited by Yong Deng and Fei-Ling Wang, 121–58. Lanham, MD: Rowman & Littlefield, 2005.

Morck, Randall, Bernard Yeung, and Minyuan Zhao. *Perspectives on China's Outward Foreign Direct Investment*. Working Paper. Washington, DC: International Monetary Fund, August 2007.

Morrison, Wayne. *China's Economic Conditions*. Report RL 33534. Washington, DC: Library of Congress, Congressional Research Service, June 26, 2012.

———. *China-U.S. Trade Issues*. Report 33536. Washington, DC: Library of Congress, Congressional Research Service, May 21, 2012.

Murray, William S. "Revisiting Taiwan's Defense Strategy." *Naval War College Review*, Summer 2008, 13–38.

Nathan, Andrew, and Robert Ross. *The Great Wall and Empty Fortress*. New York: Norton, 1997.

Nathan, Andrew, and Andrew Scobell. *China's Search for Security*. New York: Columbia University Press, 2012.

Naughton, Barry. *The Chinese Economy*. Cambridge, MA: MIT Press, 2007.

Niu Haibin. "China's International Responsibility Examined." *Xiandai guoji guanxi* (Beijing) 17 (July 2007): 81–93.

Niu Jun. *From Yan'an to the World: The Origin and Development of Chinese Communist Foreign Policy*. Steven I. Levine, ed. and trans. Norwalk, CT: Eastbridge, 2005.

O'Rourke, Ronald. *China's Naval Modernization*. Report RL33153. Washington, DC: Library of Congress, Congressional Research Service, February 8, 2012.

Pang Guang. "An Analysis of the Prospects of 'Shanghai Five.'" In *Thinking of the New Century*, edited by Ling Rong. Beijing: Central Party School Press, 2002.

———. "China's Asian Strategy: Flexible Multilateralism." *World Economy and Politics* (Beijing) 10 (2001).

———, ed. *Quanqiuhua, Fanquangiuhua yu Zhongguo: Lijie Quanqiuhua de Fuzhanxin yu Duoyangxin*. Shanghai: Renmin, 2002.

———. "SCO under New Circumstances: Challenge, Opportunity and Prospect for Development." *Journal of International Studies* (Beijing) 5 (2002): 40–52.

Paulson, Henry. "The Right Way to Engage China: Strengthening U.S.-Chinese Ties." *Foreign Affairs*, September–October 2008. www.foreignaffairs.org.

Pearson, Margaret. "China in Geneva: Lessons from China's Early Years in the World Trade Organization." In *New Directions in the Study of China's Foreign Policy*, edited by Alastair Iain Johnston and Robert S. Ross, 242–75. Stanford, CA: Stanford University Press, 2006.

Pei Jianzhang. *Yanjiu Zhou Enlai: Waijiao sixiang yu shijian* [Researching Zhou Enlai: Diplomatic thought and practice]. Beijing: Shijie Zhishi Chubanshe, 1989.

———. *Zhonghua renmin gongheguo waijiao shi, 1949–1956* [A diplomatic history of the People's Republic of China, 1949–1956]. Beijing: Shijie Zhishi, 1994.

Pei, Minxin. *China's Trapped Transition: The Limits of Development Autocracy*. Cambridge, MA: Harvard University Press, 2006.

Pei, Minxin, and Michael Swaine. *Simmering Fire in Asia: Averting Sino-Japanese Strategic Conflict*. Policy Brief 44. Washington, DC: Carnegie Endowment for International Peace, December 1, 2005.

People's Republic of China Ministry of Foreign Affairs. "China's Africa Policy." *People's Daily*. www.peoplesdaily.com.cn, January 12, 2006.

———. *China's EU Policy Paper*. Beijing: Ministry of Foreign Affairs, October 13, 2003.

People's Republic of China Ministry of Foreign Affairs, Department of Policy Planning. *China's Foreign Relations 2010*. Beijing: World Affairs Press, 2010.

People's Republic of China State Council Information Office. *China's Foreign Aid*. Beijing: People's Republic of China State Council Information Office, April 21, 2011.

———. *China's National Defense in 2002*. Beijing: People's Republic of China State Council Information Office, December 9, 2002.

———. *China's National Defense in 2004*. Beijing: People's Republic of China State Council Information Office, December 27, 2004.

———. *China's National Defense in 2006*. Beijing: People's Republic of China State Council Information Office, December 29, 2006.

———. *China's National Defense in 2008*. Beijing: People's Republic of China State Council Information Office, January 2009.

———. *China's National Defense in 2010*. Beijing: People's Republic of China State Council Information Office, March 2011.

———. *China's Peaceful Development Road*. www.peoplesdaily.com.cn, December 22, 2005.

People's Republic of China State Council Taiwan Affairs Office and Information Office. *The One-China Principle and the Taiwan Issue*. www.gwytb.gov.cn, February 21, 2000.

———. *The Taiwan Question and the Reunification of China*.www.gwytb.gov.cn, September 1, 1993.

Percival, Bronson. *The Dragon Looks South: China and Southeast Asia in the New Century*. Westport, CT: Praeger, 2007.

Pollack, Jonathan. *No Exit: North Korea, Nuclear Weapons, and International Security*. New York: Routledge, 2011.

————. "The Transformation of the Asian Security Order: Assessing China's Impact." In *Power Shift: China and Asia's New Dynamics*, edited by David Shambaugh, 329–46. Berkeley: University of California Press, 2005.

Qian Qichen. "Adjustment of the United States National Security Strategy and International Relations in the Early New Century." *Foreign Affairs Journal* (Beijing) 71 (March 2004): 1–7.

————. "Xinshiji de Guoji Guanxi." *Xuexi Shibao*, October 18, 2004.

Ranganathan, C. V. "India and China: 'Learning to Learn.'" In *Prime Minister Vajpayee's China Visit June 2003*. Occasional Studies 1, 45–54. New Delhi: Institute of Chinese Studies, October 2003.

Richardson, Sophie. *China, Cambodia, and the Five Principles of Peaceful Coexistence*. New York: Columbia University Press, 2010.

Rigger, Shelley. *Taiwan's Rising Rationalism: Generations, Politics, and "Taiwanese Nationalism."* Washington, DC: East-West Center, 2006.

Robinson, Thomas W., and David Shambaugh, eds. *Chinese Foreign Policy: Theory and Practice*. New York: Clarendon, 1997.

Rose, Caroline. *Sino-Japanese Relations: Facing the Past, Looking to the Future*. New York: RoutledgeCurzon, 2005.

Rosen, Daniel, and Thilo Hanemann. *An American Open Door: Maximizing the Benefits of Chinese Foreign Direct Investment*. New York: The Asia Society, 2011.

Ross, Robert S. ed. *After the Cold War*. Armonk, NY: M. E. Sharpe, 1998.

————.*The Indochina Tangle*. New York: Columbia University Press, 1988.

————. *Negotiating Cooperation: The United States and China, 1969–1989*. Stanford, CA: Stanford University Press, 1995.

————. "Taiwan's Fading Independence Movement." *Foreign Affairs* 85, no. 2 (March–April 2006): 141–48.

Ross, Robert, and Jiang Changbin, eds. *Re-examining the Cold War: U.S.-China Diplomacy 1954–1973*. Cambridge, MA: Harvard University Press, 2001.

Ross, Robert, and Zhu Feng, eds. *China's Ascent: Power, Security and the Implications for International Politics*. Ithaca, NY: Cornell University Press, 2009.

Roy, Denny. *China's Foreign Relations*. Lanham, MD: Rowman & Littlefield, 1998.

————. "Rising China and U.S. Interests: Inevitable vs. Contingent Hazards." *Orbis* 47, no. 1 (2003): 125–37.

————. *Taiwan: A Political History*. Ithaca, NY: Cornell University Press, 2003.

Rozman, Gilbert. *Chinese Strategic Thought toward Asia*. New York: Palgrave Macmillan, 2010.

Sa Benwang. "Some Observations on Building a Harmonious World." *Foreign Affairs Journal* (Beijing) 80 (June 2006): 37–42.

Saich, Tony. *Governance and Politics of China*. New York: Palgrave, 2001.

Samuels, Richard. *Securing Japan: Tokyo's Grand Strategy and the Future of East Asia*. Ithaca, NY: Cornell University Press, 2007.

Saunders, Phillip. "China's America Watchers: Changing Attitudes toward the United States." *China Quarterly*, March 2000, 41–65.

————. *China's Global Activism: Strategy, Drivers, and Tools*. Occasional Paper 4. Washington, DC: National Defense University Institute for National Strategic Studies, June 2006.

Scobell, Andrew. "Terrorism and Chinese Foreign Policy." In *China Rising: Power and Motivation in Chinese Foreign Policy*, edited by Yong Deng and Fei-Ling Wang, 305–24. Lanham, MD: Rowman & Littlefield, 2005.

Self, Benjamin. "China and Japan: A Façade of Friendship." *Washington Quarterly* 26, no. 1 (Winter 2002–2003): 77–88.

Shambaugh, David. *Beautiful Imperialist*. Princeton, NJ: Princeton University Press, 1991.

———. "China and Europe: The Emerging Axis." *Current History* 103, no. 674 (September 2004): 243–48.

———. *China Goes Global: Partial Power*. New York: Oxford University Press, 2013.

———. *China's Communist Party: Atrophy and Adaptation*. Washington, DC: Woodrow Wilson Center, 2008.

———. "Coping with a Conflicted China." *Washington Quarterly* 34, no. 1 (Winter 2011): 7–27.

———. *Modernizing China's Military*. Berkeley: University of California Press, 2002.

———, ed. *Power Shift: China and Asia's New Dynamics*. Berkeley: University of California Press, 2005.

———, ed. *Tangled Titans*. Lanham, MD: Rowman & Littlefield, 2012.

Sheives, Kevin. "China Turns West: Beijing's Contemporary Strategy toward Central Asia." *Pacific Affairs* 79, no. 2 (Summer 2006): 205–24.

Sheng Lijun. *China's Influence in Southeast Asia*. Trends in Southeast Asia Series 4. Singapore: Institute of Southeast Asian Studies, 2006.

Shi Yinhong. "Zhongri Jiejin yu 'Waijiao Geming.'" *Zhanlue yu Guanli* (Beijing) 2 (2003): 71–75.

Shie, Tamara. "Rising Chinese Influence in the South Pacific." *Asian Survey* 47, no. 2 (March–April 2007): 307–26.

Shinn, David, and Joshua Eisenman. *China and Africa*. Philadelphia: University of Pennsylvania Press, 2012.

Shirk, Susan. *China: Fragile Superpower*. New York: Oxford University Press, 2007.

Snyder, Scott. *China's Rise and the Two Koreas: Politics, Economics, Security*. Boulder, CO: Lynne Rienner, 2009.

Stahle, Stefan. "China's Shifting Attitude towards United Nations Peacekeeping Operations." *China Quarterly* 195 (September 2008): 631–55.

Storey, Ian James. "Living with the Colossus: How Southeast Asian Countries Cope with China." *Parameters*, Winter 1999–2000, 111–25.

———. *Southeast Asia and the Rise of China*. London: Routledge, 2011.

———. *The United States and ASEAN-China Relations: All Quiet on the Southeastern Asian Front*. Carlisle, PA: Strategic Studies Institute, U.S. Army War College, 2007.

Stueck, William W. *The Road to Confrontation: American Policy toward China and Korea, 1947–1950*. Chapel Hill: University of North Carolina Press, 1981.

Su Ge. *Meiguo: Dui hua Zhengce yu Taiwan wenti* [America: China policy and the Taiwan issue]. Beijing: Shijie Zhishi Chubanshe, 1998.

Suettinger, Robert. *Beyond Tiananmen*. Washington, DC: Brookings Institution, 2003.

Sutter, Robert. "Assessing China's Rise and U.S. Leadership in Asia—Growing Maturity and Balance." *Journal of Contemporary China* 19, no. 65 (June 2010), 591–604.

———. *China's Rise: Implications for U.S. Leadership in Asia*. Washington, DC: East-West Center, 2006.

———. *China's Rise in Asia: Promises and Perils*. Lanham, MD: Rowman & Littlefield, 2005.

———. *Chinese Foreign Relations: Power and Policy Since the Cold War*. Lanham MD: Rowman & Littlefield, 2012.

———. *U.S.-Chinese Relations: Perilous Past, Pragmatic Present*. Lanham MD: Rowman & Littlefield, 2010.

Swaine, Michael. *America's Challenge: Engaging a Rising China in the Twenty-First Century*. Washington, DC: Carnegie Endowment for International Peace, 2011.

———. "China's Regional Military Posture." In *Power Shift: China and Asia's New Dynamics*, edited by David Shambaugh, 266–88. Berkeley: University of California Press, 2005.

Swaine, Michael, and Ashley Tellis. *Interpreting China's Grand Strategy, Past, Present and Future*. Santa Monica, CA: RAND Corporation, September 2001.

Swaine, Michael, Tousheng Zhang, and Danielle F. S. Cohen. *Managing Sino-American Crises: Case Studies and Analysis*. Washington, DC: Carnegie Endowment, 2006.

Swanstrom, Niklas. "China and Central Asia: A New Great Game or Traditional Vassal." *Journal of Contemporary China* 14, no. 45 (November 2005): 569–84.

Tang Shiping and Zhang Yunling. "Zhongguo de Diqu Zhanlue." *Shijie Jingli Yu Zhengzhi* 6 (2004): 8–13.

Taylor, Ian. *China's New Role in Africa*. Boulder, CO: Lynne Rienner, 2008.

Taylor, Jay. *The Generalissimo*. Cambridge, MA: Harvard University Press, 2009.

———. *The Generalissimo's Son: Chiang Ching-kuo and the Revolutions in China and Taiwan*. Cambridge, MA: Harvard University Press, 2000.

Tian Peiliang. "China and Africa in New Period." *Foreign Affairs Journal* (Beijing) 70 (December 2003): 36–42.

———. "Nationalism: China and Japan." *Foreign Affairs Journal* (Beijing) 63 (March 2002): 63–83.

Tian Zengpei, ed. *Gaige kaifang yilai de Zhongguo waijiao* [Chinese diplomacy since reform and opening]. Beijing: Shijie Zhishi Chubanshe, 1993.

Tiang Zhongqing. *East Asia Cooperation and China's Strategic Interest*. Dangdai Yatai 5. Beijing: Chinese Academy of Social Sciences, 2003.

Tsou, Tang. *America's Failure in China, 1941–1950*. Chicago: University of Chicago Press, 1963.

Tucker, Nancy Bernkopf. "China-Taiwan: U.S. Debates and Policy Choices." *Survival* 40, no. 4 (Winter 1998–1999): 150–67.

———, ed. *Dangerous Strait: The U.S.-Taiwan-China Crisis*. New York: Columbia University Press, 2005.

———. *Strait Talk: United States-Taiwan Relations and the Crisis with China*. Cambridge, MA: Harvard University Press, 2009.

———. *Taiwan, Hong Kong, and the United States, 1945–1992: Uncertain Friendships*. New York: Twayne, 1994.

United States–China Economic and Security Review Commission. *Report to Congress 2010*. www.uscc.gov.

U.S. Congress, House Committee on Foreign Affairs. *Executive-Legislative Consultations over China policy, 1978-1979*. Washington, DC: U.S. Government Printing Office, 1980.

U.S. Congress, House Committee on International Relations. *United States-Soviet Union-China: The Great Power Triangle*. Washington, DC: U.S. Government Printing Office, 1976.

U.S. Department of Defense. *Military and Security Developments Involving the People's Republic of China, 2012*. www.defense.gov/pubs/pdfs/2012_CMPR_Final.pdf.

U.S. National Intelligence Council. *China and Weapons of Mass Destruction: Implications for the United States*. Conference Report. Washington, DC: U.S. National Intelligence Council, November 5, 1999.

———. *China's Future: Implications for U.S. Interests*. Conference Report CR99-02. Washington, DC: U.S. National Intelligence Council, September 1999.

U.S. Senate, Committee on Foreign Relations. *China's Foreign Policy and "Soft Power" in South America, Asia, and Africa*. Washington, DC: U.S. Government Printing Office, 2008.

Van Ness, Peter. *Revolution and Chinese Foreign Policy.* Berkeley: University of California Press, 1970.

Wachman, Alan. *Why Taiwan: Geostrategic Rationales for China's Territorial Integrity.* Stanford, CA: Stanford University Press, 2007.

Wan, Ming. *Sino-Japanese Relations: Interaction, Logic, and Transformation.* Stanford, CA: Stanford University Press, 2006.

Wang, Bingnan. *Zhongmei huitan jiunian huigu* [Nine years of Sino-American ambassadorial talks]. Beijing: Shijie Zhishi, 1985.

Wang, Fei-Ling. "Beijing's Incentive Structure: The Pursuit of Preservation, Prosperity, and Power." In *China Rising: Power and Motivation in Chinese Foreign Policy*, edited by Yong Deng and Fei-Ling Wang, 19–50. Lanham, MD: Rowman & Littlefield, 2005.

Wang Gungwu. *China and Southeast Asia: Myths, Threat, and Culture.* EAI Occasional Paper 13. Singapore: National University of Singapore, 1999.

———. "The Fourth Rise of China: Cultural Implications." *China: An International Journal* 2, no. 2 (September 2004): 311–22.

Wang Jianwei. "China's Multilateral Diplomacy in the New Millennium." In *China Rising: Power and Motivation in Chinese Foreign Policy*, edited by Yong Deng and Fei-Ling Wang, 177–87. Lanham, MD: Rowman & Littlefield, 2005.

Wang Jisi. "China's Search for a Grand Strategy." *Foreign Affairs* 90, no. 2 (March/April 2011): 68–79.

———. "China's Search for Stability with America." *Foreign Affairs* 84, no. 5 (September–October 2005): 39–48.

———. "Xinxingshi de Zhuyao Tedian he Zhongguo Waijiao." *Xiabdai Guoji Guanxi* (Beijing) 4 (April 2003): 1–3.

Wang Shida. "The Way to a Secure and Stable Afghanistan." *Contemporary International Relations* (Beijing) 20, no. 6 (November/December 2010): 123–31.

Wang Shuzhong, ed. *Mei-Su zhengba zhanlue wenti* [The question of contention for hegemony between the United States and the Soviet Union]. Beijing: Guofang daxue chubanshe, 1988.

Wang, Taiping et al. *Zhonghua renmin gongheguo waijiao shi, 1957–1969* [A diplomatic history of the People's Republic of China, 1957–1969]. Beijing: Shijie Zhishi, 1998.

Wang, T. Y. "Taiwan's Foreign Relations under Lee Teng-hui's Rule, 1988–2000." In *Sayonara to the Lee Teng-Hui Era*, edited by Wei-chin Lee and T. Y. Wang, 250–60. Lanham, MD: University Press of America, 2003.

Wang Xiaolong. "The Asia-Pacific Economic Cooperation and the Regional Political and Security Issues." *Dangdai Yatai* (Beijing) 4 (2003).

Wang Yizhou. *Quanqiu zhengzhi he zhongguo waijiao.* Beijing: Shijie Zhishi Chubanshe, 2004.

Weatherbee, Donald. "Strategic Dimensions of Economic Interdependence in Southeast Asia." In *Strategic Asia 2006–2007*, edited by Ashley Tellis and Michael Wills, 271–302. Seattle, WA: National Bureau of Asian Research, 2006.

Westad, Odd Arne. *Brothers in Arms: The Rise and Fall of the Sino-Soviet Alliance, 1945–1963.* Stanford, CA: Stanford University Press, 1998.

Whiting, Allen S. *China Crosses the Yalu.* New York: Macmillan, 1960.

———. *The Chinese Calculus of Deterrence: India and Indochina.* Ann Arbor: University of Michigan Press, 1975.

Wilson, Jeanne. *Strategic Partners: Russian-Chinese Relations in the Post-Soviet Era.* Armonk, NY: M. E. Sharpe, 2004.

Wishnick, Elizabeth. "Russia and China: Brothers Again?" *Asian Survey* 41, no. 5 (September–October 2001): 797–821.

Womack, Brantly. "China and Southeast Asia: Asymmetry, Leadership and Normalcy." *Pacific Affairs* 76, no. 3 (Winter 2003–2004): 529–48.

———. *China and Vietnam: The Politics of Asymmetry.* New York: Cambridge University Press, 2006.

Wong, John, and Sarah Chan. "China-ASEAN Free Trade Agreement." *Asian Survey* 43, no. 3 (May–June 2003): 507–26.

Wu Hongying. "Latin America: Key Trends and Challenges." *Contemporary International Relations* (Beijing) 20, Special Issue (September 2010): 33–42.

———. "A New Era of Sino-Latin American Relations." *Xiandai guoji guanxi* (Beijing) 17 (January 2007): 64–71.

Wu Xinbo. "Chinese Perspectives on Building an East Asian Community in the Twenty-First Century." In *Asia's New Multilateralism,* edited by Michael Green and Bates Gill, 55–77. New York: Columbia University Press, 2009.

———."The End of the Silver Lining: A Chinese View of the U.S.-Japanese Alliance." *Washington Quarterly* 29, no. 1 (2005): 119–30.

———. "Four Contradictions Constraining China's Foreign Policy Behavior." *Journal of Contemporary China* 10, no. 27 (May 2001): 293–302.

Xie Yixian, *Zhongguo Waijiao Shi: 1949–1979* [China's diplomatic history: 1949-1979]. Henan: Henan Renmin Chubanshe, 1988.

Xing Guangcheng. "Work for Mutual Trust and Mutual Benefit in Deepening Sino-Russian Relations." *Foreign Affairs Journal* (Beijing) 80 (June 2006): 8–13.

Xiong Guangkai. "Dongqian Quanqiu Fankongxing shi Jiqi Qiying Zhanwang." *Guoji Zhanlue Yanjiu* (Beijing) 2 (2003).

———. "A Review of International Strategic Situation and Its Prospects." *Guoji Zhanlüe Yanjiu* [*International Strategic Studies*, English version] 71, no. 1 (January 2004): 3.

Xu Weizhong. "Beijing Summit Promotes Sino-African Relations." *Xiandai guoji guanxi* (Beijing) 17 (January 2007): 72–79.

Yahuda, Michael. *China's Role in World Affairs.* New York: St. Martins, 1978.

———. *The International Politics of the Asia-Pacific, 1945–1995.* New York: Routledge, 1996.

———. "The Limits of Economic Interdependence: Sino-Japanese Relations." In *New Directions in the Study of China's Foreign Policy,* edited by Alastair Iain Johnston and Robert S. Ross, 162–85. Stanford, CA: Stanford University Press, 2006.

Yan Xuetong. "The Instability of China-US Relations." *The Chinese Journal of International Politics* 3, no. 3 (2010): 1–30.

———. "The Rise of China and Its Power Status." *Chinese Journal of International Politics* 1 (2006): 5–33.

Yan Xuetong et al. *Zhongguo Jueji—Guoji Huanjin Pinggu.* Tianjin: People's Press, 1998.

Yang Jianmian. *Da Mo He.* Tianjin: Renmin Chubanshe, 2007.

Yang Wenchang. "Sino-U.S. Relations in Retrospect and Prospect." *Foreign Affairs Journal* (Beijing) 80 (June 2006): 1–7.

Ye Zicheng. *Xin Zhongguo Waijiao Sixiang: Cong Maozedong dao Dengxiaoping.* Beijing: Beijing Daxue Chubanshe, 2001.

———. "Zhongguo Shixing Daguo Waijiaozhanlue Shizai Bixing." *Shijie Jingli yu Zhengzhi* 1 (2000): 5–10.

Yee, Herbert, and Ian Storey. *The China Threat: Perceptions, Myths, and Reality.* London: Routledge, 2002.

Yu Bin. "China and Russia: Normalizing Their Strategic Partnership." In *Power Shift: China and Asia's New Dynamics*, edited by David Shambaugh, 228–46. Berkeley: University of California Press, 2005.

Yuan, Jing-dong. "China's Role in Establishing and Building the Shanghai Cooperation Organization (SCO)." *Journal of Contemporary China* 19, no. 67 (November 2010): 855—70.

———. "The Dragon and the Elephant: Chinese-Indian Relations in the 21st Century." *Washington Quarterly* 30, no. 3 (Summer 2007): 131–44.

Yuan Peng. "9.11 Shijian yu Zhongmei Guanxi." *Xiandai Guoji Guanxi*, November 11, 2001, 19–23, 63.

———. "A Harmonious World and China's New Diplomacy." *Xiandai guoji guanxi* (Beijing) 17 (May 2007): 1–26.

Zagoria, Donald. *The Sino-Soviet Conflict, 1956–1961.* New York: Atheneum, 1964.

Zeng Qiang. "FOCAC: A Powerful Engine for the Continued Development of Friendship between China and Africa." *Contemporary International Relations* (Beijing) 20, no. 6 (November/December 2010): 45–59.

Zhang Biwu. "Chinese Perceptions of American Power, 1991–2004." *Asian Survey* 45, no. 5 (September–October 2005): 667–86.

Zhang Wenmu. "Quanqiuhua Jincheng Zhong de Zhongguo Guojia Liye." *Zhanlue yu Guanli* 1 (2002): 52–64.

Zhang Yunling. "East Asian Cooperation and the Construction of China-ASEAN Free Trade Area." *Dangdai Yatai* (Beijing) 1 (2002): 20–32.

———, ed. *Huoban Haishi Duishou: Tiao Zheng Zhong de Mei Ri E Guanxi.* Beijing: Social Science Departments Press, 2000.

———, ed. *Making New Partnership: A Rising China and Its Neighbors.* Beijing: Social Sciences Academic Press, 2008.

———. "New Thinking Needed to Promote East Asian Cooperation." *Foreign Affairs Journal* (Beijing) 96 (September 2010), 17–23.

———, ed. *Weilai 10-15 Nian Zhongguo Zai Yatai Diqu Mianlin de Guoji Huanjing.* Beijing: Zhongguo Shehui Kexue Chubanshe, 2003.

Zhang Yunling and Tang Shiping. "China's Regional Strategy." In *Power Shift: China and Asia's New Dynamics*, edited by David Shambaugh, 48–70. Berkeley: University of California Press, 2005.

Zhao, Suisheng. "Chinese Nationalism and Its International Orientations." *Political Science Quarterly* 115, no. 1 (Spring 2000): 1–33.

———. *A Nation-State by Construction: Dynamics of Modern Chinese Nationalism.* Stanford, CA: Stanford University Press, 2004.

Zheng Bijian. "China's 'Peaceful Rise' to Great-Power Status." *Foreign Affairs* 84, no. 5 (2005): 18–24.

Zheng Ruixiang. "New Development of Relations between China and South Asian Countries." *Foreign Affairs Journal* (Beijing) 76 (June 2005): 40–46.

Zhou Gang. "Status Quo and Prospects of China-ASEAN Relations." *Foreign Affairs Journal* (Beijing) 80 (June 2006): 14–21.

Zhou Yuhao. *Liyi Youguan.* Beijing: Zhongguo Chuanmei Daxue Chubanshe, 2007.

Zhu Feng. "Zai Lishi Gui yi Zhong Bawo Zhong Mei Guanxi." *Huanqiu Shibao Guoji Luntan*, February 28, 2002.

Zhu Tingchang et al., eds. *Zhongguo Zhoubian Anquan Huanjin yu Anquan Zhanlue.* Beijing: Shishi Chubanshe, 2002.

Zi Zhongyun. *Meiguo duihua zhengce de yuanqi he fazhan, 1945–1950* [The origins and development of American policy toward China, 1945–1950]. Chongqing: Chongqing, 1987.

————. *No Exit? The Origin and Evolution of U.S. Policy toward China, 1945–1950.* Norwalk, CT: Eastbridge, 2004.

Zou Jingwen. *Li Denghui Zhizheng Gaobai Shilu.* Taipei: INK, 2001.

Index

Afghanistan, 79, 84, 126, 202, 251, 252, 257
Africa, 313; Chinese aid, 277, 279, 281, 284; Chinese investment, 284, 285; relations with China, 5, 42, 46, 48, 86, 277–286
Agreed Framework, 93, 230
Aksai Chin, 44
Albania, 12, 153
ambassadorial talks, 41, 60, 183, 184, 187–188
Andropov, Yuri, 78, 80
Angola, 280, 285
Antarctica, 303
Anti-Secession Law, 301
"Arab Spring", 107, 277
Arafat, Yasir, 269, 270
Arctic, 303
Arkipov, Ivan, 80, 82, 82–83
Armitage, Richard, 67, 70
arms sales and embargo, 73; U.S. sales to Taiwan, 75, 76, 78, 194, 207, 228
ASEAN. *See* Association of Southeast Asian Nations
ASEAN-China Free Trade Agreement (ACTFA), 6, 163
ASEAN Regional Forum (ARF), 168, 237
Asian Development Bank (ADB), 54, 73, 77, 93; aid to China, 157, 315
Asian economic crisis, 97, 98, 237

Asia-Pacific Economic Cooperation (APEC), 93
Asia-Pacific region, 314–315; China's influence in, 1–4, 8–9, 18–19, 22, 25, 112, 149–174, 205, 207, 215–260, 311–312, 316–326; Chinese opposition to superpower dominance in, 135–143; U.S. leadership in, 321–326
Association for Relations across the Taiwan Strait (ARATS), 227
Association of Southeast Asian Nations (ASEAN), 25; relations with China, 86, 94, 163, 237–240, 319; relations with China and Japan, 220
Australia, 25; relations with China, 242

ballistic missile defense, 98, 105, 200, 202
Bandung conference, 41, 183
"Beijing consensus", 160
Belgrade, bombing of Chinese embassy, 20, 23, 95, 105, 121, 122, 197, 198
Bin Laden, Osama, 257
Bo Xilai, 99, 101, 106
Brazil, 5, 6, 289–291
Brezhnev, Leonid, 44, 152, 228; relations with China, 53–75
Brezhnev doctrine, 57, 187, 251
BRICS, 6, 163, 292
British Virgin Islands, 159
Brzezinski, Zbigniew, 65, 189

349